FEMINIST PHENOMENOLOGY FUTURES

FEMINIST PHENOMENOLOGY FUTURES

Edited by HELEN A. FIELDING
and DOROTHEA E. OLKOWSKI

INDIANA UNIVERSITY PRESS

This book is a publication of

INDIANA UNIVERSITY PRESS
Office of Scholarly Publishing
Herman B Wells Library 350
1320 East 10th Street
Bloomington, Indiana 47405 USA

iupress.indiana.edu

© 2017 by Indiana University Press

All rights reserved

No part of this book may be reproduced or utilized in any form or by any means, electronic or mechanical, including photocopying and recording, or by any information storage and retrieval system, without permission in writing from the publisher.

The paper used in this publication meets the minimum requirements of the American National Standard for Information Sciences—Permanence of Paper for Printed Library Materials, ANSI Z39.48–1992.

Manufactured in the United States of America

Library of Congress Cataloging-in-Publication Data

Cataloging information is available from the Library of Congress.

ISBN 978-0-253-02962-1 (cloth)
ISBN 978-0-253-02994-2 (paperback)
ISBN 978-0-253-03011-5 (ebook)

1 2 3 4 5   22 21 20 19 18 17

CONTENTS

A Feminist Phenomenology Manifesto / Helen A. Fielding · *vii*

Introduction / Dorothea E. Olkowski and Helen A. Fielding · *xxiii*

Part 1. The Future Is Now

1 Using Our Intuition: Creating the Future Phenomenological Plane of Thought / Dorothea E. Olkowski · *3*

2 Just Throw Like a Bleeding Philosopher: Menstrual Pauses and Poses, Betwixt Hypatia and Bhubaneswari, Half Visible, Almost Illegible / Kyoo Lee · *21*

3 Transformative Lines of Flight: From Deleuze to Masoch / Lyat Friedman · *47*

4 Crafting Contingency / Rachel McCann · *66*

Part 2. Negotiating Futures

5 Open Future, Regaining Possibility / Helen A. Fielding · *91*

6 Of Women and Slaves / Debra Bergoffen · *110*

7 Unhappy Speech and Hearing Well: Contributions of Feminist Speech Act Theory to Feminist Phenomenology / Beata Stawarska · *125*

Part 3. The Ontological Future

8 Adventures in the Hyperdialectic / Eva-Maria Simms · *141*

9 The Murmuration of Birds: An Anishinaabe Ontology of *Mnidoo*-Worlding / Dolleen Tisawii'ashii Manning · *154*

10 Trans-subjectivity/Trans-objectivity / Christine Daigle · *183*

Part 4. Our Future Body Images

11 The "Normal Abnormalities" of Disability and Aging: Merleau-Ponty and Beauvoir / Gail Weiss · *203*

12 The Transhuman Paradigm and the Meaning of Life / Christina Schües · *218*

13 The Second-Person Perspective in Narrative Phenomenology / Annemie Halsema and Jenny Slatman · *242*

14 Hannah Arendt and Pregnancy in the Public Sphere / Katy Fulfer · *257*

Part 5. Present and Future Selves

15 Is Direct Perception Arrogant Perception?: Toward a Critical, Playful Intercorporeity / April N. Flakne · *277*

16 Leadership in the World through an Arendtian Lens / Rita A. Gardiner · *299*

17 Identity-in-Difference to Avoid Indifference / Emily S. Lee · *313*

18 What Is Feminist Phenomenology? Looking Backward and Into the Future / Silvia Stoller · *328*

Index · *355*

A FEMINIST PHENOMENOLOGY MANIFESTO

HELEN A. FIELDING

In this volume we situate the future directions of feminist phenomenology in the here and now. We contend that in this moment feminist phenomenology is well positioned to take a leading role, not simply in terms of consolidating existing feminist methodologies but also in engaging the difficult task of thinking through the actual in the fullness of its relational, agential, ontological, experiential, and fleshly being, thereby opening up future possibilities. We also think there is some urgency to this claim. For many, faith in the rational human subject has been shattered by the events of the twentieth and twenty-first centuries' worldwide conflicts and increasing sectarianism. The concept of the subject as such is either obsolete or needs to be dynamically rethought. The current options appear to include resuscitating the rational liberal subject or agent, acknowledging limited agency in the performativity of language and gesture, or recognizing the agency of matter. We want to argue instead for a feminist phenomenological approach that begins with multiple, meaningful points of view on relational being.

Feminist phenomenology has emerged as a coherent discipline, as Silvia Stoller so well explains.[1] Nonetheless, accounting for living experience, which is at the heart of this methodology, is a practice central to emancipatory theorizing that both comes before and exceeds defined disciplinary borders, as Mariana Ortega points out in her work on Latina feminist phenomenology.[2] Thus, significant to our claim that feminist phenomenology is the methodology of the future is the recognition that there are multiple ways of approaching living experience, which is not to imply relativism—that is, the belief that all approaches or ways of understanding the world are equally true or equally adequate.

Instead, our claim is that we need robust accounts of embodied subjects that are interrelated within the world or worlds they inhabit, which is not to revive the vestiges of a humanism that puts humans at the center. Rather, we are reformulating the common understanding of the decentered subject as multiple rather than singular. Commensurate with this, we are reformulating the decentered subject as a point of view that moves away from the internal perspective of a singular subject in order to resituate it on the boundary between the inner realm of thought and feeling and the experiential and exterior world of political, social, and ethical forces and acts.[3] This means we account for human existence in and through the social sphere with an understanding of agency as the spontaneous capacity to begin, to set in motion what is unpredictable in its outcome with effects we cannot anticipate in advance.[4]

Writing in the aftermath of the Second World War, Maurice Merleau-Ponty describes liberalism as a failure because the *idea* of liberty is defended rather than the actual liberty of living beings: "Western humanism . . . subordinates empirical humanity to a certain idea of man and its supporting institutions" in order to perpetuate the violence of imperialism and colonization.[5] He proposes that we evaluate a politics by questioning the structure of human relations upon which it is grounded.[6] We suggest that this structure of interrelationality be extended to take into account an interrelationality of all beings while recognizing that "man has no rights over the world." The political, nonetheless, remains a human domain, which requires that human agency be addressed.[7]

Although one could arguably trace feminist phenomenology back to the early mid-twentieth century, the term itself is quite recent.[8] The first texts have been attributed variably to Simone de Beauvoir's *The Second Sex*, as well as to the works of some of the early phenomenologists such as Edith Stein.[9] These initial endeavors can now be identified as the institution of a methodology that can be recognized only after the fact, for phenomenologically it is only after something—for example, a movement or methodology—has become established that one can look back and identify the founding moment or impulse.[10] Although many of the tenets of feminist phenomenology—a focus on embodiment and the account of context, limits, and history—were central to feminist theorizing and methodologies in the latter half of the twentieth century, some feminists approached phenomenology with caution. The main reason for this was that phenomenology was largely discredited for privileging a genderless, neutral transcendental subject, and even now, as Sara Heinämaa and Lanei Rodemeyer explain, gender is still largely "taken as a factual issue" or an "empirical problem" by "most contemporary commentators," even though Edmund Husserl himself located "the problem of the sexes" as a transcendental problem.¹¹ As the locus of reason, however, the transcendental subject has too often been identified as the neutral white European privileged male subject.¹² Nonetheless, some feminists were reluctant to give up on phenomenology altogether, because it was the one methodology that provided a robust account of embodied living experience, a central starting point for many feminist analyses.¹³

We are claiming that feminist phenomenology emerges from an interrelational ontology, that not only does it offer the account of embodied experience for which it is usually recognized, but also that embodied perception underlies the production of knowledge and grounds politics. We can make this claim because we understand humans to belong to what Merleau-Ponty in his late work calls "flesh," by which he means that humans are relationally folded into a material and living world: they perceive because they too are perceptible; sensing is sedimented through engagement with the sensible; ideas, too, overlap and intertwine with the world that conditions them; and, finally, agency is not limited to the "I think," but emerges from this situated overlapping of embodied praxis, ideas, and world.¹⁴ In other words, because it begins with multiple points of view within a social, historical, and concrete sphere, feminist phenomenology establishes itself as temporally and spatially reliant and relevant. These multiple points of view do not result in relativism, however. On the contrary, because they are spatially and temporally intertwined, they overlap and encroach upon one another. They emerge simultaneously, which means they are not monads and there are possibilities for encounter.¹⁵ This claim is not modest—we are arguing that an interrelational world is also political. Even though it displaces "man" from the center, indeed displaces any notion of center, humans are nonetheless still subjects who are responsible and agents.

In short, the political is about what belongs neither solely to the world of ideas nor to that of empirical facts but is instead enacted in the realm of unpredictable human relations, which is the intertwining of ideas, experience, materiality, and action. This means we must learn "to confront ideas with the social functions they claim to articulate, to compare our perspectives with others, and to relate our ethics to our politics."¹⁶ Not knowing the future, we can take the historical context into account only when we think and act. It is, of course, always risky, for "an action can produce something else than it envisaged"—that is, the nature of human action, which is the seat of the political; nevertheless, politically we assume the "consequences."¹⁷ Because we are social and historical beings, our actions come out of the context and situation, the backdrop of history to which they belong, and thus can be judged only from within that context. So we must act in the ways that seem best given where we are now. Accordingly, we propose, "after carefully weighing everything, to push in our own direction" without knowing where it will take us.[18]

This understanding of the political comes out of an existential phenomenological approach that mediates between the excesses of empiricism and idealism—that is, the belief that either reality arises solely out of a material world, or we can never have access to a world in itself but only its representations. Instead, grounded in living existence that is both temporal and spatial, this approach provides an entirely different explanation for how we account for the world. The phenomenal subject inhabits a world that has already been constituted by others and other forces that in turn shape the subject. This "transcendental field" hence entails "a partial view and a limited power," whereby appearances, upon which phenomenology relies, are always a co-creative, spatially and temporally situated event that is nonetheless grounded in a shared world.[19] In other words, reality is creatively brought into appearance in the in-between of points of view and world(s) we inhabit.

The problem with both empiricism and idealism, as Merleau-Ponty so aptly puts it, is that for these approaches there is no point of view, "there is *no one who sees* at the center of this mass of sensations and memories . . . and, correlatively, no solid object protected by a sense against the swarm of memories."[20] Sensibility, the sense-giving of the senses, is missing, and there is no point of view for which space and time are experienced, for whom spatiality and temporality, the gathering of past, present, and future as well as milieu and situation, are given. Empiricism, which assumes to explain an objective world, ultimately does not account for the ontological structures that allow for the ways humans, other beings, and things appear and hence interrelate. The empiricist notions that the body is a "transmitter of messages," that there are pure impressions, that "red and green are not sensations," but rather sensibles, and that quality is a "property of the object," do not account for the evidence that sensation takes place within a field—that is, a figure against a ground.[21]

In other words, perception belongs to the style of being, to a larger social and cultural world to which a perceiver belongs. Even though we can have a point of view only from within the field that provides the structure, within that structure we can vary our points of view. Thus, for Merleau-Ponty, the "red patch I see on the rug is only red if the shadow that lies across it is taken into account; its quality only appears in relation to the play of light, and thus only as an element in a spatial configuration."[22] And it would not be this red "if it were not the 'wooly red'" of a carpet.[23] Empiricists might argue that light and shadow obscure our vision of this world but nonetheless an objective world remains. Phenomenologists, however, respond that light, color, and shadow actually reveal the interrelationality of things in the world according to perceptual structures where parts make sense only from within the given whole. Applying these insights to feminist concerns, Gail Weiss, for example, argues that normal phenomena such as aging and disability are too often seen as "abnormal" because they deviate from the "unrealistic" norms established by a field of expectations and ideals.[24] A feminist phenomenological perspective allows us to bring this everyday field to the foreground, shifting our perspective in order to analyze it and work toward change.

Merleau-Ponty is no more patient with the transcendental ego of idealism, for which "the world becomes the correlate of a thought about the world and no longer exists except for a constituting [Ego]."[25] In other words, we access the world only through the ways we represent it to ourselves. Indeed, the criticism launched against phenomenology—that it is reliant on the subjective view of the transcendental ego that does not take a "material" world into account—can be surmounted by attending to Merleau-Ponty.[26] Rather than either a positivist understanding of space—that is, of a world existing independently of any human perception—or the alternative of an idealist projection of concepts onto the world, Merleau-Ponty suggests that perception is a creative taking up of world, "a moment of the living dialectic of a concrete subject." Perception belongs to the "total structure," which includes not only the embodied subject but also "the actions of other human subjects" and the world(s) they inhabit.[27] To inhabit a world is thus to take it up, to gear into it and become an active part of its structure—in other words, to become an agent. "My body," Merleau-Ponty writes, "is where it has something to do."[28]

Of course, Merleau-Ponty's analysis, taken further, as feminists have done, allows us to account for how the agency of which he writes is more often denied to those whose bodies are not so well "geared into the world," whereby perception provides the "most varied and the most clearly articulated spectacle possible, [and for whom] motor intentions, as they unfold, receive the responses they anticipate from the world."[29] Beata Stawarska describes the breakdown of agency in terms of the disrespect she encountered as a fledgling lecturer who, as a woman and non-native-language speaker, deviated from the norm of what was expected in a philosophy professor. Importantly, this gearing of the body into the world lies neither on the side of an empirical world nor on the side of constituting consciousness, but rather with the embodied phenomenal subject who moves into the world and creatively takes it up. Indeed, those whose bodies do not fit well into existing "normal" structures habitually employ extraordinary creativity to navigate a too often hostile landscape.[30]

This absence of the embodied subject that Merleau-Ponty identifies at the heart of both empiricism and idealism also tends to persist in much late twentieth-century postmodernism. It is not surprising that faith in the liberal human subject was shattered by the ravages of war and the legacy of genocide, and that many philosophers wanted to think through the construction of subjectivity produced by Western humanism as its failure. Phenomenology as a tradition enabled such questioning to the extent that it allowed for accounts of living experience and a social world and did not begin with the rational thinking subject. Post-structuralist theorists coming out of this tradition took this questioning even further such that Jacques Derrida and Michel Foucault extended Martin Heidegger's radical understanding of language as the "house of Being" to the point where subjects are so shaped by language and discourse that individual agency seems to disappear.[31] For Derrida, meaning is produced through a process of differentiating, which is itself not perceptible; meaning is produced in the spaces between letters, phonemes, words, and sentences. It does not adhere to the things themselves. Foucault understands phenomenological description as producing what it was meant to describe; descriptions are not co-creative, but rather disciplinary, imposing meaning on what is there.[32] Ontology, as a study of being, or what is, is forsaken for epistemology, or how we come to know.[33]

Importantly, even as they took up and engaged with these insights, post-structuralist feminist theorists did so cautiously, for the most part avoiding the excesses of relativism, one of the consequences of abandoning ontology, while drawing on post-structuralist insights to better understand how humans are shaped by a social and cultural world and hence the movement of oppression. Thus, for example, Luce Irigaray showed how the speaking subject of Western philosophy is a masculine subject; Judith Butler, how gender is discursively or performatively produced; and Gayatri Spivak, how feminists are complicit with the colonialism they critique.[34] Importantly, phenomenological insights, though not always specifically named as such, accompanied these projects. Embodied subjectivity was never completely off the map and reappeared in such formulations as Butler's materialization of gender.[35]

Nonetheless, while the linguistic turn that is characteristic of postmodern theories focused on the play of language that allows us to make sense of cultural forces, it did so at the expense of the particularity of the individual, or for that matter any account of meaning or an empirical reality. The so-called death of the subject called into question the efficacy of representation, which was exchanged for semiotics as a play of signifiers that never actually touches upon any actual referent. And phenomenology was criticized for assuming a subject that precedes language, whose interiority is not completely shaped by the formal systems of culture and the symbolic, as well as for maintaining that there is meaning to be revealed. Although it extends our understanding of the formation of culture, semiotics as a formal system of language makes it difficult to ground either ethics or politics.

For Gilles Deleuze, another significant post-structuralist thinker, the sense-giving act of the phenomenological reduction imposes meaning structures rather than breaking them apart. For him, *Alice's Adventures in Wonderland*, a favorite of postmodern thinkers, seems to celebrate the absence of sense and the relinquishing of identity and reference.[36] Dorothea Olkowski, however, provides an alternate reading of Alice's adventures, for, as she points out, it is in the depths of Wonderland that Alice "investigates deep structures, the rules of logic."[37] And what Alice finds is that "many formal structures, such as causality, identity, reference and the logical rules of replacement . . . do not generate consequential conduct."[38] More specifically, she discovers that propositions that could be stated as linear and causal hypotheticals now follow only the rules of logic, which means they can be "transformed into a series of disjunctions bearing no causal relation to one another."[39] Without causality there is no responsibility.

This is the world of the mind in which, in Hannah Arendt's words, anything is possible, which can be both extraordinarily creative but also horrific. Arendt was referring to the concentration camps of Nazi Germany, where the unimaginable was not only imagined but also put into effect—it was an arbitrary space where consequences were not attached to actions.[40] Alice, however, is a thoughtful girl, and she leaves the depths of Wonderland, where anything is possible, and returns to her own world, where she can once again rely on thinking through what she knows and has experienced—that is, her good sense. She returns to a world where "words and deeds have unpredictable effects" and consequences that must be lived with. Rather than understanding the "disappearance of the author or the self" as the dispersal of the egoistic subject, Alice and Olkowski reveal it to be an avoidance of responsibility and hence of ethics.[41]

The more recent move to account for the agency of the material world, and to rehabilitate ontology, is a response to this emphasis on language games. Nonetheless, the living of the phenomenal being as a point of view is generally also missing from these new "material feminisms," which Stacy Alaimo and Susan Hekman define as "ways of understanding the agency, significance, and ongoing transformative power of the world—ways that account for myriad 'intra-actions' (in Karen Barad's terms) between phenomena that are material, discursive, human, more-than-human, corporeal and technological."[42] For Alaimo and Hekman, material feminisms deconstruct the "material/discursive dichotomy" upon which postmodernism has relied, eschewing the limitations of postmodern critique and returning to ontology as interrelated with epistemology.[43] Jane Bennett, an important proponent of new material feminism, calls us to attend to the "vitality of matter and the lively power of material formations."[44] Karen Barad, who is recognized as one of the central figures in this movement, argues for an understanding of agency, not as an "attribute but [rather as] the ongoing reconfigurings of the world" that belong to phenomena or "material-discursive practices."[45] Yet, as Dolleen Tisawii'ashii Manning's essay in this volume, which brings Anishinaabe ontology into dialogue with Merleau-Ponty's own, makes clear, these claims about the "agency of matter" are not new—indeed, as she suggests here and argues forcefully elsewhere, there is an established philosophical practice of taking so-called innovative ideas, including for example the concept of "other-than-human," from Indigenous thinking without acknowledgment. In her important essay that addresses Gilles Deleuze and Félix Guattari's "becoming-animal," Manning argues that although "Indigenous peoples have long waited for the West to enter this conversation," they "cannot afford to uncritically allow ideas (either about them or appropriated from them) to float freely across their borders," especially since "such encounters have consistently resulted in explicit attempts to efface divergent Indigenous practices."[46]

Indeed, perhaps paradoxically, given his postmodern roots, Deleuze's work has been central to this more recent move to account for the agency of the material world as a response to the emphasis on language games. But even for Deleuze's new empiricism, for which immanence is actually the destruction of any immanence/transcendence binary encompassing relations between materiality and sensation, there is still, it would seem, no point of view.[47] Instead, this approach traces affects and percepts as they bypass the subject—as direct intensities.[48] And for this approach, "knowing is not a human-dependent characteristic but a feature of the world in its differential becoming."[49]

Barad's agential realism similarly accounts for "ontological indeterminacy, a radical openness, an infinity of possibilities" that is "at the core of mattering."[50] The understanding of matter she seems to propose locates it at the center of sensing, whereby touching "is inseparable from the field of differential relations that constitute it.[51] Within this field there does not seem to be any consciousness as such, or if there is, as Olkowski argues, it is material: "In Barad's formulation as in Deleuze's, mind is a specific material configuration [and] differential becoming implies the repetition of a significant pattern for which there will be a variety of differences among its phenomena."[52] Phenomena or assemblages as arrangements become intelligible from the outside but not from within, and what is emphasized is the "*being* of the sensible, not sensibility itself."[53] As Barad writes:

> When electrons meet each other "halfway," when they intra-act with one another, when they touch one another, whom or what do they touch? In addition to all the various iteratively reconfiguring ways that electrons, indeed all material "entities," are entangled relations of becoming, there is also the fact that materiality "itself" is always already touched by and touching infinite configurations of possible others, other beings and times.[54]

In short, it is touching and sensing that "matter does, or rather, what matter is."[55]

While Deleuze and Barad provide the view from without, the phenomenal subject offers a perspective from within, a point of view. Merleau-Ponty notes that a melody can be transposed such that the second version holds no notes in common with the first. The melody is nonetheless recognizable as the "unity of meaning which is expressed in the juxtaposed parts, the creation of certain relations which owe nothing to the materiality of the terms which they unite."[56] Accordingly, the phenomenal subject "is not a mosaic of just any visual and tactual sensations," because there must be someone there to make sense of them, someone to gather the varied points of view.[57] This gathering takes place on many levels. There is, of course, a "central vision that joins the scattered visions, that unique touch that governs the whole tactile life of my body as a unit, that *I think* that must be able to accompany all our experiences."[58] But Merleau-Ponty also explains that what we understand as "mind or thought" is in fact "a sublimation of the flesh" in that it comes out of the anonymous and shared level of pre-personal existence, including our relations with others, as well as the sedimentation of experience that shapes the "past's structure."[59] Indeed, past events tend to remain in the background unless "the intentional threads to the horizon of the lived past" are reopened, inviting the embodied subject to once again "take up the situation that it evokes."[60] Accordingly, the subject who gathers the touching is not left behind even as it is radically and phenomenally revisited. For Merleau-Ponty, touching hands are part of a tangible world that can be felt from without but also from within.[61] As well, there can be no question of a mind/body split. He writes, "While each monocular vision, each touching with one sole hand has its own visible, its tactile, each is bound to every other vision, to every other touch; it is bound in such a way as to make up with the experience of one sole body before one sole world." Finally, the movements of touching belong not only to the embodied subject but also to the world to which they belong; they cross over and "incorporate themselves into the universe they interrogate," even as they are initiated from a point of view.[62]

Merleau-Ponty comes to call this understanding of being "flesh" and captures with his descriptions an ontology that lays out an interrelational world with points of view that are by no means autonomous; instead, they intersect and reverberate with one another in multiple ways.[63] As Eva-Maria Simms elaborates in this volume, these reverberations are a style of appearing that belong to a structure. In one rich sketch Merleau-Ponty describes how he sees the tiling of a pool through the thickness of the water not "*despite* the water and the reflections there," but rather "because of them": "If there were no distortions, no ripples of sunlight, if it were without this flesh that I saw the geometry of the tiles, then I would cease to see it *as* it is and where it is—which is to say, beyond any identical, specific place." Indeed, the "aqueous power, the shimmering element" is not contained by the pool. It "materializes itself there" as well as in the reflections, the "active and living essence" dancing across the cypress trees.[64] In other words, if we attend to what is there, we can perceive the intertwining and overlapping that is flesh. Moreover, Merleau-Ponty shares this insertion into the flesh of being with others when, for example, he speaks of the landscape with his companion and the "green of the meadow" pervades them both.[65] Our relations with others reveal we belong to a shared, perceptible world. In these short passages he thus captures some of the larger texture of an interrelated world.

The sense we make out of our sensible, motile, affective relations with the world, others, and ourselves is also political. As Hannah Arendt explains in *The Human Condition*, politically we need to rely on speech and action coming out of multiple perspectives on the world in order to decide where we want to go. This is not an easy goal, for we are witness to an age where, as Arendt observes, ideological lies can become true. Ideologues can impose their own truths upon a society, even performing the truths they proclaim to discover.[66] Just as "rational truth informs philosophical speculation," for Arendt, factual truth is political in that it can ground multiple perspectives or opinions, and so long as opinion respects factual truths, it is still "legitimate."[67] It is when factual truth is left behind that we end up with the ultimate postmodern position—that all truth is relative, described in the contemporary political climate as "alternative facts." Ultimately, an informed political position relies neither on lies nor on one perspective; rather, it comes from what Arendt calls an "enlarged mentality," whereby we take into account as many viewpoints on an issue as possible.[68] Phenomenology can account for this factual multiplicity.

It is our claim that now is the time for feminist phenomenology to come into its own—that feminist phenomenology provides the future promise for thinking through and accounting for interrelational subjects as agents who act out of situations. This entails committing to a project without knowing exactly where it will take us or whether it will succeed. But there is now a need to rethink human subjects in new ways, to displace them from the center, to think of them not only in terms of their plurality, their interrelationality, but also in terms of embodied sensibility, as inhabiting the boundary between the inner realm of thinking and feeling and the exterior, experiential world that belongs to the social, ethical, and political. Human subjects must thus be rethought of in terms of their indebtedness and responsibility to the world as "*an open or unfinished system.* . . . [For it is] *the same radical contingency which threatens it with discord* [that] *also rescues it from the inevitability of disorder and prevents us from despairing of it,*" so long as we work to preserve and multiply relations among humans, other beings, and the world.[69] Whatever our intentions, we undertake to act without knowing in advance the "objective sense" of our actions.[70] Nonetheless, because we are caught up in the larger social and historical context to which we belong, if we attend to that context, we also have the potential to enact change.[71]

NOTES

1. Silvia Stoller, "What Is Feminist Phenomenology," chapter 18 in this volume.
2. Mariana Ortega's work on inhabiting multiple worlds, "positions" or "borderlands, in *neplanta* or in-betweenness," is important for understanding not only the privilege that comes with inhabiting one world but also the richness that comes from inhabiting the in-between. See Ortega, *In-Between: Latina Feminist Phenomenology, Multiplicity, and the Self* (Albany: State University of New York Press, 2016), 3.
3. Thanks to Dorothea Olkowski for working with me to articulate this claim precisely.
4. Hannah Arendt, *The Human Condition* (Chicago: Chicago University Press, 1958), 175–78.
5. Maurice Merleau-Ponty, *Humanism and Terror*, trans. John O'Neill (Boston: Beacon Press, 1969), xxxv. As an example of this "liberal mystification," he refers to focusing on a flag or a "constitution which legitimates the classical means of police and military oppression." See *Humanism and Terror*, xxiii–xxiv.
6. Ibid., xiv.
7. Ibid., xlii.
8. See Stoller's essay in this volume (chapter 18) for a full history of this term and the emergence of the discipline of feminist phenomenology.
9. See Simone de Beauvoir, *The Second Sex*, trans. Constance Borde and Sheila Malovany-Chevallier (New York: Alfred A. Knopf, 2010). For a look at Stein's feminism, see Antonio Calcagno, *The Philosophy of Edith Stein* (Pittsburgh: Duquesne University Press, 2007).
10. Merleau-Ponty, *Phenomenology of Perception*, trans. Donald A. Landes (New York: Routledge, 2012), 414.

11. Sara Heinämaa and Lanei Rodemeyer, introduction to "Feminist Phenomenologies," ed. Sara Heinämaa and Lanei Rodemeyer, special issue, *Continental Philosophy Review* 43, no. 1 (2010): 1.
12. Linda Fisher, "Feminist Phenomenological Voices," in "Feminist Phenomenologies," ed. Sara Heinämaa and Lanei Rodemeyer, special issue, *Continental Philosophy Review* 43, no. 1 (2010): 85.
13. For example, Iris Marion Young, *Throwing Like a Girl and Other Essays in Feminist Philosophy and Social Theory* (Bloomington: Indiana University Press, 1990).
14. Merleau-Ponty, *The Visible and the Invisible*, trans. Alphonso Lingis (Evanston, IL: Northwestern University Press, 1968), 133, 264.
15. Dorothea E. Olkowski, *Postmodern Philosophy and the Scientific Turn* (Bloomington: Indiana University Press, 2012), 61; Merleau-Ponty, *Visible and the Invisible*, 266.
16. Merleau-Ponty, *Humanism and Terror*, 177.
17. Ibid., xxxvi.
18. Ibid., xxxv.
19. Merleau-Ponty, *Phenomenology of Perception*, 62.
20. Ibid., 23.
21. Ibid., 5, 10.
22. Ibid., 4.
23. Ibid., 5.
24. See Gail Weiss, "The Normal Abnormalities," chapter 11 in this volume.
25. Merleau-Ponty, *Phenomenology of Perception*, 214.
26. See, for example, Quentin Meillassoux, *After Finitude: An Essay on the Necessity of Contingency*, trans. Ray Brassier (London: Continuum, 2008); and as background, Olkowski, "Materialism, Contingency and Thought: The Limits of Meillassoux's New Materialism" in "theory@buffalo," special issue, *The Word Flesh* 17 (July 2013).
27. Merleau-Ponty, *The Structure of Behavior*, trans. Alden L. Fisher (Boston: Beacon Press, 1963), 166.
28. Merleau-Ponty, *Phenomenology of Perception*, 260. See also Eva-Maria Simms's essay in this volume (chapter 8) for a wonderful account of phenomenal structures.
29. Merleau-Ponty, *Phenomenology of Perception*, 261.
30. See Beata Stawarska's essay in this volume (chapter 7), as well as Emily Lee's and Kyoo Lee's (chapters 17 and 2, respectively), for more on this theme.
31. Martin Heidegger, "Letter on Humanism," in *Basic Writings*, ed. David Farrel Krell (London: Routledge, 1993), 217.
32. Jacques Derrida, "Différance," in *Margins of Philosophy*, trans. Alan Bass (Chicago: University of Chicago Press, 1982); Michel Foucault, *The History of Sexuality*, trans. Robert Hurley, vol. 1, *An Introduction* (New York: Pantheon, 1978).
33. We can see this move in Judith Butler's earlier work, where being a gender is replaced by performativity, gender as doing, or, ultimately, the ways gender is understood or read. See Butler, *Gender Trouble: Feminism and the Subversion of Identity* (New York: Routledge, 1990). In her later work there is a return to ontological questions. See, for example, Butler, *Frames of War: When Is Life Grievable?* (New York: Verso, 2009).
34. Luce Irigaray, *Speculum of the Other Woman*, trans. Gillian C. Gill (Ithaca, NY: Cornell University Press, 1985); Butler, *Gender Trouble*; Gayatri Chakravorty Spivak, "Can the Subaltern Speak?," in *Marxism and the Interpretation of Culture*, ed. Cary Nelson and Lawrence Grossberg, 271–313 (Urbana: University of Illinois Press, 1988).

35. See Judith Butler, *Bodies That Matter* (New York: Routledge, 1994).
36. See Gilles Deleuze, *The Logic of Sense*, trans. Mark Lester (New York: Columbia University Press, 1990).
37. Olkowski, *Postmodern Philosophy*, 104.
38. Ibid., 104.
39. Ibid., 105.
40. Arendt, *The Origins of Totalitarianism* (San Diego: Harcourt, 1968), 445.
41. Olkowski, *Postmodern Philosophy*, 117.
42. Stacy Alaimo and Susan Hekman, "Introduction: Emerging Models of Materiality in Feminist Theory," in *Material Feminisms*, ed. Stacy Alaimo and Susan Hekman (Bloomington: Indiana University Press, 2008), 5.
43. Ibid., 6.
44. Jane Bennett, *Vibrant Matter: A Political Ecology of Things* (Durham, NC: Duke University Press, 2010), vii.
45. Karen Barad, "Posthumanist Performativity: Toward an Understanding of How Matter Comes to Matter," in *Material Feminisms*, ed. Stacy Alaimo and Susan Hekman (Bloomington: Indiana University Press, 2008), 135.
46. Dolleen Manning, "The Becoming Human of Buffalo Bill," in *Intensities and Lines of Flight*, ed. Antonio Calcagno, Jim Vernon, and Stephen G. Lofts (London: Rowman and Littlefield, 2014), 188, 202. See also Chapter 9 in this volume.
47. And, as Manning points out, "Where the human is the ground of ethics, politics, capitalism, democracy, colonization and subjectivity, with becoming-animal, Deleuze and Guattari call for a disruption of humanism, through an emphasis on difference and dispersion, rather than commonality." See Manning, "Becoming Human," 188.
48. See Olkowski, *Postmodern Philosophy*, 75.
49. Ibid., 79.
50. Barad, "On Touching—The Inhuman That Therefore I Am," *Differences* 23, no. 3 (2012): 215. It is this "everything is possible" that Arendt attributes to totalitarianism, which entails the imposition of formal mathematical structures on human relations such that what is there is required to conform to the ideological structure. See Arendt, *Origins of Totalitarianism*, 440.
51. Barad, "On Touching," 216.
52. Olkowski, "Every 'One'—a Crowd, Making Room for the Excluded Middle," in *Deleuze and Queer Theory*, ed. Chrysanthi Nigianni and Merl Storr (Edinburgh: Edinburgh University Press, 2009), 57.
53. Ibid., 60.
54. Barad, "On Touching," 216.
55. Ibid.
56. Merleau-Ponty, *Structure of Behavior*, 87.
57. Ibid., 156.
58. Ibid.
59. Merleau-Ponty, *Visible and the Invisible*, 145.
60. Merleau-Ponty, *Phenomenology of Perception*, 88.
61. Merleau-Ponty, *Visible and the Invisible*, 134.
62. Rather than the view from the outside that Barad and Deleuze provide, Olkowski suggests we turn to the work of Fotini Markopoulou, who advocates instead for a theory "that refers to observations made from 'inside,' in which in evolving states,

the stage and the actors, evolve together." Markopoulou, "Planck-Scale Models of the Universe," in *Science and Ultimate Reality: From Quantum to Cosmos (Explorations Celebrating the Vision of John Archibald Wheeler)*, ed. John D. Barrow, Paul C. W. Davies, and Charles L. Harper Jr. (Cambridge, UK: Cambridge University Press, 2002), 3, as quoted by Olkowski, *Postmodern Philosophy*, 142. This approach allows for multiple and different observers living "partly different, partial views of the universe, partial views which nonetheless overlap." See Olkowski, *Postmodern Philosophy*, 142. And Merleau-Ponty writes that "the reference to a sensible or historical given is not a provisional imperfection; it is essential to physical knowledge. . . . Laws have meaning only as a means of conceptualizing the perceived world." See Merleau-Ponty, *Structure of Behavior*, 145.

63. Merleau-Ponty, *Visible and the Invisible*, 135.

64. Merleau-Ponty, "Eye and Mind," trans. Carleton Dallery, in *The Primacy of Perception*, ed. James M. Edie (Evanston, IL: Northwestern University Press, 1964), 70–71.

65. Merleau-Ponty, *Visible and the Invisible*, 142.

66. The recent political climate established by President Donald Trump provides clear evidence of Arendt's concern that the political world grounded in the factual accounts of speech and action is fragile. Though for Arendt, lying itself is action in that it can effect change, ultimately, she writes, the political realm is "limited" by that which humans "cannot change at will. And it is only respecting its own borders that this realm, where we are free to act and to change, can remain intact, preserving its integrity and keeping its promises. Conceptually, we may call truth what we cannot change; metaphorically, it is the ground on which we stand and the sky that stretches above us." Arendt, "Truth and Politics," in *Between Past and Future* (New York: Penguin Books, 1993), 264.

67. Ibid., 238.

68. Ibid., 241–42.

69. Merleau-Ponty, *Humanism and Terror*, 188.

70. Ibid., 64.

71. Ibid., 67.

BIBLIOGRAPHY

Alaimo, Stacy, and Susan Hekman. "Introduction: Emerging Models of Materiality in Feminist Theory." In *Material Feminisms*, edited by Stacy Alaimo and Susan Hekman, 1–20. Bloomington: Indiana University Press, 2008.

Arendt, Hannah. *The Human Condition*. Chicago: University of Chicago Press, 1958.

———. *The Origins of Totalitarianism*. San Diego: Harcourt, 1968

———. "Truth and Politics." In *Between Past and Future*. New York: Penguin Books, 1993.

Barad, Karen. "On Touching—The Inhuman That Therefore I Am." *Differences* 23, no. 3 (2012): 206–223.

———. "Posthumanist Performativity: Toward an Understanding of How Matter Comes to Matter." In *Material Feminisms*, edited by Stacy Alaimo and Susan Hekman, 120–54.

Beauvoir, Simone de. *The Second Sex*. Translated by Constance Borde and Sheila Malovany-Chevallier. New York: Alfred A. Knopf, 2010.

Bennett, Jane. *Vibrant Matter: A Political Ecology of Things*. Durham, NC: Duke University Press, 2010.

Butler, Judith. *Bodies That Matter*. New York: Routledge, 1994.
———. *Frames of War: When Is Life Grievable?* New York: Verso, 2009.
———. *Gender Trouble: Feminism and the Subversion of Identity*. New York: Routledge, 1990.
Calcagno, Antonio. *The Philosophy of Edith Stein*. Pittsburgh: Duquesne University Press, 2007.
Deleuze, Gilles. *The Logic of Sense*. Translated by Mark Lester. New York: Columbia University Press, 1990.
Derrida, Jacques. "Différance." In *Margins of Philosophy*, translated by Alan Bass, 3–27. Chicago: University of Chicago Press, 1982.
Fisher, Linda. "Feminist Phenomenological Voices." *Feminist Phenomenologies*. Special issue, *Continental Philosophy Review* 43, no. 1 (2010): 83–85.
Foucault, Michel. *The History of Sexuality*. Vol. 1, *An Introduction*. Translated by Robert Hurley. New York: Pantheon, 1978.
Heidegger, Martin. "Letter on Humanism." In *Basic Writings*, edited by David Farrell Krell, 213–66. London: Routledge, 1993.
Heinämaa, Sara, and Lanei Rodemeyer. Introduction to *Feminist Phenomenologies*. Special issue, *Continental Philosophy Review* 43, no. 1 (2010): 1–11.
Irigaray, Luce. *Speculum of the Other Woman*. Translated by Gillian C. Gill. Ithaca, NY: Cornell University Press, 1985.
Manning, Dolleen Tisawii'ashii. "The Becoming Human of Buffalo Bill." In *Intensities and Lines of Flight*, edited by Antonio Calcagno, Jim Vernon, and Stephen G. Lofts, 187–206. London: Rowman and Littlefield, 2014.
Markopoulou, Fotini. "Planck-Scale Models of the Universe." In *Science and Ultimate Reality: From Quantum to Cosmos (Explorations Celebrating the Vision of John Archibald Wheeler)*, edited by John D. Barrow, Paul C. W. Davies, and Charles L. Harper Jr. Cambridge, UK: Cambridge University Press, 2002, 3.
Meillassoux, Quentin. *After Finitude: An Essay on the Necessity of Contingency*. Translated by Ray Brassier. London: Continuum, 2008.
Merleau-Ponty, Maurice. "Eye and Mind." Translated by Carleton Dallery. In *The Primacy of Perception*, edited by James M. Edie, 159–90. Evanston, IL: Northwestern University Press, 1964. Originally published as *L'<OE,LIG>il et l'ésprit*. Paris: Gallimard, 1964.
———. *Humanism and Terror*. Translated by John O'Neill. Boston: Beacon Press, 1969.
———. *Phenomenology of Perception*. Translated by Donald A. Landes. New York: Routledge, 2012.
———. *The Structure of Behavior*. Translated by Alden L. Fisher. Boston: Beacon Press, 1963.
———. *The Visible and the Invisible*. Translated by Alphonso Lingis. Evanston, IL: Northwestern University Press, 1968.
Olkowski, Dorothea E. "Every 'One'—a Crowd, Making Room for the Excluded Middle." In *Deleuze and Queer Theory*, edited by Chrysanthi Nigianni and Merl Storr, 54–71. Edinburgh: Edinburgh University Press, 2009.
———. "Materialism, Contingency, and Thought: The Limits of Meillassoux's New Materialism." theory@buffalo. Special issue, *The Word Flesh* 17 (July 2013): 120–48.
———. *Postmodern Philosophy and the Scientific Turn*. Bloomington: Indiana University Press, 2012.

Ortega, Mariana. *In-Between: Latina Feminist Phenomenology, Multiplicity, and the Self.* Albany: State University of New York Press, 2016.

Spivak, Gayatri Chakravorty. "Can the Subaltern Speak?." In *Marxism and the Interpretation of Culture*, edited by Cary Nelson and Lawrence Grossberg, 271–313. Urbana: University of Illinois Press, 1988.

Young, Iris Marion. *Throwing Like a Girl and Other Essays in Feminist Philosophy and Social Theory.* Bloomington: Indiana University Press, 1990.

INTRODUCTION

DOROTHEA E. OLKOWSKI
AND HELEN A. FIELDING

THE FUTURE IS NOW

"The future is now." Google this phrase and you might be surprised to see at least 854 million results, many of which seem to announce advances in technology, although there are some song titles high in the rankings. Yet in scrolling through them, it appears that none of the results define or explain what this phrase means. The philosopher Ludwig Feuerbach did not address the future as now, but he did write about "the philosophy of the future" in a critique of G.W.F. Hegel that proposes to look at being, not as an abstraction, but as sensuous, a being involved in sense perception, feeling, and love.[1] What truly exists, Feuerbach claims, must be able to be loved, and the laws of reality must also be the laws of thought.[2] Addressing Karl Marx's later critique of Feuerbach, Maurice Merleau-Ponty picks up on Feuerbach's project in his lecture course "Philosophy and Non-Philosophy since Hegel."[3] Merleau-Ponty expands the discourse on the future to the future that is now, arguing that the concepts of subjectivity and objectivity must be recast in relation to their contact with our life.[4] This is because when philosophy is *not* detached from life, there can be a transfiguration that is "another love," "'a *new happiness.*'"[5]

In this light, the essays in part 1 of this book invoke the future but also the joyfulness and love a philosophy of the future bears. But that is not all, because although there is the sense that when such a future philosophy arrives, it arrives joyfully as a celebration and as happiness, perhaps it also arrives as a sort of revolutionary fervor. Merleau-Ponty's view of this fervor is that "one can only validly think what one has in some way lived, the rest being nothing but imagination."[6]

But it may also be important to recall that, as Merleau-Ponty states, "The idea of a continuous revolutionary effort, a social structure without inertia ... the idea of a transparent and lucid history," belongs to a system that can only be called "rationalism" and not to a truly revolutionary process.[7] An actual revolutionary future will always be full of compromises and incoherence and is not a "simple occasion for subjectivity to express its ideas and values in the world, but the commitment of the abstract moral subject to events that are ambiguous."[8] In other words, the future will arrive regardless of what subjects do, but human intervention, ideas, and values bring it into being "now."[9]

Historical and philosophical transformation are like "a traveler who moves into a changing countryside continuously altered by his own advance, where what looked like an obstacle becomes an opening and where the shortest path turns out to be the longest."[10] The way we perceive the present and the future does depend upon our wishes and our values, "but the reverse is also true; we love or hate not just in terms of previous values but from experience, from what we see, from our historical experience; and even if every historical choice is subjective, every subjectivity nevertheless reaches through its phantasms to things themselves and aims at the truth."[11]

Our vision of the future that is now does *not* seek to present "*a perception of history* which would continuously clarify the lines of force and vectors of the present," in order *not* to fall into a trajectory that would make the future merely an episode in an otherwise unchanging past.[12] We wish to account for the ambiguous "lines of force and vectors" that in the present make it such that the future,[13] while nowise determined, "is not any empty zone in which we can construct unmotivated projects," but rather that "it is sketched before us like the end of the day underway—and this outline is ourselves."[14] Thus, it is our project to situate the philosophy of feminist phenomenology within these lines of force and vectors.

To inaugurate this effort, Dorothea Olkowski discusses the perception that the human sciences—sociology, epistemology, linguistics, psychoanalysis, and logical analysis, and also the disciplines of communication, information science, technology, medicine, and neuroscience—have been seeking to overtake philosophy. She calls upon feminist phenomenological philosophers to assert our philosophies and to be clear about the plane of thought within which our concepts are placed. This is especially the case for the concept of embodiment, which has been thought and rethought through reflections on the situatedness from which we ourselves arise. She pursues the question of from what planes of thought that situatedness shall emerge now and in the future, and brings forth in a new way the manner in which we may use our intuition to carry this out.

Supporting this, Kyoo Lee's encomium to feminist philosophers past and present opens the future to new ways of doing philosophy. Echoing Simone de Beauvoir, Lee celebrates the concept that life maintains itself by surpassing itself. This essay overflows with the "emotion and declassified thoughts" of myriad feminist philosophers who, like Hypatia—who threw her bloodstained handkerchief into the faces of men—have again and again thrown the words of male philosophers back at them in order to start a new language, a "trans-fem-idiom," thinking in this way the end of this language into which they have been thrown and the beginning of that new one, first thrown but then throwing ahead.

Referring to Beauvoir, who in *The Second Sex* shows how difficult it is to cease referring to masculinity as the standard by which humanity is defined, Lyat Friedman contrasts the rigid Sadean man with the Masochistic man, who learns from the woman he initially attempts to control that he does not need "to define his manhood in relation to what he thinks women need to be or what he can do to and with them." Taking up the account of Gilles Deleuze, which overturns the oedipal readings of Sigmund Freud, Friedman shows us that by flooding the text with associative possibilities, random elements, arbitrary connections, and irregular shifts and turns, Masoch opens up the playful scenario acted out by Lou Salomé, who is photographed with a whip held over Paul Rée and Friedrich Nietzsche. Such lines of flight, Friedman finds, identify intersections, leave behind stagnant paths, and produce alternative futures for women.

This section finds its climax in Rachel McCann's exhilarating essay, which engages with contemporary architecture as a feminist phenomenological project. What structures both of these endeavors is their dynamic balance between repetition and anomaly, between the predictable and the unexpected, that links pattern work to creativity. McCann argues that in architecture as in philosophy, "patterns lacking flexibility will break against the force of larger systems, becoming isolated or disappearing altogether, and those too similar to their enveloping systems are also likely to be subsumed." And she finds these ideas originally and powerfully at work in Beauvoir and other feminists who articulate feminism to be an open system that answers to multiple demands and diverse identities.

NEGOTIATING FUTURES

Since we cannot know the future, negotiating futures phenomenally requires a commitment with no guarantees. Nonetheless, if binaries of reason and passion, internal and external, intention and action, subject and object are left behind, as we propose, then we cannot commit to a future we feel passionately about if we do not think there is a possibility of its becoming. Similarly, if we forget our passions and cynically support the future we think is inevitable, we are complicit with its eventuality.[15] In negotiating futures, we suggest that "passion and reason" become "identical" so that when others look back historically at our now, at what has been accomplished, what seemed motivated by "the obscurity of desire" will seem inevitable and will "appear as the truth of the moment."[16] We thus suggest that the "element of reason" coexist with "the elements of audacity and risk of failure" in the actions we take and the choices we make.[17]

Although negotiating futures in this book is a call for revolutionary change, it is nonetheless also temporal and reliant on context—we think and act on "the horizontal plane of existence," against the background of its "vertical dimension."[18] The actions we choose must belong to concrete situations and be evaluated accordingly; this is how change takes place, how we remain open to the new—not through breaking with the past, whereby we remain the same, but through bringing the past with us and opening it up to new possibilities.[19]

In this light Helen Fielding considers how the repetition of the same can be phenomenally shifted. Considering the phenomenon of death by suicide in response to cyberbullying, she asks how cyberspace as a system can be opened up and become more responsive to the living affect of young women subjected to abuse. At the heart of this problem is the breakdown of personal time into objective time, whereby the inexhaustible potentiality of the living world is collapsed into the indifferent infinity of the possible that, unconnected to living existence, is ultimately a closed system.

Accordingly, while the past shapes how we understand ourselves in the present, it does not necessarily determine the possibilities for our futures. Debra Bergoffen points to the insights Beauvoir provides in negotiating futures by rethinking the category of the Other in ways that it does not have to be the mark of oppression as historically defined. Instead she suggests that women's resistance—motivated by the possibility of a shared existence with all of its accompanying "pleasures and dangers . . . risks and vulnerabilities," and directed by desire—could break down the binaries of oppressor and oppressed, of imposed categories and concrete realities. Instead, the Other could become a sign of the "dignity of difference," as she so aptly describes it.

This commitment to a shared future not defined by the binaries of oppressor and oppressed is clearly articulated by Beata Stawarska in her analysis of speech act theory, the final essay in part 2. She concludes that it is not enough to attend to the "production" of speech, to be able to speak as the Other; we must also attend to the "reception of speech in a social context." With Bergoffen she imagines a shared happiness that emerges from an intersubjective world where we attend to a shared responsibility for both speaking and listening.

THE ONTOLOGICAL FUTURE

Ontology is defined as the study of the nature of being, but in this volume we are promising something more, something futural. For a long time we Western philosophers conceived of time in the manner of the ancient Greeks, Aristotle in particular, for whom time is given together with movement. So when we perceived time, we perceived that one part of time "has been" and so "is not," while another part of time is "going to be" and so also "is not." Thus, time was often thought to consist of what "is not" in relation to which the "now" serves as a boundary between past and future. For many this was replaced by Immanuel Kant's concept of an a priori intuition of space and time as the condition of the possibility of the experience of objects. These intuitions are the form of our experience, a conceptual framework that organizes it, but also a necessity in that we cannot have an experience of a physical object without intuition. Both conceptions left us with a static notion of time as the measure of space, not as futural. Thus, the phenomenological account of time proposed by Edmund Husserl supplants Kant's.

For Husserl, the internal temporality of what appears *flows away* in temporal phases that are continual and changing appearances of something that is "called" identical. Its unity is synthetic, meaning it is not the connectedness of *cogitationes* that are stuck to one another externally. Synthesis means not simply something side by side, externally related in the way physical objects are related to one another in space. Rather, what appears is *immanent in the flowing* consciousness, and this synthesis is the primal form of belonging to consciousness. This flowing away toward the future is completely unique, and any thematized object gets its identity through the flowing subjective process as an *intentional effect* of this futural temporal synthesis.[20]

But to fulfill the task of a phenomenological ontology, the futural temporal synthesis must also be related to the world and to our sensation of the world. Taking our cue from Henri Bergson, we argue that even our most minute sensations form an ontological memory, images created by the imperceptible influences of states in the world on our sensibility. It is a memory for which the entire past coexists with each new present in relation to which it is now past, as if these sensibilities were repeated again and again but *always altering*, each time opening onto something new. What catches our attention is that every new perception, every sensation alters the past and opens a new future. This is the being of what exists as a futural phenomenon.

Eva-Maria Simms, first and foremost, inquires into the potential of ontology as a feminist project. She situates this in the context of Merleau-Ponty's concept of the hyperdialectic as it manifests itself in the concrete presence of people, things, and events altering with time and permeated with absence. To articulate this Merleau-Ponty turned to Gestalt laws that express the hyperdialectical relationship of figure to ground and part to whole, but that come from the standpoint that each of us exists as a limited, interrelated part of the constellation and has only a dim intuition of the whole. Applying this principle to gender, Simms utilizes the concepts of situatedness, sexual identity, choice and destiny, temporality, diacritics, difference, and indetermination to formulate some aspects of an ontology that takes into account the specific dimensions of gendered existence as it continuously alters.

Situating her discourse from within the complex and entangled ontology specific to Algonquin language groups' centrally important concept of *mnidoo*—an unconscious conceding or an interruption of intentions, which is ingrained over generations—Dolleen Tisawii'ashii Manning weaves together the poetics of Indigenous author Linda Hogan, the phenomenology of Maurice Merleau-Ponty, and her study of and reflections on *Anishinaabe*, the "original person/being," the term utilized by the Ojibwe Indigenous peoples to name themselves. Manning contends that Anishinaabe as a "way of being" is attuned to what is there in the world in a particular way, an attitude of careful consideration toward the mnidoo-infused world as a coexistent and inherently entangled interrelationality. She draws this out in relation to the conception of prereflective knowledge of Merleau-Ponty and with Merleau-Ponty's chiasmic postulate of an "ahuman lineate," to articulate how such a prereflective unconscious mnidoo-worlding nevertheless opens onto a dialogic embodiment as expressed in the Ojibwe aphorism "We only own what we give away."

In the final essay of part 3, Christine Daigle takes up the difficult concept of human subjectivity, proposing that the human being is a "subjective multiplicity," a manifold that both makes itself through its experiences and is shaped by these experiences. Her self-described "irreverent" approach is to conceive of herself as Montaigne's bee that collects nectar from different flowers and eventually produces the honey that is its own. Her essay, both humorous and deeply serious, commences with a review of key feminist contributions to this concept. These in turn lead her to propose a feminist phenomenological ontology of trans((subj)(obj))ectivity that characterizes our gendered experience of the world and ourselves as fragmented beings whose fragments coalesce to form our being. Daigle is especially focused on how trauma and extreme experiences transform persons, alter them, and change them into completely different beings, and why this is possible ontologically insofar as they are not individual at all but always an ambiguous multiplicity.

OUR FUTURE BODY IMAGES

The body image is a vital prereflective sketch of the body's practical possibilities for engagement with the world. For this reason, it is central to our understanding of agency. There are of course different interpretations of what the term "body image" actually refers to in contemporary neurological, psychological, and phenomenological literature. One interpretation makes a clear conceptual distinction between body image and body schema, with the first referring to a "conscious reflection on my body and its possibilities," and the second to the prereflective yet "dynamic organization of the body which renders it capable of performing physical tasks."[21] Merleau-Ponty, drawing on the work of Paul Schilder, did not, however, make a sharp distinction between body image and body schema, likely because conscious images emerge from and are intertwined with the prereflective body. Challenging binaries of mind and body, internal and external, he admitted no such sharp distinctions in the embodied subject's structure.[22] Phenomenologically understood, then, the body image is, as Gail Weiss describes it in her pivotal work on the subject, "neither an individual construction, nor the result of a series of conscious choices, but rather, an active agency that has its own memory, habits, and horizons of significance."[23] It is a "system of equivalences" that allows us to transpose certain "motor tasks" that can never be understood outside the entire meaningful intertwined structure of individual and world. In other words, "the body schema is not merely an experience of my body, but rather an experience of my body in the world," which means sense and movement are never discrete.[24]

For feminist phenomenology this means our future body images emerge out of what we do now. Because it traces out how we engage with and take up the world as the system of possibilities, the body image is always both particular to each individual and yet also completely social. As a dynamic structure it is itself not perceived. Instead, it is more like a "norm or a privileged position," an attitude according to which we engage with the world and others.[25] Nonetheless, because the body image is the interpenetration of the embodied subject and the world, it is also a "certain structure of the perceived world," and its traces are inscribed within us.[26] Thus changing what we do and being shaped by social practices are inherently intertwined. Since corporeal schemas reflect the ways we take up the world, shifting these practical possibilities or embodied norms is pivotal to shifting practical possibilities, and, similarly, bringing concrete change to our world can also shift the ways we move and hence our bodily schemas. For Merleau-Ponty this means that the ways we move are absolutely intertwined with consciousness.

In her chapter for this volume, Gail Weiss extends her earlier work on body images, thinking through how the normal process of aging is socially understood to be abnormal, often leading to the stigmatization and isolation of the elderly. People with disabilities are similarly marked as abnormal. Yet, if we rethink our understanding of the normal so that norms provide a variety of structures with which we engage in the world—indeed, for the individual embodied subject, they are not atypical at all—we have new possibilities for rethinking aging and disability. Rethinking "normal abnormalities" would mean neither aging nor disability would have to be denied, and the possibilities of bodily normality could be greatly expanded. Such expansion works chiasmically with changing social attitudes, since motility and consciousness are so intricately intertwined.

Christina Schües investigates how the changing social and normative structures of the lifeworld are constituted through extraordinary biotechnological interventions. She develops her innovative bio-phenomenology in order to consider the shifting meanings of experience given the dramatic interventions of biotechnological practices such as reproductive genetics and transplantation into life itself. Bodies themselves are at the heart of new biotechnologies, so the new practices that emerge from them also shift our understandings and experiences of what it means to be embodied, as well as the social relationships that are inherently altered by these technologies. Schües is engaged with nothing less than the question of the meaning of life, a question that urgently needs to be posed anew and rethought in light of these paradigm shifts in what it means to be embodied.

While Schües is interested in the ways biotechnologies radically alter the lifeworld, Annemie Halsema and Jenny Slatman investigate shifting body images through narrative and dialogic meaning-making structures, attending specifically to the relation between health-care providers and patients. Although many people working in health and nursing studies have embraced phenomenology, the focus is usually on the first-person perspective, how the patient articulates her experiences. Halsema and Slatman propose changing the field. Drawing on women's narratives of their body images with relation to breast cancer, they instead investigate how the medical practitioners' interactions with patients, along with patients' reflections on their own meaning-making practices, can work to shift the ways they understand themselves in relation to their illness. Drawing on the work of Paul Ricoeur, they show how patients' voices, along with the interaction between medical professionals and patients, should be considered as a narrative and hence meaning-making practice.

Body images concern the local, personal, and social but also have political and ethical implications on a global scale. Katy Fulfer takes on the charged world of contract pregnancy and its implications for exploiting women in the global south. Though Hannah Arendt relegated pregnancy and labor to the private sphere, Fulfer draws on Arendt's work to argue that contract pregnancy can be understood as belonging as well to the public and hence political realm. To make this argument work, she raises the question of whether women in the global south who have contracted their gestational labor are able to exercise agency. The issues raised by Fulfer, like those raised by the others in this section, point to how phenomenology is being creatively revolutionized and taken in new directions to address pressing biotechnological, social, and political changes in the world. Through the individual to the global spheres that belong to this time and its multiple situations, they investigate the possibilities for being agents in this contemporary world.

PRESENT AND FUTURE SELVES

We speak and act before others, but for these actions not to fall away into obscurity, we build a world that endures. We fabricate things, artworks, and other structures, sometimes meant to endure. And this world in turn conditions us. Thus it is imperative that we think carefully about the world we create through our everyday and more extraordinary endeavors, since it is the one that shapes our future. Accordingly, imagining new possibilities for future selves comes out of the thinking and work in which we engage with now.

Given that women live, work, and act in a social structure that has not been thoroughly modified even by the many changes in women's condition, we insist that women wish to be part of a world that they have participated in building. This means that political and social awareness are of the greatest importance but that without real political and social opportunities, women's future selves may not be radically different from their past selves. Creating the environment for present and future selves is our task now. To some extent this is a matter of universal as well as state-driven social and political change, but such efforts usually do not come from the top. Looking at our past selves and creating our present and future now falls into the hands and minds of women who engage with new theories and practices regarding social and political life, apply the utmost scrutiny to them, and loudly and publicly announce their effectiveness for women's present and future selves. Such evaluation and scrutiny is the crucial task of the essays that complete our volume.

Posing the pivotal question of what feminist phenomenology is, in the final essay in this volume Silvia Stoller traces the concept back through its somewhat meandering journey that takes shape only through this act of looking back at the many creative works that seem to take on its form. As she brings to light, one important characteristic of feminist phenomenology is the astonishing emphasis on the political and change. Beauvoir's *The Second Sex* drew on descriptions of women's everyday lives, bringing them into view in order to transform them. Stoller shows how other feminist theorists similarly drew on this methodology to reveal such phenomena as the everydayness of racialization and the deep structures of heteronormative cultures. With this accompanying interdisciplinary vision of future directions, feminist phenomenology clearly undermines critiques of phenomenology as being merely descriptive and hence apolitical. Thus inherent to this methodology from the beginning was imagining a world that would enable future selves to emerge in multiple possible ways without being limited by the external projections that accompany oppression.

Emily Lee engages with future selves through her exploration of the intricate co-implication of sameness and difference in theorizing racial and sexual differences. As she points out, on the one side of the binary, these differences have been mobilized to support multiple oppressive practices. On the other side, practicing indifference and not taking difference into account can also be oppressive. Turning to Merleau-Ponty's concept of "identity-in-difference," Lee explores an alternative to the binary, instead thinking through the relation between identity and difference that upholds the distinction in the terms while showing how they modify each other in productive ways. In particular she is interested in thinking through an innovative approach to a phenomenology of race.

Social and political transformation demands that women take the lead in opening the future for themselves and others. For this reason Rita Gardiner's examination of leadership scholarship is crucial. She argues that for the positivist approach adopted by many authentic leadership scholars, what begins as a theoretical supposition becomes, over time, a universally valid law devoid of context and specificity that does not consider lived, embodied experience. She counters this view from nowhere with how leadership emerges in situated, embodied contexts. Drawing upon the work of Arendt, Gardiner interrogates claims put forward by "authentic leadership" scholars and proposes a relational way of conceptualizing authentic leadership that focuses on lived experience.

The penultimate essay in our volume focuses on one of the most important emerging areas in phenomenological philosophy—that is, the rapidly expanding field of cognitive science. One crucial area for phenomenology is that of the nature of perception. In a sense, nothing is more urgent insofar as how we perceive others and are perceived by them is primary with respect to how women are experienced by others and how we experience ourselves. April Flakne begins with the theory of "direct perception" and argues that its background assumptions can operate to suppress difference in the name of a meaningful coherence for those who profit from existing power relations. For this reason it may remain a species of "arrogant perception." Alternatively, she proposes that Maria Lugones's idea of "world-traveling," combined with an intercorporeity supported by direct perception's invocation of an embodied second person, and an interactionist approach to Others will provide greater opportunities for women to create present and future selves that serve their interests and those of their communities and nations, if not the world.

As witnessed by the flourishing of publications and conferences in this area, feminist phenomenology is coming into its own as a methodology. Many of the essays in this volume stem from the conference "Future Directions in Feminist Phenomenology" held at the University of Western Ontario in 2013. The idea behind this meeting was to invite international leading scholars and a few emerging scholars representing a cross-section of interdisciplinary feminist phenomenological research to provide a better understanding of the future directions of this burgeoning field. A number of the contributors belong to the Feminist Phenomenology Research Group, and this volume marks the third in a trilogy on time including *Time in Feminist Phenomenology* and *Simone de Beauvoir's Philosophy of Age*.[27] The essays in this volume provide for this understanding and demonstrate the breadth of this field.

* * *

We would like to thank Dee Mortensen and Paige Rasmussen along with Indiana University Press for their support and enthusiasm for this project. Funding for this project was provided by the Social Sciences and Humanities Research Council of Canada as well as the University of Western Ontario. We are also grateful to Rachel Bath and Kimberly Dority for their excellent work in formatting the manuscript. Finally, the editors would like to thank members of the Feminist Phenomenology Research Group for their invigorating discussion and contributions to the volume.

NOTES

1. Ludwig Feuerbach, *Principles of Philosophy of the Future*, trans. Zawar Hanfi (1972), sect. 33, https://www.marxists.org/reference/archive/feuerbach/works/future/index.htm.
2. Ibid., Sect. 45.
3. Maurice Merleau-Ponty, "Philosophy and Non-Philosophy Since Hegel," trans. Hugh Silverman, in *Philosophy and Non-Philosophy since Merleau-Ponty*, ed. Hugh Silverman (London: Routledge, 1997).

4. Ibid., 15.
5. Ibid., 12.
6. Maurice Merleau-Ponty, *Humanism and Terror*, trans. John O'Neill (Boston: Beacon Press, 1969), 127; Bryan Smyth, *Merleau-Ponty's Existential Phenomenology and the Realization of Philosophy* (London: Bloomsbury Press, 2014), 280.
7. Merleau-Ponty, *Humanism and Terror*, 74.
8. Ibid., 80, 81.
9. Ibid., 89.
10. Ibid., 94.
11. Ibid., 96.
12. Ibid., 98.
13. Ibid., 104n98.
14. Ibid., 102, 95; emphasis added; Smyth, *Merleau-Ponty's Existential Phenomenology*, 281.
15. Merleau-Ponty, *Humanism and Terror*, 40–41. Merleau-Ponty here refers to the resistance in France during the Second World War, as well as the collaborators, both having committed to a certain future—the first one that combined passion and reason as becomes evident only after the war, and the second who are shown as wrong in light of history.
16. Merleau-Ponty, *Humanism and Terror*, 41.
17. Ibid.
18. Ibid., 163.
19. Ibid., 168.
20. Edmund Husserl, *Cartesian Meditations: An Introduction to Phenomenology*, trans. Dorian Cairnes (The Hague: Martinus Nijhoff Publishers, 1973), 40–42.
21. Gail Weiss points out this distinction made by Shaun Gallagher. See Weiss, *Body Images: Embodiment as Intercorporeality* (New York: Routledge, 1999), 2. See also Gallagher, *How the Body Shapes the Mind* (New York: Oxford University Press, 2005).
22. Weiss, *Body Images*, 2; and Emmanuel de Saint Aubert, *Être et Chair* (Paris: Vrin, 2013), 40.
23. Weiss, *Body Images*, 3.
24. Maurice Merleau-Ponty, *Phenomenology of Perception*, trans. Donald A. Landes (New York: Routledge, 2012), 142.
25. Maurice Merleau-Ponty, *Le Monde sensible et le monde de l'expression: Cours au Collège de France Notes, 1953*, ed. Emmanuel de Saint Aubert and Stefan Kristensen (Geneva: MētisPresses, 2011), 143. Translations are my own.
26. Ibid., 112–14.
27. Christina Schües, Dorothea E. Olkowski, and Helen A. Fielding, eds., *Time in Feminist Phenomenology* (Bloomington: Indiana University Press, 2011); Silvia Stoller, *Simone de Beauvoir's Philosophy of Age: Gender, Ethics, and Time* (Berlin: De Gruyter, 2014). See Stoller's chapter in this volume for a further elaboration of this history.

BIBLIOGRAPHY

Feuerbach, Ludwig. *Principles of the Philosophy of the Future*. Translated by Zawar Hanfi, 1972. https://www.marxists.org/reference/archive/feuerbach/works/future.
Gallagher, Shaun. *How the Body Shapes the Mind*. New York: Oxford University Press, 2005.

Husserl, Edmund. *Cartesian Meditations: An Introduction to Phenomenology.* Translated by Dorian Cairnes. The Hague: Martinus Nijhoff Publishers, 1973.
Merleau-Ponty, Maurice. *Humanism and Terror.* Translated by John O'Neill. Boston: Beacon Press, 1969.
———. *Le Monde sensible et le monde de l'expression: Cours au Collège de France Notes, 1953.* Edited by Emmanuel de Saint Aubert and Stefan Kristensen. Geneva: MētisPresses, 2011.
———. *Phenomenology of Perception.* Translated by Donald A. Landes. New York: Routledge, 2012.
———. "Philosophy and Non-Philosophy since Hegel." Translated by Hugh Silverman. In *Philosophy and Non-Philosophy since Merleau-Ponty*, edited by Hugh Silverman, 9–83. London: Routledge, 1988.
Saint Aubert, Emmanuel de. *Être et Chair.* Paris: Vrin, 2013.
Schües, Christina, Dorothea E. Olkowski, and Helen A. Fielding. *Time in Feminist Phenomenology.* Bloomington: Indiana University Press, 2011.
Smyth, Bryan. *Merleau-Ponty's Existential Phenomenology and the Realization of Philosophy.* London: Bloomsbury Press, 2014.
Stoller, Silvia. *Simone de Beauvoir's Philosophy of Age: Gender, Ethics, and Time.* Berlin: De Gruyter, 2014.
Weiss, Gail. *Body Images: Embodiment as Intercorporeality.* New York: Routledge, 1999.

FEMINIST PHENOMENOLOGY FUTURES

PART 1
THE FUTURE IS NOW

1 USING OUR INTUITION

Creating the Future Phenomenological Plane of Thought

DOROTHEA E. OLKOWSKI

INTRODUCTION: USING OUR INTUITION

What is intuition? Both philosophical and psychological understandings of the idea of intuition may have left feminist philosophy with more questions than answers. Is intuition a sixth sense? Is it cognitive or sensory or something else? Michèle Le Doeuff has pointed out that intuition, in classical philosophical language, designates a mode of immediate apprehension, a direct *intellectual grasp* as opposed to mediated knowledge achieved through reasoning, discussion, internal debate, dialectic, experimentation, deduction, language, or proofs. Given this definition, intuition was once thought to be a valid mode of knowledge. It was thought to cooperate with these various methods of inquiry and to be what sets the process of discovery in motion as well as what completes it.

But today, according to Le Doeuff, intuition is no longer respected. Hegel is charged with having replaced intuition with conceptual analysis. Intuition, he insisted, does *not* reflect upon itself and so is nothing more than beautiful thoughts. Beautiful thoughts are not knowledge. In this way, intuition was separated from discourse, and that was its demise. For without discourse, intuition ceases to be understood as a precise method or system.[1] It ceases to have usefulness and value. Nonetheless, I am advocating that we consider intuition as a method within a structure, a structure within which feminist phenomenology can *make its future* as the future of phenomenology.

HOW TO DO THIS

Let us begin, of course, with the situated woman whose thinking sets the process of discovery in motion. The situated woman is an embodied woman. In what is by now a well-known phrase, Simone de Beauvoir asserts that the body is not a thing but a situation.[2] A body that is a situation and is not a "thing" changes. So if the body is precisely the situation in which we grasp the world and set the process of discovery in motion, the situated woman is "embodied, intersubjective, shaped by history, culture, and society," and, importantly, actively engaged with the world.[3] Thus, the situated, embodied woman's temporalization is intrinsic to her being, which is not that of an unchanging thing.

And yet in practice the situated woman's embodiment has yet to be fully recognized as her freedom, her transcendence. She is often seen as embedded in her embodiment. But this understanding can change. We can make use of "intuition" in a precise and determinate sense to make this change. But first, in order to proceed, let us look more closely at the question of embodiment.

EMBEDDED IN EMBODIMENT

If one were to ask almost any phenomenological philosopher (including those gendered/sexed male) "What is feminist phenomenology about?" one answer that would invariably be offered is "Embodiment, it's about embodiment." Feminist phenomenology is embedded in notions of embodiment possibly because prior to feminist phenomenology, there was very little discussion in philosophy about embodiment.[4]

It has been well noted that philosophy's preoccupation with reason and knowledge has recognized only somewhat recently (given its long history) that reason and knowledge were frequently defined in opposition to "feminine embodiment," an opposition that demanded exclusion, transcendence, and domination, for embodiment appeared on the philosophical scene as an obstacle to the mind's absolute demand for clear thinking and the drive for knowledge.[5] This view had the additional impact (although some perhaps thought benefit) of depriving women of a university education and, even in the case of women who did manage to obtain such an education, of devaluing their work because of their bodies.[6] For this reason, feminist phenomenologists often found their voice by bringing the body to the mind. In the Continental tradition, Edith Stein, Hannah Arendt, Simone de Beauvoir, and Luce Irigaray are frequently recognized for implicitly and explicitly raising the question of woman's place in society, politics, and philosophy in a manner that thematizes questions of embodiment.[7]

But as important as embodiment is to feminist phenomenology, its significance raises the question of why embodiment became so important in phenomenological philosophy and less so in others. This in turn raises the question of method and of the plane of thought within which this concept and the method for addressing it have arisen. Of course, feminist phenomenologists remain intensely alert to questions of method.

Maurice Merleau-Ponty, somewhat subversively, called phenomenological method a style—for example, the "style" in which this particular essay is written. It is deliberately styled so as to draw attention to certain concepts. Such alterations are unexpected in academic work but sanctioned by the methodological concept of style and the phenomenological importance of lived expression addressed by this discourse.[8]

Edmund Husserl was profoundly attuned to the meaning of his phenomenological method. Provocatively, it has been noticed that for Husserl "phenomenology *slows down* the stream of consciousness," and without this slowdown, we lose our focus on the fullness, the depth and the complexity of things, and also on the fullness of events in the world.[9] This brings us to ask what it means to slow consciousness down and how this method, this slowdown alters the naïve experience of embodiment.

Bringing the body to the mind may be more complicated than constructing a syllogism, more difficult than habituation. In our daily lives, we are often expected to play certain embodied roles. As I have noted elsewhere, "Mostly we feel joy and happiness when we are expected to, and we feel sorrow and sadness when it is required of us. Illuminating an interruption or an interval in which we can slow down or refrain from these demands is exhausting and troublesome; fragile states require separation and cushioning."[10] But taking our cue from Husserl, we may not be able to carry out the slowdown of consciousness by looking directly at embodiment. It may be that looking directly is like looking at the sun—we burn our eyes.

Husserl shows us through the epoché that looking directly does not accomplish a slowdown. For example, in the current philosophical climate, the temptation to substitute naïve psychological assumptions—those of neuroscience, for example—for philosophical ideas looms over us and threatens to produce reductive imperatives about the seemingly true nature of consciousness—and so also about embodiment, the body that is brought to mind.

This is not a slowdown. It does not give us the time to grasp our consciousness as embodiment. A true epoché would give us the opportunity, not to objectify the body, but to recognize, as Sartre argued, that consciousness *exists its body*.[11] The connection is existential, meaning lived; no thematization is necessary to bring the body to the mind if it is already a contingent point of view from which it is impossible to withdraw. From this point of view, the body is not an object; the body is the *translucent matter* of consciousness, a revelation for consciousness, a condition of consciousness, suffered as pleasure and pain, love and hate.[12] What need is there to bring this body to consciousness?

So is it not also the case that as much as phenomenology must engage with, take its orientation from, the human and natural sciences, and now more than ever from technological sciences, we might be cautious about the kinds of claims coming from these so-called rivals?[13] "To start with, the human sciences, especially sociology, wanted to replace ... [philosophy]. ... Then it was the turn of epistemology, linguistics, or even of psychoanalysis and logical analysis."[14]

But even bigger claims come from the disciplines of communication, information science, technology, medicine, and neuroscience, all of which clamor for the title "friends of the concept" so that the "simulacrum," the copy of the copy of the concept, has overtaken the philosophical concept, claimed its place. The simulacrum "indicates a society of information services and engineering."[15] In a situation where anyone can claim to be an authority, the *Idea*, the philosophical concept interrogates each claimant, exposing the simulacra, which is to say the perversion of or deviation from the Idea.

Of course, feminists have shown again and again that without non-philosophy—politics, culture, the arts and sciences—engaging with philosophy, it becomes moribund, reflecting only on itself and losing its revolutionary impetus. But if a simulacrum is all philosophy can be, then its concepts are ghostly.

Yet even if we evade the ghostly simulacrum: "Possession of the concept does not appear to coincide with revolution, the democratic State, and human rights."[16] How can this be? "As for us, we possess concepts—after so many centuries of Western thought, we think we possess them—but we hardly know where to put them because we lack a genuine plane. ... The Greeks ... possessed the plane that we no longer possess."[17]

We contemporary feminist phenomenological philosophers need to be clear about the plane of thought within which our concepts are placed. Our cherished concept of embodiment is acquired by reflecting upon the situatedness from which we ourselves arise. But on what plane of thought is that situatedness itself located? What is a plane of thought, after all? A plane of thought has been defined as a milieu populated by concepts and methods.

Gilles Deleuze asserts that the plane of philosophy has only two facets: thought and nature or speech and bodies—two facets, two faces of the same plane of philosophy. Were we to embrace this line of thought, our philosophical plane would be immanent; it would consist of a potentially infinite field of fractals, both physical molecular fractals and molecular crystalline thoughts that are attributes of bodies.[18] For example, ordinary persons caught in a shop by an armed, masked individual may find themselves in the type of situation that transforms them from shoppers into hostages. This, Deleuze claims, is an incorporeal transformation on the order of a speech act.[19] It allows for a clear distinction between nature and language—that is, between the actions and passions of bodies, and the speech acts that express this in language. Since language does not penetrate bodies, language is merely *attributed* to bodies. Nature and language—is this all we need: a material assemblage of bodies and an abstract machine of language?

In this model, each "I" is an Other. Each "I" is the affection of a passivity that experiences its own intelligence, an intelligence operating upon it but not by it.[20] It is a fractured, two-faceted, fractal "I," a passive self, always an Other, always an effect of determinations acting upon it and so never "itself." Thus situated by nature and thought, passive and fractured, situated embodiment is out of its reach. The "I am" that is Other does what it must. It thinks what it might. It cannot intuit nor can it create.

In nature and thought this is a beautiful image, an aesthetic image of a field of fractals and crystals. This field would constitute embodiment as an assemblage of physical forces or as a thought concept, but not as a lived assemblage and a lived expressed concept—not as situated, and not as a consciousness that *exists its body*.

THE PLANE OF IMMANENCE AND THE LIVED SELF

If, as Deleuze maintains, every philosophy has its place, its mental geography, then Deleuze constructs and connects his concepts on a plane of immanence. This means they do not refer to anything outside of the plane. There is no reference to an outside. Instead, on this plane the concepts associate with one another as they respond to a problem posed by thought, and they are attributed to things.

When sensibility is the problem posed by thought, it serves as the condition or form of experience in general and aesthetic experience in particular. Sensation is felt but only as an effect of the harmony or disharmony of our mental powers, in the pleasure or displeasure of our mental functioning. This distinguishes it from intuited sensibility "ensconced in our senses."[21] Thus, intuition is an easily overwhelmed sensation, and it fails to produce the Idea, the concept. Only language can do this.

By contrast, Sartre proclaimed that desire is one of the great forms assumed by the revelation of the Other's body.[22] Our passion for the Other comes to us, not from the pleasure or pain arising with our mental states, but from the world, from the light of the stars, from the temporal relations of a multiplicity of occurrences in the world, and such events reflect on us, leaving their trails, their memory images.

But we are able to localize this array of emanations in the pleasure and pain of our own body:

> In sensing ourselves subjected by the spatio-temporal arrival of events emanating through the body of the other, we feel our own body as well, our absorptions and emanations, our light and our transparency, our own skin and muscles, our own heart beat and breath, we feel them as states or images or passions engaged by the world, in danger in the world, lived as some strange, pure feeling, consciousness making itself the body which it already exists.[23]

But one is only engulfed by passion when fully engaged.

Very soon, according to Jean-Paul Sartre, what disrupts the passionate revelation of the Other's body—the engagement in sensible embodiment—is a purely cognitive awareness, as only a for-itself is able to choose itself while remaining indifferent and unchanged. This is why in the end Sartre is praised by Deleuze for having abandoned the perceptual and affective lived body, the body of the self and the body of an Other, in favor of the impersonal event, which takes place in nature and is conceptualized by thought.[24] In the end it is, for Sartre, an illusion to believe that one is not becoming in-itself or for-itself each time one is enveloped by a new circumstance, a new event.

Phenomenology and phenomenological intuition, from this point of view, naïvely yields "perceptions and affections that would awaken us to the world... as, by right, beings whose proto-opinions would be the foundations of this world.[25] In other words, the phenomenological plane of immanence is immanent to a subject whose perceptions are the basis of opinions and clichés but not concepts. Yes, such a subject is criticized for possessing only opinions, because the determinations of the phenomenologist are based on sensible intuitions, her perceptions and affections, and not on thought.

Phenomenology is also cited negatively for confusing the scientific idea—the function—with the philosophical concept, a point we must also consider. Let us approach this by examining the plane of philosophy envisioned by Merleau-Ponty. It is a form, a mental geography that demands three specific types of milieu. They are not facets, but milieus, and not two—nature and thought or language—but three: *the physical, the vital, and the symbolic*. What happens in each field is influenced by what happens in the others, and each local effect depends on its function, value, and significance in the whole.[26]

Three milieus are posited because a purely physical explanation of behavior supposes that physical forms already possess all the properties of biological and mental relations and so they are not needed.[27] But there are relevant differences between the three milieus. If there are no differences, if physical forms (nature) and their thought effects count for everything, then consciousness is indistinguishable from the brain and "becoming conscious" has no meaning whatsoever; it adds nothing at all to physical structures.

The physical milieu is powerful, for the notion of form is defined by Merleau-Ponty according to the mathematics of vector fields. It is defined on the model of an ensemble of physical forces in a state of equilibrium or of constant change such that no law can be formulated for each part taken separately and such that each vector is determined in size and direction by all the others.[28]

But the physical form "does not already exist in a physical universe and serve as an ontological foundation for perceptual structures."[29] For every natural law is an instrument of knowledge. It is an idea. Yes, it is an idea "common to an ensemble of molecular facts."[30] So there are laws in the physical structure, but there are also structures in the laws of physics. For this reason form can never be taken as a real element in the world, but only as a *limit*, something that knowledge tends toward without ever completing its journey.[31] Each form, the physical, vital, and symbolic, is a field of forces—physical, vital, or symbolic—whose law has no meaning outside of its own dynamic structure and assigns its properties to each internal point, so they belong to the system, not to individual elements or particles within the system.

But if we are to understand embodiment as a lived phenomenon and as a concept, there must be a vital realm in relation to which embodiment takes its form. Without this, there are only two facets—nature and language—ensuring that the body is either an effect of nature's forces or an effect of the attribution of language.

VITAL FORM

What is vital form? Physical form is the Idea of real and present physical conditions and physical systems. Vital form is the plane of the virtual. Every living body is subject to certain constraints, certain real and present physical conditions. There are sensible and motor thresholds for affectivity, perception, body temperature, and blood pressure. The organism as material is an "assemblage of real parts juxtaposed in space . . . which exist outside of each other as the sum of physical and chemical action."[32] But in addition, every organism differs as it "measures the action of things upon itself [and] delimits its milieu by a circular process which is without analogy in the physical world."[33] Each organism and its milieu constitute a realm of vital significance.

Current neuroscience has shown that tracing a stimulus to the cerebral cortex, which triggers a destabilization of the entire sensory cortex, results in an explosive jump from one spatial pattern of activity to a new one. The pattern expresses the nature of the class of stimulus, but it also expresses the meaning of this activity for the subject rather than for the event itself.[34] Evidence for this lies in the recognition that the ability to search for something that is rapidly changing in a context of uncontrolled and uncontrollable backgrounds has never been mechanically duplicated.

As vital and not merely physical, the organism's actions and reactions are addressed to a milieu. Every organism is a molecular entity whose analysis produces a series of physical and chemical processes attributable to any organism whatever of its type. But each organism taken as an ensemble responding to and engaged with a milieu is expressed as an Idea. It is the Idea of life. It is the expressed of its own biological functions in a physical world and "an idea, a reason in knowledge (*Erkentnissgrund*) in virtue of which all the particular facts become intelligible."[35]

The vital facts of an organism become intelligible as Ideas. Such Ideas, applicable to all organisms, include reproduction, food, and shelter, along with patterns of activity, the modes of conduct oriented by these Ideas. These categories, separable as they are and reducible to physiology, also participate in the organism's vital structure expressing as well how an organism modifies its world in accordance with its own internal milieu.

These actions are not those of purely physical entities whose behaviors can be expressed only by mathematical laws. It is absolutely true that even a complex biological organism's behavior can be violently disrupted and reduced to purely physical principles, dependent on the objective nature of the stimuli. It is also the case that living beings, such as insects, which are described as adhering to syncretic structures, are subject to the cues of their natural environments and cannot act outside of them.[36]

Brittle stars, for example, are invertebrate sea creatures with approximately ten thousand spherically domed calcite crystals covering their five limbs and central body that function as micro-lenses that collect and focus light directly onto nerve bundles, thus giving them compound-eye capability. But a brittle star is a creature without a brain, a visualizing apparatus, a metamorphosing optical system, lacking a "*res cogitans* agonizing about the postulated gap (of its own making) between itself and *res extensa*."[37] It is an organism in direct material engagement in the dynamic material configuring of the world.

But although it is relatively unproblematic to say that the brittle star brain and so the human brain are specific material configurations, this does not entail that they are somehow the *same* material configuration. Surely we are able distinguish the un-cogito of the brittle star brain from that of other species and from that of our own?

Physicists studying the movement of human beings in crowds observe that the closer two people get to colliding, the more energy they expend getting out of each other's way. From the point of view of the physicists, these are not the effects of collisions between physical particles. They refer to the process that produces these adjustments as an "instinctive mental calculation," not a physical force.[38]

Between nature and language there must be something that allows for an instinctive mental calculation. What is significant in this argument is the idea of structure, specifically vital structure as nascent intelligibility.[39] How do we know this? Extreme hunger or thirst inhibits thought and feeling. Fatigue or illness takes away intellectual passion. Intellectual interference stemming from ethical concerns dissolves sexual passion. Structure emerges intuitively in our perception in the form of the gestalt. The gestalt is the perception of a visual whole. A gestalt coheres. It makes sense on the level of perception, without the interference of logic or language.[40] The triangle is a sensible whole, even if one does not know what to call it. This is what it means to say that some signification is embodied. This is the intersection, the intertwining of nature and language. This is the meaning of embodiment.[41]

Embodiment is the sensible and perceptible that make sense. On its own, the body is limited. No body can ever see itself seeing. Touch some objects with your hand, and it reveals the qualities of those objects but not in the same moment those of your own hand.[42] You cannot see your eye seeing nor feel your hand touching, otherwise they would be objects. Your own bodily senses are inapprehensible to you. You cannot be an object for yourself, but the things in the world indicate that you are there.[43] They are promises or indications of possible actions. This too is embodiment.

For this reason, sense perceptions are never subjective. They are objective variations of the perceptual field. Either you see the pen on the table, or if it is covered with a piece of paper, you see the paper. The truth of what you see is objective.[44] The empty cup on the table, the tantalizing aroma, each beckons the embodied human to take up the gestalt it promises. Embodiment takes place on the vital plane of existence. It is the link between nature and language.

INTUITION AND LINGUISTIC FORM

In *The Ethics of Ambiguity*, Simone de Beauvoir argues for a structure that is an implicit critique of the Sartrean idea that the engagement in sensible embodiment is a purely cognitive awareness because only a for-itself is able to choose itself. Her objection to this model is rooted in a critique of Sartrean temporality, which she defines as the Lucretian notion of the clinamen. Sartre, she implies, uses this concept to describe the acts of a for-itself that chooses itself only by escaping the causal determination of the past. Thus, the Sartrean for-itself operates moment by moment, nihilating each previous position, moving from nothingness to nothingness, where each new moment is a choice that breaks completely with that past so as to be defined by Sartre as nothingness.[45]

By contrast, Beauvoir insists that moral freedom requires a past and a future, and that in order to prevent a moral choice from being just an opaque and stupid fact, we must justify it, not as a unique, atomistic decision with no connection to the past or future, but as belonging to the temporal unity of our current project. Beauvoir objects to the Sartrean model because, as she states in *The Second Sex*, in their dealings with men in society, women too often are simply told some facts and are then told "either you agree or you do not agree" with these facts, so the middle option is excluded.[46] The ambiguity of an open future is eliminated when one must choose between this fact and that. Moreover, she argues that failure on the part of women to accept this so-called choice results generally in insults and severe treatment, hostility, deprivation, or aggression. Women and men both know that in a male-organized society, at any moment a man can exercise his freedom, transcend his current situation, and negate the past by objectifying another and declaring this or that fact to be the truth. But the situated, embodied woman recognizes that there is no fixed truth of this nature.

As Merleau-Ponty indicates, a body without meaning is a mere physiochemical mass. This is why it is not possible to simply negate a previous embodied situation; doing so would deprive that embodied situation of meaning. This is the lesson of embodiment, of the vital plane of existence. How, then, do we make the transition from the vital plane of embodiment to language and action? How is it that language expresses an internal law of the organism? What lies between the physical stimuli that act on the organism and the expression of the vital significance of the milieu for that organism? Merleau-Ponty refers to an "embodied dialectic" that "grasps unities of signification which a consciousness finds and sees unfolding in it."[47] In other words, as Beauvoir has indicated, this transition must take place in time. And in time we may retrieve the understanding and reality of intuition anticipated at the beginning of this essay.

In *Matter and Memory* Henri Bergson articulates how time unfolds in a present moment. The present, he states, occupies a duration, but this duration is not an atomistic unit; it is double. It arises on each side of a so-called present point, with one foot in the past and the other in the future. It is "both a perception of the immediate past and a determination of the immediate future."[48] But the perception of the immediate past is not yet a gestalt; rather, it is *sensation*, the translation of a long succession of immediate vibrations localized in the body that prepare the body in its sensorimotor capacity for the future, which is action.

It is the case, as Sartre noted and then apparently forgot, that in the present, consciousness *exists its body*, exists it as a structure of sensations and movements.[49] The gestalt can be said to arise at the intersection of this "two-ness" of duration and the simultaneous existence of objects in space, which is the moment of perception. But this takes place insofar as the whole of our past psychical life does not simply evaporate but conditions our present state—although not absolutely, as the present is precisely what is being made in the upsurge between the past and the future.[50] This occurs in and through sensation as the long train of vibrations from out of the past are localized in the body, which, situated as a center of action, calls upon those vibrations, those particular images necessary for action into the future.[51]

It is in the upsurge of this twofold nature of time that intuition may once again take its place to guarantee that action is not merely the enactment of a preexisting pattern, an invariable response to a specific set of facts, but is truly creative.[52] Insofar as the creative act still calls for a structure to organize it, we may find this given to us in intuition. The mathematician L. E. J. Brouwer, concerned that formalism—a method for which properties of time and space that were familiar regularities of experience, although approximate, were nevertheless deemed to be invariable—had started to be projected onto nature in spite of the inability of ordinary spoken or written languages to formulate them, as natural languages cannot satisfy their requirement for logical consistency.[53]

Brouwer credits Henri Bergson with the originating insight of intuitionism, which is the primordial intuition of time, Bergson's *durée*. The mathematical nature of causality and the primordial intuition of time as the fundamental creative act of mathematics are the central theses of Brouwer's analysis of nature and language.[54] Brouwer refers to intuition as a time-bound process beginning in the past, existing in the present, and evolving into an open future. Above all, once constructed, such formulations remain, as Bergson argued, alive in mind or memory.

Brouwer states that "*intuitionist mathematics is an essentially languageless activity of the mind having its origin in the perception of a move of time, i.e. the falling apart of a life moment into two distinct things, one of which gives way to the other, but is retained by memory.*"[55] Removing all qualitative contents from this falling apart, this "two-ity," gives the ordinal "two-oneness" and leaves us with the "empty form" of time, the "*basic intuition of mathematics*," self-unfolding and introspectively realized.[56] This means that for intuitionists, time is non-atomic; it is more like a "fluid paste from which points cannot be picked out with atomist accuracy."[57] The intuitionist is always able to choose how to construct any given sequence; thus every element in a construction has an indeterminate future.

For this reason, for intuitionists, among logical axioms, the principle of excluded middle is called the most flawed and obvious misstatement of fact. A given proposition such as "either 'P' or 'not-P' must be true" affirms the fundamental principle of binary thinking and the logic of identity.[58] Since for the intuitionist, statements, whether affirmative or negative, express the completion of the intuitionist's own inner time in a temporality that "flows with the flux," with an open future and unpredictable free choices, there can be no a priori fixed determination of the elements of that proof.[59] Surely this structure reaffirms Le Doeuff's account of intuition as what sets the process of discovery in motion as well as what completes it. And although Brouwer does concede that the principle of the excluded middle may apply to an extensive group of phenomena of the exterior world, this does not mean that blind or universal applications of the principle are permissible.[60]

Brouwer therefore argues that given the primordial intuition of temporal flow, intuitionists must forego the excluded middle and thereby open the endless and primordial flow of time. When this is applied to language, it means that when a proposition no longer has to be either true or false but remains indeterminate or ambiguous, then something new can still take place. In this way also, intuition is reconnected to discourse and language, to making statements whose truth or falsity lies in the future or may remain indeterminate, statements that reflect the indeterminacy of nature as much as of human existence yet still hold out the possibility of truth.

For Bergson, the indeterminacy of the future arising in the primordial flow of time is clearly an embodied indeterminacy:

> Here I am in the presence of images, in the vaguest sense of the word, images perceived when my senses are open to them, unperceived when they are closed.... Yet there is *one* of them which is distinct from all the others, in that

> I do not know [*connais*] it only from without by perceptions, but from within by affections: it is my body. I examine the conditions in which these affections are produced: I find that they always interpose themselves between the excitations that I receive from without and the movements I am about to execute.[61]

Bergson examines the conditions under which sensory images are produced. He concludes that most perceptions are perceived from "without," but that the image of the body is also given from "within" through affections, and each affection is conditioned by a movement that contains a multiplicity. That is, every affection is situated at the "interval" between a multiplicity of excitations received from "without" and the movements about to be executed through the body.

Within affectivity, Bergson finds nothing that constrains choice. Feeling and sensation affirm this, for they are activated whenever the human being takes the initiative, and they fade when behavior becomes automatic. Affectivity thus arises in the interval between excitation and action.[62] This is because bodily affections persist in the form of memory images.

> In the fraction of a second which covers the briefest possible perception of light, billions of vibrations have taken place, of which the first is separated from the last by an interval which is enormously divided. Your perception, however instantaneous, consists then in an incalculable multitude of remembered elements; and in truth every perception is already memory.[63]

The memory of the past, localized in the body, offers to the sensorimotor mechanisms of the body all the recollections capable of guiding them in their task and gives to the motor reaction the direction suggested by the lessons of experience. But the sensorimotor apparatus also furnishes to memories the means of taking on a body, of materializing themselves, thus of becoming present. In order for a recollection, for some of the long succession of vibrations to appear in consciousness, it is necessary that they descend from the heights of pure memory down to the precise point where action is taking place. In other words, it is from the present, by means of the intuition of two-ness or *two-ity* that there comes an appeal to which memory responds, and it is from the sensorimotor elements of present action that a memory "borrows the warmth which gives it life."[64]

For Bergson, as for Merleau-Ponty and Beauvoir, it is the vital realm of embodiment and the affirmation of intuition and ambiguity that make possible a link between nature and language and that make possible an open future, not subject to purely physical forces, where language can do no more than describe attributes of bodies. As Beauvoir argues, when one completes a project, the value of this provisional end will be confirmed indefinitely only insofar as it too is acted upon and becomes the starting point for another project. This is how creative freedom develops without congealing into facticity.[65] Thus, conceptualized, we may indeed take up embodiment as the link between nature and language that feminist phenomenology embraces in order to move into its own future as the future of phenomenology.

DOROTHEA E. OLKOWSKI is Professor and former Chair of Philosophy at the University of Colorado, Colorado Springs, and Director of the Cognitive Studies Program. She is the author of *Postmodern Philosophy and the Scientific Turn* (Indiana University Press, 2012), *The Universal (In the Realm of the Sensible)* (Edinburgh University Press, 2007), and *Gilles Deleuze and the Ruin of Representation* (University of California Press, 1999).

NOTES

1. Michèle Le Doeuff, *The Sex of Knowing*, trans. Kathryn Hammer and Lorraine Code (New York: Routledge Press, 2003), 4, 6–7; originally published as *Le Sexe du savoir*, 1998. Le Doeuff cites G.W.F. Hegel, *Lectures on the History of Philosophy*, trans. E. S. Haldane, vol. 3 (London: Routledge and Kegan Paul, 1955), 550. Le Doeuff focuses on how the intuitive came to be opposed to the discursive and attributed to women. See also Henri Bergson, *The Creative Mind*, trans. Mabelle L. Andison (New York: Philosophical Library, 1946), 140–41; and Henri Bergson, *Oeuvres* (Paris: Presses Universitaires de France,1991), 1356.

2. Simone de Beauvoir, *The Second Sex*, trans. H. M. Parshley (New York: Vintage Books, 1989), 34.

3. Margaret A. Simons, "Beauvoir's Philosophical Independence in a Dialogue with Sartre," *Journal of Speculative Philosophy* 14, no. 2 (2000): 89.

4. See, for example, the excellent collection by Janet Price and Margrit Shildrick, eds., *Feminist Theory and the Body* (Edinburgh: Edinburgh University Press, 1999), which contains many important phenomenological essays and critiques of phenomenology, including those of Margrit Shildrick, Janet Price, Eve Kosofsky Sedgwick, Anne Balsamo, Elizabeth Spelman, Helen Marshall, Luce Irigaray, Judith Butler, and Christine Battersby. See also Christina Schües, Dorothea E. Olkowski, and Helen A. Fielding, eds., *Time and Feminist Phenomenology* (Bloomington: Indiana University Press, 2011), with essays on the body by Sara Heinämaa, Christina Schües, Linda Fisher, Annemie Halsema, Helen A. Fielding, and Dorothea E. Olkowski.

5. Linda Martin Alcoff, "Phenomenology, Post-Structuralism, and Feminist Theory on the Concept of Experience," in *Feminist Phenomenology*, ed. Linda Fisher and Lester Embree (Dordrecht: Kluwer Academic Publishers, 2000), 39–55, 40–42.

6. Ibid., 43.

7. Eva-Marie Simms and Beata Stawarska, "Introduction: Concepts and Methods in Interdisciplinary Phenomenology," *Janus Head* 13, no. 1 (2014): 6–16, 7.

8. Ibid., 9.
9. Ibid.
10. Dorothea E. Olkowski, *The Universal (In the Realm of the Sensible): Beyond Continental Philosophy* (Edinburgh: Edinburgh University Press, 2007), 104.
11. Jean-Paul Sartre, *Being and Nothingness*, trans. Hazel E. Barnes (New York: Washington Square Press, 1984), 434; originally published in French as *L'Être et le néant*, 1943.
12. Sartre, *Being and Nothingness*, 437–44.
13. Gilles Deleuze and Félix Guattari, *What Is Philosophy?*, trans. Hugh Tomlinson and Graham Burchell (New York: Columbia University Press, 1994), 10; originally published in French as *Qu'est-ce que la philosophie?*, 1991.
14. Deleuze and Guattari, *What Is Philosophy?*, 10.
15. Ibid., 11.
16. Ibid., 103.
17. Ibid., 101.
18. Ibid., 38.
19. Gilles Deleuze and Félix Guattari, *A Thousand Plateaus: Capitalism and Schizophrenia*, trans. Brian Massumi (Minneapolis: University of Minnesota Press, 1987), 97; originally published in French as *Mille Plateaux, Capitalisme et Schizophrénie*, 1980.
20. Gilles Deleuze, *Difference and Repetition*, trans. Paul Patton (New York: Columbia University Press, 1994), 86. "The activity of thought applies to a receptive being, to a passive subject which represents that activity to itself rather than enacts it . . . which lives it like an Other within itself."
21. Gilles Deleuze, "The Idea of Genesis in Kant's Aesthetics," trans. Daniel W. Smith, *Angelaki* 5, no. 3 (2000): 61.
22. Sartre, *Being and Nothingness*, 502. Crucial here is the idea of revelation rather than fascination.
23. Olkowski, *The Universal*, 117.
24. Deleuze and Guattari, *What Is Philosophy?*, 47.
25. Ibid., 150.
26. Maurice Merleau-Ponty, *The Structure of Behavior*, trans. Alden L. Fisher (Boston: Beacon Press, 1963), 131; originally published as *La structure du comportement*, 1942.
27. Merleau-Ponty, *Structure of Behavior*, 134.
28. Ibid., 137.
29. Ibid., 144.
30. Ibid., 143.
31. Ibid., 142.
32. Ibid., 151.
33. Ibid., 148; emphasis added.
34. Walter J. Freeman, *Societies of Brains: A Study in the Neuroscience of Love and Hate* (Hillsdale, NJ: Lawrence Erlbaum Associates, 1995), 66.
35. Kurt Goldstein, *The Organism: A Holistic Approach to Biology Derived from Pathological Data in Man* (Cincinnati: American Book Company, 1939), 375, 378; cited in Merleau-Ponty, *Structure of Behavior*, 153.
36. Merleau-Ponty, *Structure of Behavior*, 104.
37. Karen Barad, *Meeting the Universe Halfway* (Durham, NC: Duke University Press, 2007), 379. Barad suggests that the brittle star brain can serve as a model for human con-

sciousness. This does not seem to be to be an appropriate comparison, since humans have brains and brittle stars do not, so the two belong to very different structures.

38. Kevin Hartnett, "In Crowds, Human 'Particles' Follow Laws of Movement: Science Starts to Unlock the Physics of People," *Boston Globe*, December 14, 2014.

39. Merleau-Ponty, *Structure of Behavior*, 207.

40. See the excellent design website "Gestalt Theory of Visual Perception," http://www.users.totalise.co.uk/~kbroom/Lectures/gestalt.htm.

41. Merleau-Ponty, *Structure of Behavior*, 211.

42. Sartre, *Being and Nothingness*, 402.

43. Ibid., 419.

44. Ibid., 420.

45. Simone de Beauvoir, *The Ethics of Ambiguity*, trans. Bernard Frechtman (New York: Citadel Press, 1976), 26.

46. Beauvoir, *Second Sex*, 614–615.

47. Merleau-Ponty, *Structure of Behavior*, 161.

48. Henri Bergson, *Matter and Memory*, trans. Nancy Margaret Paul and W. Scott Palmer (New York: Zone Books, 1988), 178.

49. Ibid.

50. Ibid., 191.

51. Ibid., 198.

52. This system, known as formalism, originated in a method for which properties of time and space that were familiar regularities of experience, though approximate, were nevertheless deemed to be invariable. Such invariables are called axioms, and from them were developed systems of properties following principles of classical logic, which was considered to be autonomous. These mathematical entities exist neither in nature nor in our conception of nature, yet such relations and laws of reasoning are frequently projected onto nature in spite of the avoidance of ordinary spoken or written languages in formulating them, as natural languages cannot satisfy the condition of consistency available only through the series of relations that form symbolic logic. See L.E.J. Brouwer, "Intuitionism and Formalism," in *Collected Works* (Amsterdam: North-Holland 1975), 125–26.

53. Brouwer, "Intuitionism and Formalism," 125–26.

54. Walter P. Van Stigt, "Brouwer's Intuitionist Programme," in *From Brouwer to Hilbert: The Debate on the Foundations of Mathematics in the 1920s*, ed. Paolo Mancosu (Oxford: Oxford University Press, 1997), 1–22, 7.

55. Brouwer, "Intuitionism and Formalism," 510.

56. Ibid.

57. Van Stigt, "Brower's Intuitionist Programme," 1–22.

58. Vladimir Tasić, *Mathematics and the Roots of Postmodern Thought* (Oxford: Oxford University Press, 2001), 40–41.

59. Ibid., 40.

60. Brouwer, "Intuitionism and Formalism," 510–11.

61. Bergson, *Matter and Memory*, 17.

62. Ibid., 18.

63. Ibid., 194.

64. Ibid., 197.

65. Beauvoir, *Ethics of Ambiguity*, 8.

BIBLIOGRAPHY

Alcoff, Linda Martin. "Phenomenology, Post-Structuralism, and Feminist Theory on the Concept of Experience." In *Feminist Phenomenology*, edited by Linda Fisher and Lester Embree, 39–55. Dordrecht: Kluwer Academic Publishers, 2000.

Barad, Karen. *Meeting the Universe Halfway*. Durham, NC: Duke University Press, 2007.

Beauvoir, Simone de. *The Ethics of Ambiguity*. Translated by Bernard Frechtman. New York: Citadel Press, 1976.

———. *The Second Sex*. Translated by H. M. Parshley. New York: Vintage Books, 1989.

Bergson, Henri. *The Creative Mind*. Translated by Mabelle L. Andison. New York: Philosophical Library, 1946.

———. *Matter and Memory*. Translated by Nancy Margaret Paul and W. Scott Palmer. New York: Zone Books, 1988.

———. *Oeuvres*. Paris: Presses Universitaires de France, 1991.

Brouwer, L.E.J. "Intuitionism and Formalism." In *Collected Works*. Amsterdam: North-Holland, 1975.

Deleuze, Gilles. *Difference and Repetition*. Translated by Paul Patton. New York: Columbia University Press, 1994.

———. "The Idea of Genesis in Kant's Aesthetics." Translated by Daniel W. Smith. *Angelaki* 5, no. 3 (2000): 57–70.

Deleuze, Gilles, and Félix Guattari. *A Thousand Plateaus, Capitalism, and Schizophrenia*. Translated by Brian Massumi. Minneapolis: University of Minnesota Press, 1987. Originally published in French as *Mille Plateaux, Capitalisme et Schizophrénie*. Paris: Les Editions de Minuit, 1980.

———. *What Is Philosophy?* Translated by Hugh Tomlinson and Graham Burchell. New York: Columbia University Press, 1994. Originally published in French as *Qu'est-ce que la philosophie?* Paris: Les Editions de Minuit, 1991.

Freeman, Walter J. *Societies of Brains: A Study in the Neuroscience of Love and Hate*. Hillsdale, NJ: Lawrence Erlbaum Associates, 1995.

Hartnett, Kevin. "In Crowds, Human 'Particles' Follow Laws of Movement: Science Starts to Unlock the Physics of People." *Boston Globe*, December 14, 2014.

Hegel, G.W.F. *Lectures on the History of Philosophy*. Vol. 3. Translated by E. S. Haldane. London: Routledge and Kegan Paul, 1955.

Le Doeuff, Michèle. *The Sex of Knowing*. Translated by Kathryn Hammer and Lorraine Code. New York: Routledge Press, 2003. Originally published as *Le Sexe du savoir*. Paris: Aubier, 1998.

Merleau-Ponty, Maurice. *The Structure of Behavior*. Translated by Alden L. Fisher. Boston: Beacon Press, 1963. Originally published as *La structure du comportement*. Paris: Presses Universitaires de France, 1942.

Olkowski, Dorothea E. *The Universal (In the Realm of the Sensible): Beyond Continental Philosophy*. Edinburgh: Edinburgh University Press, 2007.

Price, Janet, and Margrit Shildrick, eds. *Feminist Theory and the Body*. Edinburgh: Edinburgh University Press, 1999.

Sartre, Jean-Paul. *Being and Nothingness*. Translated by Hazel E. Barnes. New York: Washington Square Press, 1984. Originally published in French as *L'Être et néant*. Paris: Gallimard, 1943.

Schües, Christina, Dorothea E. Olkowski, and Helen Fielding, eds. *Time and Feminist Phenomenology*. Bloomington: Indiana University Press, 2011.

Simms, Eva-Marie, and Beata Stawarska. "Introduction: Concepts and Methods in Interdisciplinary Phenomenology." *Janus Head* 13, no.1 (2014): 6–16.

Simons, Margaret A. "Beauvoir's Philosophical Independence in a Dialogue with Sartre." *Journal of Speculative Philosophy* 14, no. 2 (2000): 87–103.

Tasić, Vladimir. *Mathematics and the Roots of Postmodern Thought*. Oxford: Oxford University Press, 2001.

Van Stigt, Walter P. "Brouwer's Intuitionist Programme." In *From Brouwer to Hilbert: The Debate on the Foundations of Mathematics in the 1920s*, edited by Paolo Mancosu, 1–22. Oxford: Oxford University Press, 1997.

2 JUST THROW LIKE A BLEEDING PHILOSOPHER

Menstrual Pauses and Poses, Betwixt Hypatia and Bhubaneswari, Half Visible, Almost Illegible

KYOO LEE

> Life maintains itself only by surpassing itself.
> —Simone de Beauvoir, *The Second Sex*

W<small>HAT IS THIS</small> thing, that stuff underneath of which some of us would talk only softly, quietly, killingly?

"Speaking of which, do you happen to have a tampon with you?," whispers a fellow conference-goer, or -comer, to me, gingerly, prompting me to rummage through my 24/7 emergency Ziploc in my daypack, where usually three tampons of three sizes are found lying promiscuously betwixt pens, pencils, erasers, clips, maybe trying to blend in, hidingly, yes, yes, I do, ain't I a woman ready to go?

First, FACT #1: Menstruation as a monthly corporeal event, the cyclical shedding of the uterine lining (endometrium), is part of "biological data/facts/given (*les données de la biologie*)" for a majority of women during their years of reproductive capacity, ages roughly thirteen to fifty.[1]

FACT #2: According to Aristotle, the thinker of life, "If a woman looks into a highly polished mirror during the menstrual period, the surface of the mirror becomes clouded with a blood-red colour." Really? Perhaps it depends on where and when the "red clouding" takes place.[2] To turn to M. Descartes for directions, another amateur clinician, who saw "copulation" as "a disorganized mixture of two fluids which act on each other as a kind of yeast, generating mutual heat":[3]

> Spirits are exhaled through the eyes as can be seen in menstruating women whose eyes are said to emit vapours. The whole body of a woman is full of

vapours when she has her days. The heavier humour is purged through the vagina, the subtler humour is purged higher up, namely through the eyes.[4]

One underlying point, among many, particularly worth noting in this semi-anatomical fragment (1631) attributed to Della Porta and René Descartes, a semi-parody of Aristotelian biological sexism, is that a woman, especially a modern-ish one, "having her days" tends to become a sign, a semiotic event to read, not some ancient, tragic "uterus crying for the lack of a baby."[5] As a thing to factualize (that is to say, to decode, monitor, process, manage, project, intervene, etc.) rather than more simply to fear, the menstrual body in the modern heterosexist patriarchal capitalist imaginary still functions as a production site that is failed or else fanning out of control—that is, useless or horrible.[6] "Spirits are exhaled through the eyes of menstruating women": disclosed in this rather sarcastic remark by the modern philosopher known for his metaphysically "inappropriate" or "unintegrated," and somehow radically egalitarian, "sexless" view of the human animal are the gender-ideological traces of Aristotelian hylomorphism.[7] As Luce Irigaray writes in the *Speculum of the Other Woman*:

> Outside of this process is nothing: outside of this process is the nothing that is the woman. She alone is in a position—perhaps?—to question her function in this all-powerful "machine" we know as metaphysics, in that omnipotent "technique" of onto-theology. She functions—still—as choice, but a choice that has always already been made by "nature," between a male pleasure and her role as a vehicle for procreation. The latter role is most clearly apparent in "menstruation" which "belongs in the realm of the prōtē hylē." By coming back to the cycle of the mother, at least in its potentiality, one will have turned again to the first matter and her mysteries. But the male individual must take care not to slip back there. For his form is unlikely to profit thereby. It is rather by distance and separation that he will affirm his self-identity.[8]

These scenes of inherited, lensed reading point to a kind of meta-fact or meta-factualized body in which the female kind vis-à-vis its matrixial menstruality and instrumentality forms a certain auto-fabricated scaffolding for the "primal matter," persisting as and through a mélange of myths and facts that are framed and flavored by the narrative interests and layers of hereditary patriarchy as well as speculative projections and anxieties.

FACT #3, probably a counter-fact for some folks: "Not all women menstruate, and not only women menstruate. Post-menopausal women, women post-hysterectomy, and some athletes, for example, do not menstruate, and some preoperative transmen do menstruate (as do many intersexuals)."[9]

Now, while I find the third fact interesting too, here I will be focusing on the first two, an eclipsed banality and sub-metaphysical mystery about the female menstruating body as well as the female menstrual body in general. Not being so well versed or engaged in any centralist, essentialist, majoritarian, ideological, or minoritarian, or autobiographical, or even mystical discourses about that subject, I shall spend some time just staring at it mind-body-fully, say, phenomenologically, feminist phenomenologically: what is this, a menstrual event, a pause?

ENTER M. M: "ALL RIGHT, DOUBTING LADIES . . . HERE'S FREE PROOF!"

Most notably, the job of a menstruator, menstruat*ing* or menstru*al*, is both part-time and full-time. Once on board, one is on call 24/7, as it were, especially if the call tends to come at irregular intervals despite the lunar mandates built into the very concept, *menses, period*. Then roughly at least a quarter of your so-called prime time—that's about ten years total—is spent on dealing with this periodic private mess(iah), start to finish; and every so often, that's (bloody) on your mind, whether you're on "it" or not. But, now, the thing is ("All right, Doubting Ladies,"[10] and girls, and girls and boys, and gentlemen too, whoever you are, just suspend your identities and any sort of politics and think about this, nice and simple): you, they, we, I, whoever—anyone hardly talks about "it" unless, every so often, under the breath, as "Twenty-something Tuesday," "a Crime Scene in My Pants," "Aunt Flo visiting from Reading," "The Communist Coming," and so on.[11] If this is some kind of linguistic sneeze caused by the "Girl Flu," again the thing is we don't even hear it, let alone about it, since most of us just know, which in part provokes such a proto-Cartesian clinical demand for legibility and mastery, a clear and distinct demonstration followed by some sort of solution or at least resolution.[12]

Where, when? Before it happens, it's gone. No talk, only winks and whispers. No one asks, no one tells. Don't tell, don't ask—so says the socio-discursive contract, subtle and simple. "These two messages," put together, "easily cohere," however.[13] Positively queer:

> Strong social pressures and our own internalized sense of decency tell us that we must vigilantly guard against revelation of our bleeding, especially in public and to strangers. . . . The message that a menstruating woman is perfectly normal *entails* that she hide the signs of her menstruation. The normal body, the default body, the body that every body is assumed to be, is a body not bleeding from the vagina. Thus, to *be* normal and to be taken as normal, the menstruating woman must not speak about her bleeding and must conceal evidence of it. The message that the menstruating woman is normal makes her deviant, a deviance that each month puts her on the other side of a fear of

disorder, or the subversion of what is right and proper. It seems apt, then, in this normatively masculine, gender-egalitarian society, to say that the menstruating woman is queer. As with other queers, the price of a woman's acceptance as normal is that she stay in the closet as a menstruator.[14]

What's going on in that W. C.? What's up with this womanly closetry? I agree: "If we can't *talk about* menstruation, how can we possibly make productive noise about menstrual culture and its intervention?" Chris Bobel is so on it.[15]

"We," note. Taking place in the female human body that is also a "social body" (where networks of individual physical behaviors and psychosomatic experiences including affects and symptoms are socially recognized, codified, regulated, emulated, encouraged, or discouraged, with the activation of interpersonal feedback and surveillance systems such as mediations, interventions, innovations, etc.), the monthly discharging of blood and associated matter that, once done, might not seem to matter much to anyone except maybe Joe the Plumber, does become a manifold feminist issue, immediately, in sociology, politics, economy, and ethics, just to name a few, and more broadly, aesthetics, ecology, phenomenology, ontology, metaphysics, inter alia.[16] The list goes on, bleedingly, yes. Not exactly "a problem that has no name" but in fact too many, this menstrual event seems to make sense almost only in the world of evasive abstractions and redemptive euphemisms, where "furtive talks about supplies" socialize with diffused and diversified personal jokes often drenched in (un)sharable psychosomatic "female complaints" and abjections.[17] Instantly, intimately, women get it. Today we see the networked theorization and increasing prominence of menstrual activism (e.g., Society for Menstrual Cycle Research) along with the mainstreaming of menarche parties and even the niche marketing of menopausal tours and so on, but we also still see the female menstrual body (womb, uterus) remaining such a taboo subject, the one that bleeds through the vagina, specifically *that*, that "unmentionable." Metaphorically cosmeticized and metaphysically ignored, the menstrual subject, linguistically non-concretized as such, practically appears to live and die all alone, naturally, constantly, lingeringly, disappearing into its own crimson shadows.[18] The message? Again, menses should become merrily mentionable as, say, neighboring words such as "men's," "men," or "Moses," as clearly, distinctly, totally, infinitely, universally, cosmically as possible, in various languages, including and especially philosophical. We all get that . . . or do you?

Philosophy, too, although still rarely, attends to such special recursive hemorrhage as a main female corporeal feature, not just an amusing aside to whisper about among those in the know or flow. Take Iris Marion Young's

"Menstrual Meditations," previewed above, on the analogously "queer" identity and normativity of Mademoiselle-Madame Menstruation or Ms. Modest Mode, who is also in a dialogue with *The Second Sex* (*Le deuxième sexe*) of Simone de Beauvoir, the chapter on puberty in particular, which we will also revisit shortly. Young, with Beauvoir, shows how "the menses inspire horror in the adolescent girl because they throw her into an inferior and defective category. This sense of being declassed will weigh heavily upon her. She would retain her pride in her bleeding body if she did not lose her pride in being human."[19]

Is philosophy still in its puberty with respect to its own menstrual (non-) thought? Philosophy may still be too premature to be able to ask, let alone answer, such reflexive questions about its own growth, developmental perplexities. I am asking a question of the other not so much *of* or *to* philosophy but *in*: not an issue of some classical or classified "other" invading a body, proper, of philosophical knowledge or the philosophical knower per se, often ex-appropriated, extra-territorialized, externalized as such in the name of the "Other," but the issue of its own onto-phenomenological authenticities inextricably bound up with innate alterities. That is to ask: how does philosophy *as* feminist philosophy face its own "feminist(-masculinist)" complex, doing justice to its own coded, corded complexity?—all sorts, affective, objective, agential, eventual, lingering.[20] Will the real Ms. Modern please stand up or just sit down to do some real thinking, reading, writing, breathing, being in the doing and undoing of all of that and more, or less as needed?

For now, as "I, too, overflow," with certain emotions and declassified thoughts, I shall continue to dwell on this issue of queer (in)visibility or (il)legibility vis-à-vis menstrual speech and phenomena.[21] In part, the disconcertingly subtextualized phenomenological subjectivity of female menstrual experiences that Young explores with exemplary lucidity, and Beauvoir with sardonic concision, is what took me or brought me here. In this line of interrogating the internally exposed, perversely convoluted *ex*teriority of the menstrual primal scene, traceable also to Luce Irigaray's neo-Platonic cave that she turns inside out, what stands out most intriguingly for me now as a function of what keeps me thinking to this day is menstrual *ex*istence itself. What, exactly, is (this that is) coming *out*, regardless, no matter what?

THAT EXISTS

To be clear, I am not looking for any empirically compelling, culturally desirable, or ecologically restorative reasons why menstruators should carry on even if they had a choice not to, as in choosing between breastfeeding and formula feeding, or between eye glasses and contact lenses. Nor am I inquiring about the medical or politico-economic pros and cons or risks and benefits of monthly menstrual calls and biotechnological manipulations of them. Such, while interesting and important, is beyond my analytic scope and thematic expertise. Also, the broadly psychocultural and mythopolitical dimensions of menstrual practices that accompany the conspiratorial concealment of them, while more immediately in line with my pursuit here, are not my primary concern. I too wonder, "Why, exactly, do nearly all women hate their periods more than their other bodily process? How do culture, gender ideology, and consumerism shape these reactions?"[22] And if indeed nearly one-third of women would "eliminate their periods permanently if they could," if no one, especially no woman, seems to enjoy menstruating anyway, I too remain curious about the origin and destination of this phenomenal hate.[23] Yet, my focus lies more specifically in detecting and drawing out a kind of conceptual, interlingual language of menstruation that scaffolds all of those subterranean negativities under constant semi-erasure: again, what is there for one to *read*, to begin with?

What I am seeking is a kind of philosophical justice to menstruation itself, if not exactly a justification for or against it, this particular part of abjected, debased, subalternized female animality, bloody mammality that appears to and disappears into collective consciousness somehow unnaturally, despite being a natural bodily function. If public urination or defecation is an issue of public hygiene, and public sex or masturbation a matter of public nuisance and safety, to the extent that they concern the sensorial boundaries and socio-legal spaces of individuals and communities in need of regulated protection and promotion, wouldn't public menstruation—that is, a publicly visible menstrual event taking place in and through a body, just like a life and a death—be less of an offense? "Menstruation in progress": why and how would such a sign be different from David Beckham showing off his Calvin Klein boxer shorts beneath his slightly baggy trousers, especially if and "when he has his days" à la Descartes's menstrual woman? "If men could menstruate," as Gloria Steinem imagined so spectacularly, they might indeed brag, as in "Yeah, man, I'm on the rag!"[24] Right on, girl. And if that is about "the power of justifications" across histories and cultures, we would also want to know what this need or impulse not to see just *is*, this structured turning away from menstrual happening in the body that is, after all, part of everyone, every one of us in flesh.[25]

Just what is at the core of that nullified quiddity of female menstrual embodiment—its contagious (un)touchability, audible (un)speakability, obvious (in)visibility? By now it should be clear to any—especially (non)menstruating—one that the usual "if-then logic of geometry" just does not apply to the world of female menstruation, this "Girl thing" half veiled, riddled, with all of those "psychologically disorienting," culturally sanctioned contradictions.[26] If, however, this ontological "curse" rhyming with mytho-cultural, even under deconstruction, would still *be* something different from a "common cold" (Karen Houppert's "modest futuristic scenario," still quite stimulating, I must say), what could be a way in to and out of this menstrual conundrum, a philosophically mindful way to respond to this common dream on pause?[27] Like Young on the queer "coherence" of menstrual in/visibility, Sara Ruddick, another philosopher for life, is putting a finger on that pattern of lively-deadly duality, with a focus this time on its material temporality, "the latent horror of motherhood (that) survives," "this lurking below the surface," as Beauvoir put it: "in many cultures birthing labor, the menstruation associated with it, and at times even breast-feeding evoke disgust. . . . It is disturbing in itself and because it forces on any onlooker the intimate knowledge of his or her own fleshly beginning."[28] More exactly at issue, looked at more closely, with Elizabeth Grosz, and Beauvoir again, is *fluid* fleshliness that remains unboxed, ultimately unboxable: "leaking, uncontrollable, seeping liquid; as formless flow; as viscosity, entrapping, secreting; as lacking not so much or simply the phallus but self-containment"; this "spontaneous mingling . . . of . . . hostile disgust . . . with . . . carnal tenderness," "the Mother" on her way, "coming" in or/and out, with or without her Tupperware.[29] A phallic lack turning into a menstrual leak: where is this switch, and where exactly is ur-motherly lacking-leaking leading, headed?

Just go soak the world? Womyn, what should be the next move in our menstrual activism? Recycled recreationism? Another pause, I'm sensing. As Christine Delphy warns, "It is essential to recognize that the meaning of periods, for instance, is not *given* with and by the flow of body, but like *all* meaning, by consciousness and thus by society."[30] I share such measured concerns about some unfiltered—or shall we say, unpadded or uncorked—proliferations of French(y) "feminine writing (*l'ecriture feminine*)," basically fluid (milky, orgasmic, oceanic), not solid, which, in counter-masculinist gestures, recycles and reinscribes some archaic "menstrual" marks all over in one way or another, enacting a sort of literary Jackson Pollocking of menstrual blood, in some compensatory or recuperative modes.[31] Woman or man, one can then easily fall into the trap of reactionary or retrograde gender essentialism or semio-capitalism, going all the way, and mainly one way, as if the meaning of the "the flow of body" were now, suddenly, irreversibly renaturalized. Yet it has also been genealogically concocted, culturally orchestrated, historically sedimented, already: "given how the human body sees and hears itself in its reversibility . . . what remains quite mysterious here is how that mute world ever receives a structure, that is, is the body biological or psychological or cultural in its linguistic orientation?," in its *linguistic* orientation, wonders Dorothea Olkowski, as I do here, with Maurice Merleau-Ponty of *The Visible and Invisible*.[32] What would be that very connective tissue ("reversibility") for bidirectional relationality, which "borders the body and language"?[33]

The point of that question transposed here also functions as a critical reminder that menstrual theorizing or gazing, going forward or backward, either way or in anyway, has to take place on some open-ended two-way streets at least ideally, not just at some well-organized cul-de-sac. Critical menstrual feminist textualizing—thinking, writing, reading, living, pausing—is to be interlingual or translingual in its very material density and discursive vitality so as to produce dynamic, affectively integrated, interactively intelligible, and intellectually interdisciplinary enterprises. It cannot be just contained in or channeled through some pure gynocentric fury over the phallogocentric mutation and conquest of the mother earth; alternative universal reflections from ecofeminism or New Age feminism are necessary and might be insufficient. Nor can the gushing, leaking, or eventual non-flowing of menstrual blood along with the biomedical and political manipulation of it, these quotidian intricacies and urgencies, be relegated to or circuited through some discursive networks of waste management issues, the neoliberal "hygienic crisis" and public health "imperative," the "'American way' to menstruate," which immigrant groups should also learn, and so on, each of which matters gravely but not independently. It is in fact in such a now increasingly techno-industrialized, massive garbage dump that one can richly excavate the "matter-language," not meta-, but rather wasted, wasteful "waste-language," of triviality, unintelligibility, absurdity, redundancy, as do avant-garde modern artists such as Marcel Duchamp and Gertrude Stein.[34] Unlocking and unleashing this way the irreducible pricelessness and ontological primal-ness of the stuff the world is made of, one would also get closer access to senses of the surface-to-depth, one-to-the other, semiotico-material "reversibility" of the flesh just noted. Truly, every one of these menstrual-excremental brownie points, connected and concocted in one way or another, counts deeply, sharply, vibrantly, which is partly what philo-SOPHIA should sense and register in particular if nothing else—with a view to reversing the ontological order of displaced justice such as patriarchy. How? By, as I envisage, reorderingly disordering or disorderingly reordering the world by creating an alternative hyper–waste basket or innermost outhouse of being itself, of beings otherwise being-ed, not binged, as "emptying filling is creating (creative?) action," to recycle Gertrude Stein's philopoetic formulation here.[35]

The issue, again, is how we should understand such a cross-cultural menstrual constant conceptually while respecting the corporeal diversity, complexity, and originality of each and every menstrual event that drives this query forward as well as backward. What sustains this search for one idea, one thing, one line that remains even when moving, that remains oddly even yet unevenly singular, is this question already repeated that I am trying to keep open(-ended): given this near universal aversion to the volatile fluidity, formless subjectivity, promiscuous plasticity of the female menstrual body, what is "this" pervasive yet unreadable menstrual thing often unembraced or else embellished by the menstruators themselves, and what, or who, endures it temporally or otherwise? And why and how does such a contextually analytic attention matter, that phenomenological look at the flip side of avoidance? Where could such durational, durationally syncopated menstrual events be located in a greater scheme of universal ontology, the being of the universe that is renewed every month or so individually and collectively? Obviously, we need to know more about this originary and recursive disgust over menstrual fluids oozing out of and back into the female corporeal universe, this phenomenally monstrous, psycho-culturally indemonstrable, strictly private affair itself, this sudden hidden outsideness or sliding-out-ness of menstrual thrush that is wirelessly linkable to a highly unsexy blush.[36] Back to that blinded spot, this invisiblized red ink: let us try to see the why of this not-seeing, the gesture—structure, genesis, idiomaticity—of that documentary evasion that disclosingly disguises the life of menstruation. Back to the basics, then, here is another inspirational passage, from Beauvoir:

> She becomes an object, and she sees herself as object; she discovers this new aspect of her being with surprise: it seems to her that she has been doubled; instead of coinciding exactly with herself, she now begins to exist *outside*.[37]

Shifting the categorical focus from "experience" to "existence," from the first-person central-marginal experience (Young) "back" to the subhuman or subterranean existence (Beauvoir) as in "back to the things themselves," the well-recycled Husserlian phenomenological slogan, we can touch more deeply the phenomenological sobjectivity of menstrual temporality, this marvelous, mobile intricacy. There in the neo-Cartesian circle or ellipsis, I see a menstrual modality of the "sobject that exists in a perpetual procedural loop, a perpetual substantive eclipse": the recursivity of the menstrual subjectivity-cum-objectivity of the female body, the subject that bleeds as a bleeding object, the subject that bleeds into a bleeding object it instantly becomes.[38] Gliding half-knowingly, early or late, into an auto-hetero-hemorrhaging mode, in a psychosomatic holding pattern, the reproductively inscribed body hosts "a dead person that has never lived" each time anew, carrying it around every time it lives its dead life and dies its living death.[39] The menstruator enters *and* exits the cycle of life simultaneously while bleeding herself into a revolving door she herself becomes, beginning to exist and exit at once in syncopation that seems to have a will, a script, of its own:

> Unlike the other bodily excretions, however, menstrual "discharge" is not subject to voluntary regulation by the menstruating woman. . . . In the popular view menstruation also puts the menstruating woman in the company of the incontinent—the infant, seriously ill, or frail elderly—who must bind, hide, or have hidden for them the expressions of their bodies. Regarded suspiciously, menstrual "incontinence" is closely allied with irregularity, and therefore unreliability. Even when the cycle is regular, menstruation makes the body "irregular," a fact that has excluded women from psychological experiments as well as employment or posts that require stability.[40]

The blood in her flows out of her; the blood belonging to her escapes her. Her blood disowns itself, floods out without, and despite, her will or wishes. She splits herself almost at a split second, perpetually punctually; perpetually punctuated throughout the course, she slides back into what appears to be herself. She becomes double, self-self-conscious, "the double *cogito*," sometimes thinking of her menstrual table while sitting at a writing table, as "a table means does it not my dear it means a whole steadiness. Is it likely a change," and some other times, finding herself at that writing table reading her own periodic thoughts into the periods of modern philosophy or high modernist lit stuff, garbage, depending on which mood-mode she is in.[41] In any event, she would be anchored somewhere between and will find herself occasionally asking this: one menstruates—so what?

Any menstrual event or affair, pre-/post-inclusive, is a window onto a world of waves, half covered, half heard, there still, steady still. In a used tampon about to be thrown into a garbage can, naked and unloved, is the trembling flesh of the world, forgotten and flowering anyhow. Someone, some one, still there, reading, witnessing, hearing, dreaming, singing, without signing, the auto-generative semiotic inscription and subscription of the femalely bleeding body. "When Beauvoir talks rather sadly about puberty," Michèle Le Doeuff observes:

> she is speaking for herself alone and the chapter on this issue in *The Second Sex* should be read in the light of the *Memoirs of a Dutiful Daughter*. She counts her experience twice: once in the mode of the universal and once in that of an autobiographical narrative. Obviously for her it was a sad fate. In women's groups, we discovered together that we cannot be certain that there is something that can be called puberty.[42]

Again, without isolating or valorizing sobjectivity of "the 'I bleed, therefore I am' discourse" of uncontested womanhood or philosophic queenliness, but rather extrapolating from each case a singular event that remains overcharged and overlooked at once, we are here following through that philopoetically infused line of "menstrual meditations" or mediations held open by Stein, Beauvoir, Douglas, Young, Ruddick, Battersby, Bobel, Cixous, Grosz, Irigaray, Olkowski, and others, as well as Descartes in principle, hoping to find some ways to think, link, life-death (*bios-thanatos*) anew along the way, to "access being" afresh, which has both onto-phenomenological and datalogical imports.[43] Some philosophical attention paid this way to menstrual phenomenality and its whole spectrum including so-called menopausal transition (perimenopause), a murderously derogatory term as I will explain later, will yield guiding insights into existential matters of transitory and transformative transcendence, on both macro and micro scales.

For "there are two movements that come together in life," as Beauvoir observes in reference to the ovum and the sperm, "and life," she goes on to say:

> maintains itself only by surpassing itself. It does not surpass itself without maintaining itself; these two moments are always accomplished together. It is academic to claim to separate them: nevertheless, it is either one or the other that dominates.[44]

Continuing to cogitate "menstrual," with and after Beauvoir, I see this passage addressing something else too, something *ex*tra in or *ex*ternal to the shadows of reproductive copulation: what if one takes the life of a flowy, not just juicy, breathing vagina for what it is, accepting it at its face value, with its full life cycle in view and its rhythm intact, not necessarily in relation or conjunction to the penis as a measuring stick?[45] Note further the critical potency of Beauvoir's deconstructive debunking of the double life of *Homo Erectus*: on the one hand, she demonstrates how a boy-man aspires to transcend into Super *Homo Mensura* by mobilizing that "foreign . . . double" as a psycho-physical leverage or rule for himself, himself mirrored in the female-feminine other he controls, kneads, by his measure. On the other hand, more curiously, Beauvoir embraces the other side of this penile-phallic drama, conceptually, by spotlighting its fluidly ambiguous indeterminacy therein, its being, in fact, "midway between voluntary process and spontaneous process" (meaning, as Debra Bergoffen explains, "the penis is not always erect. Its ejections are not always within the boy's/man's control."[46]). Now recall: one is not always menstruating, either, as has been acknowledged from the start. Then, as Bergoffen goes on to affirm, we have this post-Beauvoirean lesson, an effect of that phallic deconstruction:

> It is also the case that these flows, as signatures of the birthing body, are marks of transcendence—signs of an openness to the future and the other. Again patriarchy is forgetful. Instead of registering the ambiguities of the female body it erases all the marks of transcendence.[47]

Following this line, we are reminded to ask ourselves how and where we should meet this menstrual frenemy, her immeasurably complex temporality, when it is on the move, making its way in and out.

Who, what, is this little femme personae, this resident alien that keeps alerting and alienating us with its strangely communal color, red, this familiarly foreign correspondent from and to the otherworldly tabulated time that accompanies many a woman, young and old, dawn to dusk, cradle to grave? I am being hysterical—or hypothetical? For she, say, this little femuncula we haven't yet even made up, is not human, not even a woman. But she is in her, passes through her, disappears with her and into her new her, survives her, moves onto another, an o*ther* like a *mother*, her mother, via parasitical pauses and poses, initiating and producing and sustaining the indivisible fluctuating realities of the female body, seemingly one too many. This ongoing gesture to respect and recodify the underbelly transcendence of menstruation and undercover menstruators to find "a new language invented by nature, secreted by 'womanhood,'" should continue to propel feminist thinking, and what follows traces some indelible watermarks drawn by such menstrual soul-bodies in action, some illuminating examples—two philosophical menstruators, both singular.[48]

THAT YOU CAN AND DID THROW THIS THING, "A HANDKERCHIEF . . . USED ON THAT OCCASION"

In *The Female Worthies* (*Biographium Faemineum*), a compilation, the subtitle says, of "memoirs of the most illustrious ladies of all ages and nations . . . containing (exclusive of foreigners) the lives of above fourscore British ladies," there is a Greek Alexandrian philosopher (a naturalized British subject?) appearing in some curiously curated detail. That worthy female—"a lady of such beauty, modesty, wisdom and virtue . . . eagerly sought for by many in marriage," "daily surrounded with a circle of young gentlemen, many of them distinguished by their fortune or quality," so already well known to many learned gentlemen then, is Hypatia (350/370–415), head of the Platonist School at Alexandra, who, like Socrates (469–399 B.C.), died a famous death except more cuttingly, being killed by a Christian mob.[49] Here goes the legendary story of Hypatian menstrual fit, worth following at every step of the way, especially in this "modern," also "early" modern, version:

One of her own scholars, made warm love to her, whom she endeavoured to cure of his passion by the precepts of philosophy. The spark vehemently urging his suit (pleading no doubt the irresistible power of beauty) at a time when she happened to be under an indisposition common to her sex, she took up a handkerchief, of which she had been making some use on that occasion, and throwing it into his face, said, *This is what you love, young fool, and not any thing that is beautiful.* For the *Platonic* philosophers hold goodness, wisdom, virtue, and such like things, whole intrinsic worth are desirable for their own sakes, to be the only real *beauties*, of whose divine symmetry, charms, and perfection, the most superlative that appear in *bodies*, are but faint resemblances. This is the right notion of *Platonic love.* And therefore *Hypatia*'s procedure might well put a student of philosophy at *Alexandria* to the blush, and quite cure him too, as *Suidas* assures us, it did, whatever effect such an action might have upon any of the young students in our modern universities.[50]

Where shall we start? Or stop? Or swerve? Do smile but study more.

Among many lessons to be extracted from this unusually explosive "occasion" allusively abstracted here, I too shall offer some modest philosophic thoughts on just this case, this point: Upon hearing that "*this* is the right . . . *Platonic love*" (love, not move), what do you hear? "Any of the young students in our modern universities" too would wonder whether that means any menstruating or menstrual body, not so much a thing of "divine symmetry, charms or perfection" as some sort of bloody clutter of mystery, can be a Platonic sobject in the first place, whether as an agent (one, the subject, thinking of it) or as a topic (one, the object, being thought of). Or are we saying that all of "this" is acceptable as it is insofar as we, the institutionalized Platonic lovers, don't-tell-don't-ask about such messy-testy (testy, not tasty) matters and remain happily ignorant or ignored thereafter?[51] Positively queer again and again already a deeper Platonic question is being raised right there, hidden in plain sight: What is "this," after all? What does it refer to or amount to? Are you there? Are we on the same page or plane? Or planet?

How about this? What "that" is, if anything, is that Hypatia doing justice, menstrual justice. She is doing triple justice: to herself, to the man in question, to Plato(nism). Here is a visual aid, a modern version of the Hypatian cogitator interrupted, this time a scene from Denise Riley:

> It's not possible to live twenty-four hours a day soaked in the immediate awareness of one's sex. Gendered self-consciousness has, mercifully, a flickering nature. Yet even here there are at once some puzzles; because to be hit by the intrusions of bodily being—to be caught out by the start of menstruation, for instance—is just not the same as being caught up unexpectedly in 'being a woman.' . . . You walk down a street wrapped in your own speculations; or you

speed up, hell-bent on getting to the shops before they close: a car slows down, a shout comments on your expression, your movement; or there's a derisively hissed remark from the pavement. You have indeed been seen 'as a woman,' and violently reminded that your passage alone can spark off such random sexual attraction-cum-contempt, that you can be a spectacle when the last thing on your mind is your own embodiedness. But again, the first thought here, surely, is not, 'Now, humiliatingly, I've become a woman,' but rather that you have been positioned antagonistically as a woman-thing, objectified as a distortion.[52]

Now, *this* is more like it, is it not, I mean, what we are talking about here. *This* is the philosophical model of the situation Hypatia is facing as a gender-embodied thinking being. A non-Platonic move made to her, Hypatia is making a bold countermove that is indeed (as well as in deed) closer to Platonic love; "take it, this is the beauty you are admiring," take it, in the name of Plato. The irony of "Platonic love" is being hurled at that bunch of fine young male mind-bodies in this very Platonic game: note this non-Platonic interval *of* the Platonic scene to be continued and move on.

Hypatia is throwing "it," performing it, "like her," just like that, as a girl—almost overthrowing—but what, exactly?[53] Is she renouncing or repressing her lady parts here? Hardly. Is she then flaunting her girliness or womanliness? Again, not quite. Is she demonstratively transcending her femininity or womanliness by transporting something out of her vaginal closet? Harder to tell. One thing for sure: she is writing something else into this scene of unrequited love, impossible affairs, or, plainly, sexual harassment. What is transgressive, risking transitory illegibility, is the very move she is making—namely, that she threw something. T.H.R.O.W. she did, "like a girl or not," shamelessly, finally. She's had enough of it. She is not throwing it away but at it, back at the smug face of philosophy that says one thing and does another or the other. Exactly.

What was she counter(-do)ing? How and why does Hypatia throw it like she means it? Start with her pitching. Just unfold "it," that euphemized "handkerchief," the twice-used, heavily textured matter now thrown at some hapless chap, one who suffers from Platonic love deficiency or excess, as some might still argue—and I will just leave you there, fine, go play with yourself then. Again, what does "it" disguise and disclose, that "not-so-beautiful" thing in and now out there?

1. The sobjectivity of menstrual acts and reproductive potentials as an allegorized (cat-)call for be(com)ing, a summarized "reminder," cosmic or otherwise;

2. The in/visibility and il/legibility of the menstruating female body and her double consciousness phenomenologically embodied as such;
3. The materially compressed echo-temporality of menstrual events that is not only cyclical but also surgical, not only cyclically monumentalizable into a measure of archaic-futural time rhythmically self-distanciated as such, the mode Julia Kristeva sees in "Women's Time," but also punchier, pointier than that, present in itself and presented to itself via a searing now, with its subterranean continuity eruptively suspensive, surging, cuttingly (sur)real.[54]

Follow, let us, this line of counteraction by one unusual spinster (1) who "died a maid" after possibly throwing many a handkerchief upon emergent occasions.[55] See Hypatia reemerging, a philosopher (2) who, out of cogito-menstrual frustration, semi-outs herself as a bleeder in actuality, and Hypatia, a woman of some Medusan breeding (3) whose "beauty," as Hélène Cixous would say, "will no longer be forbidden," who would not have become "menopausal," a tamed linear notion that flattens a pause into a programmed ending, practically a stop button.[56] But who says it's over? Rather, this furious, hilarious Hypatia now comes to us as a flaming figure of menstrual pause, a syncopated embodiment of the menstrual woman's time, time of auto-hetero-compression, not just quasi-messianic future anteriority.

Following the example of the im/patient Hypatia, with those "not . . . ashamed of their torrents," we could start a new language, a new trans-fem-idiom, say, of menstrual pause, the sort of internal, tonal, somewhat oddly rooted pause in and of this auto-transfixing formulation by Gertrude Stein, a poet of the modernity of the right-now[57]: "Each one is one. Each one is being the one each one is being. Each one is being one. Each one is being the one that one is being. Each one is being one. Each one is one."[58] Yes, go back and read again, each one. Just note, for now, "the austere verity of . . . 'Being' as the absolute occupation . . . revealed . . . with uninterrupted insistence," as Mina Loy aptly points out, with one of the keenest sets of eyes and ears for the Steinian detail of literary modernism, its subterranean massiveness if not straightforward messiness. Thinking, writing, living, breathing, dying, being with and in a pause, each pause being each one and being the one that one is being: holding in sight a pair of parallel bars as those seen in media players, imagining walking through some unnamed two columns that would support a sheltering roof (*stoa*) for communal being, I suggest we return to the Hypatian scene of performative or demonstrative menstruation so as to single out, extract, the very power of the female body, its near tautological auto-connective forces: I suggest we hold not only in sight but in breath its being and being what it is and becoming part of female bodies in intersubjective liquidity—its being inclusive of intergenerational blood stream beginning at the end on "firstdays" à la Cixous, the mourner and learner of impossible deaths, deaths lying between the "first" and a "day" with an eventuation of the two crossing, merging many times all the time with no discrimination between a day and a day except aesthetic and sometimes ascetic discernment of each and every time passing by.[59] For truly "first" days come unannounced first, outside, and through the invisible grid of projections, anticipations, desperations, all such temporal safety nets and traps. That is, when starting to menstruate, joyfully or painfully, she, or more precisely her minding, pauses for her bodily calls and needs and quirks. When the other time comes, this or that pause is mobilized otherwise, so she would make herself pause and pace herself for some other matters as well, scribbling more on her hankies, if necessary, or writing herself into many a "biography" of "the people inside," "irregular vines covering / the cottages / concealing the entrance ways" where you're (not) welcome not because of your beauty but regardless of.[60]

Menstruating or not, furiously or not, Hypatia 2.0 keeps herself busy drafting, getting transfigured into, "a mother's law" of continuous counting where one connects another one, where "nothing is allowed to interrupt the mere continuation of communication," not so much the law of the Father, where one bars and dominates the other, where something would block something else and someone should blame someone else for something that happens inside/outside the father's control.[61] And so on. Again our trailblazing Stein, of and in each one of us, sums it up, and this time in *A Long Gay Book* (1909–1912) like this: "what is secretion, secretion is that amusement which every little mark shows as merit," each and every little ink mark counting as progress, as work in progress, as in every little monthly mark and link on calendar as something that merits a double look, mark.[62]

If and when Hypatia appears or disappears, what she is, is that she is on menstrual pause, anyway, either way, as are many women at this very moment, their "pockets filled with words," choke-full of unmentionables already mentioned and marching away anyway.[63] Listen, I repeat: she is not on menopause, but on menstrual pause, always, all ways, all the way. She is not reproductively (un)ready, she is ready (un)productively. On pause, she lives and dies. She flows. She is a flow and is a gate that itself starts flowing, fading in and out. She flows into a flow out of which she flows, followingly. She becomes a flow, part of one, each one becoming one that is being one, each one that each being is, each bleeding being bloody is. Hypatia's handkerchief, every single one she must have used, actually or hypothetically, is in and circulates through every menstruatingly measured woman's body and time.

THAT REMAINS TO BE SEEN, OBSCENE

Hypatia has come out as a menstruator in a semi-self-outing mode, out of necessity, both in principle and in real time, "right now." Her self-identity as a female philosopher dually marked by the seemingly unalterable, gendered embodiment of feedback system, a.k.a. "(male) philosophers," is performatively redeployed with a critical intent. Yes, throwing herself out there, she was and is in your face, obscenely, but the thing is, she is already in your body, has been, in fact. If they say "thy righteousness is but a menstrual clout," she will not just say that my hysteric reaction is thy construction.[64] She will also say that my menstrual busyness is (not) thy business. When speaking her mind, she talks back, volleys back, *and* says something else, throwing the ball elsewhere at once, letting it be somewhere, so it tends to appear later—emerging from her tomb, "wombs tombs."[65] The scene of womanly demonstration becomes monstrously, wantonly, double, temporally slit, (in)visibly split. What is she on about? What does she want—to say? This (annoyingly parenthetical, seemingly trivial or peripheral) doubleness of her echo, if audible to an extent, tends to come, materialize, first in the form of recalcitrant il/legibility—that is, surface legibility and folded illegibility. This is some other phenomenal phenomenology that arrives with no apology, thrown like an effigy.

Meet Bhubaneswari (or Bhuvaneswari) Bahduri, "a young woman of sixteen or seventeen" who

> hanged herself in her father's modest apartment in North Calcutta in 1926. The suicide was a puzzle since, as Bhubaneswari was menstruating at the time, it was clearly not a case of illicit pregnancy. Nearly a decade later, it was discovered, in a letter she had left for her elder sister, that she was a member of one of the many groups involved in the armed struggle for Indian independence. She had been entrusted with a political assassination. Unable to confront the task and yet aware of the practical need for trust, she killed herself.[66]

So, she, too, "died a maid." And then?

Time itself goes back. This menstrual code, rediscovered and recracked from a suppressed family archive (pertaining to the younger sister of Gayatri Chakravorty Spivak's grandmother's, Raseswari Debi), comes to demonstrate the counter-writing of the female body undertaken for itself, including the futural self that can only bank on archival hopes. Simply, remarkably, Bhubaneswari waited for that time to come—to menstruate. Inserting into the counter-narrative its own "blooded" forensic precision, *the* temporal footprint, this chrono-topological body in the final act was "writing resistance in" and into "itself" in the face of insurmountable, interlocked structures of oppressions such as patriarchal violence, class system, and the colonial rule that would systematically, totally, misread it, "it," this

> highly developed, class-marked feminist individualism: first to join a terrorist group and then to commit suicide are successive marks of free will and independence for anyone anywhere, but particularly for a Hindu middle-class woman in the 1920s in India. Spivak describes it as a "frightening, solitary, and 'Clytemnestra-like' project for a woman."[67]

Why? Especially because it operates within the specific contours of discourses of sanctioned suicide that are linked to a Hindu regulative psychobiography in which such a death is permitted only to men—with the exception of *sati*. And by timing her death to coincide with the onset of menstruation, Bhubaneswari "reverses the interdict (in the Dharmaśāstra) against a menstruating widow's right to immolate herself." Spivak reads this act therefore as "an ad hoc, subaltern rewriting of the text of sati-suicide."[68]

So this example of a Brahmin girl's "subaltern" suicide or a subalternized girl's Brahmin-like noble suicide, as widely recognized and extensively discussed, has also become part of Spivak's ongoing projects to deconstruct—disclose by displacement, analyze to the core to a haunting effect—the discursive axiomatics of Euro-Anglo-American imperialism and its redemptive gendered fantasies that feed themselves on the moralized horrors of the subjugated subject/other mother, such as the practice of widow burning (*sati*) in colonial India, which the British colonial government banned.

"This" lucid dreaming, to which reading *reverts* out of slumber, to recall our earlier discussion on the phenomenological reversibility of the body and language, this female body of interlinguality or intercorporeality that gets fundamentally unread or misread by the colonial-patriarchal epistemology of subjectivity, is being rearchived as if relieved, although not restored per se. Almost with nothing else at hand, not even a handkerchief or a hand, Bhubaneswari wrote with her body, the totality, the infinite minimality of it, using her menstrual blood as her ink, her Steinian ink and link. She rewrote her body through her last menstruation that save her other life, her afterlife, her honor, her integrity, her consistency, her politics, her ethics, her soul, her anguish now partially rendered visible. The suicidal reinscription of her irreducible agency, her paradoxically knotted being, her final *sum* shows in the form of a speech act: I am, I am *not* pregnant, I am *not* the woman you/they as*sum*e I am. A "priority given" by Spivak

> to *this* message over the expressed and explicit reason for her death (i.e., remorse over failure to carry out an assassination) must be sought not in the literary

critic's characterological analysis . . . but rather in the feminist historian's legitimate habit of reading gendered behavior in terms of its social conditioning. That Bhubaneswari found it insufficient to declare the true cause of her death via a suicide note but sought to convey, *in addition*, a coded message via her body solely in order to remove any misunderstanding about an illicit pregnancy: *this* is the sign of her gendered subalternity. Whatever the transgressive potential of the sexuate body's excess (here its menstruating, unclean condition in death), it is canceled in this instance by the woman's submission to the violence of a social system's insistent demand to be satisfied about a female subject's chastity—even in death.[69]

Again, the meaning of *"this"* example is constantly, instantly, dualized as a Brahmin girl's "subaltern" suicide or a subalternized girl's Brahmin-like suicide, and thus il/legible to that extent, that way.

"This" rupture, this irresolution, this perpetual lining, this discursive cross-firing, this insidious watermarking, is not "Platonic love" or the same as, although a case could be made if one were to stick or re-revert to that usual line of reading, where a body or a boy-like body is supposed to go through and transcend its impure origin of copula love through gestures of sacrificial sublimation or supernatural self-rectification. Hypatia gesturing toward Bhubaneswari this way or that way, across the pond, without necessarily becoming her, however, as each remains singular in her anchored materiality and historico-existential specificity, what we see is something like a circular-Platonic "womb tomb" turning into a post-Kantian womb bomb. She had her own body expire, having it live its afterlife instead. The core of the young girl's ontology, both her suicidal identity and absent presence, remains quite literally unlocatable within that grand tableau of phallogo-colonial reading of "a history of the vanishing present," at the very moment of its inscription. Spivak says this, in sum:

> Whereas the British Indian reform of sati is much celebrated, when a young, single girl attempted to write resistance in her very body, she could not be read. If only I could occupy with desire, *that singular inscribed body*, I have tried to understand how she felt as she waited for her periods to begin, so she could disprove what she knew would be the conclusion drawn from her hanged body—illicit pregnancy.[70]

The impossible sub-ontology of Bhubaneswari is theoretically linkable to that of, say, "two girls alone" sitting at a bar, drinking, and chatting, referred to as such by a man behind the bar, the bartender. Recall the way in which Bhubaneswari's ontological singularity, not ontic numeric singleness, is erased from the historical memories and narratives. In this vein, Spivak, a couple of decades on, sitting there at a bar, wonders back half-jokingly about the grammatological oddities of such "two girls alone" rendered natural, massively natural, by the hegemonic epistemology of gendered recognition. Musingly, she asks, "Do we need a special analytic category for female collectivities? For lesbian couples? For single lesbians? Is the antonym of single–double? Multiple? Or always–married?"[71] The discourse of reproductive heterosexist couplehood, immediately apparent with such a riddling density, is still pervasively normative. "Thy righteousness is but a menstrual clout": no one would be genuinely surprised, if only still shocked, to hear such a notion of situationally naturalized "bitchiness" hurled back, habitually, at the sexually harassed, even the tragically hanged or butchered. Hypatia and Bhubaneswari, dead or alive, are among countless female bodies lodged in various corners of the "humanimal" archives of this not-so-Platonic world, where the end of "this" flows into the beginning of "that," with such singular, menstruating bodies disclosed anew in the counter-archives of I-was-here-and-will-be-there-if-i-am-not-seen-present.[72] Perhaps we could then also flip that conceptual slur to say instead, to show: "My (up)rightness could be in a menstrual clout," a tomb bomb. If I am thrown in a situation, I am back in certain acts of throwing.

THAT COMES IN A PMS (PERIODIC MENTAL SYNTHESIS):
I THINK I AM [ON(,) A PERIOD].

> I am
> I am just throwing this out
> I am just throwing this back out
> Again
> At it
> Like "a woman having her days"
> As René Descartes says
> ...
> I think
> I think I am
> I think I am on
> I think I am on a period
> I am
> Yes, I am, a period.
>
> > The scene in which every scene has its origin
> > in languageless invisibility is a ceaselessly active actuality.
> > —Pascal Quignard, *The Roving Shadows*[73]

KYOO LEE is Associate Professor of Philosophy at John Jay College, City University of New York, and author of *Reading Descartes Otherwise: Blind, Mad, Dreamy, and Bad* (Fordham University Press, 2013).

NOTES

1. Simone de Beauvoir, *The Second Sex*, trans. Constance Borde and Sheila Malovany-Chevallier (New York: Alfred A. Knopf, 2010), 28–29.
2. Cited in William Shea, "Descartes and the Rosicrucian Enlightenment," in *Metaphysics and Philosophy of Science in the Seventeenth and Eighteenth Centuries*, ed. R. S. Woolhouse (Dordrecht: Springer, 1988), 96.
3. René Descartes, *The Philosophical Writings of Descartes*, trans. John Cottingham, Robert Stoothoff, Dugald Murdoch, and Anthony Kenny (Cambridge, UK: Cambridge University Press, 1985), 1:322.
4. Shea, "Descartes and the Rosicrucian Enlightenment," 84.
5. Katie Conboy, Nadia Medina, and Sarah Stanbury, *Writing on the Body: Female Embodiment and Feminist Theory* (New York: Columbia University Press, 1997), 29.
6. Ibid.
7. Tom Sorell, *Descartes Reinvented* (Cambridge, UK: Cambridge University Press, 2005), 148; Sara Heinämaa, "The Soul-Body Union and Sexual Difference: From Descartes to Merleau-Ponty and Beauvoir," in *Feminist Reflections on the History of Philosophy: The New Synthese Historical Library* 55 (2004): 137–51, 138.
8. Luce Irigaray, *Speculum of the Other Woman*, trans. Gillian C. Gill (Ithaca, NY: Cornell University Press, 1985), 166.
9. Chris Bobel, *New Blood: Third-Wave Feminism and the Politics of Menstruation* (New Brunswick, NJ: Rutgers University Press, 2010), 11–12.
10. Modess menstrual napkin (pad) advertisement, "All right, Doubting Ladies . . . here's FREE proof," 1933, http://www.mum.org/mod33fe.htm.
11. Kirstie Renae, "15 Euphemisms for your Period," *Literally Darling* (blog), January 28, 2014, http://www.literallydarling.com/blog/2014/01/28/euphemisms-period.
12. Ibid.
13. Iris Marion Young, "Menstrual Meditations," *On Female Body Experience: "Throwing Like a Girl" and Other Essays* (New York: Oxford University Press, 2005), 107.
14. Ibid.
15. Bobel, *New Blood*, 8.
16. Christine Daigle, "Beauvoir's Politics of Ambiguity," paper presented at the Canadian Political Science Association, Ottawa, Canada, May 29, 2009.
17. Betty Friedan, *The Feminine Mystique* (1963; New York: W. W. Norton, 2001), 57–78; Bobel, *New Blood*, 7; Laurent Berlant, *The Female Complaint: The Unfinished Business of Sentimentality in American Culture* (Durham, NC: Duke University Press, 2008).
18. Crimson Movement, http://crimsonmovement.com.
19. Beauvoir, *Second Sex*, 329, cited in Young, "Menstrual Meditations," 97.
20. Dorothea Olkowski, "Introduction: What Are Feminist Enactments?," *Resistance, Flight, Creation: Feminist Enactments of French Philosophy* (Ithaca, NY: Cornell University Press, 2000), 1.

21. Hélène Cixous, "The Laugh of the Medusa," *Signs* 1, no. 4 (1976): 876.
22. Bobel, *New Blood*, 7.
23. Ibid.
24. Gloria Steinem, "If Men Could Menstruate," *Ms. Magazine*, October 1978, 110.
25. Ibid.
26. Karen Houppert, *The Curse: Confronting the Last Unmentionable Taboo: Menstruation* (New York: Macmillan, 2004), 239, 9, 241.
27. Ibid., 243.
28. Beauvoir, *Second Sex*, 192; Sara Ruddick, *Maternal Thinking: Toward a Politics of Peace* (Boston: Beacon Press, 1989), 190.
29. Elizabeth Grosz, *Volatile Bodies: Toward a Corporeal Feminism* (St. Leonards, Australia: Allen and Unwin, 1994), 203; Beauvoir, *Second Sex*, 192.
30. Christine Delphy, *Feminism and Sexual Equality* (New York: Monthly Review Press, 1984), 195.
31. Cixous, "Laugh of the Medusa."
32. Dorothea Olkowski, "The End of Phenomenology," *Hypatia* 15, no. 3 (2000): 76.
33. Dorothea Olkowski, "Merleau-Ponty: The Demand for Mystery in Language," *Philosophy Today* 31, no. 4 (1987): 355.
34. Joan Brumberg, "Something Happens to Girls: Menarche and the Emergence of the Modern American Hygienic Imperative," *Journal of the History of Sexuality* 4, no. 1 (1993): 99–127, cited in Bobel, *New Blood*, 7, 104; Houppert, *The Curse*, 105–109; Lisa Ruddick, *Reading Gertrude Stein: Body, Text, Gnosis* (Ithaca, NY: Cornell University Press, 1990), 152.
35. Gertrude Stein, *Matisse, Picasso, and Gertrude Stein with Two Shorter Stories* (Barton, VT: Something Else Press, 1972), 215.
36. Christine Battersby, *The Phenomenal Woman: Feminist Metaphysics and the Patterns of Identity* (New York: Routledge, 1998), 39.
37. Beauvoir, *Second Sex*, 361; emphasis added.
38. Robert Fitterman and Vanessa Place, *Notes on Conceptualisms* (New York: Ugly Duckling Press, 2009), 38.
39. Mary Douglas, *Purity and Danger: An Analysis of Concepts of Pollution and Taboo* (1966; New York: Routledge, 2001), 97.
40. Ruddick, *Maternal Thinking*, 190.
41. I thank Dorothea Olkowski for this formulation of the double cogito and discussion around it. See also Stein, "A Table," in *Tender Buttons: Objects, Food, Rooms* (Auckland: Floating Press, 2009), 26. I thank Dee Morris for this reference and discussion around it.
42. Le Doeuff, "Beauvoir and Feminism," 2000, 54.
43. Bobel, *New Blood*, 12.
44. Beauvoir, *Second Sex*, 28.
45. Ibid., 57–58.
46. Ibid., 57; Debra Bergoffen, "Simone de Beauvoir: Disrupting the Metonymy of Gender," in *Resistance, Flight, Creation: Feminist Enactments of French Philosophy*, ed. Dorothea Olkowski (New York: Cornell University Press, 2000), 104.
47. Bergoffen, "Simone de Beauvoir," 104.
48. Michèle Le Doeuff, "Beauvoir and Feminism," in *French Feminism Reader*, ed. Kelly Oliver (Lanham, MD: Rowman and Littlefield, 2000), 53.

49. *The Female Worthies*, 36–37.
50. Ibid., 37.
51. Nancy Tuana, "Coming to Understand: Orgasm and the Epistemology of Ignorance," *Hypatia* 19, no. 1 (2004): 194–232.
52. Denise Riley, *"Am I That Name?": Feminism and the Category of "Women" in History*, (Minneapolis: University of Minnesota Press, 2003), 96–97.
53. Young, "Menstrual Meditations," 27–45.
54. Julia Kristeva, "Women's Time," *Signs* 7, no. 1 (1981): 13–55.
55. *Female Worthies*, 36.
56. Cixous, "Laugh of the Medusa," 876.
57. Olkowski, "Introduction: What Are Feminist Enactments?," 6.
58. Mina Loy and Roger L. Conover, *The Last Lunar Baedeker* (Highlands: Jargon Society, Distributed by Inland Book Co., 1982), 289.
59. Hélène Cixous, *First Days of the Year*, trans. Catherine A. F. MacGillivray (Minneapolis: University of Minnesota Press, 1998).
60. Barbara Guest, "One," *The Collected Poems of Barbara Guest* (Middletown, CT: Wesleyan University Press, 2008), 183.
61. Rüdiger Campe, "Continuing Forms: Allegory and the Translatio Imperii in Caspar von Lohenstein and Johann Wolfgang Goethe," *Germanic Review: Literature, Culture, Theory* 77, no. 2 (2002): 136.
62. Stein, *Matisse, Picasso, and Gertrude Stein*, 110.
63. Guest, "One," 183.
64. Sara Read, "Thy Righteousness Is but a Menstrual Clout: Sanitary Practices and Prejudice in Early Modern England," *Early Modern Women: An Interdisciplinary Journal* 3 (2008): 1–25.
65. Cixous, *First Days of the Year*, 41–58.
66. Gayatri Chakravorty Spivak, "Can the Subaltern Speak?," in *Marxism and the Interpretation of Culture*, ed. Cary Nelson and Lawrence Grossberg (Urbana: University of Illinois Press, 1988), 307; Spivak, *Can the Subaltern Speak?: Reflections on the History of an Idea*, ed. Rosalind Morris (New York: Columbia University Press, 2010), 291, 62–63.
67. Gayatri Chakravorty Spivak, "If Only," *The Scholar and Feminist Online* 4, no. 2 (2006): http://sfonline.barnard.edu/heilbrun/spivak_01.htm; Rajeswari Sunder Rajan, "Death and the Subaltern," in Spivak, *Can the Subaltern Speak?*, 123.
68. Rajan, "Death and the Subaltern," 123.
69. Ibid., 125–26.
70. Spivak, "If Only"; emphasis added.
71. Ibid.
72. Bhanu Kapil, *Humanimal: A Project for Future Children* (Berkeley, CA: Kelsey Street Press, (2009); Kalpana Seshadri, *HumAnimal: Race, Law, Language* (Minneapolis: University of Minnesota Press, 2012), 198.
73. Pascal Quignard, *The Roving Shadows* (London: Seagull Books, 2012), 7.

BIBLIOGRAPHY

Battersby, Christine. *The Phenomenal Woman: Feminist Metaphysics and the Patterns of Identity*. New York: Routledge, 1998.

Beauvoir, Simone de. *The Second Sex*. Translated by Constance Borde and Sheila Malovany-Chevallier. New York: Alfred A. Knopf, 2010.
Bergoffen, Debra. "Simone de Beauvoir: Disrupting the Metonymy of Gender." In *Resistance, Flight, Creation: Feminist Enactments of French Philosophy*, edited by Dorothea Olkowski, 97–110. New York: Cornell University Press, 2000.
Berlant, Laurent. *The Female Complaint: The Unfinished Business of Sentimentality in American Culture*. Durham, NC: Duke University Press, 2008.
Bobel, Chris. *New Blood: Third-Wave Feminism and the Politics of Menstruation*. New Brunswick, NJ: Rutgers University Press, 2010.
Brumberg, Joan. "'Something Happens to Girls': Menarche and the Emergence of the Modern American Hygienic Imperative." *Journal of the History of Sexuality* 4, no. 1 (1993): 99–127.
Campe, Rüdiger. "Continuing Forms: Allegory and Translatio Imperii in Caspar von Lohenstein and Johann Wolfgang Goethe." *Germanic Review: Literature, Culture, Theory* 77, no. 2 (2002): 128–45.
Cixous, Hélène. *First Days of the Year*. Translated by Catherine A. F. MacGillivray. Minneapolis: University of Minnesota Press, 1998.
———. "The Laugh of the Medusa." *Signs* 1, no. 4 (1976): 875–93.
Conboy, Katie, Nadia Medina, and Sarah Stanbury. *Writing on the Body: Female Embodiment and Feminist Theory*. New York: Columbia University Press, 1997.
Daigle, Christine. "Beauvoir's Politics of Ambiguity." Paper presented at the special panel on "Simone de Beauvoir's Political Thought: Freedom, Ambiguity and Politics," Annual Meeting of the CPSA (Canadian Political Science Association), Ottawa, May 29, 2009. https://www.cpsa-acsp.ca/papers-2009/Daigle.pdf.
Delphy, Christine. *Feminism and Sexual Equality*. New York: Monthly Review Press, 1984.
Descartes, René. *The Philosophical Writings of Descartes*. Vol. 1. Translated by John Cottingham, Robert Stoothoff, Dugald Murdoch, and Anthony Kenny. Cambridge, UK: Cambridge University Press, 1985.
Douglas, Mary. *Purity and Danger: An Analysis of Concepts of Pollution and Taboo*. 1966. New York: Routledge, 2001.
The Female Worthies or, *Memoirs of the most illustrious ladies of all ages and nations . . . Containing (exclusive of foreigners) the lives of above fourscore British ladies . . . Collected from history, and the most approved biographers, and brought down to the present time . . .* London: Printed for S. Crowder, 1766.
Fitterman, Robert, and Vanessa Place. *Notes on Conceptualisms*. New York: Ugly Duckling Press, 2009.
Friedan, Betty. *The Feminine Mystique*. 1963. New York: W. W. Norton, 2001.
Grosz, Elizabeth. *Volatile Bodies: Toward a Corporeal Feminism*. St. Leonards, Australia: Allen and Unwin, 1994.
Guest, Barbara. "One." *The Collected Poems of Barbara Guest*. Middletown, CT: Wesleyan University Press, 2008.
Heinämaa, Sara. "The Soul-Body Union and Sexual Difference: From Descartes to Merleau-Ponty and Beauvoir." *Feminist Reflections on the History of Philosophy: The New Synthese Historical Library* 55 (2004): 137–51.
Houppert, Karen. *The Curse: Confronting the Last Unmentionable Taboo: Menstruation*. New York: Macmillan, 2004.

Irigaray, Luce. *Speculum of the Other Woman*. Translated by Gillian C. Gill. Ithaca, NY: Cornell University Press, 1985.
Kapil, Bhanu. *Humanimal: A Project for Future Children*. Berkeley, CA: Kelsey Street Press, 2009.
Kristeva, Julia. "Women's Time." *Signs* 7, no. 1 (1981): 13–55.
Le Doeuff, Michèle. "Beauvoir and Feminism." In *French Feminism Reader*, edited by Kelly Oliver, 39–58. Lanham, MD: Rowman and Littlefield, 2000.
Loy, Mina, and Roger L. Conover. *The Last Lunar Baedeker*. Highlands, NC: Jargon Society, 1982.
Modess. "All right, Doubting Ladies . . . here's FREE proof." Magazine advertisement in *Collier's* magazine. Johnson & Johnson, February 18, 1933. http://www.mum.org/mod33fe.htm.
Olkowski, Dorothea. "The End of Phenomenology." *Hypatia* 15, no. 3 (2000): 73–91.
———. "Introduction: What Are Feminist Enactments?" *Resistance, Flight, Creation: Feminist Enactments of French Philosophy*, edited by Dorothea Olkowski, 1–21. Ithaca, NY: Cornell University Press, 2000.
———. "Merleau-Ponty: The Demand for Mystery in Language." *Philosophy Today* 31, no. 4 (1987): 352–58.
Quignard, Pascal. *The Roving Shadows*. London: Seagull Books, 2012.
Rajan, Rajeswari Sunder. "Death and the Subaltern." In *Can the Subaltern Speak?: Reflections on the History of an Idea*, edited by Rosalind Morris, 117–38. New York: Columbia University Press, 2010.
Read, Sara. "Thy Righteousness Is but a Menstrual Clout: Sanitary Practices and Prejudice in Early Modern England." *Early Modern Women: An Interdisciplinary Journal* 3 (2008): 1–25.
Renae, Kirstie. "15 Euphemisms for your Period." *Literally Darling* (blog). http://www.literallydarling.com/blog/2014/01/28/euphemisms-period.
Riley, Denise. *"Am I That Name?": Feminism and the Category of "Women" in History*. Minneapolis: University of Minnesota Press, 2003.
Ruddick, Lisa. *Reading Gertrude Stein: Body, Text, Gnosis*. Ithaca, NY: Cornell University Press, 1990.
Ruddick, Sara. *Maternal Thinking: Toward a Politics of Peace*. Boston: Beacon Press, 1989.
Seshadri, Kalpana. *HumAnimal: Race, Law, Language*. Minneapolis: University of Minnesota Press, 2012.
Shea, William. "Descartes and the Rosicrucian Enlightenment." In *Metaphysics and Philosophy of Science in the Seventeenth and Eighteenth Centuries*, edited by R. S. Woolhouse, 73–99. Dordrecht: Springer, 1988.
Sorell, Tom. *Descartes Reinvented*. Cambridge, UK: Cambridge University Press, 2005.
Spivak, Gayatri Chakravorty. "Can the Subaltern Speak?" In *Marxism and the Interpretation of Culture*, edited by Cary Nelson and Lawrence Grossberg, 271–313. Urbana: University of Illinois Press, 1988.
———. *Can the Subaltern Speak?: Reflections on the History of an Idea*. Edited by Rosalind Morris. New York: Columbia University Press, 2010.
———. "If Only." *The Scholar and Feminist Online* 4, no. 2 (2006). http://sfonline.barnard.edu/heilbrun/spivak_01.htm.
Stein, Gertrude. *Matisse, Picasso, and Gertrude Stein, with Two Shorter Stories*. Barton, VT: Something Else Press, 1972.

———. *Matisse, Picasso, and Gertrude Stein, with Two Shorter Stories*. Paris: Plain edition, 1933.
———. "A Table." In *Tender Buttons: Objects, Food, Rooms*. Auckland: Floating Press, 2009.
Steinem, Gloria. "If Men Could Menstruate." *Ms. Magazine* (October 1978): 110.
Tuana, Nancy. "Coming to Understand: Orgasm and the Epistemology of Ignorance." *Hypatia* 19, no. 1 (2004): 194–232.
Young, Iris Marion. "Menstrual Meditations." *On Female Body Experience: "Throwing Like a Girl" and Other Essays*, 97–122. New York: Oxford University Press, 2005.
———. "Throwing Like a Girl." *On Female Body Experience: "Throwing Like a Girl" and Other Essays*, 27–45. New York: Oxford University Press, 2005.

3 TRANSFORMATIVE LINES OF FLIGHT

From Deleuze to Masoch

LYAT FRIEDMAN

> "Give me your little truth, woman!" I said.
> And thus spoke the little old woman:
> "You go to women? Do not forget the whip!"
>
> —Nietzsche, *Thus Spoke Zarathustra*

Simone de Beauvoir's *The Second Sex* poses a challenge: Because "humanity is male, and man defines woman, not in herself, but in relation to himself," then, we must ask, Can women define themselves, in themselves, without falling into the trap set up by such prior definitions.[1] Can one overcome dyads such as male–female, subject–object, culture–nature in order to demarcate difference in non-negating terms? Can differences be understood without reimposing opposites? It is a simple challenge, and yet complex, as de Beauvoir notes:

> The categories masculine and feminine appear as symmetrical in a formal way on town hall records or identification papers. The relation of the two sexes is not that of two electrical poles: the man represents both the positive and the neuter to such an extent that in French *hommes* designates human beings.... Woman is the negative, to such a point that any determination is imputed to her as limitation, without reciprocity.[2]

The pair masculine–feminine forms a simple logical opposite. However, other paired opposites are superimposed on top of it and aligned. The opposite, masculine–feminine, is stacked upon male–female, and then upon yet another pair, men–women, giving the impression of being equivalent, predetermined, and substantiated qualities. Because of the alignment, the opposites are not contested. Disentangling one pair of opposites implies disentangling a much too long series of dyads, such as nature–culture; subject–object; active–passive; rational–irrational; predator–victim; mobile–motionless; omnipotent–lacking; sadist–masochist; independent–dependent; strong–weak; worker–domestic caretaker; master–slave, to name a few. Such opposites, assembled into permanent axes, have been used, as de Beauvoir shows, throughout history to justify the necessity of control and power of the privileged.

The challenge posed by *The Second Sex* is still more complex because it exposes an overlooked factor in the consolidated axes. Women, de Beauvoir claims, are not the opposite of men, they are Other to men. She writes, "She is Other at the heart of a whole whose two components are necessary to each other."[3] While the pair defines women as opposite to men from men's perspective—as his supplement—women, de Beauvoir argues, remain outside the two opposing poles. The privileged define women in accordance with their needs and desires as their negative, leaving women outside the axes of what humanity is or could be. In formal terms, the Otherness of women makes it impossible for women to entangle the opposing axes, if only because Otherness is not a part of the pair. The alignment of opposite pairs, such as men–women and self–other, cannot be disentangled, because the category of women functions as both opposite of men and other to them, as well as having their own selves. If we follow this line of logic, we would need to conclude that women are other to their own Otherness, and such a conclusion makes no sense at all.

The problem de Beauvoir puts forth is further complicated because when an opposition undergoes disentanglement, its effect does not serve to unravel the alignment of axes; rather, it serves to readjust the axes and produces new and subtle oppositions. Thus, if one can show that the opposite of sadism, for example, is not masochism, then one will work hard at trying to find an appropriate opposition to both sadism and masochism. This move allows one to overlook the fact that "sadism" is used to define extreme manly behavior and "masochism" is allocated to all women. Severing the opposition sadism-masochism does not logically conclude with the inference that women are not men's opposites.

While de Beauvoir attempts to explain how throughout history women have found themselves in the position of the Other while being defined as opposite to and of men, she does not answer her own challenge. She does not lay out a strategy for change, nor does she offer means to advance women. Although feminists' demands and activities have certainly helped improve the lives of many women, the category of thought, the opposition female–male, and its corresponding axes have remained unhindered. De Beauvoir writes, "If woman discovers herself as the inessential and never turns into the essential, it is because she does not bring about this transformation herself."[4] Women, according to de Beauvoir, have not and could not bring about change because of the particular position they found themselves in.

In this essay I would like to propose one possible course of action. It is an odd method, and yet it is designed to circumvent oppositions. It does not contest the oppositions; rather, it provides "lines of flight" that complicate them—for example, that of sadism–masochism. It does not disentangle the dyad, as it merely presents the intricacies of the qualities associated with the dyad and, in so doing, transforms the condition for the possibility of the opposition men–women. It is a method proposed by Gilles Deleuze in an article from 1961 and later developed into a full text in 1967.[5]

Gilles Deleuze begins by opposing the opposition: masochism is not the opposite mechanism of sadism, as Sigmund Freud had claimed in his early essays on sexuality.[6] Masochism, he argues, has nothing in common with sadism. Even later, Deleuze adds, when Freud discovered primary masochism, and "gave up trying to derive masochism from sadism," he continued to explain masochism on the basis of the death drive.[7] Freud, as de Beauvoir summarizes in her chapter on "Sexual Initiation," claims there are three forms of masochism: one linking between pain and sexual pleasure, another producing feminine acceptance of erotic dependence, and a third, generating self-punishment. "Woman is masochistic because pleasure and pain in her are linked through defloration and birth, and because she consents to her passive role."[8]

What Freud, according to Deleuze, did not understand is that masochism is not a defensive reaction to a sadist father or an innate death drive—a neurotic mechanism; rather, masochism entails a different type of psychic structure. For Deleuze, it is a schizoid mechanism that employs "the perception of the maternal image or of the devouring mother," defying paternal law.[9] The masochist, Deleuze asserts, circumvents the figure of power—the oedipal figure of the father—by acting out on behalf of a cold, severe, and oral motherhood, which patriarchy forbids. The masochist utilizes images of mothers and women that oedipal law denies. Masochism is the arousal of "the pathological protest of a part of ourselves that has been wrecked by the law."[10] It is a subversive mechanism that disrupts what appears as necessarily natural and brings to light figures of women that a neurotic, like Freud, cannot imagine are possible.

It is an enlightening argument. Unlike de Beauvoir, who attempts to defend women who have been reduced by patriarchy to the position of masochism, Deleuze attempts to show that masochism has nothing to do with women. Despite an insistence on father-mother imagery, by distinguishing between sadism and masochism, two perversions that are not necessarily prevalent, Deleuze is able to show that there is a real alternative to the universalizing oedipal construction. The alternative is not a variation on similar old themes or a negation of a given model. It is a completely different type of psychic or behavioral structure. Despite its uniqueness, masochism is not recommended by Deleuze; rather, what is of interest in this case is the fact that masochism exemplifies how one can work with and disable oedipal oppositions. In other words, if masochism is completely different from neurosis, then exploring the method by which the masochist deviates from oedipal mechanisms is a significant step toward disentangling ourselves from hyper-determined oedipal axes. I would like to explore here what makes it possible to move away from neurosis, without relapsing into a dialectical construction. To use Deleuze's terms, I want to examine the method of deterritorializing patriarchic standards and reterritorializing alternatives. What interests me is the process of transformation (the conversion of self, as Foucault terms it) that does not require oedipal evolution and binary oppositions. I am looking for independent moments of transmutation and possible alternative choice making. If we can identify the means by which to break away from oedipal domination rather than submit to them by attempts to resist them, then we can begin to delineate alternative routes to patriarchal order and plan a future.

In order to understand the suggested transformative mechanism, let me first present Deleuze's argument and provide a short outline to Masoch's "Venus in Furs."[11] I do so in order to examine not only how these texts provide useful information but also how they are designed to produce an effect on the reader. They are what I would like to call working texts. They are not only performative accounts, reiterating a situation or acting out a posture by repeating and validating "necessarily natural" choices.[12] They are also texts aimed at generating a transformation in the reader. What transformation is is a question I cannot possibly provide an answer to—it is a question that requires a novel type of scientific methodology. Instead, let us follow Deleuze's transformative texts and identify some of the transformations as they occur in the text. By showing that masochism is a unique psychic structure that enables the reader to detect change, without reverting to repetitive oedipal performances, I hope to expose and focus a moment in a process of transformation.

DIFFERENCES

Deleuze's argument is simple. And it is both instructive and effective because it undermines a very simple assumption: Sade and Masoch are both men. The masochist is neither a woman nor a feminine man. Freud's writings suggest that women tend to acquire a masochistic attitude once castration sets in;[13] that Masoch's tale is assumed to expose femininity rather than masculinity—much has been written by feminists about Freud's inability to characterize women's "nature" on its own terms and de Beauvoir's *The Second Sex*—shows how difficult it is to cease referring to masculinity as the standard by which humanity is defined. Perhaps Freud was inspired by the Austrian psychiatrist Richard Freiherr von Krafft-Ebing, who coined the term "sadomasochism" in 1886, demarcating sadism and masochism as opposites. That is not the case. Masoch's protagonist is a man seeking empowered women, not a frail woman seeking to be dominated by a man or, as de Beauvoir notes, a woman whose "desire for effacement leads to masochism."[14] Although the women in both perversions are there to serve obligatory tasks, necessary to satisfy and accommodate men—after all, Sade and Masoch are both men writers who cannot imagine writing from a woman's perspective—nonetheless, the women are not identical. The women they write about play traditional roles—to be desired by men, as they will—but they are not of the same type. The argument, for Deleuze, is quite basic. He writes:

> The woman torturer of masochism cannot be sadistic precisely because she is *in* the masochistic situation; she is an integral part of it, a realization of the masochistic fantasy. . . . The same is true of sadism. The victim cannot be masochistic, not merely because the libertine would be irked if she were to experience pleasure, but because the victim of the sadist belongs entirely in the world of sadism.[15]

Sade's masochist woman is entirely distinct from Masoch's protagonist or the negative of his sadist mistress. Alternatively, Masoch's sadist is incompatible with Sade's sadistic men. She is not a sadist, despite the fact that the masochist implores her to become one. Deleuze's argument is a rejection of doubling negatives and dialectic logic: to not be a non-sadist is not to be a sadist or a masochist. And yet Masoch's beloved is not Other to his desires and fantasies, to use de Beauvoir's term. She is independent of his pathology. She has multiple alternatives.

Deleuze lists eleven distinctive differences between Sade's and Masoch's writings. He writes:

1. "Sadism is speculative-demonstrative, masochism dialectical-imaginative."[16] Sade shows and demonstrates. He displays the full force of masculine operations and makes a spectacle of how such acts of violence enable men to transcend life and overcome nature. Men, in Sade's tales, declare, act, and display their actions. They do not deliberate or consider options. They have no

need to think about others or ponder the effects of their deeds on others. Their act is a fact, and it shows—they are men of action. Masoch does not act. He convinces his admired woman to engage with him in staging imaginary settings. He implores and lingers in the discussion. He enjoys hearing the woman object to him. He wants her to dislike liking the performance of the fantastic scenario. He asks her to fulfill his favorite fantasy because she loves him and because she does not like performing his fantasies, yet he is careful not to neglect her needs and feelings. Every expression on the woman's face is considered and celebrated. Masoch enjoys conversing and staging fantasies.

2. "Sadism operates with the negative and pure negation, masochism with disavowal and suspension."[17] Sade is set to destroy. From a partial process of destruction, he proceeds to full obliterations. He systematically progresses from domination, humiliation, damaging, and crushing his victims to a full annihilation of life itself. He has a target and accomplishes it. Action, from a sadist perspective, is the performance of brutal force and demolition. Nothing else can be considered. Masoch does not act; he stages. And when he does, he does not fully complete the fantasy. He suspends the finale. He clings to the few moments before the fantasy can conclude and dwells in anticipation. Sade completes the act of destruction; Masoch defers completion and holds on to a sense of expectation and suspense.

3. "Sadism operates by means of quantitative reiteration, masochism by means of qualitative suspense."[18] Sade repeats the same deed endlessly. He executes with precision a progressive and detailed program. Each session is a minute accumulation of previous operations of torture, intensified and broadened. What counts is the magnitude and extent of the destruction, while the means of its achievement are inconsequential. Masoch aims to stage qualitatively different scenes of suspense. Each fantasy, despite some common traits, is different in type. There is no progression of fantastic suspension; it is a staging of distinct types of anticipations, each unique, leaving the reader wanting. In that sense, it is clear to the reader of Sade what men desire. The reader of Masoch is left with a sense of incomprehension; because the fantasy is never complete, the reader cannot fully understand the masochist.

4. "There is a masochism specific to the sadist and equally a sadism specific to the masochist, the one never combining with the other."[19] The sadist does not care for his victims. Though he wants them terrified, suffering, and screaming, he is not interested in their perspective or their experience of the torture. Masoch cares deeply for his sadist mistress. Her feelings are of utter importance. No act is done without her consent. As Masoch tries to teach his lady to enjoy administering pain and humiliation, he values her hesitant reac-

tions, as does she. She is not a sadist from Sade's perspective. She hesitates, dislikes torture and pain. She is a woman in love, gentle and caring. Sade's sadists do not see the women they torture; Masoch's masochist cares deeply for his beloved.

5. "Sadism negates the mother and inflates the father; masochism disavows the mother and abolishes the father."[20] Sade obliterates all women. Women with children, as well as those who are pregnant or breastfeeding, are particular targets for annihilation. Masoch ignores father figures and escapes men of authority. He rejects the role of motherhood for women and empowers them with attributes that are incompatible with castration. For Sade the protagonists are men of action, judges, priests, authoritative figures who forcefully execute their free will by annihilating all women; for Masoch the women are hunters, whores, goddesses. Their roles are nontraditional. The woman in Masoch's tale is admired because she is not staged as an object of desire. She is free to determine for herself her desire. She is a woman independent of men and their regulative authority. Her independence is not defined by a man who is aroused by independence in women.

6. "The role and significance of the fetish and the function of the fantasy are totally different in each case."[21] The fetishist, in psychoanalytic terms, is someone who disavows and rejects the notion and image of the castrated mother.[22] While Sade performs castration, "the little death," literally, Masoch disavows the castration. Sade determines that obliteration of all women must be performed. According to the fetish logic, if women have not been castrated, Sade is set to carry out the necessary task in order to maintain the desired order. For Sade the fetish is the penis, empowered by the act of mutilating women. Masoch, on the other hand, rejects the notion of castration altogether and fantasizes empowered mistresses, not phallic, but powerful and enabled. According to the fetish logic, Masoch disavows the reality of castration and substitutes for the "horror" by dressing his beloved woman with a fur coat and providing her with a whip. But a close reading of Masoch's text shows that these objects are not fetishized. They are not the focus of Masoch's desire. They merely serve as stage props for the fantasy. It is the attitude of his mistress that Masoch is attentive to. She is empowered, and by being so, she proves to Masoch that she is not castrated. In other words, for Masoch there is no substitute for the castration. It is completely rejected.

7. "There is an aestheticism in masochism, while sadism is hostile to the aesthetic attitude."[23] Sade destroys. Masoch is a careful director who chooses the setting and scenic props with care and attention to detail. Events filled with magic and natural beauty are abundant.

8. "Sadism is institutional, masochism contractual."[24] Sade's men are men of authority setting up an orderly society in which destruction is the agenda. Everything is determined and controlled for the purpose of satisfying the men. It is an extreme exaggeration of tyranny: an orderly program executed with military precision, no questions asked. Masoch draws contracts with his beloved mistress. He ensures that before she takes on her dominating role, she is on equal footing with him. The contract is based on conscious and rational consent of two equal adults. It also determines that both the masochist and his mistress are free to do as they please when they are not engaging with the staged fantasies, but, more importantly, that each can terminate the contract at will. Sadism is based on a closed institution; masochism, on free will and mutual consent.

9. "In sadism the superego and the process of identification play the primary role, masochism gives primacy to the ego and to the process of idealization."[25] Sade's men operate in accordance with a moral obligation. They rule. A superego declares a categorical imperative that must be followed without exception. The law is clear. Everyone must comply with the acts of the master. Masoch attempts to perform an ideal fantasy with the help of an admired woman. He does not try to establish a society enforced by the moral law; rather, he tries to set a staged performance, knowing very well the social norms of his reality. They both fail. By failing, ego, that part of oneself that tries to accommodate both desires and reality, regulates impending events. Ego puts everything in suspense. It is attuned and accommodating.

10. "Sadism and masochism exhibit totally different forms of desexualization and resexualization."[26] Sadism annihilates its objects of sexual desire, making thought pure and resistant to desire. Yet by obliterating all women and all possible stimuli, the men can perform only a single act, one that thought determines for itself: the sexual act performed on all possible objects. By neutralizing thought, sadism resexualizes all aspects of life and thus exists as pure negation. Sade obliterates everything and in so doing makes every object an object of desire. Masoch, on the other hand, does not sexually perform in his staged fantasies, if only because he suspends the moment prior to it as his mistress is oozing with sexuality, adorned with fetishized objects. Masoch seeks to suspend sexuality and thus makes everything sexually enticing. While Masoch rejects the notion of the castrated mother, desexualizing her, he nonetheless provides his mistress with resexualized powers. Only she can determine, according to Masoch, her sexual pleasures and is unashamed by it.

11. "Finally, summing up all these differences, there is the most radical difference between sadistic *apathy* and masochistic *coldness*."[27] Sade does not

A Table of Distinctions

	SADE	MASOCH
1	Speculative—Demonstrative	Dialectical—Imaginative
2	Negative & Pure Negation	Disavowal & Suspension
3	Quantitative Reiteration	Qualitative Suspense
4	Victim, not masochist	Mistress, not sadist
5	Inflated father	Disavowed mother
	Negated mother	Abolished father
6	Performance of castration	Empowered Woman
7	Aesthetics of destruction	Majestic beauty
8	Institutional administration	Contract
9	Super Ego: The Law	Ego: Attunement
10	Destruction of sexual object—	Sexualized ideal—
	Pure Thought	Deferred Body
11	Apathy	Coldness

care about the women he tortures and kills. He enjoys administrating pain to women and is unmoved by their cries and suffering. He does not see them. Masoch's mistress is a beloved woman in love, filled with sexual desires, who enjoys her body and celebrates life. She treats her servant and humiliated masochist with harsh coldness, like a loving oral mother who does not want to spoil her child. She is cold because she freezes the moment before full completion. She is cold and severe, because she is determined to teach the masochist how to become a man. She is severe but full of life. Sade does not care about the living; he is administering death. Masoch's mistress is preparing him for life.

When assembled into a table (table 3.1), the differences noted appear as opposites, aligned and consolidated into a symmetrical axis. As if each is a negation of the other. They are not. Deleuze sets each trait with other possibilities, easily thought of. For example, vision and speech, the first difference, have a long history in dialectic thought. And yet, because vision can be demonstrative, imaginative, educative, judgmental, or even compassionate, and speech can be emotional, instructive, harsh, or even precise, the complexity of the links between vision and speech undermines the opposition. Each difference is defined by the aggregate of possible incompatibilities. Each trait is set to produce a proliferation and a variety of patterns.

But even the simple opposition is dispersed by the text. Even though sadism and masochism are originally designed to construct traditional opposition between men and women, by the end of the text we understand that they do not share a common feature whatsoever—they are male perversions, not female. Sadism and masochism are male fantasies, and women's perspectives are always presented from the standpoint of the male protagonist, as de Beauvoir argues. When considered, the women of these male fantasies diverge, if only because one is the negative figure of the sadist, the other is not—just like the dyad vision and speech. Sade's sadist is the figure of power; his victim is the figure of his prey, awaiting torture and death. She is his opposite. Masoch's masochist thrives on humiliation and suffering; his sadist woman is put off by the humiliation. As he tries to convince her to enjoy her role, she attempts to cure his perversion. If he desires to be reduced to being a servant, she refuses to act from her position of power. Masoch's mistress is idealized because she is not his opposite. He admires her as a person of independence who is not defined by his fantasy.[28] The pairs are incompatible.

The method proposed by Deleuze is articulated in clear terms in a text he has written with Félix Guattari, *Kafka: Toward a Minor Literature*. There they describe the transformative process as one in which the motif of a bent head or a straightened head appears in much of Kafka's work. It is a simple opposition, and Kafka dismantles it by producing different sets of arbitrary associations linked to the opposing pair (table 3.2):

bent head	straightened head
portrait-photo	musical sound

By misaligning the corresponding signifieds (portrait-photo–musical sound) with respect to the repetitious signifiers (bent head–straightened head), Kafka offers the reader, Deleuze and Guattari argue, "lines of flight" or "lines of escape." It is a way out of the consolidation of oppositions. It discerns connecting lines to other signifieds and to a multiplicity of possibilities overlooked by the opposing axes. Deleuze and Guattari write:

> These examples sufficiently show that in the realm of expression, sound is not opposed to the portrait, *as* the straightened head was opposed to the bent head in the realm of content. If we consider the two forms of content abstractly, there is undeniably a simple formal opposition between them, a binary relation, a structural or semantic quality that scarcely let us out of the realm of the signifiers and that is more a dichotomy than a rhizome.[29]

Lines of flight divert the dichotomy by producing "nonlinear" associations. By making partial connection to non-opposing motifs, Masoch and Kafka transform the systematic binary structure. Deleuze and Guattari conclude with a warning: "It isn't a question of liberty as against submission, but only a question of a line of escape, or rather, of a simple *way out*, 'right, left or in any direction,' as long as it is as little signifying as possible."[30] Even the warning operates with the same logic: liberty becomes related to a way out; submission remains caught in the given opposition.

TRANSFORMATION

"Venus in Furs" is the tale of Severin, who dreams about Venus and falls in love with Wanda, a woman next door. They meet and fall in love. Patiently he tells her of his desire to be humiliated and beaten. He asks her to allow him to become her servant. Slowly she begins to accept her role. He buys her a fur coat and a whip, but on the evening she tries to administer a beating, she is unable to perform and leaves crying. He sets up a contract with her. He asks for two things: that she will not leave him and that she will not allow another man to treat him in the same way. Gradually she begins to comply, showing signs of cold enjoyment, but nonetheless, she finds her role difficult and always stops short of fulfilling his desires. A Russian suitor causes Severin to be jealous, so Severin and Wanda decide to move to Italy, to a place where no one knows them. Severin travels as Wanda's servant. In the house they rent, he takes the role of the gardener and a new contract is set up. It is agreed that he will give up his life in her service. She agrees. To humiliate him, she seeks lovers whom he needs to serve. She finds a German painter who paints her in her fur coat as she beats Severin with the whip. (The painter becomes so excited by the scene that he too requests to be lashed.) Then she meets a Greek man who is cruel to Severin. What is different this time is that the Greek enjoys his own cruelty. She does not. At one point, she ties Severin to a stake in the garden with the help of servant girls and strikes him with the whip, leaving him bleeding all night long. But it is when the Greek man uses the whip on Severin that he runs away, seeking to end his life. He discovers that he cannot kill himself, not even for his mistress's sake. Severin takes leave and returns to his home.

Three years later, Severin receives a letter from his beloved mistress. She writes, "I can admit that I loved you deeply. But it was you who stifled my feelings with your romantic devotion and insane passion."[31] She ends her letter saying, "I hope that my whip has cured you, that the treatment, cruel though it was, has proved effective." Severin admits being cured. He ends his tale with a moral:

> Woman, as Nature created her and as man up to now has found her attractive, is man's enemy; she can be his slave or his mistress, but never his companion. This she can only be [until] she has the same rights as he and is his equal in education and work.[32]

Masoch's tale is about a masochistic man who learns, by perverted means, how to become independent and self-determined. In the process, Masoch learns about the fundamental misconceptions men have about women. It is not another tale about what men think of women, but a criticism of men and their ideas of women. The masochist is cured and the cure implies that he does not need to define his manhood in relation to what he thinks women need to be or what he can do to and with them. The conversion that Severin undergoes teaches him "with alarming clarity how blind passion and lust have always led men."[33] What is transformed is Severin's understanding that his relation to women and to the world is determined not by whom he interacts with as given, but by how he imposes himself on those he interacts with.

The method of change is quite simple. Unlike Sade with his repetitious deeds, slowly progressing and linearly advancing, Masoch sets up a series of distinct yet random events: fixation on the coldness of a woman in a fur coat, operating as a servant, or laboring as a gardener. There is no progressive theme running through these positions. The additional characters are just as coincidental: a female friend who visits Wanda, the mistress; a Russian suitor; a German painter who becomes excited by the lashing; and a sadistic Greek who enjoys humiliating—these participants do not show a progressive advancement in the plot. These are arbitrary threads, leading the plot, but leading without a constructive organization. They are haphazard occurrences, indiscriminate events forming waves in the narrative. They are what Deleuze terms "lines of flight"—the irregular occasions shifting the narrative and leading it in a different direction. They are random dots on a linear web, opening unexpected routes that lead in a variety of directions. Deleuze and Guattari write:

> Lodge yourself on a stratum, experiment with the opportunities it offers, find an advantageous place on it, find potential movements of deterritorialization, possible lines of flight, experience them, produce flow conjunctions here and there, try out continuums of intensities segment by segment, have a small plot of new land at all times. It is through a meticulous relation with the strata that one succeeds in freeing lines of flight, causing conjugated flows to pass and escape and bringing forth continuous intensities.[34]

Lines of flight are the non-regularities, unexpected or unplanned. They are the means out of habitual sets of progressive imperatives. They are the way to escape a given path and to break away with constraining limitations. They are the multiple possibilities averted by moral laws. Always already there, but undetected.

For Freud, the method of transformation is very precise, always the same. By causing his patient, and reader, to object to an oedipal interpretation, Freud is able to identify the mechanism of resistance at work. Almost all of Freud's patients object to his interpretation. He then uses their objection in order to detect the form of resistance: how they reject or deny his claims. Then Freud employs the same mechanism of resistance to reflect back onto his patient, like a mirror. He resists his patients by employing the same means of resistance. In so doing, Freud is blocking the ability of his patients to use a given mechanism of defense. By obstructing and preventing the mechanism, Freud is hoping to disintegrate the hold that mechanism has over contained unconscious desires and thoughts—the mechanism that holds the id from flooding consciousness. The problem is that in the process of disintegration, Freud's patients, and readers, find themselves without an alternative mechanism by which to bind the free energy and form conscious narratives that re-grounds the unconscious. Without options, Freud's patients internalize the oedipal interpretation Freud had used in order to provoke the transformative operation. In the process, Freud's patients become oedipalized—trapped in a system that was only supposed to provoke resistance.[35]

For Deleuze, as well as Masoch, the method of transformation does not require systematic negations and resistances. It does not eliminate possible alternatives. In fact, it is set to produce a multiplicity of possible routes. Lines of flight are multiple exits on a particular path awaiting actualization, intersections that have been ignored or overlooked because of oedipal impositions. By flooding the text with associative possibilities, random elements, arbitrary connections, irregular shifts and turns, Deleuze and Guattari, as well as Masoch, form breaches in the predetermined histories. Deleuze and Guattari write:

> We may be more interested in a certain line than in the others, and perhaps there is indeed one that is, not determining, but of greater importance . . . if it is there. For some of these lines are imposed on us from outside, at least in part. Others sprout up somewhat by chance, from a trifle, why we will never know. Others can be invented, drawn, without a model and without chance: we must invent our lines of flight, if we are able, and the only way we can invent them is by effectively drawing them, in our lives. Aren't lines of flight the most difficult of all?[36]

Lines of flight form a transformative method. Deleuze, in his article on Masoch, construes a binary structure and sets up a table of dyad possibilities, all the time inundating the construction with numerous variations. It showers the reader, patient, person, with random imagery, alternative possibilities, and divergent options. Faced with increasing inconsistencies, a mistaken route generates countless transformations.

In a 1966 article titled "Must We Burn Sade?" de Beauvoir answers her own challenge. In her reading of Sade's works, she performs a unique line of flight. Despite the hatred of women, acts of extreme cruelty, and murderous tortures, she attempts to understand Sade by assembling a complex set of traits inconsistent with Sade's assertions. Sade, de Beauvoir argues, was bored and chose the imaginary; expressed his ethics in works of literature"; attempted to grasp "existence in one's self and in the other"; "felt himself to be feminine and resented the fact that women were not the males he really desired"; "a favorite fantasy of his [was] to be penetrated and beaten while he himself was penetrating and beating"; "gained insight into himself as passive flesh"; "[it] was not murder that fulfilled Sade's erotic nature: it was literature"; "[if] he set himself the duty of shocking, it was because in this way truth might be made manifest"; "precursor of psychoanalysis"; "a great moralist"; "conceives the free act only as an act free of all feeling."[37] By complicating the reading of his literature, de Beauvoir shows that being patient with Sade's writing and listening to his fantasies unravel the human behind the man who was determined to expose the hypocrisy of humanity.[38] What is of interest in her article is the fact that de Beauvoir provides lines of flight, breakups in the binary oppositions, and a multiplicity of variables in order to present Sade as a writer more complicated than what he has been given credit for.

A LINE OF FLIGHT

In an article from 1998, Adrian del Caro argues that the notorious quote from Friedrich Nietzsche cited at the beginning of this text has a radically different explanation.[39] Nietzsche has an old woman give Zarathustra advice: When "you go to women? Do not forget the whip!"[40] Nietzsche, Caro argues, not only read Masoch's texts, but he also staged a photographed scene with Paul Ree and Lou Salomé. In the photo Nietzsche is pulling a wagon while Lou Salomé is holding the whip. The scene, writes Caro, is staged by Nietzsche a day after Lou Salomé has rejected Nietzsche's proposal to her.[41] Nietzsche, Caro argues, gave Lou Salomé, like Masoch, the whip. Yet, unlike Wanda, Lou Salomé did not cure him.

Readers of Nietzsche do not tend to identify this particular line of flight—there are numerous ones in his texts. It is embedded in our reading practices to

FIG. 3.1. Photograph of Lou Andreas-Salomé, Paul Rée, and Friedrich Nietzsche in Basel, May 1882. By Helen Wolff and Kurt Wolff. Retrieved from Beinecke Rare Book and Manuscript Library, Yale University.

consolidate binaries in accordance with established structures, despite Nietzsche's resilient attempts to produce transformations. And yet, we must learn— from his attempts, as well as attempts by Masoch, Deleuze, de Beauvoir and others—how to transform the categorical imperative to read texts by performing the norm. We must learn to avoid reiterating oppositions even as we disagree with them. We must find lines of flight, identify intersections, and leave given paths, if only to produce alternative futures for women and men. The purpose is not to escape from the norm, the acceptable and the conventional. Rather, the purpose is to transform pre-given customs by endorsing a proliferation of lines of flight. Deleuze and Guattari write:

> Lines of flight, for their part, never consist in running away from the world but rather in causing runoffs, as when you drill a hole in a pipe; there is no social system that does not leak from all directions, even if it makes its segments increasingly rigid in order to seal the lines of flight. There is nothing imaginary, nothing symbolic, about a line of flight. There is nothing more active than a line of flight.[42]

LYAT FRIEDMAN is Chair of the graduate program in Policy and Theory of the Arts at Bezalel Academy of Arts and Design in Jerusalem. She is the author of *In the Footsteps of Psychoanalysis: A Postmodern Gendered Criticism of Freud's Thought* (Tel Aviv: Bar Ilan University Press, 2013).

NOTES

1. Simone de Beauvoir, *The Second Sex*, trans. Constance Borde and Sheila Malovany-Chevallier (New York: Random House, 2011), 5.
2. Ibid.
3. Ibid., 9.
4. Ibid., 8.
5. Compare Gilles Deleuze, "De Sacher Masoch au Masochism," *Arguments* 5e année 21, no. 1 (1961): 40–46; Gilles Deleuze "From Sacher Masoch to Masochism," trans. Christian Kerslake, *Angelaki* 9 (2004): 125–33; and Gilles Deleuze, *Le Froid et le Cruel* (Paris: Éditions de Minuit, 1967), 967.
6. Compare Sigmund Freud, "Three Essays on the Theory of Sexuality"; "A Child Is Being Beaten"; "Fetishism"; and "Female Sexuality," all in *The Standard Edition of the Complete Psychological Works of Sigmund Freud*, ed. and trans. by James Strachey (London: Hogarth Press, 1953).
7. Deleuze, "De Sacher Masoch au Masochism," 130.
8. Beauvoir, *Second Sex*, 411.
9. Deleuze, "De Sacher Masoch au Masochism," 161, 131.
10. Ibid.

11. English translation of Masoch's tale can be found in Gilles Deleuze, *Masochism: Coldness and Cruelty*, trans. Jean McNeil (New York: Zone Books, 1989).

12. They are not performative texts in the sense Judith Butler uses the notion. Deleuze's and Masoch's texts do not prove to be "constituting the identity [they are] purported to be." They are texts that cause a transformation in the reader, sending her or him to seek alternatives. Butler is quoting Nietzsche a few lines down in her text, writing, "there is no 'being' behind the doing, effecting, becoming; 'the doer' is merely a fiction added to the deed—the deed is everything." See Judith Butler, *Gender Trouble* (New York: Routledge, 1990), 25; quote is taken from Friedrich W. Nietzsche's *Genealogy of Morals*, trans. Walter Kaufmann (New York: Random House, 1967), part 1, sec. 13. Butler understands the quote to mean that there are no women behind the expression "women." However, she ignores the second part of the quote: the doing can transform the performance of the subject. It is an effecting expression. It does the deed.

13. According to Freud, in "The Economic Problem of Masochism" (from 1924), there are three types of masochism: sexual, moral, and feminine. What is central to all three types is a desire by the masochist to regress into a dependent position, a proper "feminine" attitude. The masochist seeks, according to Freud, to be a child and to be the bad child who is punished by his authoritative mother, administering discipline in the name of the father. Masochist fantasies express the need to be subjugated by a dominating father. In "A Child Is Being Beaten" (from 1919), Freud lists three stages of evolution for the sadist. In the first stage, a child sees the father beat up another child—producing an unintentional active sadistic pleasure; in the second, the father beats up the child—generating a passive masochistic stance; in the third stage, the child sees another adult beat up another child—it is an active sadistic stance, active because the child seeks to find another child being beaten. What is important, according to Freud, is the fact that the child translated the beating into statements about himself. The father beating another child is understood to mean "father loves me." The girl learns that she is loved in reference to whom a man "beats." The boy must learn to take the role of beater.

14. Beauvoir, *Second Sex*, 690.
15. Deleuze, *Coldness and Cruelty*, 41.
16. Ibid., 134.
17. Ibid.
18. Ibid.
19. Ibid.
20. Ibid.
21. Ibid.
22. In Freud's terms, "the boy refused to take cognizance of the fact of his having perceived that a woman does not possess a penis . . . for if a woman had been castrated, then his own possession of a penis was in danger." The boy maintains, what seems to Freud as an illusion, that women have a penis. "In his mind the woman *has* got a penis, in spite of everything," Freud writes, "but this penis is no longer the same as it was before." Something else has been "appointed its substitute." See Freud, "Fetishism," 150, 152.
23. Deleuze, *Coldness and Cruelty*, 134.
24. Ibid.
25. Ibid.

26. Ibid.
27. Ibid.
28. By the end of Masoch's tale, his mistress's voice is clearly heard, in and for itself.
29. Gilles Deleuze and Félix Guattari, *Kafka: Towards a Minor Literature*, trans. Dana Polan (Minneapolis: University of Minnesota Press, 1986), 6.
30. Ibid.
31. Leopold von Sacher-Masoch, "Venus in Furs," in *Masochism: Coldness and Cruelty*, trans. Jean McNeil (New York: Zone Books, 1989), 270.
32. Deleuze, *Coldness and Cruelty*, 271.
33. Ibid., 269.
34. Gilles Deleuze and Félix Guattari, *A Thousand Plateaus: Capitalism and Schizophrenia*, trans. Brian Massumi (Minneapolis: University of Minnesota Press, 1987), 161.
35. Lyat Friedman, "Anti-Oedipus: The Work of Resistance," in *Deleuze and Psychoanalysis*, ed. Leen Bolle (Leuven, Belgium: Leuven University Press, 2010).
36. Deleuze and Guattari, *Thousand Plateaus*, 202.
37. Simone de Beauvoir, "Must We Burn Sade?," trans. Annette Michelson, in *The Marquis de Sade* (New York: Grove Press, 1966), 9, 6, 21, 25, 27, 29, 33, 35, 39, 40, 55.
38. Butler finds Beauvoir's reading to be sympathetic. See Judith Butler, *Giving an Account of Oneself* (New York: Fordham University Press, 2005), 45–46.
39. Adrian del Caro, "Nietzsche, Sacher Masoch, and the Whip," *German Studies Review* 21, no. 2 (1998): 241–61.
40. Friedrich W. Nietzsche, *Thus Spoke Zarathustra*, trans. Adrian del Caro (New York: Cambridge University Press, 2006), 49–50.
41. Caro, "Nietzsche, Sacher Masoch, and the Whip," 284.
42. Deleuze and Guattari, *Thousand Plateaus*, 204.

BIBLIOGRAPHY

Butler, Judith. *Gender Trouble*. New York: Routledge, 1990.
———. *Giving an Account of Oneself*. New York: Fordham University Press, 2005.
Beauvoir, Simone de. *Le deuxième sexe*. Paris: Éditions Gallimard, 1949.
———. "Must We Burn Sade?" Translated by Annette Michelson. *The Marquis de Sade*. New York: Grove Press, 1966.
———. *The Second Sex*. Translated by Constance Borde and Sheila Malovany-Chevallier. New York: Random House, 2011.
Caro, Adrian del. "Nietzsche, Sacher Masoch, and the Whip." *German Studies Review* 21, no. 2 (1998): 241–61.
Deleuze, Gilles. *Le Froid et le Cruel*. Paris: Éditions de Minuit, 1967.
———. "From Sacher Masoch to Masochism." Translated by Christian Kerslake. *Angelaki* 9 (2004): 125–33.
———. *Masochism: Coldness and Cruelty*. Translated by Jean McNeil. New York: Zone Books, 1989.
———. "De Sacher Masoch au Masochism." *Arguments* 5e année, 21, no. 1 (1961): 40–46.
Deleuze, Gilles, and Félix Guattari. *Kafka—Pour une literature mineure*. Paris: Éditions des Minuit, 1975.
———. *Kafka: Towards a Minor Literature*. Translated by Dana Polan. Minneapolis: University of Minnesota Press, 1986.

———. *Mille Plateaux: Capitalisme et Schizophrénie*. Paris: Éditions de Minuit, 1980.
———. *A Thousand Plateaus: Capitalism and Schizophrenia*. Translated by Brian Massumi. Minneapolis: University of Minnesota Press, 1987.
Freud, Sigmund. *The Standard Edition of the Complete Psychological Works of Sigmund Freud*. Edited and translated by James Strachey. London: Hogarth Press, 1953–1974.
Friedman, Lyat. "Anti Oedipus: The Work of Resistance." In *Deleuze and Psychoanalysis*, 83–102, edited by Leen Bolle. Leuven, Belgium: Leuven University Press, 2010.
Nietzsche, Friedrich W. *The Genealogy of Morals*. Translated by Walter Kaufmann. New York: Random House, 1967.
———. *Thus Spoke Zarathustra*. Translated by Adrian del Caro. New York: Cambridge University Press, 2006.
Sacher-Masoch, Leopold von. "Venus in Furs." In *Masochism: Coldness and Cruelty*. Translated by Jean McNeil. New York: Zone Books, 1989.

4 CRAFTING CONTINGENCY

RACHEL McCANN

THIRTEEN YEARS INTO the twenty-first century, much of the promise of the postmodern era has begun to materialize for the field of architecture. Technology has caught up with imagination, and our tolerance for evanescence, contingency, and multiplicity has found consonances in a world of informatics and bioengineering that transgress old boundaries of form, order, and identity. In the field of architecture, the chaotic character of earlier decades (when we drew sharp angles with dissonant relationships to show that we were no longer seeking a singular truth) is morphing into an appreciation and understanding of deep pattern. In contrast to the formal dissent of ten years ago, architects are now making beautiful sense out of complexity.

This architectural sense is rooted in a growing understanding of pattern, inspired by the work of Gilles Deleuze, pioneered by architectural theorists Greg Lynn and Lars Spuybroek, and given form by architects Lisa Iwamoto, SHoP, and BIG, to name a few. Although at first glance this pattern work's emphasis on mathematics and abstraction may seem out of step with social concerns and deeply out of step with a phenomenological approach such as Maurice Merleau-Ponty's phenomenology of the "flesh," a number of fertile connections exist. Based in an understanding of the social and ethical implications of Merleau-Ponty's flesh, this chapter explores how the principles of parametric architectural design, with its complex structures that draw strength from anomaly and deformation, constructively overlap some of the key tenets of feminism and manifest a productive model for effecting social change. Salient attributes include a dynamic balance between internal logic and outside forces; questions of identity, contingency, and adaptability; applicability to different energetic, material, and life forms; and always change over time as the patterns disperse, disrupt, bifurcate, coalesce, and reconfigure.

RELATIONAL FIELDS

Ilya Prigogine, a Nobel Laureate chemist whose work focuses on systems theory, describes a self-organizing system as a process where local interactions bring large-scale order to a previously disordered system; examples include crystallization, convection patterns, market patterns, neural networks, even animal swarming. The initial local ordering of the system is spontaneous, either stemming from a condition of the system itself or responding to a condition set up by an outside agent. Local ordering springs up in a decentralized way distributed throughout the system, "triggered by random fluctuations [and] amplified by positive feedback." Because it is spontaneous and widespread, a self-organizing system is typically robust and has the energy and the directional focus to repair internal disturbances or damage.[1]

When a system's boundaries are permeable to outside influences, they become sites of exchange that allow the system to evolve toward greater complexity and order. We can view life as such an open system and observe its constant and often cataclysmic give-and-take between growth and order.[2] Nonequilibrium, or open system thermodynamics, provides a framework for observing such complex systems that shift in response to gradients in pressure, temperature, or chemical makeup, and whose degree of disequilibrium may induce "sudden transitions or bifurcations" before the system reconfigures into a new state of stability. Prigogine's description of a self-ordering system is reflected in Deleuze's conception of existence as a sphere of immanence, or "manifold," with a vector field or set of rules for interaction wherein elements of the field move and change in response to a stable attractor or goal. A radical break or bifurcation in the system (Deleuze's "catastrophe") may occur as the evolving pattern moves toward the limits of the system or, alternatively, responds to an exterior force or unstable attractor. After the catastrophe, the system reorients itself and redirects itself to a new attractor.[3]

Deleuze advocates the destabilization (deterritorialization) of knowledge and of the self, and he describes things as existing in the immanent field with singularity and irreducible alterity by means of differential relations.[4] His system is formal, universal, and abstract, and unmuddied by questions of the flesh, although its structure can be appropriated into the social and natural realms as enfleshed ideas with each domain differentially structured. The universe is thus a field of difference, "a system of multiple, nonlocalizable, ideal connections, a differential calculus corresponding to each Idea, where each Idea differentiates the field" and all of its elements.[5] In this system, as Dorothea Olkowski characterizes it in *Postmodern Philosophy and the Scientific Turn*, "every subject or object is an event, . . . the result of the contingent encounters of [transcendent] affects and percepts," and the world is "an ongoing process of trajectories differentiating themselves [through] predictable motions and unpredictable perturbations" that cause or allow events and intelligence.[6]

Merleau-Ponty's flesh is just such a dynamic system, whose myriad elements seek encounter, difference, and mutual transformation. Envisioned as a continually evolving relational field, the flesh is a medium of transformative encounter founded in the body's sensory openness to, and interrogative attitude toward, the lived world. "My body, the human other, and material things are variations" of this "general relational condition," and there is no emphasis on binary oppositions or cataclysmic bifurcations as the flesh undergoes a continual process of transformation based on both difference and assimilation.[7] Other elements of the flesh, along with (myself as) a perceiver, are participants in an enveloping perceptual field, and perceptual interaction with them results in a paradoxical doubling in which perceived things breach the perceiver's boundaries to exist simultaneously in the world and within the perceiver's own carnal schema.[8] And yet the doubling happens with an offset or *écart* (Deleuze's non-gathering), and so, for Merleau-Ponty, Deleuze's bifurcation and catastrophic systemic restructuring are continual small restructurings, the mutual transformation that results from every interaction in the "strange proximity" between perceiver and (an often co-perceiving) perceived.[9]

Écart, a concept that is central to Merleau-Ponty's vision of relationships in the flesh, describes an offset, an interval or distance, a difference in value, and even restructuring one's direction to gain such an interval. In *Merleau-Ponty's Philosophy*, Lawrence Hass describes écart as "a difference-spacing-openness at the heart of perceptual experience" enfolded in a condition of reversibility that intertwines and coheres difference without opposition. The flesh understands contradictory elements as ongoing enigmas that enable growth, not oppositions to resolve, as its conceptualization remains mired in carnality.[10]

In contrast to Deleuze's formal and abstract viewpoint that allows difference to remain unreconciled, Merleau-Ponty takes multiple interior viewpoints that allow for the same enigma. Deleuze's manifold, on the molar or general level, contains machines that may be social, technical, or organic, and these machines manifest on the molecular or particular level "as single objects and living organisms that appear as single subjects."[11] Merleau-Ponty's flesh (the general field) has social, technical, and organic aspects as well, and its elements can appear as single perceivers and perceived things. Despite their many similarities, the two systems are somewhat oppositional, for in each philosopher's work the other's principal construct is considered secondary. To Deleuze, Merleau-

Ponty's flesh is one of many molar machines with its own particular relational calculus, not sufficiently formal to ground a universal or grand style of thought.[12] Yet Deleuze's pure, formal, un-enfleshed system operates on a level that to Merleau-Ponty is a subset of the larger flesh, a manifestation of embodied intellect that has emancipated itself from its carnal origin through abstraction. In the flesh, Deleuze's manifold is a "singing of the world" that, like a geometric proof, once it has taken shape, seems self-evident and inevitable but is one of many possible secondary constructs springing from the pre-personal, anonymous level of the flesh.[13]

Hass calls perceptual experience "a field of contact" where we mingle with things, others, and the larger environment. In this vital, carnal coupling, the things we experience have "sense-directions," an "open . . ., charged indeterminacy" with inherent logic that suggests pragmatic and ideational possibilities. The field of possibilities is always in motion, and Hass sees a pulse from "indeterminacy to configuration and back again [as] the living body [organizes] coherent things into sense-laden configurations" in an ongoing state of receptive communication.[14] Once a certain sense is made of the possible directions offered up by the perceived, a new idea "'transcends and transfigures' the initial situation" and reorganizes it into an ideational sense that brings with it a certain sense of inevitability, often obscuring its own contingency.[15] Such momentary crystallizations of the lived world's contingent meanings can also take on a semblance of purity and permanence, and Merleau-Ponty invites us "to discern beneath thinking that basks in its acquisitions, and offers merely a brief resting-place in the unending process of expression, another thought which is struggling to establish itself." Any formalizations or abstractions are "not a genuine eternity and a participation in the One, but concrete acts of taking up and carrying forward by which, through time's accidents, we are linked in relationships with ourselves and others."[16] As long as we understand its carnal origins and its carnal contingency (insisted on by Merleau-Ponty and denied by Deleuze), a formalized expression or concept such as Deleuze's manifold fits within Merleau-Ponty's thought, allowing for a fruitful furtherance of the consideration of becoming.

Painter and art theorist György Kepes, whose work investigates the visual logic of scientific and industrial processes, construes patterns as temporary boundaries between past and future acts or states of energy, and characterizes patterns as "meeting-points of action." Informed by physicist Fotini Markopoulou, Olkowski discusses Deleuze's manifold in terms of quantum causal histories in which actors and stage evolve together. Drawing from Merleau-Ponty and Simone de Beauvoir, she reconfigures Deleuze's "crowd" as "a point of view according to which different observers 'see' or 'live' [partial and overlapping] views of the universe." Olkowski restyles Deleuze's manifold as crowdsourced reality, a field whose attributes (patterns and particles) create a point of view made of "a crowd of influences." Changes in the particulars can alter the field as a whole, and the arrangement suggests the possibility of an ethics in which we view others as opportunities for transformation and mutual influence rather than opposition.[17]

Merleau-Ponty's philosophy of interrogation opens us to the Other, to the crowd-sourced field. In the flesh, he maintains, "there is an intersection of my universe with that of the other" in which "we must understand life as the opening of a field of action."[18] In this field, "I experience my own body as the power of adopting certain forms of behavior and a certain world . . . now, it is precisely my body that perceives the body of another, and discovers in that other body a miraculous prolongation of my own intentions, a familiar way of dealing with the world. . . . The anonymous existence of which my body is the ever-renewed trace henceforth inhabits both bodies simultaneously."[19] In *The Retrieval of the Beautiful*, Galen A. Johnson elucidates: "The lines of my life are overlaid with the 'dotted lines' inscribed by others. . . . So we are drawn and in a double sense. We are drawn upon by Others as they shape our lives, and we are drawn toward Others as we encounter them in our world."[20] Thus we see Merleau-Ponty's flesh providing the framework for Olkowski's "crowd of influences" and Kepes's patterns as "meeting-points of action," as different bodies in the flesh influence both one another and the larger field.

THE AESTHETICS OF RELATION

These strong interconnections are echoed in the ideas of anthropologist, linguist, and cyberneticist Gregory Bateson, who worked in a sustained way to connect systems theory with the social-behavioral sciences, and who contends that "patterns operate according to an aesthetic logic—one that is based on 'recognition and empathy' rather than rationality." Bateson's thinking frames pattern theory in a way that highlights the visual and spatial aspects of pattern and thus brings it into the realm where we can examine it architecturally. In describing the tendency of patterned systems to proliferate while maintaining their dynamic equilibrium, he characterizes them as generally recursive (manifesting or responding repeatedly to the same rule or motif, even if across different scales), redundant, and predictable. A pattern's repetition and redundancy allow us to observe and understand—or at least intuit—the rules for interaction between pattern components. Once we understand the system, "any deviation [in the pattern] will stand out (and is coded positively as information or negatively as a mistake)."[21]

It is the dynamic balance between repetition and anomaly, between the predictable and the unexpected, that links pattern work to creativity, as Paul Andersen and David Salomon explain in *The Architecture of Patterns*. The predictability and redundancy of a pattern allow it to receive and accommodate new information, which in its turn morphs the pattern into something new but still coherent by either inflecting or disrupting it. "Thus," according to Andersen and Salomon, "far from maintaining homogeneity or encouraging pandemonium, patterns establish favorable conditions for creativity and learning to occur." We read and assimilate any new information against the previously understood background pattern and reconceive the meaning of the larger pattern along with its informational interlocutor.[22] The ability of the pattern's internal logic to accommodate deformation in the face of an external force (in this case, the new information) gives it an adaptive, contingent identity that can flex to meet a variety of demands and accommodate difference with relative equanimity. Thus a balance between stasis and transformation, between overarching idea and individual goals makes a strong architectural patterned system. Order is needed; too much entropy makes a system unremarkable or useless, and complexity demands intricate and ordered relations.[23]

Olkowski, through Beauvoir, asks that we come to understand the Other as "a crowd and not an atom" and to live in a state of mutual influence accepting the trajectories of others and allowing them to change us and take our work forward. She asks us to (make systems that do) not exploit others or deprive them of opportunities for meaningful cultural and social contribution. She also advocates for openness and ambiguity in our projects, which allows others in the crowd to transform them, echoing Merleau-Ponty's discussion of the carnal linkages in expressively "taking up and carrying forward" ideas.[24]

Perception in the flesh is characterized by the same openness, ambiguity, and adaptive contingency. Merleau-Ponty says that perceived things "offer themselves . . . only to someone who wishes not to have them but to see them, not to hold them as with forceps, or to immobilize them as under the objective of a microscope, but to let them be and to witness their continued being—to someone who therefore limits himself to giving them the hollow [*le creux*], the free space they ask for in return, the resonance they require."[25] Johnson expressly links this posture to the ethics that pervades Merleau-Ponty's work: "In between the heat of grasping and the cold of indifference, there is a kind of caring for things and others that opens up both self and other to an uncharted richness."[26]

Bateson's "aesthetic logic . . . based on 'recognition and empathy'" resonates with this view and with that of mathematician Norbert Weiner, the originator of cybernetics, who views pattern as "an arrangement of information" that transforms in response to interaction with other patterns. To Weiner, information exists not as a stable identity or static essence, but as a flexible pattern or message that interacts with and transmits to surrounding patterns. Both internal properties and external forces determine the pattern's degree of environmental flexibility and its ability to self-organize, which Weiner views in terms of homeostasis.[27]

FEMINIST ETHICS: THRIVING WITHIN A STRONG SYSTEM

Strong external environments make it more difficult for local patterns to maintain self-determination in their identity. Negative or neutral feedback from its external environment may dampen a system to a state of insignificance or oblivion. And as Andersen and Salomon point out, even positive feedback, which reinforces and magnifies attributes of the system, "actively adds destabilizing information into exchanges between organisms and their environments, producing states that are far from equilibrium, far from the status quo, and hard to predict."[28] In the face of destabilizing positive feedback, homeostasis may convert to a dynamic equilibrium, with change built in as system components, organisms, or people make choices about the best configuration to maintain their purpose or identity—alternatively, the pattern may cataclysmically disrupt or simply phase out of existence.

In these dynamic states, a pattern is dependent, though not entirely, on its environment within yet larger systems. Patterned systems, especially those involving human lives and thus agency, can adapt according to their own interior logic—if they are not "too simple or inflexible"—to exist as active arrangements that are "more than just the index of other forces." Patterns lacking flexibility will break against the force of larger systems, becoming isolated or disappearing altogether, and those too similar to their enveloping systems are also likely to be subsumed.[29] These outcomes apply to natural interactions, chemical reactions, political organizations, neighborhood groups, building panel systems, and urban landscapes alike.

One of the central tenets across a broad spectrum of feminism thought is robust accommodation of difference. We have already discussed, if briefly, Olkowski's advocacy of approaching the Other in a spirit of transformation rather than opposition. In consonance with pattern theory, Donna Haraway's "Cyborg Manifesto" emphasizes the dynamic balance between internal logic and outside forces, questions of identity, contingency, and adaptability. Taking the mechanical-biotic hybrid cyborg as an instructive form, she envisions a politics that enfolds "permanently partial identities and contradictory standpoints" and calls for feminism to form alliances and contingent unities that transgress and knit together previous boundaries of identity. Rather than appealing to categories of truth or falsity, Haraway asks that we eschew grand bargains and elegantly simple solutions to attune to the subtle, shifting matrix of "emerging pleasures, experiences, and powers with serious potential for changing the rules of the game." She calls for noise, imperfection, and pollution in our communications and stresses that feminism must avoid casting its aims as a revolutionary struggle in which we have staked out a position of moral superiority. Instead, she advocates assuming the contingent identity of a "bastard race" that "teaches about the power of the margins."[30]

Feminist author bell hooks also writes powerfully about impure identities, reminding us that in order to effect social change, we must position ourselves at once on society's margin and at its center. Cultivating a position in the center gives us the power to effect change, but remembering our position in the margin allows us to recall that change is necessary.[31] Drawing from Elizabeth Janeway's *Powers of the Weak*, hooks contends that recreation of one's own identity outside of the tropes given by voices of power is one of the most fundamental freedoms we possess.[32]

In addition to the importance of an Other surviving within a strong external system, hooks understands that the system itself will thrive by fostering the flexibility to embrace difference. Unless we redefine power from its traditional form, we will be seduced and corrupted by it. Instead of power as the ability to dominate and control, hooks, following Nancy Hartsock, promotes "understandings of power that are creative and life-affirming," aligned with energy, action, and accomplishment. She further believes that groups struggling for societal change will gain momentum insofar as they manifest the life-affirming power that aims to transform and benefit society as a whole.[33] The écart at the heart of the flesh allows for the offset of identities in which such difference can thrive, and pattern theory underscores the importance of both flexibility and difference in the continued evolution of a system.[34]

Finally, in terms of creative expression, allowing the differences among gendered, ethnic, classed, abled, and aged bodies to inform our society and our phenomenology feeds the creative, transformational, sense-making capacities of the lived body. Merleau-Ponty writes, "We are collaborators in a consummate reciprocity. In the present dialogue, I am freed from myself, for the other person's thoughts are certainly his. . . . And indeed, the objection which my

FIG. 4.1. NOX/Lars Spuybroek, The Three Graces, hotel and conference center, Dubai, 2007 (by permission of NOX/Lars Spuybroek).

interlocutor raises to what I say draws from me thoughts that I had no Idea I possessed, so that at the same time that I lend him thoughts, he reciprocates by making me think too."[35] True creativity is a vulnerable, dangerously open state where one's world can be flipped, leading to a catastrophe in the manifold. This vulnerability lies at the heart of artistic endeavor, which Johnson discusses in terms of beauty: "Human self-awareness requires being questioned and challenged from the outside, even obstruction by the outside, and this is a gift of the beautiful.... The experience of the beautiful is the experience of a fundamental openness to Being."[36] As Merleau-Ponty sums it up, "love . . . leads us just to what can tear us."[37]

ARCHITECTURE AND PATTERN LOGIC

The profound recent shift in architectural design methods reflects the complexity, contingency, and impure identity of the different threads this chapter has drawn together. In the new paradigm of parametric design, old categories of floor and ceiling, wall and window are no longer stable concepts. Architects'

FIG. 4.2. Zaha Hadid Architects, Madrid Civil Courts of Justice, Madrid, 2007 (by permission of Zaha Hadid Architects).

questioning of such givens as horizontal and vertical, opaque and transparent has transformed our understanding of perceiving and inhabiting space. Lynn's and Spuybroek's inquiries into computer-generated pattern (fig. 4.1) are paralleled by designs from architecture firms such as Zaha Hadid Architects (fig. 4.2) and Iwamoto Scott (fig. 4.3) for civil buildings and skyscrapers that transgress— even abandon at times—the boundaries of these age-old categories. Traditional proportion systems and spatial visualization from hand-drawn perspectives are no longer adequate design devices in the postmodern era, where emphasis has shifted from proportionally regulating Platonic masses and volumes to tweaking computer-generated, asymmetrical, amorphous, and dynamic forms. Structure is no longer limited to bearing wall or post and beam, but has now been reconfigured into thin webs that can track the surface of a wall or even become tubes of space. And above all, architects are filling the surfaces of their unorthodox forms with intricate patterns.

In consonance with the systems discussed above, parametric architecture achieves strength through deformation—structural, spatial, and ideational.

FIG. 4.3. Iwamoto Scott, Edgar Street Towers, New York, 2009 (by permission of Iwamoto Scott).

Lynn refers to parametric design as "animate" because its formal conception is based in the intertwining of motion and force. As intersecting forces generate mathematical information stored as three-dimensional form, architecture changes from a static geometric frame for the movement of time and space to something that, as Lynn phrases it, "can be modeled as a participant immersed in dynamical flows."[38] Formal abstraction based on the x, y, and z axes gives way to "gradients, flexible envelopes, temporal flows and forces," allowing the architect to include "issues of force, motion, and time" in her design process.[39] The process gives architectural form flexibility in responding to multiple generative forces, and it finds middle ground between the extremes of either standing firm against the "stress of difference" or breaking under its tide. Allowing for deformations under force adds to the complex intricacy of the system, leading Lynn to describe its pliancy as "a cunning submissiveness." The dynamic origins of parametric design and the resultant form's contingency and flexibility allow architecture to become dynamically complex.[40] The resultant form is often beautiful, resists conceptualization, is structurally strong, and generates unexpected and surprising reformulations of once-inviolate categories. As such, it provides an instructive model for its larger society.

For example, Lynn describes formal systems where "a point change is distributed smoothly across a surface so that its influence cannot be localized at any discrete point" and "vector sequences whose regions of inflection produce singularities on a continuous surface."[41] He could just as well be writing of the dynamics of social change when he describes architecture: "It may be possible to neither repress the complex relations of differences with fixed points of resolution nor arrest them in contradictions, but sustain them through flexible, unpredicted, local connections. . . . A more pliant architectural sensibility values alliances, rather than conflicts, between elements [and benefits from] first an internal flexibility and second a dependence on external forces for self-definition."[42] Internal flexibility allows feminism to work with partial identities and contingent partnerships, and dependence on external forces allows feminist ideals and actions to effect a slow but steady deformation and reshaping of societal patterns.

DAMPENING AND DOUBLING WITHIN A SYSTEM

Thus far we have been considering a pattern's ability to incorporate the effect of an external force. But such forces are often systems in themselves, and the negotiations between repetition and difference become even more intricate when two systems of influence overlap, or when a pattern's intrinsic systems intersect multiple external forces. The "aesthetic logic of connection" can yield unexpected and intricate beauty as multiple systems reinforce and magnify one another in some ways and dampen or de-articulate in others. Andersen and Salomon see these interactions as "point[ing] the way toward new forms of identity and intelligence in architecture in particular and in culture in general." In pattern-based design, the greatest beauty often comes from "impure and complex blends," and Andersen and Salomon contend that "combining multiple patterns . . . opens up a project's aesthetic identity and organizational logic" and gives an intricate postmodern complexity to the work.[43]

The work of the designer often involves creative leaps in which she adapts a pattern to fit a new set of contingencies, or adjusts the scale of a component to fit in with or transform the overall pattern. Andersen and Salomon call this way of working a "productive misalignment," in which the architect exploits the tension of overlapping patterns and puts it to productive use. In their words, "Establishing links between otherwise disparate cultural, intellectual, and technological categories has long been the job of the architect. . . . The ability to produce relationships where none existed before is endemic to both the production and experience of architecture, [and] the aesthetic power of patterns promotes this synthetic activity."[44] It is just this sort of categorical slippage that infuses the relational thinking of Haraway and hooks.

The architectural patterns of today's intricate buildings and landscape interventions respond to multiple demands at once: structure, climate response, light conduction, thermal insulation, ventilation, electrical and mechanical systems, solar collection, exhaust, and circulation, to name a few. Once a pattern is engineered to function structurally, its redundancies form a field for the overlaying of additional functions.[45] As these additional functions are overlaid on the structural pattern, it morphs—sometimes imperceptibly and sometimes quite noticeably—to incorporate them. Depending on how the systems overlap, these deformations can be localized or distributed throughout the pattern. When layered functions coincide or double (with positive interference), they may produce moments or areas of high intensity or large inflection; when they offset (with misalignments or negative interference), effects can dampen each other to provide very subtle articulation or a small disruptions on the surface. Sometimes the patterns syncopate enough to produce anomalies that seem idiosyncratic but are in fact integral to the form's aesthetic logic.

All of these effects can be adjusted with precision by designers adjusting code.[46] With the right degree of redundancy and complexity, patterned systems can simultaneously contain both short- and long-term aspects that accommodate fluctuating needs and desires ranging from changes in the physical site to societal shifts. Their coherence persists in the face of complexity, anomaly, and the shifting perceptions of their observers and inhabitants.

The pattern's redundancy and complexity give it "the capacity to simultaneously blur, reveal, gradate, and accentuate distinctions" among its parts. And since they can be infinitely reproduced, they are always open systems. Finally, form doesn't follow function, nor is it always indicative of the underlying structure of the pattern itself, so the pattern does not essentialize. Its structure assembles connections between "typically discordant . . . systems" and mediates gradations between typically binary oppositions.[47]

CREATIVE SOCIETAL MISALIGNMENTS

Such a structuring of society would allow for diverse discourses and interests to inform the public sphere. Devonya N. Havis outlines the benefits of richly articulated societal patterns that allow space for multiple voices. She characterizes black feminism as drawing from ancestral and communal as well as mainstream and academic sources, blending "varied contexts for making sense of the world" that include the lives and decisions of ordinary women. These varied sources of knowledge, which thread through the black community in both formal and informal ways, provide "a repository of ideas and practices, strategies, and tactics for negotiating life and framing experiences associated with living in a racialized context." This layered communal wisdom considers the wider implications of ideas and actions, and Havis calls on us to identify "blind spots" and understand the personal, relational, and communal implications of our thoughts and deeds.[48]

Any ethnic or gendered minority understands how to navigate within society on dual levels. hooks describes switching back and forth between black and white dialects when operating in academia and in home communities.[49] Sarah L. Webb's evocative poetry delineates the constrictive act of dwelling in societal structures built for others. "By Design" describes how the architects of culture "blocked our vision with exquisite facades" while "the public pupil adjusted to the blight"—a culture that then urges its occupants "decorate these hollow structures."[50] "Invisible Buildings" concretizes the struggle of outgrowing an oppressive structure's confines:

> Sometimes my limbs don't fit inside of these spaces.
> I try to gather myself in, tuck everything really tight, and suck in my breath.
> But I'm suffocating inside of this grand palazzo.
> And why, when there is so much sky outside?[51]

Alisa Bierria describes the divide between the intentional acts of societally disenfranchised minorities and the construal of those acts by the dominant social discourse. In particular, she takes up the "criminalization of black action" within existing American patterns of power.[52] She cites the example of Janice Wells, a black schoolteacher who called the police to report a prowler and was herself tasered by the responding police officers. Bierria details the reasonable sequence of actions Wells took as the encounter unfolded and the misinterpretation of those actions by the responding police officers due to the "historically constituted, socially reinforced, and institutionally authorized" view of black women as "criminal, uncontrollable, untrustworthy, and pathological." In the encounter, Wells's personhood, authority, and intentions were erased and written over by a dominant social narrative underpinned by a systemic structure of "violence and domination."[53]

Bierria asserts that women of color live "within political and theoretical frameworks unequipped to reflect their experiences and insights."[54] Drawing from Angela Y. Davis, she points out that "action meant to meaningfully transform oppression is regularly and actively countered with state violence," and "even those actions that are within the boundaries of the law remain vulnerable to being criminalized and punished."[55]

Bierria proposes that such exterior-imposed narratives can be resisted and destabilized by "a heterogeneous framework of agency—*agencies*" that takes into account the enveloping social structure: "whether an agent's action will be legible to others as she intends, whether she has institutional backup for her account of her actions . . ., and if the agent's intention is vulnerable to being replaced by some other constructed explanation of her action that conforms to an oppressive schema." Such a schema might describe the officers' actions as "hegemonic agency." In contrast, "black women who act intentionally within [a dominant power structure] must discern how to employ agency on the margins of legibility and legitimacy, in the context of different kinds of resistance, and, sometimes, with the expectation of certain failure." Bierria describes "insurgent agency" as "a kind of resistant agency that does not aim to transform the conditions of oppression, but instead temporarily destabilizes, circumnavigates, or manipulates those conditions in order to reach specific ends."[56]

Havis describes the lives and actions of black women as "creative negotiations" within oppressive societal structures.[57] She draws from Audre Lorde (and aligns with bell hooks) in advocating for "difference and creativity" within a relational community, urging us to allow our differences with others to spark creativity and form community.[58]

FIG. 4.4. Ieshia Evans and Baton Rouge police, Baton Rouge, Louisiana, 2016 (© Jonathan Bachman, Reuters).

Havis draws from Saidiya Hartman, who proposes "simulated compliance" as a means to challenge structures of domination by manipulating appearances.[59] Havis also cites Lisa Jones's notion of the "Bulletproof Diva," who uses power creatively "to contest and disrupt" societal ideas of her place, her role, and her intrinsic dignity. She dwells within the boundaries she is not allowed to cross, but creatively reconfigures them, and "she could be any Black woman who chooses to invent, fashion, and refashion herself with a liberatory interest." All such liberation eventually positively restructures the larger world.[60]

The "productive misalignment" that architects use creatively to exploit the tension of overlapping patterns resonates with these visions of civic agency and resistance. One brief, salient example arose during a period of heightened racial tension between the police force and the black community in Baton Rouge in the summer of 2016. Divergent views of agency and intention led the Baton Rouge police force to respond in riot gear to a black community protest of prior police brutality. In a stunning and literal example of a Bulletproof Diva, Ieshia Evans stood peacefully and gracefully before a host of riot-clad officers and instantly became an emblem of peaceful yet powerful resistance to authority (fig. 4.4).

The events in Baton Rouge leading up to this iconic moment can be viewed in terms of pattern theory, as a series of local interactions that formed a dynamic balance between the internal logic of black community, in pain over the loss of yet one more of their own at the hands of police, and outside forces of state-sanctioned power. Questions of identity and strategies of contingency and adaptability governed the coalescing protest and the police response to it. Prigogine's notion of a robust, self-organizing system aptly describes the ongoing events in Baton Rouge, as local actions coalesced in a decentralized fashion throughout the system, "amplified by positive feedback," culminating in a massive protest met by a massive police response.[61] The system's boundaries became sites of (potentially cataclysmic) exchange that continually reconfigured the evolving pattern of local actions along with the larger pattern of world opinion about American racial relations and systems of power. The "charged indeterminacy" of Merleau-Ponty's flesh is very much in play in this series of fundamentally carnal encounters with injury and even death on the line, but his vision of coexistence within the flesh also contains the potential for mutually transformative, positive encounters with Others and with the pattern as a whole.[62]

To some extent, the social patterns here are recursive, redundant, and predictable, following Bateson's characterization of patterns in general, as people on all sides reiterate entrenched ideologies. But the creative misalignments of a few intentional agents can tweak the predictability and redundancy of the pattern, prodding it to subtly reconfigure and opening cracks in the system that allow a greater number of people to move society forward in a meaningful way. Thus, Merleau-Ponty's "consummate reciprocity" allows an Other to plant seeds of change within each of us as we creatively and collectively reconfigure existing patterns, upending age-old categories, reconceptualizing orthodox systems of power, forming contingent partnerships, creatively deforming a constantly evolving pattern.[63] As in architectural design, the overall pattern morphs to assimilate and accommodate new events and actions. If a society's patterns are sufficiently flexible to permit creative deformation, yet stable enough to avoid collapse under the deformation, they can change and thrive while responding to typically binary oppositions.

LACE-WORKS

Beauvoir, hooks, and other feminists call for feminism as an open system that answers to multiple demands and diverse identities—structural and functional redundancies built on a broad commitment to giving to others "the hollow . . ., the free space," and the safety they need to participate meaningfully in the larger culture. A strong armature then allows layering of other actions and ideas to morph the overall pattern in subtle and salient ways.

In the unfinished draft of his final work, Merleau-Ponty compares our relational existence in the flesh to "lace-works."[64] This arresting image for interacting and creating within the flesh calls to mind the intricate patterns and adaptability of parametric architecture. Strong, flexible, beautiful, and economical of material but requiring an eye for design and care in construction, lace simultaneously veils and transmits light, covers and allows air to pass through its porous boundaries. It flexes in response to external forces, admits variety in its pattern, and draws strength from a web of connections.

Of the intimacy and transformative power of fleshly connections, Merleau-Ponty writes, "If I am close enough to the other who speaks to hear his breath and feel his effervescence and his fatigue, I almost witness, in him as in myself, the awesome birth of vociferation."[65] If I am close enough to a voice, I feel the breath and energy behind it, I witness the beginning point of the clamor that the whole world makes together, I feel it echo with my own voice. This close, dangerously open creative state is a structure that can create and sustain social justice.

RACHEL MCCANN is Professor Emerita at Mississippi State University School of Architecture, and currently singer/songwriter fronting the vocal jazz/R&B band *Carnal Echo*. She is editor (with Patricia Locke) of *Merleau-Ponty: Space, Place, and Architecture* (Ohio University Press, 2015).

NOTES

1. Paul Andersen and David Salomon, *The Architecture of Patterns* (New York: W. W. Norton, 2010), 54, 56.
2. Dorothea E. Olkowski, *Postmodern Philosophy and the Scientific Turn* (Bloomington: Indiana University Press, 2012), 53.
3. Ibid., 62–67.
4. Ibid., 70–72.
5. Gilles Deleuze, *Difference and Repetition*, trans. Paul Patton (New York: Columbia University Press, 1995), 81; cited in Olkowski, *Postmodern Philosophy*, 73–74.
6. Olkowski, *Postmodern Philosophy*, 75.
7. Maurice Merleau-Ponty, *The Prose of the World*, trans. John O'Neill (Evanston, IL: Northwestern University Press, 1973), 136–37. Merleau-Ponty's "variations" could be construed to correspond to Deleuze's molecular realm of constant differentiation, and his "general relational condition," or flesh, sets out overarching principles in the same manner as Deleuze's molar level. But Merleau-Ponty's flesh differs fundamentally from Deleuze's manifold in ways that will be discussed below.

8. I have previously taken up this theme at length along with its ethical implications for social interaction. See Rachel McCann, "A Sensuous Ethics of Difference," in "Ethics of Embodiment," special issue, *Hypatia* 26, no. 3 (2011): 497–517.

9. Maurice Merleau-Ponty, *Signs*, trans. Richard C. McCleary (Evanston, IL: Northwestern University Press, 1964), 15.

10. Lawrence Hass, *Merleau-Ponty's Philosophy* (Bloomington: Indiana University Press, 2008), 137, 128. Hass says that Merleau-Ponty's phenomenology attempts to "honor and express the enigmatic weave of 'wild being' without . . . deforming it."

11. Olkowski, *Postmodern Philosophy*, 80.

12. Ibid., 64.

13. Hass, *Merleau-Ponty's Philosophy*, 152–54.

14. Ibid., 59–61, 63, 79. Note the similarities to an open or nonequilibrium thermodynamic system in this conceptualization.

15. Maurice Merleau-Ponty, *Phenomenology of Perception*, trans. Colin Smith (London: Routledge and Kegan Paul, 1962), 388; cited in Hass, *Merleau-Ponty's Philosophy*, 151, 164, 155, 160. Hass considers expression an "embodied, creative way of arriving at truths and communicating with others." He stresses that, for creators, "the work of expressing the world is contingent through and through, . . . contingent upon their ability and commitment to being creative, when so much around them is mimetic. And it is contingent upon previous cultural acquisitions, upon the material and political conditions amid which such people are thinking."

16. Maurice Merleau-Ponty, *The Visible and the Invisible*, ed. Claude Lefort and trans. Alphonso Lingis (Evanston, IL: Northwestern University Press, 1968), 389, 394–95; cited in Hass, *Merleau-Ponty's Philosophy*, 161–63.

17. Olkowski, *Postmodern Philosophy*, 142–43, 152.

18. Merleau-Ponty, *Visible and the Invisible*, 80; Maurice Merleau-Ponty, *Nature*, trans. Robert Vallier (Evanston, IL: Northwestern University Press, 2003), 173; cited in Galen A. Johnson, *The Retrieval of the Beautiful: Thinking through Merleau-Ponty's Aesthetics* (Evanston, IL: Northwestern University Press, 2010), 176.

19. Merleau-Ponty, *Phenomenology of Perception*, 354. Or, as Johnson puts it, "When we think of the Other, it must be the case that there is a divergence (*écart*) between the opening onto the world experienced by each of us, but also a fundamental common envelopment shared between us from which the divergence originates. Merleau-Ponty expresses this in terms of interrogation, the question mark. The other is a question mark that puts to the test the right I might arrogate to think the world for all: 'The other's gaze on the things is a second openness.'" Merleau-Ponty, *Visible and the Invisible*, 58; cited in Johnson, *Retrieval of the Beautiful*, 152.

20. Merleau-Ponty, *Phenomenology of Perception*, 61; cited in Johnson, *Retrieval of the Beautiful*, 155.

21. Andersen and Salomon, *Architecture of Patterns*, 56–58.

22. Ibid., 60–61. The response recalls Merleau-Ponty's transformative flesh and Deleuze's crowd.

23. Olkowski, *Postmodern Philosophy*, 52–53.

24. Ibid., 152–55; Merleau-Ponty, *Phenomenology of Perception*, 394–95.

25. Merleau-Ponty, *Visible and the Invisible*, 101; cited in Johnson, *Retrieval of the Beautiful*, 159.

26. Johnson, *Retrieval of the Beautiful*, 159. Johnson posits "the essential relation to things and others," then, "not as indifference, or as grasping, whether physical or intel-

lectual, but as letting appearances, aspects, perspectives, and nuances—what Merleau-Ponty noted as the hollows, free space, and resonance of things—be nourished in the process of sensitive questioning and appreciation" (160).

27. Anderson and Salomon, *Architecture of Patterns*, 57, 63.
28. Ibid., 50.
29. Ibid., 50–54.
30. Donna Haraway, "A Cyborg Manifesto: Science, Technology, and Socialist-Feminism in the Late Twentieth Century," *Simians, Cyborgs, and Women: The Reinvention of Nature* (New York: Routledge, 1991), 154, 173, 176.
31. bell hooks, "Choosing the Margin as a Space of Radical Openness," *Yearning: Race, Gender, and Cultural Politics* (Boston: South End Press, 1990), 145–53.
32. bell hooks, *Feminist Theory: From Margin to Center* (New York: South End Press, 2000), 92. Otherwise, cultural restraints will continue to limit expressive human agency. Gail Weiss illuminates the dangers of cultural devaluing of difference, arguing that such devaluation engenders a destructive, rather than therapeutic, kind of impure identity. See Gail Weiss, *Body Images: Embodiment as Intercorporeality* (New York: Routledge, 1999).
33. hooks, *Feminist Theory*, 90–92. She is drawing from Nancy Hartsock, "Political Change: Two Perspectives on Power," *Quest: A Feminist Quarterly* 1 (1974).
34. Andersen and Salomon, *Architecture of Patterns*, 54.
35. Merleau-Ponty, *Phenomenology of Perception*, 354.
36. Johnson, *Retrieval of the Beautiful*, 176, 192.
37. Maurice Merleau-Ponty, *In Praise of Philosophy and Other Essays*, trans. John Wild and James Edie (Evanston, IL: Northwestern University Press, 1963), 75; cited in Johnson, *Retrieval of the Beautiful*, 196.
38. Greg Lynn, *Animate Form* (New York: Princeton Architectural Press, 1999), 11.
39. Ibid., 17.
40. Greg Lynn, "Architectural Curvilinearity: The Folded, the Pliant, and the Supple," *Architectural Design* 63, no. 3–4 (1993): 8–15, 8, 10.
41. Lynn, *Animate Form*, 29.
42. Ibid., 8. The emphasis on flexible alliances recalls Haraway's approach.
43. Andersen and Salomon, *Architecture of Patterns*, 68, 79. This open "identity and organizational logic" resulting in a beautiful, strong, and "intricate postmodern complexity" applies equally to the work of social transformation.
44. Ibid., 72–73, 92.
45. Ibid., 108.
46. Ibid., 96, 107.
47. Ibid., 118, 121, 132, 125.
48. Devonya N. Havis, "'Now, How You Sound': Considering a Different Philosophical Praxis," *Hypatia* 29, no. 1 (2014): 238, 240, 246.
49. hooks, "Choosing the Margin," 146–48.
50. Sarah L. Webb, "By Design" (unpublished poem).
51. Sarah L. Webb, "Invisible Buildings" (unpublished poem).
52. Alisa Bierria, "Missing in Action: Violence, Power, and Discerning Agency," *Hypatia* 29, no. 1 (2014): 131.
53. Ibid., 132–34.
54. Ibid., 138. Inspired by Norma Alarcón, "The Theoretical Subject(s) of *This Bridge Called My Back* and Anglo-American Feminism," in *Making Face, Making Soul/Haciendo*

Caras; Creative and Critical Perspectives by Feminists of Color, ed. Gloria Anzaldúa (San Francisco: Aunt Lute Books, 1990), 359.

55. Angela Y. Davis, "Political Prisoners, Prisons, and Black Liberation," in *The Angela Y. Davis Reader,* ed. Joy James (1971; Malden, MA: Blackwell, 1998); cited in Bierria, "Missing in Action," 139.

56. Bierria, "Missing in Action," 137, 139–40.

57. Havis, "'Now, How You Sound,'" 239.

58. Ibid., 247. Drawing from Audre Lorde, *Sister Outsider: Essays and Speeches* (Berkeley, CA: Ten Speed Press, 1984), 113.

59. Saidiya V. Hartman, *Scenes of Subjection: Terror, Slavery, and Self-Making in Nineteenth-Century America* (New York: Oxford University Press, 1997), 8; cited in Havis, "'Now, How You Sound,'" 249.

60. Havis, "'Now, How You Sound,'" 244–45. Drawing from Lisa Jones, *Bulletproof Diva: Tales of Race, Sex, and Hair* (New York: Anchor Books, 1995).

61. Andersen and Salomon, *Architecture of Patterns,* 56.

62. Hass, *Merleau-Ponty's Philosophy,* 59–61.

63. Merleau-Ponty, *Phenomenology of Perception,* 61; cited in Johnson, *Retrieval of the Beautiful,* 155.

64. Merleau-Ponty, *Visible and the Invisible,* 270.

65. Ibid., 144; cited in Johnson, *Retrieval of the Beautiful,* 124.

BIBLIOGRAPHY

Alarcón, Norma. "The Theoretical Subject(s) of *This Bridge Called My Back* and Anglo-American Feminism." In *Making Face, Making Soul/Haciendo Caras: Creative and Critical Perspectives by Feminists of Color,* edited by Gloria Anzaldúa. San Francisco: Aunt Lute Books, 1990.

Andersen, Paul, and David Salomon. *The Architecture of Patterns.* New York: W. W. Norton, 2010.

Bierria, Alisa. "Missing in Action: Violence, Power, and Discerning Agency." *Hypatia* 29, no. 1 (2014): 129–45.

Davis, Angela Y. "Political Prisoners, Prisons, and Black Liberation." In *The Angela Y. Davis Reader,* edited by Joy James. 1971. Malden, MA: Blackwell, 1998.

Deleuze, Gilles. *Difference and Repetition.* Translated by Paul Patton. New York: Columbia University Press, 1995.

Haraway, Donna. "A Cyborg Manifesto: Science, Technology, and Socialist-Feminism in the Late Twentieth Century." *Simians, Cyborgs, and Women: The Reinvention of Nature,* 149–81. New York: Routledge, 1991.

Hartman, Saidiya V. *Scenes of Subjection: Terror, Slavery, and Self-Making in Nineteenth-Century America.* New York: Oxford University Press, 1997.

Hartsock, Nancy. "Political Change: Two Perspectives on Power." *Quest: A Feminist Quarterly* 1 (1974). Reprinted in *Building Feminist Theory: Essays from* Quest. New York: Longman, 1981.

Hass, Lawrence. *Merleau-Ponty's Philosophy.* Bloomington: Indiana University Press, 2008.

Havis, Devonya N. "'Now, How You Sound': Considering a Different Philosophical Praxis." *Hypatia* 29, no. 1 (2014): 237–52.

hooks, bell. "Choosing the Margin as a Space of Radical Openness." In *Yearning: Race, Gender, and Cultural Politics*, 145–53. Boston: South End Press, 1990.
———. *Feminist Theory: From Margin to Center*. New York: South End Press, 2000.
Janeway, Elizabeth. *Powers of the Weak*. New York: William Morrow, 1981.
Johnson, Galen A. *The Retrieval of the Beautiful: Thinking through Merleau-Ponty's Aesthetics*. Evanston, IL: Northwestern University Press, 2010.
Jones, Lisa. *Bulletproof Diva: Tales of Race, Sex, and Hair*. New York: Anchor Books, 1995.
Lorde, Audre. *Sister Outsider: Essays and Speeches*. Berkeley, CA: Ten Speed Press, 1984.
Lynn, Greg. *Animate Form*. New York: Princeton Architectural Press, 1999.
———. "Architectural Curvilinearity: The Folded, the Pliant, and the Supple." *Architectural Design* 63, nos. 3–4 (1993): 8–15.
McCann, Rachel. "A Sensuous Ethics of Difference." *Ethics of Embodiment*. Special issue, *Hypatia* 26, no. 3 (2011): 497–517.
Merleau-Ponty, Maurice. *In Praise of Philosophy and Other Essays*. Translated by John Wild and James Edie. Evanston, IL: Northwestern University Press, 1963.
———. *Nature*. Translated by Robert Vallier. Evanston, IL: Northwestern University Press, 2003.
———. *Phenomenology of Perception*. Translated by Colin Smith. London: Routledge and Kegan Paul, 1962.
———. *The Prose of the World*. Translated by John O'Neill. Evanston, IL: Northwestern University Press, 1973.
———. *Signs*. Translated by Richard C. McCleary. Evanston, IL: Northwestern University Press, 1964.
———. *The Visible and the Invisible*. Edited by Claude Lefort. Translated by Alphonso Lingis. Evanston, IL: Northwestern University Press, 1968.
Olkowski, Dorothea E. *Postmodern Philosophy and the Scientific Turn*. Bloomington: Indiana University Press, 2012.
Webb, Sarah L. "By Design." Unpublished poem. www.slwrites.com and www.colorismhealing.org/author/sarah.
———. "Invisible Buildings." Unpublished poem.
Weiss, Gail. *Body Images: Embodiment as Intercorporeality*. New York: Routledge, 1999.

PART 2
NEGOTIATING FUTURES

5 OPEN FUTURE, REGAINING POSSIBILITY

HELEN A. FIELDING

Openness to the world and to the future belongs to personal time intertwined with impersonal or natural time, which is at the heart of phenomenology. Humans, as phenomenal subjects, make sense of the world they encounter, and in so doing they have the potential to enact change. However, as embodied, they also have the ability to be shaped by it—and in this age the world that shapes humans is largely indifferent to this phenomenal potential. They gear into a world that too often does not connect personal and impersonal time with the processes or systems in which they are increasingly absorbed, and for which individual phenomenal subjects are largely irrelevant. At stake are the ways we make sense of the world, both individually and methodologically—that is, the relationship between meaning and structure, between living, sensible, and hence unpredictable existence and natural, cyclical processes. Phenomenology allows us to describe such structures and to account for enacting change precisely because we are phenomenal subjects who encounter and engage with the world. In contrast, although postmodern approaches are able to explain how subjects are shaped by formal structures of culture and language, they are not able to account for the meaningful ways particular embodied subjects take up the world.

Surprisingly, there is overlap between postmodern theorists, for whom words gain significance through function, entailing a move from truth to formal demonstrability, and modern science, which has replaced sensual perception or intuition with "logical constructs of immediate experience," as Dorothea Olkowski has argued.[1] In other words, both rely on objective time—that is, time disconnected from sensual experience that does not allow for encountering the world and others. Importantly, these theoretical ways of understanding science and culture belong to the being of our age, which means they also condition and define the world we live so that phenomenal perception and living experience are no longer trusted. Individual perspectives are understood to be relative to one another and unable to provide accounts of the real. Accordingly, in this postmodern world, the breakdown of personal and impersonal time into objective time allows for the infinity of what is possible, where what is possible is not connected to living existence but rather to often arbitrary systems; in fact, objective time entails the closing down of the virtual world of inexhaustible potentiality. I examine this closing down through considering two cases of death by suicide resulting from cyberbullying. In considering situations where an open future breaks down, I argue that regaining possibility requires the reintegration of personal time into the structure of anonymous existence or impersonal time that allows for encounters. In other words, I claim that feminist phenomenology is a means for both explaining the world and changing it.

Maurice Merleau-Ponty describes impersonal time as the flow of new perceptions, of the new content of experience. It belongs to the world that offers itself up to be perceived, the natural world as the "horizon of all horizons, and the style of all styles." Impersonal time "ensures my experiences have a given, not a willed unity beneath all of the ruptures of my personal and historical life." The sensory functions that are the body support this "given, general, and pre-personal existence."[2] Alternatively, personal time is given in the "point of view," which is an insertion into the world that does not limit existence but makes it possible. A point of view is not thought of what is there or its representation; it is rather an engaged, relational, temporally thick hold on the world in which one is immersed. Without this hold or point of view, there would be no existence as such. For Merleau-Ponty, artwork provides such a point of view: "When I gaze upon the brilliant green of Cézanne's vase, it does not cause me to *think* of pottery, it presents it to me, it is there, along with its thin and smooth outer surface, and its porous interior, in the particular manner in which the green is modulated."[3] Merleau-Ponty could not perceive the particularity of this green vase if he had not already encountered and been beckoned by other vases on sunlit tables in his everyday life. Indeed, his fascination with Paul Cézanne centered on the artist's ability to capture the ways the particularity of perception emerges from everyday living experience, how something takes shape meaningfully for someone from the anonymous flow of existence, with all of its ambiguities.

Personal time is, thus, this gathering together and the integration of what is perceived, along with cognition, motricity, and sensitivity in the structure of the intentional arc of existence.⁴ This intentional arc allows us not only to engage meaningfully with the world but also to withdraw from it, which is to give ourselves over to the anonymous life that motivates personal existence, which we do, for example, when we sleep. As Merleau-Ponty explains, it is "precisely because" the body "can shut itself off from the world" that it also has the capacity to open "up to the world."⁵ Thus, both impersonal time and personal time are inherent to embodied phenomenal existence.

Objective time is of another order. It is the time of empiricism and "intelligence as understood by classical physics," which entails the assumption that eternal physical laws of nature are not affected by human action, culture, or time, and that the best way to understand them is by standing back from the world, observing from what Hannah Arendt calls the "Archimedean Point."⁶ Objective time thus consists of "successive moments," because in circumventing the phenomenal subject, there is no one there to experience time as the "thickness" of the past and the future in the present.⁷ Objective time is understood in terms of space, for time is the spacing of moments—the past is merely a present moment now past—it is not retained along with the future in the thickness of the present. In the attempt to account for reality once and for all, lived temporality is necessarily collapsed. Merleau-Ponty writes:

> If the synthesis could be actual, if my experience formed a closed system, if the thing and the world could be defined once and for all, if the spatio-temporal horizons could (even ideally) be made explicit and if the world could be conceived from nowhere, then nothing would exist. I would survey the world from above, and far from all places and times suddenly become real, they would in fact cease to be real because I would not inhabit any of them and I would be nowhere engaged. If I am always and everywhere, then I am never and nowhere.⁸

The problem with this closed system, then, is that rather than providing an account of reality, there is no reality. Without a point of view, simultaneity is understood according to classical physics in terms of space that is relative.⁹ As Arendt points out:

> The general relativism that results automatically from the shift from a heliocentric to a centerless world view—conceptualized in Einstein's theory of relativity with its denial that "at a definite present instant all matter is simultaneously real . . . was already contained in, or at least preceded by, those seventeenth-century theories according to which blue is nothing but a "relation to a seeing eye" and heaviness nothing but a "relation of reciprocal acceleration."¹⁰

Experientially, however, simultaneity is given to us as the emergence of beings and phenomena gathered relationally in "the thickness of time," which "involves a certain 'indeterminacy.'"[11] Understood phenomenologically, "things coexist in space because they are present to the same perceiving subject and enveloped in a single temporal wave." Things "spring forth," not relatively, but rather in relation to one another, and bring a past and a future together in their temporal thickness.[12] Summertime in Provence brings flowers, which are gathered every year, fragrantly spilling from vases; the artist, caught up in this temporal wave that resounds with past and future summers and the drive to account for the real, responds with his paintbrush.

It is precisely this gathering of the past and future in the present experienced from a point of view by someone who perceives, feels, thinks, and acts that is at the heart of phenomenology. This phenomenological subject has come under attack for its associations to a liberal humanist one, but they are not the same subject; for one, the phenomenal subject is not autonomous, since it is integrally intertwined with a sensuous and interspecies world and emerges with this world in the thickness of time. Indeed, it is in the present understood in terms of temporal plenitude that the inexhaustible potentiality of the world opens up. It is in the present we corporeally cleave to the world, where we have contact with the world that rises up at the same time, and we have the potential to creatively respond and relate to it affectively, perceptually, and through action. It is in the present where we do not have to rely upon cognitive projections and associations, and where the virtual and the actual, as well as the anonymous and personal of our lived existence, come together, allowing us to reckon with new possibilities.

There are, however, situations where this experience of the present of personal time as inexhaustible potentiality breaks down. Catherine Malabou, for example, writes about phenomena such as brain injury, Alzheimer's disease, and war trauma closing down this potential.[13] For Merleau-Ponty it is these moments when what is inherent to the phenomenal body breaks down that we are better able to grasp how the phenomenal world opens up meaningfully to us in the ways we act, engage, and encounter things, people, and relations, against a generality of existence that intervenes and mediates "our presence to ourselves."[14] He takes up at length, for example, the case of the patient Schneider, who suffered a wartime head injury that limited his ability to respond to the world. Unlike "the normal subject [who] immediately has several 'holds'" on the world, Schneider's contact was "stripped of all practical signification." Due to his injury, he was "enclosed in the actual," whereas "normally" the phenomenal body is open to a virtual world of possibility:[15]

> Whereas for the normal person each motor or tactile event gives rise in consciousness to an abundance of intentions that run from the body as a center of virtual action either toward the body itself or toward the object, for the patient [Schneider], on the contrary, the tactile impression remains opaque and closed in upon itself.[16]

In other words, for Schneider, the world of possibilities that belongs to personal time has closed down, and the world he encountered was purely empirical or concrete. Schneider lost the phenomenal experience whereby each moment is full of the living possibilities with which we "reckon," possibilities that are actualized as possibilities, "crystallized into a situation," yet retain their place in the virtual.[17]

I want to turn to another instance of trauma to more fully understand this closing down of phenomenal potentiality—specifically, the phenomenon of teen suicides resulting from depression initiated by online bullying. Adolescence is a time when future possibilities should be open, unlike old age, which is weighed down by the past.[18] The depression in question seems to be, like old age, experienced phenomenologically as the closing down of possibilities.[19] Whereas for old age the closing down comes with the weight of a life lived, for adolescents in this situation it seems to be linked to a traumatic event or series of events. What is interesting about this particular phenomenon is that the bullying takes place predominantly (though not exclusively) through the mediation of cyberspace.

Consider, for example, the 2013 death by suicide of Rehtaeh Parsons, a seventeen-year-old girl from Nova Scotia, who was "allegedly assaulted" by four young men at the age of fifteen.[20] An image made of this "alleged" assault was circulated on the internet, sparking harassment and cyberbullying of Parsons from classmates. At the time, the young men involved were not subjected either to cyber censure or to a judicial process, although more recently two of the young men were convicted of child pornography charges.[21] The challenge of seeing pornography charges progress through the judicial system lies in establishing "who" took the images and "who" posted them. On the one hand, the seeming anonymity of the internet makes the specific instances of the crime hard to establish, the origin difficult to pin down. The particularity of her death, on the other hand, sparked an event: a public discussion of online bullying that revealed how young women are not only vulnerable as always to assault, and to the challenges of charging those accused, but now also to another kind of injury, the repetitive circulation of a representation or image of the assault, whose endless reiterability is indifferent to living time and space.[22] Parsons's death by suicide brought this case into public discourse, but what has come under review in this case and others like it is not the initial assault so much as the recirculation of images and text through the internet and social media.

I do not want to argue that it is the technologies themselves that are responsible. Susan Kozel (following Martin Heidegger among others) has shown convincingly that technologies can facilitate encounters, only differently.[23] Nonetheless, communication in cyberspace tends to belong to what Arendt calls "the social," which is the collapse of the private and public realms of existence, where one can be alone among many. I would argue that this is because, similarly to objective time, on the internet temporality is collapsed into space, even though this is not the case for the phenomenal subjects who use it. There is a kind of *at the same time* of the past, the present, and the future structured as the past, but it is not the same as the thickness of time experienced in the phenomenal present. Phenomenologically, the past informs the present, but it also begins to fade and to become indistinct. On the internet, however, objective time is taken one step further. It is no longer simply the progression of successive moments, but instead the spatial aspect of objective time comes to full realization in the coexistence of these moments in different internet "spaces"; the past can be revisited through the click to a URL or can arbitrarily disappear.

At stake here is the simultaneous existence of the indifference of the social world of cyberspace and the deeply felt point of view understood as the boundary between the "inner realm of thought and feeling and the experiential and exterior world of political, social and ethical forces and acts."[24] Rehtaeh Parsons, it seems, did not experience her situation as one in which she existed, as one where her inner realm interwove with her exterior world—in other words, a world that could change—although she did try to shift things. According to her mother, Parsons moved away for a while, saw a therapist, took antidepressants—attempted to find a future in an apparently closed system.

In French the word for "meaning" is *sens*. This word *sens* has a particular significance phenomenologically, as Merleau-Ponty shows us, because it is directional; it implies sense or meaning as well as the senses themselves. Sense, as meaningful, is oriented because it is intentional and thus implies an anticipated future. I reach for my water assuming the fulfillment of the quenching of my thirst. Parsons moves away from her home, attempts to build a life in anticipation of a future. But this future is not fulfilled as future in terms of the unknown possibilities lying open before her—she is instead, it would seem, submerged in a closed present that appears infinite, like the internet itself, without limits but lacking in potentiality.

This closing down of the present seems to be characteristic of trauma. Merleau-Ponty explores this aspect of traumatic temporality in *Phenomenology of Perception*. For someone who has experienced a trauma, as Parsons did, one present moment among all others "acquires an exceptional value. It displaces the others and relieves them of their value as authentic present [and hence open] moments."[25] Even though the content of experience is replaced by new perceptions and new emotions, the new structure established by the trauma remains the same: "Impersonal time continues to flow but personal time is arrested." As a structure, this past moment is not a representation attached to a specified date. Instead, it shapes the person's whole existence—the traumatic moment "remains" a "true present" hiding behind the gaze. It persists as a "style of being and only to a certain degree of generality" that is itself more like a "particular anxiety."[26] It persists as a closed system.

Importantly, though, not only is Rehtaeh Parsons suffering from a traumatic event that seems to have affected the structure of her personal time, but also, I would suggest, the internet itself is structured somewhat like a traumatic event. In other words, it is a closed system that does not give over either to the flow of anonymous pre-personal time that belongs to generalities and grounds us in the world, or to the specificity of the living personal time that helps shape it. In a world where Rehtaeh Parsons is available as a Google search, there is, as Drew Nelles points out, no remembering and no forgetting, in the ways that humans allow some events to recede and others to be remembered;[27] instead, with the internet there is just the endless possibility of digitized access, whereby some URLs persist and others abruptly disappear.[28] Time is for the most part collapsed into space, and living experience, which is inherently temporal, becomes indifferent.

When an open structure gives way to a closed system, the world of possibility also closes down. Let us turn to Amanda Todd, who also died by suicide at age fifteen, in 2012.[29] She similarly describes a world closed off from possibility. Like most contemporary youth, Todd led a life that clearly overlapped and intersected with cyberspace in a way that dissolved boundaries between private and public. A month before she died, she posted a nine-minute video on YouTube; it is a narrative describing the bullying and abuse she endured both online and off, initiated through her use of social media.[30] She never actually speaks in the video. Instead, she holds up a series of cue cards, one by one (seventy-six in total), each carefully paced, furthering her story with a sentence or two, set to music.[31] She begins, "I have decided to tell you about my neverending story." Established as a story that has no closure but is nonetheless, as a system, not open, she describes her use of a webcam in the seventh grade with friends, "to meet people." She then recounts how a one-time flash of her breasts began a trail of sextortion and cyberbullying, leading eventually to physical assault, depression, alcohol, drugs, cutting, further abuse, and changing schools several times. As she describes the events, she tries to move on, to initiate a future, but finds that she cannot: "I can never get that photo back. [New card] It's out there forever. . . . [Another card] I'm stuck. . . . I have no one. I need someone." She ends her narrative with one sentence: "My name is Amanda Todd." Her face remains in shadow, her eyes hovering just outside the frame; she holds the cards in front of her upper body.

YouTube, like other social media, is primarily a social realm in Arendt's sense of the term, whereby, to recall, we can be alone among many. For Arendt the social is a modern phenomenon. For the Greeks, as she describes it, the important distinction was between the private realm of the home—which was a place of deprivation but also a place of withdrawal and sheltering—and the public realm, where one appeared before others.[32] In the modern age, the private realm has become opposed not to the public but to the social.[33] In the social, humans do not distinguish themselves as individuals; they are types or statistics, one among many. The social does, then, retain the notion of privation from public relations, as a space of indifference that encourages sameness and conformity.[34] Alternatively, the public space (or the political) is one of difference and differentiation, where people individuate, both becoming and showing who they are through acting and speaking before others. They accomplish this appearing through encountering others with shared interests, which "can relate and bind them together."[35]

Amanda Todd's video seems to be an attempt to speak and act in the public space of appearance. Telling a story is a way of trying to make sense of events, to give them a form, a structure and meaning, and thus belongs to personal time. Accordingly, it would seem Todd's video was more than a cry for help; it was an attempt to speak before others. Nonetheless, the act of inserting her voice in written narrative form into the space of the social does not lead to her appearance as someone. First, it is a story posted among many on YouTube. Second, as a video it is not an event as such; it has both the aspects of reiterability that belong to the social and private realms, where repetition and cyclicality prevail, and the aspect of a work that is made, such as an artwork.

However, Todd does try, it would seem, to appear as someone. It is significant that she identifies herself with her full name, and not her face or her body nor the sound of her own voice; for on the internet, the affective lived existence of the body is too easily obscured. We also cannot ignore that her Asian ethnicity feeds into racialized and sexualized scripts imposed on her from the start. Indeed, it was an image of her body—"a what" and not a "who," a representation that was endlessly circulated, switched about, and redeployed—that caused her so much suffering. Her name, on the other hand, identifies the narrator to others; in this case it announces who she is and defies anonymity.

A month after posting the video, nothing had changed and Todd completed her suicide. Apparently her school was aware of the video, and she had been sent to counseling, but nothing, it would seem, was done to address the bullying itself. In other words, the violence was addressed in the private and not the public realm, where realities are recognized. Arendt writes that "to be deprived" of a space of appearance "means to be deprived of reality, which humanly and politically speaking, is the same as appearance." Reality is thus "guaranteed by the presence of others."[36] Todd's suicide was perhaps the one way she could act in order to appear as an individual in the public realm of appearance. In the social, the relational and public aspect of having one's reality confirmed by others is missing, even if the personal aspects of our lives can be laid bare to others who are largely indifferent. The man who was subsequently charged with allegedly distributing the image and blackmailing Todd was apparently later located in The Netherlands; the relation between the two was apparently arbitrary.[37] It could have been any girl, or any perpetrator, whoever, wherever. It just happened to be Amanda Todd.

We can never know precisely what these young women were thinking and feeling before they died, but it would seem that the inexhaustible present did not appear to them as an open structure. Instead it appeared as a closed but infinite system, and the only possibility for escape was to leave the system altogether, for a system does not allow for the here and now that grounds reality in an open present. The circulation of images and texts in these cyberbullying accounts are, on the one hand, part of the living existence or structure of these young women, but on the other hand, their circulation allows for them to be detached from their milieu or situation, to be switched about and stockpiled in an internet "cloud," where they can live on indefinitely, in the way that digital files can, or randomly disappear. This means these images and texts do not "presence" in the way of coming into appearance and fading away that belongs to the personal and even impersonal time of living beings and things. Indeed, Amanda Todd's YouTube video was taken down for a while and then reposted. They are arbitrarily accessible, effectively without limit in a system where they can appear at the same time, but where the emergent temporality of the simultaneous necessary to an encounter is difficult to achieve. Perhaps Amanda Todd was searching for that when she tried to meet people with her webcam at twelve years old. But it was not what she found. Though there are other individuals caught up in the system, what seems to be a place for encounters too often does not allow for them; for in such a system, "there is [effectively] *no one who sees* at the center of this mass of sensations and memories."[38]

Such an endless or infinite system that belongs to objective time is one that is ultimately closed; there is no temporality, no intentionality, no milieu or meaningful structure, and no emerging into appearance or fading away. Hence, there is no potentiality that belongs in the present with an unknown but open future. In a sense, the way images are circulated and hence appear within a heteronormative and racialized system (since we cannot understand the systematic appropriation of women's sexuality outside of an always already racialized, classed, ableist, and heteronormative system) is for the most part indifferent—it refers to individuals, but only in the ways they are taken up in the system. Individuals, like Todd, are deeply affected, but that affect itself becomes part of the system rather than connecting them relationally with others.

Heidegger's name for this systematization, "enframing" (*Gestell*), refers to the endless or infinite processes that mark the way of being in the modern age to which objective time belongs. As with objective time, there is no emergence into existence (and no fading away)—in other words, presencing. Instead there is the imposition of a systematizing measure on everything that is, and humans, who meaningfully encounter and respond to being—they are, after all, conditioned both corporeally and cognitively by the world they inhabit—in turn reveal the actual, or nature, as a storehouse of energy, standing or stockpiled in reserve, ready to be efficiently switched around. What is particular to these systematic processes is that they never actually touch upon what is there. For example, pharmaceutical companies are largely about making profit for the process of making profit, and not for healing disease and ending suffering. There is no time-space here for an encounter that touches upon anything or anyone. And modern physics, which is supposedly the study of *physis*, or nature, "sets nature up to exhibit itself as a coherence of forces calculable in advance." Experimental science sets up in advance the framework that delimits "how nature reports itself when set up in this way."[39]

We see this shift in Newton's first axiom, "every body left to itself moves uniformly in a straight line"; it is an axiom that denotes a complete shift in the way that nature is understood.[40] Heidegger sums up this new understanding as follows: "all natural bodies are essentially of the same kind"; "motion in a straight line becomes decisive"; place becomes interchangeable; force is that which deflects "rectilinear, uniform motion"; indeed, motion becomes merely "a change of position and relative position," which means that ultimately the "concept of nature changes. . . . It is no longer the inner principle out of which the motion of the body follows."[41]

What occurs with this process is the subjection of living existence to forms of systematic and indifferent measurement. Time becomes objective and space interchangeable. Heidegger refers to this indifferent measuring of distances or spaces as "parametrics"; the parameters of time as a "sequence of 'nows,'" and space as a "spatial side-by-side," do not allow for the relational movement of encountering. Measured parametrically there can be successions of moments in time, but these "now" moments will never encounter one another face-to-face. Similarly, if space is measured in terms of a continuum of "unbroken and consecutive" sequences, then face-to-face encounters among the elements are also foreclosed.[42] Calculating space as measurable means there is no actual distance and "everything becomes equal (*gleich*) and [hence] indifferent (*gleich-gültig*)"—in other words, relative.[43] Accordingly, space and time understood parametrically do not bring us closer to the nature of space and time that allows for presencing relationally into appearance, what Heidegger also calls "nearness." This nature is ultimately "inaccessible to calculative thinking."[44]

Importantly, it is not science itself that is the problem, but rather the separation of science from philosophy, which allows for the assumption that there are mere facts rather than understanding that facts are tied to concepts.[45] Accordingly, in modern science "the physical world" is taken up "as if it were an intersecting of linear causal series in which each keeps its individuality," and science remains cut off from "a history of the universe in which the development is discontinuous."[46] This separation of science from philosophy and history is mirrored in the decisive cut between personal and impersonal time and what is understood as the objective time of science. It is also this split, Olkowski has argued, that is repeated in postmodern philosophies, which take up science beyond Newtonian physics. For in the case of classical physics, one can calculate both the velocity and the position of bodies in a system in advance.[47] But with what Heidegger refers to as "atomic physics," motion can be determined in terms of either position or velocity, but not both at the same time. Whereas with classical physics nature can be "calculated in advance," with atomic physics the guarantee is necessarily statistical.[48] What both approaches to physics share is that nature is set up and secured in advance. However, as Heidegger points out, in atomic physics "even the *object vanishes*," and instead of a "subject-object relation," there is a "pure relation" or system that secures subjects and objects as standing reserve.[49]

From Arendt we know that statistics belong to the realm of the social, "where large numbers and long periods are involved, and acts or events can statistically appear only as deviations or fluctuations."[50] If you stand back far enough from the particularity and uniqueness of living existence, patterns will emerge that provide us with predictability. Thus, for example, we can now see the phenomenon of young women completing suicide precipitated by cyberbullying and assault as a kind of type, since we are now able to draw back far enough to generate statistics; but this does not give us the particularity of each death.[51] Amanda Todd's and Rehtaeh Parsons's deaths provide us with a general phenomenon, but phenomenologically we can understand the phenomenon only by considering the particularity of each life lived. As Olkowski points out, with Arendt, statistically "nothing interesting, remarkable, or unusual can happen."[52]

It is this relativity rather than simultaneity that is characteristic of postmodern thinking.[53] Postmoderns have rightly dispensed with the Cartesian subject who applies the axiom of reason, the "I think" as "the ground upon which hereafter all certainty and truth are based," or in other words, the "I" as "the special subject, that with regard to which all the remaining things first determine themselves as such."[54] But in not replacing the subject as the arbiter of reason with one who provides a sensible or intuitive account of the world from a situated point of view, the formal structure that belongs to mathematics prevails. Indeed, postmodern philosophy also relies on mathematical formalism, which "equates truth with demonstrability."[55] For, as Olkowski shows, this drive to dismiss meaning, living experience, and intuition, one that characterizes "postmodern" philosophers, is merely the fulfillment of the formalism or functionalism whose beginnings can be traced in modern science.[56]

The problem is that formal systems, unlike living beings, are ultimately closed. And the move from the determinism of Newtonian or classical mechanics to the statistical probability of classical thermodynamics does not imply a shift away from closed and isolated classical systems, since it introduced the state of equilibrium, "where no further changes take place."[57] Because thermodynamics is a study of energy, work, and heat, it applies to processes rather than things.[58] Accordingly, as Olkowski explains, a postmodern thinker like Gilles Deleuze, who relies on classical thermodynamics and differential calculus, has the event coming not out of the space of experience, but rather occurring in n-dimensional abstract space.[59] The "formal mathematical name" for an event in this system is the "catastrophe," which is a shift in the fixed point of the system. The shift will cause instability, but it is only temporary, since the system then shifts to the area of the new fixed point. For Deleuze, "every subject or object is an event, nothing but the result of contingent encounters of affects and percepts," whereby affects and percepts are liberated from subjects and objects.[60] There is no space of experience within this system, and time is reversible. Ultimately, then, dynamical systems prioritize space over time. They are characterized by a "trajectory" that negates each preceding point, which means the past does not affect the present. Indeed, "each past point is a unique, infinitesimal position on an x/y axis."[61] In this world, "space and time are given, not emergent."[62]

This is the logical space of objective time, the space of the mind that leaves behind the intentional arc of embodied existence. It is a space in which, in Arendt's words, "everything is possible." Arendt was referring to the concentration camps of Nazi Germany, where it was not simply that "everything is permitted," but, more importantly, that anything could happen—it was an arbitrary space where consequences were not attached to actions, where lies could be made true.[63] This was not a space where the virtual was tied to the actual, to context or situation. As the ultimate modern or even postmodern space, it was tied to ideological thinking, which emancipates "thought from experience through certain methods of demonstration" so as to "order facts into an absolutely logical procedure which starts from an axiomatically accepted premise, deducing everything else from it." It is a process that is not connected to "the realm of reality."[64]

The phenomenological method, alternatively, connects living experience to knowledge, bringing the world to appearance through showing, which entails intuition, including perceptual, affective, and motile engagement intertwined with reason. What is perceived is not merely sensation but also touches on the actual (*Wirklichkeit*). What has shifted in this age of technology, as Heidegger calls it, is the relation between the showing and what is shown. Categories of reference are now imposed rather than allowing what is to emerge out of itself as relational. Importantly, there are two different ways to understand the relation, the first as referential (*Beziehung*), the second as being held (*Verhältnis*). The first is connected to placing (*stellen*), which is the root of Gestell, or enframing; the second is connected to holding (*halten*), which we can understand in terms of a relationship in the sense of a mutual shaping that emerges over time. Phenomenal subjects are not thinking subjects in the Cartesian sense; rather, they engage and comport themselves (*sich verhalten*) within and with the world. But this phenomenal aspect of being is itself not brought to appearance in this age.[65] What we see instead is a shift in the sign, according to Heidegger, from "something that shows which allows the emphasis on the showing from out of itself, to something that designates" where the emphasis is on imposing from the outside.[66]

Trinh T. Minh-ha calls this the difference between speaking about "the other" and speaking nearby.[67] The first imposes what is supposed to be an "objective" truth, whereas the second creates meaning in the time-space of the relational encounter. This does not mean that being touched, being moved, or being near to someone or something requires spatial proximity. Nearness has nothing to do with the measuring of distances or spaces. Instead, nearness incorporates embodied appearing—that is, letting something be perceived for what it is through the ways that it concerns us, touches us, and moves us. This means there is simultaneity at the heart of nearness that includes emerging at the same time, a touching and being touched in the same way at the same time. Because it is a touching that concerns us, it is not at all indifferent, unlike the time-space of parametrics, where there are no encounters. Nearness, which cannot be set out or calculated in advance, belongs to the ecstatic and embodied present.[68]

What does this mean for Amanda Todd? She was evidently deeply touched by the circulation of these images and texts, but not in a way that allowed her to come into her own, to be relationally held. Instead she was subjected to referential structures and representations that denied her reality, contributing to her psychic dispersal, as well as physical assault. In her note posted beneath the YouTube video, she writes, "I'm struggling to stay in this world, because everything just touches me so deeply." She struggled, it seems, to adhere to a meaningful structure or milieu, to stay in the here and now of her world, of personal and impersonal or natural time, even as she was touched deeply by the system of objective time that was largely indifferent to who she was.

Phenomenally, then, we can understand the present as full of potentiality in the here and now. It is the very openness, the sheer potential, that marks a present that is temporally ecstatic in the phenomenological sense of presencing—that is, the simultaneous emerging together of (*das Gleich-Zeitige*) the past, the present, and the future, which keeps the past and the future as open, the past in terms of the ways it informs the present, always anew, and the future as open to what cannot be known in advance.[69] Objective time, understood as a succession of nows, cannot account for how the past, present, and future encounter each other at the same time, in the same space, in the same emergent way; indeed it is this sameness and simultaneousness that allows encounters to take place at all.[70] The present, then, can be understood as full of potentiality, inexhaustible and nevertheless meaningfully structured in terms of the situation, phenomenon, or milieu. To have a future is to be open to a range of possibilities even as one cannot know in advance what the future will be; it is this openness in the present, experienced phenomenally as the here and now, that holds the promise of a future and the possibilities for change.

Feminist phenomenology entails bringing into appearance phenomena that have previously been passed over, silenced, or made invisible within imposed discursive and meaning-making structures. In bringing phenomena to appearance, it brings them near—that is, into relation with the public world—so that we can engage with them, be affected and changed by them, and in turn effect change. It is about shifting perception, shifting how we understand the world we live, bringing logos or reason into relation with living realities rather than imposing them from without, and thereby opening up virtual possibilities. Accordingly, in the movement of showing, and thus bringing to appearance, feminists alter reality by shifting the relational structures of personal and natural time that provide the web of the real.

What does this mean for opening the future and regaining possibility? The future is not one that can be planned in advance. It comes out of the inexhaustible fullness of the present moment of personal and natural time, which Merleau-Ponty refers to as "a zone of generalized existence and of already completed projects, significations scattered between us and the things."[71] Opening the future thus entails cultivating our attention to this zone of existence, of personal as well as impersonal time, to being attentive to the here and now that emerges in the particular experiences that modulate the shared and generalizable—in other words, the "single structure that is the concrete subject."[72] To do so is to open up the inexhaustible potentiality of the virtual world rather than living the isolating system of objective time. Opening the future comes out of the virtual possibilities of where we actually are, which must be shared, relational, and acknowledged by others.

Rehtaeh Parsons's and Amanda Todd's deaths marked the closure of their lives, but they were events that initiated discussion, on the internet and beyond, bringing into appearance this phenomenon of cyberbullying leading to death by suicide.[73] In doing so, they allow us to think them through in the fullness of the present and to challenge the systems that perpetuate abuse. In order to experience the future as open means considering where we actually are, and thus where we want to go, as well as what actions we need to take. Regaining possibility is thus grounded in the fullness of the here and now, the interrelation of personal and impersonal or natural time as the space-time of simultaneous encounters.

HELEN A. FIELDING is Associate Professor of Philosophy and Women's Studies and Feminist Research at the University of Western Ontario. She edited (with Christina Schües and Dorothea E. Olkowski) *Time in Feminist Phenomenology* (Indiana University Press, 2011).

NOTES

1. See Dorothea E. Olkowski, *Postmodern Philosophy and the Scientific Turn* (Bloomington: Indiana University Press, 2012), xiv.
2. Maurice Merleau-Ponty, *Phenomenology of Perception*, trans. Donald A. Landes (New York: Routledge, 2012), 345.
3. Ibid.
4. Ibid., 137.
5. Ibid., 168.
6. Ibid., 232; Hannah Arendt, *The Human Condition* (Chicago: Chicago University Press, 1958), 11.
7. Merleau-Ponty, *Phenomenology of Perception*, 288.
8. Ibid., 347.
9. Olkowski, *Postmodern Philosophy*, 61.
10. Arendt, *Human Condition*, 263–64.
11. Merleau-Ponty, *Phenomenology of Perception*, 232.
12. Ibid., 288.
13. She writes about this phenomenon in terms of "destructive plasticity," since she is concerned with the neuroplasticity of the brain. See Catherine Malabou, *Ontology of the Accident*, trans. Carolyn Shread (Malden, MA: Polity Press, 2009), 2–3.
14. Merleau-Ponty, *Phenomenology of Perception*, 476. Merleau-Ponty's habit of turning to those with disabilities in order to explain the "normal" embodied subject has been extensively criticized in disability studies.
15. Ibid., 111.
16. Ibid., 111–12.
17. Ibid., 112, 476.
18. See Beauvoir, *Coming of Age*, trans. Patrick O'Brien (New York: Putnam, 1972), 382.
19. Adolescent death by suicide has reached crisis levels in some Indigenous communities in Canada. As reported by CTV News, "according to a 2000 report from the Canadian Institute of Health, suicides among First Nations youth (aged 15 to 24) was about five to six times higher than non-aboriginal youth in Canada." Michael Shulman and Jesse Tahirali, "Suicide among Canada's First Nations," *CTV News*, April 11, 2016.
20. Parsons died on April 7, 2013, after she was taken off life support while in a coma after hanging herself. Her death is not an isolated event. Cyberbullying and its link to suicide is now a recognized occurrence and can likely be considered statistically.
21. "Rehtaeh Parsons Suspects in Court to Face Child Porn Charges," *CBC News*, August 15, 2013.
22. Of course with more traditional forms of media this iterability was always present, but what is different about social media is this collapse of private and public and the ongoing accessibility of the images and stories.
23. See Susan Kozel, *Closer: Performance, Technologies, Phenomenology* (Cambridge: MIT Press, 2007), 72–77.
24. See Helen Fielding, "Feminist Phenomenology Manifesto," in this volume. This articulation of the subject is co-conceived with Olkowski.
25. Merleau-Ponty, *Phenomenology of Perception*, 85.
26. Ibid.

27. Drew Nelles, "The Internet Dilemma: Do People Have a Right to Be Forgotten," *Toronto Globe and Mail*, May 3, 2013. Nelles cites a blog post by Parsons's father that reads, "I don't want her life to be defined by a Google search about suicide or death or rape. I want it to be about the giving heart she had."

28. Thanks to Katharina von Radziewsky for pointing out the arbitrariness of URL persistence.

29. "Amanda Todd Suicide: RCMP Repeatedly Told of Blackmailer's Attempts," *CBC News*, November 15, 2013. A documentary was also made about Todd's case. See *The Fifth Estate*, "The Sextortion of Amanda Todd," 2013.

30. See "B.C. Girl's Suicide Foreshadowed by Video," *CBC News*, October 11, 2012, for the account, as well as Todd's video, which is available at https://www.youtube.com/watch?v=vOHXGNx-E7E&feature=youtu.be.

31. The first piece is by Jimmy Eat World, "May Angels Lead You In," and the second by Sia, "Breathe Me."

32. Arendt, *Human Condition*, 50.

33. Ibid., 38.

34. Ibid. My thanks to Veronica Vasterling for her helpful suggestions on how to deepen this distinction between social and public space.

35. Arendt, *Human Condition*, 182.

36. Ibid., 199.

37. "Amanda Todd's Alleged Tormentor Loses Another Lawyer," *CBC News*, April 28, 2016.

38. Merleau-Ponty, *Phenomenology of Perception*, 23; emphasis in original.

39. Martin Heidegger, "Question Concerning Technology," in *Question Concerning Technology and Other Essays*, trans. William Lovitt (New York: Harper and Row, 1977), 21.

40. Martin Heidegger, "Modern Science, Metaphysics, and Mathematics," in *Basic Writings*, ed. David Farrell Krell (San Francisco: HarperSanFrancisco, 1993), 286.

41. Ibid., 286–88.

42. Martin Heidegger, *On the Way to Language*, trans. Peter D. Hertz (San Francisco: Harper Collins, 1971), 104–105; Martin Heidegger, *Unterwegs zur Sprache* (Pfullingen, Germany: Günther Neske, 1959), 200.

43. Heidegger *On the Way to Language*, 105; *Unterwegs zur Sprache*, 200 (translation adjusted).

44. Heidegger, *On the Way to Language*, 105; *Unterwegs zur Sprache*, 200–201.

45. Heidegger, "Modern Science," 272.

46. Merleau-Ponty, *Structure of Behavior*, trans. Alden L. Fisher (Boston: Beacon Press, 1967), 139.

47. Olkowski, *Postmodern Philosophy*, 27.

48. Martin Heidegger, "Science and Reflection," in *Question Concerning Technology*, 172. See also Olkowski, *Postmodern Philosophy*, 26.

49. Heidegger, "Science and Reflection," 172–73.

50. Arendt, *Human Condition*, 42.

51. See, for example, a list of cyberbullying statistics at "Cyberbullying Rampant on the Internet," *CyberBully Hotline*, http://www.cyberbullyhotline.com/07-10-12-scourge.html.

52. Olkowski, *Postmodern Philosophy*, 52.

53. Ibid., 61.

54. Heidegger, "Modern Science," 303–304.
55. Olkowski, *Postmodern Philosophy*, 10.
56. As Arendt describes it, "This mathematical operation does not serve to prepare man's mind for the revelation of true being by directing it to the ideal measures that appear in the sensually given data, but serves, on the contrary, to reduce these data to the measures of the human mind, which given enough distance, being sufficiently remote and uninvolved, can look upon and handle the multitude and variety of the concrete in accordance with its own patterns and symbols." Arendt, *Human Condition*, 266–67.
57. Olkowski, *Postmodern Philosophy*, 46.
58. Ibid., 48.
59. Deleuze conceptualizes an immanent system, which means it is still closed and deterministic as well as atomistic. Since its processes occur at the molecular level at speeds beyond that of light, it is at least not "immediately reduced to entropic equilibrium." However, although it is chaotic, it is still deterministic, because "once established, the rules governing the field of thought do not alter." Olkowski, *Postmodern Philosophy*, 66.
60. Ibid., 75.
61. Ibid., 121.
62. Ibid., 85.
63. Hannah Arendt, *The Origins of Totalitarianism* (New York: Harcourt Brace, 1952), 471; Arendt, "Truth and Politics," *Between Past and Future* (New York: Penguin, 1968), 238.
64. Arendt, *Origins*, 471.
65. Heidegger, *On the Way to Language*, 120; *Unterwegs zur Sprache*, 240.
66. Heidegger, *On the Way to Language*, 115; *Unterwegs zur Sprache*, 234.
67. Trinh T. Minh-ha, "Speaking Near-by: A Conversation with Trinh T. Minh-ha," *Visual Anthropology Review* 8, no. 1 (1992): 87.
68. Heidegger, *On the Way to Language*, 131; *Unterwegs zur Sprache*, 151.
69. Heidegger, *On the Way to Language*, 106; *Unterwegs zur Sprache*, 201–202.
70. Heidegger, *On the Way to Language*, 106; *Unterwegs zur Sprache*, 201–202.
71. Merleau-Ponty, *Phenomenology of Perception*, 476.
72. Ibid., 477.
73. It also brings into appearance the perseverance of these sexualized scripts of good girl/bad girl that obscure the culpability of those who harass, let alone assault.

BIBLIOGRAPHY

Arendt, Hannah. *The Human Condition*. Chicago: Chicago University Press, 1958.
———. *The Origins of Totalitarianism*. New York: Harcourt Brace, 1952.
———. "Truth and Politics." *Between Past and Future*, 227–80. New York: Penguin, 1954.
Beauvoir, Simone de. *The Coming of Age*, translated by Patrick O'Brian. New York: Putnam, 1972.
CBC News. "Amanda Todd Suicide: RCMP Repeatedly Told of Blackmailer's Attempts." November 15, 2013. http://www.cbc.ca/news/canada/amanda-todd-suicide-rcmp-repeatedly-told-of-blackmailer-s-attempts-1.2427097.
———. "Amanda Todd's Alleged Tormentor Loses Another Lawyer." April 28, 2016. http://www.cbc.ca/news/world/amanda-todd-aydin-coban-trial-1.3557566.

———. "B.C. Girl's Suicide Foreshadowed by Video." October 11, 2012. http://www.cbc.ca/news/canada/british-columbia/b-c-girl-s-suicide-foreshadowed-by-video-1.1217831.

———. "Rehtaeh Parsons Suspects in Court to Face Child Porn Charges." August 15, 2013. http://www.cbc.ca/news/canada/nova-scotia/rehtaeh-parsons-suspects-in-court-to-face-child-porn-charges-1.1320435.

Deleuze, Gilles. *The Logic of Sense*. Translated by Mark Lester. New York: Columbia University Press, 1990.

Fielding, Helen A. "Beyond the Surface: Towards a Feminist Phenomenology of the Body-as-Depth." PhD diss., York University, Canada, 1996.

Heidegger, Martin. "Modern Science, Metaphysics, and Mathematics." In *Basic Writings*, edited by David Farrell Krell, 267–305. San Francisco: HarperSanFrancisco, 1996.

———. *On the Way to Language*. Translated by Peter D. Hertz. San Francisco: Harper Collins, 1971.

———. "Question Concerning Technology." In *Question Concerning Technology and Other Essays*, translated by William Lovitt, 3–35. New York: Harper and Row, 1977.

———. "Science and Reflection." In *Question Concerning Technology and Other Essays*, translated by William Lovitt, 155–82. New York: Harper and Row, 1977.

———. *Unterwegs zur Sprache*. Pfullingen, Germany: Günther Neske, 1959.

Kozel, Susan. *Closer: Performance, Technologies, Phenomenology*. Cambridge: MIT Press, 2007.

Malabou, Catherine. *Ontology of the Accident*. Malden, MA: Polity Press, 2009.

Merleau-Ponty, Maurice. *Phenomenology of Perception*. Translated by Donald A. Landes. New York: Routledge, 2012.

———. *The Structure of Behavior*. Translated by Alden L. Fisher. Boston: Beacon Press, 1967.

Nelles, Drew. "The Internet Dilemma: Do People Have a Right to Be Forgotten." *Toronto Globe and Mail*, May 3, 2013. http://www.theglobeandmail.com/life/the-internet-dilemma-do-people-have-a-right-to-be-forgotten/article11715854/?page=all.

Olkowski, Dorothea E. *Postmodern Philosophy and the Scientific Turn*. Bloomington: Indiana University Press, 2012.

Shulman, Michael, and Jesse Tahirali. "Suicide among Canada's First Nations: Key Numbers." *CTV News*, posted April 11, 2016. http://www.ctvnews.ca/health/suicide-among-canada-s-first-nations-key-numbers-1.2854899.

Trinh T. Minh-ha, and Nancy Chen. "'Speaking Near-by': A Conversation with Trinh T. Minh-ha." *Visual Anthropology Review* 8, no. 1 (1992): 82–91.

6 OF WOMEN AND SLAVES

DEBRA BERGOFFEN

If the sentence "On ne naît pas femme: on le devient," translated in 1952 by H. M. Parshley as "One is not born but becomes a woman," and by Constance Borde and Sheila Malovany-Chevallier in 2010 as "One is not born but becomes woman," is considered the most famous feminist legacy of Simone de Beauvoir's *The Second Sex*, the category of the Other may stand as its most enduring bequest to the philosophy of oppression. Its value, however, depends on attending to its nuances, for if we fail to see that Beauvoir provides different accounts of the ways that a person can be designated as the Other, we will fail to see how specific mechanisms of othering produce different modes of oppression with different consequences for those who are oppressed. Further, if we read Beauvoir's idea of the Other only in terms of oppression, thereby demonizing the othering through which the Other comes into being, and, implicitly or explicitly, calling for the eradication of the category of the Other, we will lose sight of the role the Other plays in the dialectic of intersubjectivity and end up supporting the idea that only one type of subjectivity is legitimately human. In analyzing the unique mode of othering through which women are oppressed, in detailing the distinct otherness of the sexual difference, and in speaking of the Other as a category of reciprocity that is betrayed by the politics of oppression, *The Second Sex* shows us that in their demand to be recognized as fully human, women can transform the Other from a mark of oppression to a sign of the dignity of difference.

THE CATEGORY OF THE OTHER

Beauvoir introduces the category of the Other through the words of Claude Lévi-Strauss and the ideas of G.W.F. Hegel. Quoting Lévi-Strauss, she writes,

"The passage from the state of Nature to the state of Culture is defined by man's ability to think [of] biological relations as systems of oppositions; duality, alternation, opposition and symmetry."[1] Claiming that if humanity were solely a *Mitsein* (being with others) of solidarity and friendship, the thought systems described by Lévi-Strauss would not be possible, Beauvoir (perhaps forgetting that she did not preclude the possibility of humanity being a Mitsein of solidarity and friendship but only precluded the possibility of it being *solely* a Mitsein of solidarity and friendship) draws on Hegel to convert Lévi-Strauss's systems of oppositions that included alternation and symmetry into systems of oppositional hostility. Instead of the multiple possibilities of oppositional thinking offered by Lévi-Strauss, she confronts us with a monological system of antagonisms where the subject "asserts itself as the essential and sets up the Other as the inessential, the object."[2] Continuing in this Hegelian vein, Beauvoir argues that the subject who asserts itself as essential cannot sustain its claim. Those designated as inessential refuse this designation. They assert their subjectivity. Sometimes their assertions create new inessential others perpetuating the cycle of violence. Sometimes, however, those who overthrow their oppressors reject the temptation to oppress those they designate as Other and embrace the phenomenological truth of their intersubjective ambiguous condition—subject and Other are shifting, relational, and relative positions.[3]

In arguing for this phenomenological truth of subjectivity—that subject and Other, as ambiguous, are relative and related to each other—Beauvoir embeds the subject in the flows of intersubjectivity. The ambiguity of being a subject who perceives the world and of being perceived as an object within it becomes in *The Second Sex* the interchangeability of being a subject for myself and an Other to you. The anonymity of perceptual ambiguity is particularized. It is only in relation to me that you are Other. You are not *the* Other; you are my other. As my Other you are the horizon against which my unique mode of subjectivity unfolds. As my Other who reveals the relativity of my subjectivity, however, you are also the one who challenges my taken-for-granted truths and ways of being. You are my question mark. I am vulnerable to your challenge to my way of life. How I respond to this vulnerability is undecidable. Whether I experience it as initiating a questioning that interrupts the seductions of the desire to be the absolute subject or as triggering the fortification of my position as the absolute subject—whether I welcome your strangeness or attempt to destroy it—cannot be determined in advance. Hence the fact that humanity cannot be solely a Mitsein of solidarity and friendship. What can be said, however, is that given this phenomenological account of the Other, the hostility to the Other and the declaration of absolute subjectivity are neither original nor spontaneous moments of consciousness. What is immediately given is ambiguity. The hostility to the Other and the assertion of absolute subjectivity are reactionary flights from the inherent vulnerability of our intersubjective, ambiguous condition.

The logic of this flight is fairly straightforward. The ambiguity of subjectivity is bifurcated. Instead of the intersubjective subject-Other flow, the positions of subject and Other are severed and frozen. One type of subjectivity establishes itself as absolute with exclusive claims to legitimacy. Those who fail to embody this mode of subjectivity are either dehumanized and reduced to the being of a quasi-thing, as in slavery, or recognized as human but inferior, and subordinated, as in the case of non-slave women. The cycles of violence that define human history may be read in terms of both the tactics used to enforce claims of absolute subjectivity and their ultimate failure. The positions of subject and Other cannot be stabilized. The Other, or at least some Others, slave others, class others, colonized others, rebel. They (re)claim their humanity. Women others, however, are an anomaly. They do not rebel. Thus a question that haunts *The Second Sex*: why don't women rebel?

Beauvoir provides several possible answers to this question: economic dependency; complicity; the fact that women are divided by race, class, religion, ethnicity, and nationality, and that they identify with the men of their race, class, religion, ethnicity and nationality rather than crossing these lines to identify with one another.[4] But, as I shall argue here, these reasons, important as they are, do not get to the heart of the matter. They are symptoms of a more fundamental issue: the bond of the sexual difference that promises to fulfill our desire for intimacy. Beauvoir describes this bond as rooted in what she calls "an original *Mitsein*." She writes:

> The proletariat could plan to massacre the whole ruling class; . . . but a woman could not even dream of exterminating males. The tie that binds her to her oppressor is unlike any other. The division of the sexes is a biological given, not a moment in human history. Their opposition too took place in an original *Mitsein*, and she has not broken it. The couple is a fundamental unit with the two halves riveted to each other: cleavage of society by sex is not possible. This is the fundamental characteristic of woman: she is the Other at the heart of a whole whose two components are necessary to each other.[5]

This reference to the original Mitsein of the heterosexual couple is bookended by two other Mitsein citations in *The Second Sex*. One, toward the end, where Beauvoir speaks of women's desire to be included in "'the human *Mitsein*,'" the other, in the introduction and cited above, where Beauvoir challenges the idea of the possibility of a humanity characterized solely by a Mitsein of solidarity and friendship.⁶ These Mitsein references call to each other in interesting ways. In speaking of an original Mitsein, which could have produced a Mitsein of solidarity and friendship but failed, and of a human Mitsein that women wish to join, Beauvoir indicates that if it is the case that humanity cannot be characterized solely as a Mitsein of solidarity and friendship, it is also the case that the utopian possibility of this Mitsein is central to women's desire for liberation. This Mitsein hope sets women's demands for freedom apart from other revolutionary movements.

In telling us that the cleavage of society by sex is not possible, and that if "the proletariat could plan to massacre the whole ruling class; . . . a woman could not even dream of exterminating males," Beauvoir indicates that although the sexual bond has, to date, kept women from rebelling, in teaching women that subjects exist relative to and in relationship with each other, this bond shows them that their rebellion cannot follow the usual routes to freedom. If it is the case that slaves can hope to free themselves only by destroying those absolute subjects called masters, it is also the case that by eradicating the occupants of the position of the absolute subject while leaving the place of the absolute subject vacant, former slaves may be tempted to inhabit it. The hope offered by a revolution begun by those who exist in an original Mitsein is that, knowing that there are no absolute subjects, but only relative, relational, and ambiguous ones, their demand for freedom will not succumb to this temptation. A rebellion aimed at restructuring intersubjectivity in terms of the relationship between ambiguous subjects will neither destroy some subjects so that others may exist, nor equate freedom with claiming the rights of the absolute subject. Further, coming from the original Mitsein of the sexual difference, women will speak of something more than the ethical ideal of friendship and solidarity. They will speak of the pleasures offered by the presence of the Other.

Though Beauvoir is most focused on the fact that, to date, the original Mitsein has been the source of women's exploitation, she is also attentive to the fact that this Mitsein has been the site of erotic and sensual pleasure. She sees these pleasures playing a key role in the promise of this Mitsein, for unlike the pleasures of mastery claimed by the absolute subject, the pleasures of the erotic are the gifts of an ambiguous subject. The refusal of the risks of intersubjective vulnerability has no place here. In Beauvoir's words:

> In fact man is, like woman, a flesh, . . . and she, like him, in the heart of carnal fever, is consent, voluntary gift and activity; each of them lives the strange ambiguity of existence made body. . . . The same drama of the flesh and spirit and finitude and transcendence plays itself out in both sexes; . . . they have the

same essential need of the other. . . . If they knew how to savor it, they would no longer be tempted to contend for false privileges; and fraternity could be born between them.[7]

The phrase "original *Mitsein*" has disappeared; the idea has not. Returning in the form of "the drama of the flesh" and tied to the idea of fraternity between the sexes, we discover that the revolution that liberates women will clip the wings of the flight from vulnerability embodied in the desire to be an absolute subject by tying the value of sexual equality to the erotica of the sexual difference. To see that for all of her stress on the necessity of women's economic independence, Beauvoir finds that this independence is a necessary but not sufficient condition for undoing patriarchy, we need to return to the idea of an original Mitsein for the clues it offers to the difference between the situation of the "free" woman and the slave and to the significance of this difference for the type of oppression they endure.[8] These clues may be framed in terms of the question, How did the sexual difference, originally the site of erotic intimacy and desire, come to betray this desire and become the place where women are alienated from their humanity?

WHAT SORT OF OTHER IS WOMAN?

Over the years, I have struggled with Beauvoir's idea of an original heterosexual Mitsein. What does Beauvoir mean by "original"? Given her chapter on biology, it cannot refer to an immutable natural state. Further, given that Beauvoir cannot find an origin that could account for woman as Other, it cannot be read as the origin of her situation as the Other. Though it seems to suggest a heterosexual mandate, this too seems unlikely, for this would equate human sexuality with its reproductive function, a position explicitly rejected by Beauvoir. Beauvoir's endorsement of this Mitsein can be read neither in terms of a biological destiny responsive to the reproductive demands of the species nor as sanctioning heteronormative sexuality, for her descriptions of heterosexual sexual initiation, of marriage, and of motherhood are indictments of the ways that normative heterosexuality is responsible for the oppression of women. One of the points of *The Second Sex* is that until these norms are dismantled, women's status as the inessential Other will prevail.

Pulling this together, I read Beauvoir's reference to an original Mitsein pointing to an abiding human desire for intimacy expressed in the relationship of the couple. Further, when Beauvoir writes that the true form of the couple has yet to emerge, she signals that the coupled form this desire originally took was not the blueprint for its realization. Its true form is yet to come.[9] *The Second Sex* makes it clear that far from taking us on a path toward this realization, current configurations of the sexual difference thwart it. In poisoning heterosexual relationships and denying the legitimacy of lesbian, gay, bisexual, and transgender couples, normative heterosexuality corrupts the meaning of human sexuality by defining it biologically in terms of body parts rather than understanding it polymorphously as the desire for the unique sexual embodiment of the other.

Reading Beauvoir's references to an original Mitsein as an expression of an originally given desire for intimacy that has yet to find its true form contests the idea that in appealing to this Mitsein, Beauvoir endorses heteronormative sexuality. What cannot be contested, however, is the fact that this idea of the Mitsein identifies the couple as the site where this desire is fulfilled. On this matter, advocates of communal living or multiple partner intimacies will find it necessary to part ways with Beauvoir. For those who are convinced that the couple is the privileged site of intimacy, however, Beauvoir's references to an original Mitsein stands as a utopian promise that is kept alive by women who forfeit the demands of reciprocity for the value of this intimate bond. *The Second Sex* may be read as an argument for the value of this couple bond and as a condemnation of the current devil's bargain that protects it.

In coming to these conclusions about the original Mitsein, I have come to understand it in terms of the materiality of the polymorphous sexual difference. As original, this materiality is indigenous to our embodiment. As a human materiality, however, the sexual difference must be taken up and made meaningful. It is lived through human invention and intervention. The original givenness of the sexual difference will be the thing that disrupts the attempt to equate "free" women and slaves. Though woman's sex can and has been used to alienate her from her humanity, it can be used to destroy her humanity only if it is overridden by such non-original, historical, factors as race, religion, or ethnicity. Like her male counterpart, as a slave she is reduced to a quasi object, terrorized, and exploited for profit. When it is advantageous to her owner, her sex is ignored and her body is used as a work machine. When it profits her owner, her sexed body is put into play for its reproductive value and she is bred as an animal. Though she is identified as female, she is not recognized as a woman who deserves to be treated as a human being. Reading Sojourner Truth's "Ain't I a Woman" through this lens, I hear her saying (at least) two things: one, the white idea of woman is racist; and two, because she is a woman, her humanity must be respected.

OF WOMEN AND SLAVES

The family resemblance between the situations of women and slaves invites us to compare them. The idea of an original Mitsein stops us from carrying this comparison too far. Though Beauvoir often compares "free" women to slaves and sometimes equates "free" women with slaves, at critical points in her texts she establishes the difference between "free" women who as Other are alienated from their humanity and slaves who as Other are severed from theirs.

In *The Ethics of Ambiguity*, Beauvoir argues that both slaves and "free" women share the condition of being reduced to the status of the child. They are "kept in a state of servitude and ignorance"; "they can only submit to the laws, the gods, the customs and the truths created by [others]."[10] Insofar as this identity of slave and "free" woman is intended to establish that the original mark of oppression is being condemned to live in the world of the Other, this identification remains in force throughout *The Second Sex*. Thus, in discussing the independent woman, Beauvoir writes, "While today's customs impose fewer constraints on her than in the past, such negative licenses have not fundamentally changed her situation; she remains a vassal imprisoned in her condition [of living in a world that has] always belonged to men and still retains the form they have imprinted on it."[11] So long as she lives in a world whose meaning and values are defined by men, woman's freedom is an illusion.

References to the shared condition of the "free" woman and the slave are found throughout *The Second Sex*. Beauvoir identifies woman as her husband's prey, who, like the slave, is considered his property.[12] She says that a woman is a "slave to her husband, children and home."[13] She argues that "if men were content to love a peer instead of a slave[,] women would be far less obsessed with their femininity and discover themselves as women—which after all they are."[14] In calling women men's vassal, however, and in finding that "they are on the whole still in a state of serfdom. . . . Her being-for-man is one of the essential factors of her concrete condition,"[15] Beauvoir alerts us to the mistake of equating the situation of the "free" woman with that of the slave. Though dictionaries cite "slave" as a second definition of "vassal," the first definition describes the vassal as a person living in the feudal era who exists in a condition of dependency where loyalty is given in exchange for protection. Women as vassals, not slaves objectified by masters, but dependents who, in exchange for loyalty, receive male protection—is there a more apt description of the patriarchal protection racket? Give deference to male privilege and you will be provided for and safe.

Some of you, not all. Some of you, not just those who are openly enslaved, will be exploited for pleasure and profit. Though the married woman, essential to her husband's fantasy of a "freely enslaved companion," will be respected as a person and saved from the extremes of oppression, her "safety" will come at the expense of the prostitute.[16] In Beauvoir's words: "The existence of a caste of 'lost women' makes it possible to treat the 'virtuous woman' with the most chivalric respect. The prostitute is a scapegoat: man unloads his turpitude onto her and he repudiates her.... She is treated like a pariah.... The prostitute does not have the rights of a person; she is the sum of all types of feminine slavery at once."[17]

This talk of women and slaves—of wives who are respected as persons and of prostitutes who are not—and of different types of female slavery points to a more complex way of thinking about women that is sometimes pursued, but more often than not passed over, in *The Second Sex*. Beauvoir's Marxism made her attentive to the class differences among women and to how these differences could determine whether a woman was treated like a person or vilified as a prostitute. She did not, however, alert us to other factors that might determine whether a woman could clothe herself in those myths of femininity that accorded her the dignity given to a person, or whether she was destined to embody myths of women that left her at the mercy of men's sexual and aggressive fantasies. Though Beauvoir took note of her privileged situation and, adopting a variation on the Marxist theme of the truth of the proletariat's perspective, claimed that her situation as a privileged woman allowed her to expose the oppressions of patriarchy, she did not see that her critique of patriarchy was limited by the ways that it reflected her identification with the men of her race, class, and intellectual status. We might see this as a matter of her feminist Marxism overshadowing the phenomenological demands of the epoché, as well as a reminder of the impossibility of discerning all of the assumptions that find their way into our work.

Contemporary feminists have noted this problem in Beauvoir's thought in particular and in second-wave feminism in general and have moved to address it.[18] They have analyzed the intersections among one's identity as a woman and one's religious, ethnic, race, class, and national identity to make the case that, contra Beauvoir, we cannot say that being a woman is the primary source of a woman's oppression in that being a woman is also simultaneously and necessarily being a woman of a certain ethnicity, race, class, and religion.

Feminists of color have been especially vocal in challenging Beauvoir's and white women's explicit or implicit assertion of epistemic privilege. Situating themselves as the Other of the white feminist perspective but not as the Other of feminism, by revealing the limits of white feminist positions they are the question mark that challenges the idea of woman. They are revising Beauvoir's

"One is not born but becomes (a) woman" to read, "One is not born but becomes women." Speaking in their own voices, black feminists such as Kathryn Gines and bell hooks argue that we need a feminist framework that reveals the multiple realities of women's sexed and gendered lives. Gines identifies Anna Julia Cooper as pioneering the creation of this framework. According to Gines, Cooper's critique of the sexism of white and black men and the racism of white women and men exposes the inadequacy of seeing black women as the second sex, the one who has one strike against her humanity, rather than seeing her as embodying the burden of the one who has two.[19] Margaret Simons's critique of Beauvoir's focus on female dependency and passivity makes it clear that operating in this feminist frame is not dependent on the color of one's skin, for Simons, like Cooper, finds that the idea of absolute patriarchy obscures the fact that some white women have had power over minority women and men.[20] As Beauvoir argued that postmenopausal women were the third sex, these women suggest that there are four, five, and many other sexes.

According to hooks:

> Much feminist theory emerges from privileged women who live at the center, whose perspectives on reality rarely include knowledge and awareness of the lives of women and men who live in the margin. As a consequence, feminist theory lacks wholeness, lacks the broad analysis that could encompass a variety of human experiences. Although feminist theories are aware of the need to develop ideas and analysis that encompass a larger number of experiences, that serve to unify rather than to polarize, such theory is complex and slow in formation. At its most visionary, it will emerge from individuals who have knowledge of both margin and center.

This observation speaks to the importance of seeing this expanded frame of feminist thought as a challenge to rather than a rejection of earlier feminist analyses.[21] In making this statement, hooks reminds us that as feminists committed to the dignity of difference, we are engaged in what Maurice Merleau-Ponty calls dialogue, where "in throwing the other toward what I know which [s]he has not yet understood, or in carrying myself toward what one is going to understand," I trespass upon the other as she trespasses upon me.[22] In this observation, hooks also reminds us that our different situations share this: we live in male-dominated societies, and so long as this is the case, we will be subjected to certain shared forms of abuse. Violence against women is a fact of life for women whether they live at the center or on the margin.

Beauvoir's assessment of the different roles allotted to respected women and "othered" women reveals, however, that the threat and reality of violence toward women in the center and the violence inflicted on women living in the margins serve different purposes. The long history of enemy women being reduced to sex slaves by victorious armies, the Japanese army's use of colonized non-Japanese women as sex slaves in World War II, and the current ubiquity of sex trafficking, where "exotic" women are favorite targets, is used to support the idea of men's uncontrollable aggressive sexuality and to make the point that these women are disposable. It is also used to remind women at the center that they can be evicted from their status as persons by being accused of being whores and that as whores they are legitimate targets of abuse.

In giving us two ends of the continuum of women's oppression—the vassal and the slave—that contemporary feminists are complicating, Beauvoir, like today's feminists, alerts us to the mistake of collapsing the difference between the subjugation of the vassal woman living at the center and the oppression of the slave woman existing on the margin. Pushing the analogy between the "free" woman and the slave too far misses the fact that it would be counterproductive to the patriarchal project to reduce all women to slaves. To preserve the fantasy of the masculine absolute subject, some women must be seen as wanting to submit to masculine authority. Given that this appearance belies the fact that "halfway between revolt and slavery she unwillingly resigns herself to masculine authority . . . [and that he must resort to] force to make her shoulder the consequences of her reluctant submission," when force is used it will be dissimulated.[23] Domestic violence, the dirty secret of married and cohabitation life, will be called something else by the husband/male partner and the wife/female partner. He will explain it in terms of a justifiable response to a valid grievance. She will explain it as something he did not mean. Both will conspire to preserve the appearance of her status as a person: him because securing the myth of her freedom fulfills his desire to be recognized as the sovereign subject; her because it saves her from being reduced to a prostitute.

THE MYTH OF FEMININITY

Finally we find it. The crux of the failure of the analogy between "free" women and slaves lies in the shoals of men's desire. If Hegel's account of slavery is belied by its realities—masters are interested in their slaves' commercial value, not their recognition—it accurately describes the relationship between "free" women and men in a male-dominated world. Here, the mechanisms of violence are not, as in slavery, aimed at the destruction of freedom, but at its domestication. Free women's otherness must be constructed in such a way as to secure her ability to grant recognition. Destroying all women's freedom would end the game. Only a free person can credibly recognize another as a subject.

A free person's recognition, however, cannot be guaranteed. It comes with the risks of intersubjective vulnerability. Fleeing these risks while desiring their profit, men create the myth of femininity. Insofar as they are seen as embodying this myth, some women are given the illusion of freedom. It may be the case that these women are seduced by the promises of the myth and willingly succumb to its allure. However, the mechanisms of violence in the service of this myth suggest that self-preservation as well as seduction lure "free" women to embrace their feminine status. Whatever the reason, in accepting the counterfeit freedom of femininity, these women fulfill men's desire. Existing as sexed and sexualized objects paradoxically endowed with freedom, they assure men that their status as the absolute subject is secure.[24] In Beauvoir's words, "[Woman] appears as the privileged other through whom the subject accomplishes himself; one of the measures of man, his balance, his salvation, his adventure, his happiness."[25] By giving some women the option of several ways to embody the "privileges" of femininity, the multiple and often contradictory myths of femininity fortify the illusions of freedom that secure men's happiness. As illusionary, this freedom is limited to the right to foster the status and authority of men. In the evening dress of her choice, Beauvoir writes, "woman is disguised as woman for all the male's pleasure and pride of her owner."[26] Existing as vassals whose freedom is constrained by loyalty, women secure men's status as the absolute subject.

The relationship between man as subject and woman as docile freedom repeats Lacan's account of the mirror stage to invert it. According to Lacan, the infant, seeing its reflection in the mirror and its mother's eyes, looks to her to confirm its identity as integrated and whole, an imaginary identity at this stage of its existence but an object of desire that persists throughout our lives. Like the child gazing into his mother's eyes, man looks to woman to reflect him back to himself in the image of his desire. In looking to her to replay the mother's role, however, he is no longer the helpless infant facing an all powerful presence. The adult man can demand woman's compliance. Where the mother was free to affirm or reject the infant's desire to be identified with its image, woman, as an inessential other—a docile freedom ensnared in the myth of femininity—can be counted on to affirm man's desire to be recognized as the essential subject.

Of course this is only part of the story. The global epidemic of violence against women makes it clear that the consequences of refusing to play the role of the mirror can be disastrous. This violence suggests that the seduction of women's freedom is not as secure as it seems. Women may not be as docile as they appear. Threats are necessary to keep them in their place. Here, as in the case of slavery, the mechanisms of violence meet resistance, perhaps even provoke it. Slaves rebel. Women reject the illusions of freedom for the real thing.

CLOSING, IF NOT NECESSARILY CONCLUDING, THOUGHTS

In *The Ethics of Ambiguity* the comparison between women and slaves is untroubled. That work, which Beauvoir later criticized for being too abstract, did not note that despite their shared situation of living in a world not of their making, "free" women's and slaves' oppression took different forms. In *The Second Sex* the meaning of oppression is materialized. Though freedom still means living in a world where one's values count, where one's desires are recognized as legitimate, and where one's projects have a chance to succeed, the difference in their status as oppressed others reveals that the "free" woman's and the slave's route to this freedom will be different. Beauvoir makes this clear when she finds that privileged women, women who have secured their freedom, are still haunted by myths of femininity. These women find that "their successes are in contradiction with [their] femininity."[27] Where slaves easily resolve the contradiction between being free and being a slave by rejecting their slave identity, women, finding that "their successes are in contradiction with [their] femininity," discover that divorcing their identity as women from the ideals of femininity, from how they became (a) woman, is no easy task.[28] In alerting us to the limits of economic liberation, Beauvoir shows us that it is as women that women want to become part of the human Mitsein and that this requires divorcing the contours of femininity from women's sexed materiality. Thus Beauvoir writes, "[Women] would not think of eliminating [themselves] as a sex: [they] only ask that certain consequences of the sexual difference be abolished."[29]

The project of liberating women from the myth of femininity so that the meaning of the sexual difference given in the materiality of the original Mitsein may emerge indicates that the original givenness of this Mitsein refers not to some earlier utopian moment (a garden of Eden once upon a time) but to the givenness of the human desire for intimacy. As expressed in the sexual difference, the life of this desire speaks to a future where women and men "recognizing each other as subject, . . . will remain *other* for the other; reciprocity in their relations will not do away with the miracles that the division of human beings into two separate categories engenders . . . [rather] the division of humanity will reveal its authentic meaning and the human couple will discover its true form."[30] Liberating women from the myth of femininity also means freeing them from the idea that only men can confirm them in their sexual difference(s). Further, insofar as the authentic meaning of the human couple requires that the position of the absolute subject is abolished and the ambiguities of human subjectivity—its shifting, relative, and relational intersubjective realities—are acknowledged, realizing the true meaning of the couple will free men from needing vassals to affirm their masculinity. As liberated to recalculate their masculine and feminine identities, both sexes will also confront the risks and vulnerabilities of their intersubjective condition. Whether or not the promise of intimacy borne in the original Mitsein comes to pass will be determined by the willingness of each sex to affirm the dignity of the difference(s) of the other.

DEBRA BERGOFFEN is Professor Emerita of Philosophy at George Mason University and the Bishop Hamilton Philosopher in Residence at American University. She is the author of *The Philosophy of Simone de Beauvoir: Gendered Phenomenologies, Erotic Generosities* (State University of New York Press, 1997), and *Contesting the Politics of Genocidal Rape: Affirming the Dignity of the Vulnerable Body* (Routledge, 2012). Her essays on Simone de Beauvoir, human rights, sexual violence in armed conflict, and feminist theory appear regularly in journals and anthologies.

NOTES

1. Simone de Beauvoir, *The Second Sex*. Translated by Constance Borde and Sheila Malovany-Chevallier (New York: Vintage Books, 2010), 7.
2. Ibid.
3. Ibid.
4. Ibid, 8, 10.
5. Ibid., 8–9. Monique Wittig, speaking as a materialist lesbian, rejects this reading of the promise of the Mitsein. She argues that breaking the heterosexual relationship is the path to women's liberation, that it enforces the myth of woman and is inherently exploitive. See Wittig, "One Is Not Born a Woman," *The Straight Mind* (Boston: Beacon Press, 1992), 8–20.
6. Beauvoir, *Second Sex*, 17.
7. Ibid., 763.
8. In making it clear that the analogy between "free" women and slaves cannot be taken too far or used to claim that their situations are interchangeable, Beauvoir's discussions of women and slaves is distinct from the politics of nineteenth-century U.S. feminists who, Elizabeth Spelman argues, in equating the subordination of women to the exploitation of slaves silenced those who suffered under slavery. However, whether in describing the situation of enslaved women Beauvoir implied that they could not speak for themselves is a more complicated matter, which I will leave for another time.

See Spelman, *The Fruits of Sorrow: Framing Our Attention to Suffering* (Boston: Beacon Press, 1997), 113–14.

9. Beauvoir, *Second Sex*, 766.

10. Simone de Beauvoir, *The Ethics of Ambiguity*, trans. Bernard Frechtman (New York: Philosophical Library, 1948), 37.

11. Beauvoir, *Second Sex*, 721.

12. Ibid., 171.

13. Ibid., 657.

14. Ibid., 726.

15. Ibid., 721, 156.

16. Ibid., 651, 600.

17. Ibid., 599.

18. See, for example, Patricia Hill Collins, *Black Feminist Thought: Knowledge, Consciousness, and the Politics of Empowerment* (New York: Routledge, 1991); bell hooks, *Feminist Theory: From Margin to Center* (Boston: South End Press, 1984); Audre Lorde, *Zami, Sister Outsider, and Undersong* (New York: Quality Paperback Club, 1993); and Elizabeth Spelman, *Inessential Woman: Problems of Exclusion in Feminist Thought* (Boston: Beacon Press, 1988).

19. Kathryn T. Gines, "Sartre, Beauvoir and the Race/Gender Analogy: A Case for Black Feminist Philosophy," in *Convergences: Black Feminism and Continental Philosophy*, ed. Maris del Guadalupe Davidson, Kathryn T. Gines, and Donna-Dale I. Marcano (New York: State University of New York Press, 2010), 35–52.

20. Margaret Simons, "Richard Wright, Simone de Beauvoir, and *The Second Sex*," in *Beauvoir and* The Second Sex: *Feminism, Race, and the Origins of Existentialism* (Lanham, MD: Rowman and Littlefield, 1999), 167–84.

21. hooks, *Feminist Theory*, ix.

22. Maurice Merleau-Ponty, "Dialogue and the Perception of the Other," in *The Prose of the World*, trans. John O'Neill (Evanston, IL: Northwestern University Press, 1973), 131, 133.

23. Beauvoir, *Second Sex*, 651.

24. Ibid., 755.

25. Ibid., 262.

26. Ibid., 575.

27. Ibid., 273.

28. Ibid., 273

29. Ibid., 66.

30. Ibid., 766.

BIBLIOGRAPHY

Beauvoir, Simone de. *The Ethics of Ambiguity*. Translated by Bernard Frechtman. New York: Philosophical Library, 1948.

———. *The Second Sex*. Translated by Constance Borde and Sheila Malovany-Chevallier. New York: Vintage Books, 2010.

Collins, Patricia Hill. *Black Feminist Thought: Knowledge, Consciousness, and the Politics of Empowerment*. New York: Routledge, 1991.

Gines, Kathryn T. "Sartre, Beauvoir, and the Race/Gender Analogy: A Case for Black Feminist Philosophy." In *Convergences: Black Feminism and Continental Philosophy*, edited by Maris del Guadalupe Davidson, Kathryn T. Gines, and Donna-Dale I. Marcano, 35–52. New York: State University of New York Press, 2010.

hooks, bell. *Feminist Theory: From Margin to Center*. Boston: South End Press, 1984.

Lorde, Audre. *Zami, Sister Outsider, and Undersong*. New York: Quality Paperback Club, 1993.

Merleau-Ponty, Maurice. "Dialogue and the Perception of the Other." In *The Prose of the World*, translated by John O'Neill, 131–46. Evanston, IL: Northwestern University Press, 1973.

Simons, Margaret. "Richard Wright, Simone de Beauvoir, and *The Second Sex*." *Beauvoir and* The Second Sex: *Feminism, Race, and the Origins of Existentialism*, 167–84. Lanham, MD: Rowman and Littlefield, 1999.

Spelman, Elizabeth. *The Fruits of Sorrow: Framing Our Attention to Suffering*. Boston: Beacon Press, 1997.

———. *Inessential Woman: Problems of Exclusion in Feminist Thought*. Boston: Beacon Press, 1988.

Wittig, Monique. "One Is Not Born a Woman." *The Straight Mind*, 8–20. Boston: Beacon Press, 1992.

7 UNHAPPY SPEECH AND HEARING WELL

Contributions of Feminist Speech Act Theory to Feminist Phenomenology

BEATA STAWARSKA

THIS ESSAY IS an attempt to grapple with an experience I had upon entering the academic profession about a decade ago and teaching a large undergraduate lecture class at a state university for the first time in my career. I often felt that my speech during my lectures sounded hollow, that it lacked resonance with my audience (composed in part of students with a strong sense of white male entitlement, compounded with commitment to stereotypical gender norms, ageism, and expectations of a familiar "native" accent), despite the fact that I enunciated well and occupied an official position of authority in the classroom. I felt that what I was saying systematically failed to translate into a speech well heard and that I was perpetually at the risk of being devalued. I found that the requests tied to my authority position in the classroom, such as to be in class on time, to contribute to classroom discussion, and to not chat when class was in session, were systematically at risk of being undone by an absence of minimal receptiveness on the part of my students. The latter was sometimes expressed in a hostile and confrontational gaze, enacted bewilderment that punctuality and classroom participation were in fact expected, continued chatting, smirking, and so on. In this setting, my speech felt significantly inferior compared to my usual communicative and cognitive abilities. I often felt *unhappy* as a speaker.

A decade later, I would like to diagnose this sense of unhappiness of speech gendered feminine (and also marked by age and nationality) within an institutionalized context of public education in philosophy. Even though there is an obvious autobiographical and anecdotal dimension to such a project, I also heard similar reports about challenges to public speaking from my female junior colleagues often enough to believe that it may be used as a case study with greater applicability. I will open with Simone de Beauvoir's account of speaking as a woman from *The Second Sex* in order to underscore the risk of being silenced, a risk that is faced by women philosophers within an established tradition of gender-based power inequity within the field. I will therefore be taking the reader over fairly familiar territory in the opening section of this essay but with the goal of highlighting Beauvoir's unique perspective on gendered speech. I acknowledge that the unveiled sexism reported by Beauvoir as a strategy used by the male interlocutors in order to undermine the validity of her philosophical claims is no longer common practice. I will therefore draw on resources from contemporary feminist speech act theory in the remainder of the essay in order to salvage Beauvoir's insight that women's speech is systematically at risk of being silenced within a non-egalitarian social context, and to demonstrate that the mechanism of silencing may assume more subtle and diffuse forms than direct attempts to undermine the credibility of the woman speaker. These subtle forms of silencing occur when women's speech is systematically received or taken up in an unintended sense or is not taken up at all and therefore deprived of effectiveness or "illocutionary force." I contend that the experience of *unhappy speech* reported above can be deciphered if we attend not only to the production but also to the reception of speech in a social context, including a failure to receive. This implies that any emancipatory strategy geared toward bringing greater felicity to language in the social world must also involve the task of *hearing well*, and I will conclude with a plea to that effect.

BEAUVOIR ON SPEAKING AS A WOMAN

Simone de Beauvoir opens her introduction to *The Second Sex* by expressing a doubt about the task at hand: "I have long hesitated to write a book on woman." The subject she pursues is an irritating one, as are the many debates trailing behind it. Having surveyed some of that thorny terrain, Beauvoir changes focus from the subject matter of the question to her own implication in the process of raising the question itself: "It is significant that I pose it."[1] The significance of Beauvoir, a woman, raising the question of what a woman is has to do with this: being a woman is how she first identifies herself; it is the "basic truth" from which all the other assertions will arise.[2]

As Toril Moi has noted, it would be easy to dismiss this initial moment of self-identification as a slide from the terrain of theory to autobiography, with Beauvoir opting for a mode of confession instead of analysis.[3] This would explain why Beauvoir does not succeed in effectively theorizing sexual difference but only in accumulating "more or less positivist" information about it.[4] Yet rather than force the cited passage into an opposition between theory and autobiography, we can perhaps investigate it as *a speech act*—that is, an act of doing things with words that is mindful of the contextual setting within which this act is performed. Understanding this passage as a speech act means that in raising the question of "what is a woman," and appending that "it is significant that I pose it," Beauvoir reflects on the situation within which this question is raised (and on how this situation shapes the process of raising the question anew) as well as foregrounding her own subject position within the terrain to be covered by the question about what a woman is. As a woman, she finds herself situated in a determinate way within the gender-based distribution of power: *she* is the negative pole in relation to the positive one occupied by a *he*; *she* is the particular while *he* is the universal; *she* is a deviant while *he* is the standard. This preexistent asymmetry implies that Beauvoir raises her question from a position already inflected by gender-based power differentials, wherein to speak as a woman is to speak from a position of a non-universalizable particular, with her claims always tainted with the specificity of her sex. As she pursues this: "I used to get annoyed in abstract discussions to hear men tell me: You think such and such a thing because you're a woman."[5] The reminder of Beauvoir's subject position is here deployed by a male interlocutor as a strategy that seeks to deprive her statements of general validity. To think such and such *because* one is a woman means, within the distribution of power mapped out above, to make a hopelessly un-philosophical claim, to speak in the mode of autobiography, literature, or confession. The subject position gendered feminine is therefore perceived (by a male interlocutor) as a block on the way toward universality; it is exploited for the sake of silencing the speaker, and the foregrounding of sex can effectively choke her voice.[6]

How does a speaker gendered feminine respond to these attempts of silencing? The range of options is limited and unsatisfactory. To retort to the man, "I think it because it is true," Beauvoir writes, is to eliminate her subjectivity—to pretend that words can be detached from who is speaking and in what context. Clearly, Beauvoir does not believe that such a detachment is possible or even desirable. Furthermore, it must be possible to have one's speech be gendered without simultaneously rendering one's statements relative, partial, and insignificant. Finding oneself in a situation where one's words risk falling flat because one speaks *like* or *as* a woman is why recourse to a neutral, objective truth is an unsatisfactory one. Furthermore, the access to neutral, objective truth has already been claimed by the *he*; as Beauvoir notes, the man does not understand being man as a particularity (and that is why retorting that he thinks the contrary because he is a man is "out of the question").

Identifying the subject's gendered position in language is therefore like playing a game with loaded dice: its effect for a woman is a forced foregrounding of her sexual specificity, but for a man it is a trivial reminder of unlimited access to generality. The woman's position in language is not that of a neutral subject indicated by the shifter *I*, but of a sexed Other. As soon as she opens her mouth, her words are vulnerable to being silenced, and even before she ventures to speak, her language is inscribed as non-serious, as gendered in a way that seems to make an entry into philosophical ("abstract") speech complicated. Silencing in the present can be so effective because it belongs to a habituated history of power imbalance tied to gender.

Admittedly, Beauvoir's example of explicit references to her gender no longer serves as a common strategy of silencing a woman speaker. Yet I believe that the mechanism of silencing Beauvoir diagnoses remains in force, albeit its more usual form is a failure of uptake—that is, a failure to receive speech gendered feminine in the manner appropriate to the locutions she employs. As a result, the speech act will be emptied of requisite force to carry an effect and hence vulnerable to being silenced even in the absence of overtly sexist statements. I will describe this process by drawing on feminist speech act theory because I believe that it can offer resources to feminist phenomenology for spelling out the process of gender-based disempowerment in language in more detail. To be sure, the classic speech act theory formulated by J. L. Austin pays little heed to the social and cultural forces that shape the ways a speech act is attended to and received, but this is where feminist speech act theory and feminist phenomenology serve as a much needed corrective. They both emphasize that gendered speech is informed by its situated context, including the inherited history of power imbalance.

SILENCING AS A FAILURE OF UPTAKE

Contemporary feminist speech act theory engages Austin's groundbreaking research on linguistic performativity to spell out the political and social dimensions of speech. Austin approaches language as an utterance embedded in a conversational context and tied to the speech participants rather than a free-floating statement. He assigns language to the domain of action or doing things in the world rather than simply stating facts from a disengaged viewpoint. Austin distinguished between three interconnected layers within the speech act: *locution*, the saying of certain words with a certain meaning or content;

illocution, performing an act *in* saying these words; and *perlocution*, producing certain effects *by* saying these words. Consider an example borrowed from Jennifer Hornsby and Rae Langton.[7] A woman says to a man who is making advances toward her, "I am not interested." The locutionary act consists in the meaningful content of the woman's utterance—that is, in the fact that she does not produce mere noise but conveys meaning. The illocutionary act in this case is the woman's refusal to engage in sexual intercourse. The perlocutionary act includes the effects and consequences of the woman's utterance and, if she is successful, the withdrawal of the man. Needless to say, the speaker's utterance of the appropriate locution for an act of refusal does not necessarily yield the intended illocutionary force. A "no" uttered by a female speaker may be received by a male hearer as a titillating invitation to press on, especially in light of the practice pervasive in pornographic speech to have the "no" mean anything but. Following Hornsby and Langton, "Pornographic speech acts help create a communicative climate in which the felicity conditions for some of women's speech are not met."[8] That means that the felicity conditions for a speech act of refusal, but possibly other speech acts tied to the exercise of authority and autonomy, are not met within the communicative climate where women's speech is systematically deprived of the illocutionary force that the appropriate locutions are likely to produce when uttered by socially dominant speakers. Hornsby and Langton term the process that makes certain speech acts effectively unspeakable for women "illocutionary disablement" or "silencing." The silencing occurs at the illocutionary level, meaning that even though the speaker effectively produces an articulate and intelligible utterance indicating refusal, still her speech fails as illocution—that is, it fails to enact the force needed to turn her utterance into an effective speech *act* (of refusal in this case). Therefore this infelicity befalling the otherwise appropriate and audible speech cannot be accounted for in terms of the subjective utterance alone; the failure is a socially modulated fact.

Let me flesh out this point by expanding upon Austin's classical distinctions. Austin distinguishes between different kinds of infelicity effecting conventional speech acts. The infelicity can effect, first, the conventional procedure (say, a marriage ceremony), and, second, the persons and circumstances involved (say, the minister, and the couple), who must in a given case be deemed appropriate for the invocation of the particular procedure. For example, the words uttered by the couple during the ceremony must include the conventional "I do." Furthermore, the couple must be deemed appropriate for the invocation of the marriage procedure based not only on prior marital status (as acknowledged by Austin) but also on gender and sexuality. For example, only recently have same-sex couples been granted marriage equality in the entire United States and their "I do" endowed with the illocutionary force of a mutually binding speech act. The third and fourth infelicities affecting speech acts have to do with the procedure needing to be executed by all participants correctly and completely.

For example, the utterance "I divorce you" said by a Christian does not enact an existing procedure, and therefore it fails. However, Austin notes, it would be effective if uttered by a Mohammedan.[9] Austin refers here to the divorce procedure under Islamic law, which consists in the *Talak* invocation (or some equivalent thereof, with the implied meaning of "divorced"). What Austin fails to notice is that the *Talak* procedure is traditionally enacted by men and becomes ineffective when uttered by women (a woman can reserve in her marriage contract the right to divorce, but in practice few women do).[10] The existence of a conventional procedure does not therefore guarantee its general accessibility. A woman may utter the right words and yet her utterance be deprived of illocutionary force. In cases of both an infelicitous refusal and divorce, the judgment regarding appropriateness ties to the pervasive social norms relative to gender in male-dominated societies rather than to determinate rules and conventions. It is the gender-based power inequity that accounts for the infelicity of some of women's speech acts, and not, say, a legal standing that can in principle be reversed—as in the case of marriage, where a previously married person can become appropriate for the invocation of marriage vows to a new partner by going through a divorce, and so a previously infelicitous act can meet felicity conditions.

In the case of women's disempowered speech, there is no readily available legal or other procedure that would make the relevant speech act felicitous. The perceived inappropriateness of the person for the invocation of the speech act here is largely based on unwritten social mores. Yet these social mores effectively determine who has the power and authority to refuse unwanted sex or terminate an unwanted marriage, among the many things we do with words. Furthermore, a minimum of power and authority is required for a felicitous enactment of most speech acts (other than acts of deprecating or deriding oneself), and if femininity is systematically entwined with powerlessness, then women's speech is routinely at risk of failure. As Miriam Meyerhoff notes, expanding on Lakoff's and Langton's views, "You have to be a serious person with your own views to satisfy the felicity conditions for most speech acts, and if women are socially and discursively constructed in roles that preclude having serious views, then as far as some speech acts go, their attempts to act are silenced."[11]

It follows that the existing status quo directly affects the felicity of women's speech. Unwritten habitual practices relative to gender and power, and not just the official and legal status, may impact the perceived appropriateness of persons in speech. Therefore a speech act theory that is sensitive to the real world of speech acts needs to transcend a procedural focus in order to include these social conditions of illocutionary success and failure, and to shed the illusion of an unmarked universal speaking subject to include gender as well as class, race, nationality, and ability. Socially inclusive analyses of speech acts have been developed by scholars such as Kristie Dotson, who develops an epistemology of testimony in conjunction with feminist speech act theory to underscore speaker dependency upon audiences and to identify correlated practices by which members of oppressed groups are silenced on account of their gender and race. Dotson focuses especially on the failures of audiences to communicatively reciprocate in linguistic exchanges by means of what she terms "testimonial quieting" (an audience fails to identify a speaker as a knower) and "testimonial smothering" (speaker truncates her testimony to match the audience's limited testimonial competence). In this essay I focus on the audience failure to identify a speaker as an authority on account of gender, age, and nationality. My analysis thus shares Dotson's (and Hornsby's) central emphasis on communicative reciprocity in linguistic exchanges; I develop the latter by highlighting the central role played by audience uptake within Austin's own speech act theory.

AUSTIN REVISITED: UPTAKE AS A FELICITY CONDITION FOR SPEECH ACTS

In the lectures, Austin continually returns to one additional infelicity, although, surprisingly, he does not include it in his formal list.[12] It is "a sort of infelicity of misunderstanding"—or uptake, which complicates the distinction between the illocutionary and the perlocutionary dimensions of speech and thus further illuminates the cases of silencing referred to here.[13] For example, my speech act of ordering someone to do something is vulnerable to the infelicity of misunderstanding if it has not been heard or taken up by the addressee as an order. Austin notes that an order to, for example, go and pick up wood on a desert island will be disregarded if the speaker does not have sufficient authority to pass orders, unlike a captain on a ship, who genuinely has authority.[14] Needless to say, speakers may have conventionally recognizable authority and yet be perceived as inadequate leaders, as discussed above. Austin seems to assume that the officially and legally specified status (for example, captain versus the purser, unmarried versus married person) suffices to regulate success in speech. Still, his emphasis on hearer dependency can be extended to cover cases where infelicity is tied to gender-based power inequity, regardless of official titles and status. Austin notes, "It is always possible, for example, to try to thank or inform somebody yet in different ways fail, because he doesn't listen, or takes it as ironical, or wasn't responsible for whatever it was, and so on. This distinction will arise, as over any act, over locutionary acts too; but failures here will not be unhappiness as there, but rather failures to get the words out, to express ourselves clearly, etc."[15]

Here Austin distinguishes between locutionary and illocutionary failure, a failure at the level of the physical act itself—for example, speaking in sotto voce—and an illocutionary failure located at the level of the speech act properly so called.[16] The former infelicity seems bound to the utterance narrowly construed as the sound sequence issuing from the speaker's mouth, while the latter is a socially modulated act, constituted by the speaker's vocal productions *and* the hearer's uptake of these productions in a certain sense. According to Austin, "Unless a certain effect is achieved, the illocutionary act will not have been happily, successfully performed. This is not to say that the illocutionary act is the achieving of a certain effect. I cannot be said to have warned an audience unless it hears what I say and takes what I say in a certain sense. An effect must be achieved on the audience if the illocutionary act is to be carried out. . . . The performance of an illocutionary act involves the securing of *uptake*."[17]

This passage is intriguing on multiple counts. First, Austin complicates the distinction he is keen to preserve elsewhere between the speech act and its effect, or the illocution and the perlocution.[18] The speaker is not in control of the effects of her speech on others, and the former cannot be simply derived from the latter. Still, the felicity of the speech event is contingent on an intrinsic interrelation between the two, insofar as the effect of securing uptake helps to convert an *attempted* speech act into an effectively *achieved* one. We find here an interesting case of retroactive constitution of the force of the utterance by the audience who must receive it in a certain sense for the utterance to take effect. This is not a (solely) subjective constitution of meaning, but a socially modulated one. The hearer's uptake is both the effect of what is being said *and* the condition of the saying acquiring the force of a speech act. The accomplishment of the speech act is thus contingent not only on the speaker's actions but also on the hearer's participatory involvement in the speech event and on actively attending to what the speaker is up to. Receiving speech in an appropriate way is as much a speech-related *act* as producing it is.

The infelicity resulting from insufficient uptake impacts most illocutionary acts. As Hornsby and Langton put it, reciprocity provides a background condition of speech as a whole. In their words:

> Language use . . . relies on a mutual capacity for uptake, which involves a minimal receptiveness on the part of language users in the role of hearers. This minimal receptiveness does not mean that a hearer will agree, or is even capable of agreeing, with what a speaker is saying; but it does mean that a hearer has a capacity to grasp what communicative act a speaker might be intending to perform. When reciprocity is present, the speaker's utterance works as she means it to. Its working so appears to depend on nothing more than speaker and hearer being parties of a normal linguistic exchange, in which a speaker's attempt to communicate is successful. A speaker tries to do an illocutionary thing; a hearer recognizing that the speaker is trying to do that thing is then sufficient for the speaker to actually do it.[19]

To extend Hornsby and Langton's insightful analysis further, a speech act includes not only the three dimensions previously discussed (locution, illocution, perlocution) but also an interlocutionary one, co-involving the speaker and the hearer in similar measure. Austin may not have recognized the importance of interlocution, because his conception of illocution is narrowly tied to the *issuing* of utterance, at partial neglect of the receiving end. This focus on the active doing explains why the infelicities included on the master list all have to do with the production and not the reception of the utterance. It also explains why the infelicity of misunderstanding or misrecognition does not get included in the master list despite being taken up—excuse the pun—over and over during the lectures. Austin states overtly that his primary interest lies in illocution or action, separated off from perlocution.[20] However, as we have seen, a speech act is intrinsically interconnected with its effect on the hearer, and the infelicity relative to this effect shapes the force of the speech act itself. If so, then illocution and perlocution are more intimately interwoven than the initial classification suggests.[21] Therefore, Austin's formal distinction between the speaker and the hearer domains, between the force and the effect of speech, turns out to be more permeable as well. The two are linked via interlocution, which may need but not always be formally manifest within the utterance, since I do not always (need to) employ a direct form of address to nonetheless speak *to you*. You, the listener, partake in the success or failure of my efforts. My speech act exists in the flight from my mouth to your ear, and if unheard or unheeded, it drops dead somewhere in between. Speech is oriented to the addressee even when it does not explicitly *say it*, so the search for formal criteria of felicity, and for formal distinctions between meaning, force, and effect, is only surface based. These formalisms are bound to miss the lived experience of unhappiness in speech unheard or unheeded despite meeting all the procedural criteria of success.

This is where feminist phenomenology, as developed by Beauvoir, is useful: it serves as a reminder that a speech act is not a purely linguistic matter but is shaped by the inherited history of social and cultural forces that affect the ways the speech act is attended to and received. The granting or the withdrawal of uptake—which, according to the reading of Austin offered above, belongs to the list of necessary conditions of felicity in speech—remains undecipherable outside of the situated context within which these acts unfold. A philosophical account of speech acts must therefore pay heed to the received, gender-based distribution of power within the social world if it is to remain concrete, and if it is to make sense of its own basic categories, such as the illocutionary force of an utterance. The latter is not generated ex nihilo in the present moment by using the appropriate formula but depends on the reception and recognition of the act for it to work its magic; furthermore, the efficacy of this magic is itself shaped by the inherited standards of gender norms and views related to what is appropriate for each gender to do with words. Any individual utterance is therefore inscribed within a larger context than its immediate one, and historically weighed.

CONCLUDING REMARKS

I opened this essay with an autobiographical example of hollowed speech from the classroom. Using the terms from speech act theory, this example can be deciphered as *diffuse* illocutionary disablement, or silencing, to indicate a pervasive stance of un-receptiveness toward a female speaker deploying an authority position in a public space—as distinguished from the more focused illocutionary disablement of specific speech acts, as in the "no" or *Talak* illocutions previously discussed. Both the diffuse and the focused instances of illocutionary disablement can be described as unhappy speech using the categories of felicity from Austin if one agrees that the reception and recognition of a speech act contribute to its illocutionary success. Furthermore, if we accept Beauvoir's claim that the traditional construals of femininity and epistemic authority are at odds with each other within a patriarchal society, where women are cast as the dependent Other of men, then not only may women's speech contain elements indicative of lesser power, but also, importantly, it may systematically fail to find the minimal receptiveness necessary for speech to carry force. Whether it is because women are raised to speak in sotto voce or because our speech goes unheeded despite being audible, the felicity of women's speech is systematically endangered in a non-receptive communicative climate.

It follows that an emancipatory strategy geared at rectifying the infelicity of misrecognition in language must include both the audience and the speaker. The infelicity of misrecognition is a double failure, since it is in part an infelicity of the *hearing act*, a failure to hear and heed the speaker in the right way, despite the felicity conditions relative to the production of the speech act being met. This failure may not register phenomenologically as a loss on the hearer's part, and it would require a lot of good faith to recognize one's own *mishearing* as a shortcoming to be rectified. However, that is exactly what the above analysis implies: felicitous speech is speech well heard. It follows that the feminist quest for women's own voice has as an indissociable counterpart a quest and cultivation of an ear that is attentive to the other. This cultivation of attentive listening shares the illocutionary force of a speech act well received, and it can be empowering at the receiving end too. I hear you, I heed you, because I am responsible for our shared happiness.[22]

BEATA STAWARSKA is Professor of Philosophy at the University of Oregon. She is author of *Saussure's Philosophy of Language as Phenomenology* (Oxford University Press, 2015) and *Between You and I: Dialogical Phenomenology* (Ohio University Press, 2009).

NOTES

1. Simone de Beauvoir, *The Second Sex*. Translated by Constance Borde and Sheila Malovany-Chevallier. (New York: Random House Digital, 2012), 5.
2. Ibid.
3. Toril Moi, *Sex, Gender, and the Body: The Student Edition of* What Is a Woman? (Oxford: Oxford University Press, 2005), 191.
4. Ibid.
5. Beauvoir, *Second Sex*, 5.
6. Moi, *Sex, Gender, and the Body*, 215.
7. See Jennifer Hornsby and Rae Langton, "Free Speech and Illocution," *Legal Theory* 4, no. 1 (1998).
8. Ibid., 27.
9. John Langshaw Austin, *How to Do Things with Words* (Oxford: Oxford University Press, 1975), 27.
10. See Miriam Meyerhoff, "Doing and Saying: Some Words on Women's Silence," in *Language and Woman's Place: Text and Commentaries*, by Robin Lakoff, ed. Mary Bucholtz (Oxford: Oxford University Press, 2004), 214.

11. Ibid., 213.

12. I do not discuss the two last infelicities of persons having certain thoughts and feelings, and so conducting themselves (e.g., being sincere in making a promise), as they have no direct bearing on this discussion.

13. Austin, *How to Do Things with Words*, 22.

14. Ibid., 28.

15. Ibid., 106.

16. Ibid., 139.

17. Ibid., 116–17, 139.

18. For an example, see ibid., 118.

19. Hornsby and Langton, "Free Speech and Illocution," 25.

20. Austin, *How to Do Things with Words*, 103.

21. While I cannot fully develop this point within the limits of this essay, the general focus in Austin's lectures on performativity is on the procedural aspect of speech acts, which could in principle be formalized. The commitment to formal criteria animates Austin's search for explicit performatives whose grammatical form (such as first-person singular, present indicative) would help to disambiguate them from constatatives or descriptive statements (to be cast in the third-person singular or plural indicative). As every student of speech act theory knows, this quest for formal criteria ultimately fails, and language qua speech turns out to be performative through and through, with even the most mundane declarative statements such as "The cat is on the mat" still doing things with words. The explicit failure of Austin's project (to identify explicit performatives) is thus a measure of its success, since the scope of performativity turns out to be greater than initially assumed, expanding to language as a whole. I would like to suggest that a similar productive failure affects Austin's formal distinction between illocution and perlocution.

22. Elsewhere I make a case for a performativity of active listening as a potential emancipatory strategy that can reverse the historically sedimented habitus of silencing the members of socially oppressed groups. See Beata Stawarska, "Linguistic Encounters: The Performativity of Active Listening," in *Body/Self/Other: The Phenomenology of Social Encounters*, ed. Luna Dolezal and Danielle Petherbridge (New York: State University of New York Press, forthcoming).

BIBLIOGRAPHY

Austin, John Langshaw. *How to Do Things with Words*. 1955. Oxford: Oxford University Press, 1975.

Beauvoir, Simone de. *The Second Sex*. Translated by Constance Borde and Sheila Malovany-Chevallier. New York: Random House Digital, 2012.

Dotson, Kristie. "Tracking Epistemic Violence, Tracking Practices of Silencing." *Hypatia* 26, no. 2 (2011): 236–57.

Hornsby, Jennifer, and Rae Langton. "Free Speech and Illocution." *Legal Theory* 4, no. 1 (1998): 21–37.

Meyerhoff, Miriam. "Doing and Saying. Some Words on Women's Silence." In *Language and Woman's Place: Text and Commentaries*, by Robin Lakoff. Edited by Mary Bucholtz, 209–215. Oxford: Oxford University Press, 2004.

Moi, Toril. *Sex, Gender, and the Body: The Student Edition of* What Is a Woman? Oxford: Oxford University Press, 2005.

Stawarska, Beata. "Linguistic Encounters: The Performativity of Active Listening." In *Body/Self/Other: The Phenomenology of Social Encounters*, edited by Luna Dolezal and Danielle Petherbridge. New York: State University of New York Press, forthcoming.

PART 3
THE ONTOLOGICAL FUTURE

8 ADVENTURES IN THE HYPERDIALECTIC

EVA-MARIA SIMMS

IN AN EARLY feminist phenomenological paper, Jeffner Allen interpreted Maurice Merleau-Ponty's "hyperdialectic" or "good dialectic" through the I–other, men–women opposition and criticized Merleau-Ponty for his androcentric, sexist assumptions of a gender-neutral body as the foundation for his ontology.[1] Since then phenomenological feminists have stayed away from Merleau-Ponty's concept of the hyperdialectic, even though Allen, at the end of her paper, points out possibilities for a new beginning for the "good dialectic" in feminist thinking.

Despite a consistent critique of Merleau-Ponty's androcentrism, feminist thinkers have found his philosophy to be productive because it provides conceptual access to the field of human experience, the situatedness of gendered life and oppression, and the varied manifestations of human embodiment and material culture.[2] Most of the Merleau-Pontean concepts borrowed by feminists, however, come from *Phenomenology of Perception*, a philosophy that Merleau-Ponty himself critiqued in his later work for being too much tied to the perspective of human perception and consciousness. His turn toward ontology and concepts like "chiasm," "flesh," and "hyperdialectic" were attempts to overcome the limitations of a philosophy of consciousness and to engage thought with "a whole architecture, a whole complex of phenomena 'in tiers,' a whole series of 'levels of being.'"[3] This raises a number of questions: If Merleau-Ponty's process of philosophical inquiry moved into ontological territory because *it had to* in order to stay true to itself, what happens to feminist phenomenology beyond *Phenomenology of Perception*? Can we follow Merleau-Ponty into a philosophy that complicates and multiplies existential structures and erases

141

the very separation between perceiver and perceived, body and world, self and other in its ontological move? Can ontology be a feminist project?

In this essay I will move through some of Merleau-Ponty's ontological "wild region," as Allen calls it, and embark upon the adventure of tracking the development of his ontological turn through the concept of the hyperdialectic.[4] I will argue that from early on Merleau-Ponty had a conflicted and ambivalent relationship with the Hegelian dialectic and its Marxist manifestations, particularly its tendency to assume an abstract "high-altitude thinking" that did not take into account the ontological entanglement of the embodied mind with the stream of history. The hyperdialectic as a method developed in tandem with Merleau-Ponty's evolving understanding of gestalt, structure, or *forme* and the transformational rules that govern wholes, which he encountered in his work with gestalt psychology, Claude Levi-Straus's structuralism, and Ferdinand de Saussure's linguistics. The method of the hyperdialectic, which Merleau-Ponty developed only in outline, suggests a way for investigating complex systems where changes in individual elements affect the web as a whole—and vice versa. I intend to bring together the diverse hyperdialectic rules that Merleau-Ponty gathered from his structuralist readings (such as figure/ground, pivot/field, whole/difference, being/non-being, immanence/transcendence, etc.), which were filtered through his readings of Edmund Husserl and Martin Heidegger. At the end I hope to be in a better position to address the question: can ontology be productive for feminism?

DIALECTIC

Merleau-Ponty encountered and applied dialectical thinking throughout his writing life but did not explicitly confront dialectical thought until the opening chapters of *The Visible and the Invisible*, as Jacques Taminiaux has pointed out.[5] Merleau-Ponty's thinking developed in conversation with Alexandre Kojève's lectures on Hegel's dialectic and the dialectical materialism of Marxism, which Merleau-Ponty encountered in his political work with Jean-Paul Sartre. In *The Structure of Behavior*, Merleau-Ponty investigated the dialectical relationship between an organism and its milieu and introduced the notion of gestalt as a dialectical confrontation between perceiving organism and world. In *Phenomenology of Perception*, existence and being-in-the-world became the framework for dialectical thought, but little was said about the philosophical foundations of dialectics itself. Even in the explicitly political writings that deal with Marxism and Hegelianism, "it is striking to verify," says Taminiaux, "just how little these writings bother to translate themselves into the texts of Hegel or Marx, and how zealously, instead, they scurry to translate these texts into the terms of *The Structure of Behavior* or *Phenomenology of Perception*."[6] Taminiaux summarizes Merleau-Ponty's relationship with dialectics in this way: "Dialectical thinking is not thematized as such, but hailed in passing insofar as Merleau-Ponty believes an existential tenor can be recognized in it, and cast aside insofar as it is unfaithful to the conditions of Being-in-the-world."[7]

In *The Visible and the Invisible*, however, Merleau-Ponty does thematize dialectics and stops hailing it as a friendly fellow traveler. He launches a full-scale attack on Sartre and on Hegelian dialectics. He calls Sartre's thinking "a totalizing thought, a high-altitude thought" (*pensée de survol*), because it removes itself from the thickness of being and surveys it as if from above.[8] The same challenge is made against the Hegelian dialectic: it is an "abstract dichotomy" that covers over "a swarm of relations with double meaning," whose "complex totality" is the "actual truth" that underlies the simplifications of the dialectic.[9] The dialectician falls into "the trap of the dialectic" and is haunted by an "evil genius": Hegel recognizes the powerful transformational movement within systems but turns it into an explicative principle that casts "a spell over the world" and makes it appear in a limited and dualistic way.[10] This abstract, high-altitude, bad dialectic "imposes an external law and framework upon the content and restores for its own uses the pre-dialectical thought."[11] The bad dialectic loses touch with the "concrete constellation" of the world and fails philosophy in three significant ways:[12]

1. It functions as an autonomous thought system that becomes a methodological formalism, which is ultimately unresponsive to the complexity of phenomena.
2. It remains unreflective of its own structure as a product of human consciousness and the limitations this imposes.
3. It maintains the illusion that it can completely capture being in its idealized verbal statements.

What was it in Merleau-Ponty's thought that caused first the hailing and then the strong attack against the dialectic? In this essay I will show that the reckoning with Sartre and Hegel can be understood through the evolution of Merleau-Ponty's understanding of gestalt principles and the attempt in his late writings to formulate a post-structuralist structuralism. I have found that reading Merleau-Ponty as a "neo-structuralist" or "neo-gestaltist" clarifies many of the more obscure terms and concepts in his mature work, and it illuminates what Merleau-Ponty had in mind when he called for the "good dialectic," the hyperdialectic.

WHAT IS A GESTALT?

It can be argued that Merleau-Ponty is the first philosopher to truly grasp the importance of the gestalt principle for Western philosophy. The thread of the concept of gestalt/structure/form weaves through his writing from beginning to end, but it has a different appearance and function at different periods in his philosophy.

In *The Structure of Behavior*, structure and form allowed Merleau-Ponty to articulate a new dimension or order that "lies on this side of the split into pure nature and pure consciousness, pure externality and pure internality."[13] In his first definition of the term "gestalt" (translated into French as *forme*), form/gestalt is defined as "a total process" and a system that is more than the sum of its parts: "systems are defined as transposable wholes."[14] Any change in one part of the system affects the whole, and the total form/gestalt can maintain its identity in change when the relationship between parts remains the same.

After working through the findings of the gestalt psychologists and finding them limited and reductionist in their application of gestalt principles to higher forms of consciousness, Merleau-Ponty nevertheless came to the conclusion that the notion of gestalt captures most profoundly "the joining of an idea and an existence which are indiscernible, the contingent arrangement by which materials begin to have meaning in our presence, intelligibility in its nascent state."[15] For him, the "joining of an idea and an existence which are indiscernible" delineates a place for philosophy on this side of empiricism and intellectualism: existence and the material world are already ideal and meaningful structures; ideas and the products of consciousness are already material and existential structures.

In *Phenomenology of Perception*, the gestalt principle of figure/ground is "the very definition of the phenomenon of perception, that without which a phenomenon cannot be said to be perception."[16] It becomes a major theme of reflection and a way of examining the relationship between the perceiver and the larger field of the perceived world. Gestalt designates the "physiognomy" or the "style" of appearances and the complex web of other things that form the ground of any entity that comes to attention in consciousness. Things, for Merleau-Ponty, are "field-beings"—that is, entities that have no clear boundary in perception but hidden profiles and concealed relationships to other things and the world as a whole. They are figures on a transcendental ground. Color perception, for example, becomes possible because each color exists as a field that transcends what the eye sees: there are the wooly reds of dresses, the glossy reds of billiard balls, the leafy reds of autumn trees, and the dusky reds of sunsets; they appear as red only in relation to adjacent fields of green, yellow, or blue. The wholeness or totality of the gestalt and the impact of parts upon one another becomes the model for an immanent, existential transcendence into which the perceiving, embodied subject is inserted.

According to Merleau-Ponty's own analysis, however, one of the philosophical shortcomings of *Phenomenology of Perception* was that "the tacit cogito is impossible" because it maintained the perspective of the subjective perceiver, a "mythology of a self-consciousness to which the word 'consciousness' would refer."[17] In reality experience is not "an absolute flux of singular *Erlebnisse*; there are fields and a field of fields, with a style and a typicality," and Merleau-Ponty challenged himself to "describe the existentials that make up the armature of the transcendental field—and which are always a relation between the agent (I can) and the sensorial or ideal field."[18]

In *The Visible and the Invisible*, Merleau-Ponty attempted to follow through with this project, and we have a shift in terms of the gestalt principle. He stepped away from the perspective of the part, which sees the world arranged around it in a changing tableau—the field of consciousness—as we find it in *Phenomenology of Perception*. His thinking now aims for the relationship between the field of perception and the "field of fields," which is the whole sensorial and ideal field, which he sometimes calls "world," sometimes "totality," and sometimes "Being." Simple causality and a straightforward, progressive dialectic of thesis, antithesis, and synthesis cannot describe the complicated operations of complex systems.

FROM DIALECTIC TO HYPERDIALECTIC: A GESTALT METHOD

In order to think about the nature of field-beings and their relation to Being, Merleau-Ponty invented the hyperdialectic. The hyperdialectic is a method that keeps in view and satisfies the complexities of gestalts/structures and their transformations. If we imagine Being as the whole, and the existing beings as the interrelated parts, Merleau-Ponty's hyperdialectic, and his resistance against the dialectic, becomes clear:

> Being is not made up out of idealizations or of things said, as the old logic believed, but of *bound wholes* where signification never is except in tendency, where the inertia of the content never permits the defining of one term as positive, another term as negative, and still less a third term as absolute suppression of the negative itself.[19]

Being is made up out of bound wholes. Merleau-Ponty's hyperdialectic is an attempt to conceive of a set of principles that describes the complexity and transcendence of Being as the constellation of bound wholes. It manifests itself in the concrete presence of people, things, and events as they morph in time. This presence, however, is permeated with absence. The unconcealed is surrounded by the concealed. Things show some of their profiles but withhold others. Human perspectives on the world are always partial, and the greatest irony for the philosopher is that we humans are "lacunary" and not transparent to ourselves: we are transcendent beings and much of ourselves is concealed even from ourselves, and that is true for every other human being we encounter. Transcendence is one of the qualities of every gestalt: each part is unique and related to every other part and to the gestalt as a whole, but no two relationships between parts and between parts and the whole are the same. The whole transcends the parts, but the parts are also transcendent to one another. Inserted into Being, humans can never not be a part of it and cannot surpass it in thought.

In order to describe the workings of the complex intersections between perceptual presences and what surrounds them as their horizon of ideality, Merleau-Ponty borrowed the German term *"es west"* and Heidegger's description of the "worlding" of an old high school building from the *Einführung in die Metaphysik*.[20] When Merleau-Ponty, in *The Visible and the Invisible*, renounces the idealist phenomenology of consciousness and essences, where essences are added as a "transversal dimension" to a material world of "spatio-temporal atoms," a new complex, structural, dynamic understanding of Being emerges. Being is a morphological event (*morphé* in Greek means form or structure), "a whole architecture, a whole complex of phenomena 'in tiers,' a whole series of 'levels of being,'" that is entangled and active as the invisible field with every visible and tangible manifestation.[21] Like Heidegger's old high school building, every thing, every body, every visible is related to everything else in a complex pattern of nearness and distance, impact and quiescence, presence and absence. In order to make this complex invisibility of the visible thinkable, Merleau-Ponty has to push his language to its limits. He describes what it is like being immersed in Being:

> Being no longer being before me, but surrounding me and in a sense traversing me, and my vision of being not forming itself from elsewhere, but from the midst of Being—the alleged facts, the spatio-temporal individuals, are from the first mounted on the axes, the pivots, the dimensions, the generality of my body, and the ideas are therefore already encrusted in its joints. There

is no emplacement of space and time that would not be a variant of the others, as they are of it; there is no individual that would not be the representative of a species or of a family of beings, would not have, would not be a certain style, a certain manner of managing the domain of space and time over which it has competency, of pronouncing, of articulating that domain, of radiating about a wholly virtual center—in short a certain manner of being, in the active sense, a certain *Wesen*, in the sense that, says Heidegger, this word has when it is used as a verb.[22]

When Being is no longer described as being before me, as high-altitude thinking does, but from the midst of its forms and traversed by it and entangled with other beings, philosophy has to begin anew. It becomes a continual interrogation of Being and of the thinker as a being within Being. It aims for the subject *x*, the totality of Being, which is ultimately unreachable.

But how should the philosopher proceed? Do we end up with a useless metaphysics of Being where every entity, every act is dissolved in the ultimate oneness of the whole? And here Merleau-Ponty turned again to the gestalt laws. If we keep the hyperdialectic relationship of figure to ground, of part to whole, and of the thing with its transcendental field in mind, we can begin to understand the philosophical ground that necessitated the language of the intertwining, the chiasm, the flesh, but we can also look for the rules, laws, and principles that govern complex systems of being. Being is not an unformed mass, a swirling of nothingness, but it manifests in things. Things have a gestalt, a way of appearing, a style, a morphology. They "crystallize" out of the flow of being and reveal themselves to our perspective, but never completely: "and thereby we can see how the world comes about."[23] This coming about of the world "takes form under the domination of certain structural laws," and interrogation discerns the where, when, and how of these astonishing "articulations in the world":[24] this was the lesson Merleau-Ponty learned from Saussure's structural linguistics.[25] But what are these structural laws that Merleau-Ponty has in mind? Let us examine his hyperdialectic analysis of a red dress.

THE RED DRESS: A HYPERDIALECTIC ANALYSIS

Merleau-Ponty begins the chapter "The Intertwining—The Chiasm" with a riff on the redness of a red dress in order to push the phenomenology of color to its limits.[26] The appearance of red follows structural laws: Red is tied to the configuration or texture of the fabric. It is not just a physiological response of the eye or a quale in the mind, but an existential event, tied to the "there is" of the red dress and the "there is" of the perceiving body.

1. Red exists in a shifting web of relations, depending on the colors, textures, and lights around it. They are the transcendent field or ground on which red appears as red.
2. Red forms a constellation with other colors. The red dress as a gestalt is the "pivot" or "central hinge" around which a system is distributed and which is open to its transcendental field. However, despite this openness, it is "a bound and not a free possibility."[27]
3. Red changes in relation to this constellation: "It is a certain node in the woof of the simultaneous and the successive."[28] Small changes in other, even distant parts of the field (e.g., the street lights come on at dusk), can impact the color of the red dress.
4. Red relates to other colored appearances because it is differentiated from them—that is, it is part of the diacritical structure of the visible: "We have to pass from the thing (spatial or temporal) as identity, to the thing (spatial or temporal) as difference."[29] Merleau-Ponty uses the example of the pairs of eyes or ears to show the productivity of difference: "Consider the two, the pair, this is not two acts, two syntheses, it is a fragmentation of being, it is a possibility for separation (two eyes, two ears: the possibility for discrimination, for the use of the diacritical), it is the advent of difference (on the ground of resemblance therefore, on the ground of the *omou en panta*)" ("all things are together," Anaxagoras).[30] "What do I bring to the problem of the same and the other? This: that the same be the other than the other, and identity difference of difference—this 1) does not realize a surpassing, a dialectic in the Hegelian sense; 2) is realized on the spot, by encroachment, thickness, spatiality—."[31] Difference, divergence, dehiscence, *écart*: all terms describe a divergent, diacritical positionality within a web of gestalt relationships.
5. Red is a manifestation in the total field of the visible that contains what is not yet or never can be seen: "The red dress a fortiori holds with all its fibers onto the fabric of the visible and thereby onto a fabric of invisible being."

Clearly, Merleau-Ponty recapitulates here not only the lessons learned from gestalt psychology and structural linguistics but also the modifications and innovations that his own studies required. The red dress pushes him to the limits of our familiar concepts. Colors and things are no longer discrete beings, but "ephemeral modulations of this world."[32] His language is forced to invent terms that can capture the mysterious appearance of being without dissolving everything into the all: "Between the alleged colors and visibles, we would find anew the tissue that lines them, sustains them, nourishes them, and which for its part is not a thing, but a possibility, a latency, and a flesh of things."[33] The "flesh of things," finally, is the web of relationships of visible things and what exists invisibly between them but would not be without them. The flesh, in other words, is a poetic term for gestalt and for the whole that binds and separates all things, that is never congruent with things, and that, from the perspective of the parts, is always concealed and only a possibility on the horizon. But the flesh is also a term for the concreteness of the parts, the existential density that allows them to appear and relate to each other, that which is between them.

The radicalness of Merleau-Ponty's gestalt concept is that he places himself (and philosophy) into the middle of gestalt dynamics, where we are a limited, interrelated part of the constellation and have only a dim intuition of the whole. Being, as we saw before, is "the field of fields," the ultimate, and within its purview we interrogate the world that is coexistent with us. Perceptual faith can be understood as the fundamental, prereflective sense that we are of Being: we are part of the whole and one of its styles of manifestation.

TRYING IT OUT: HYPERDIALECTIC AND GENDER

In *The Visible and the Invisible*, gestalt principles were one of the tools Merleau-Ponty used to think Being. The principles of the hyperdialectic reminded him to keep the complex web of relations between beings and their relation to the whole in mind. The structural linguistic method of looking for difference and placement in the diacritical structure of wholes provided a place for individuality, rupture, and non-coincidence. It also allowed Merleau-Ponty to think Being in a dynamic, structural, temporal, morphological way: not as a fully disclosed presence, but as something that is always already here and yet always on the way. Taken in this sense, the hyperdialectic, the "good dialectic," fulfills what the Greek word "*dia-legein*" promises: to speak about things and to welcome differences.

But what are the implications of Merleau-Ponty's ontology for feminism? It goes beyond the framework of this essay to answer this question in depth, but I will make a small attempt to structure the inquiry. Following the hyperdialectic laws from the analysis of the red dress, we can extrapolate what this might mean for gender and feminism.

> 1. My gender is tied to the complex configuration of places, people, and events and exists as a semiotic, meaning-making activity in the context of my culture's history. It is an existential event, tied to the "there is" of my female body (its situatedness), but also to the perceptions, discourses, and practices of others. It is, in a certain sense, *not* "mine," and my own awareness and knowledge of it is latent and lacunary.

2. My gender exists in a shifting web of relations and depends on its transcendent field. Sometimes the near impingement of the explicitly sexual dimensions of the field (through the male gaze or cultural imperatives of dress or manner) forces the female person to assume the female form; other times sexual identity recedes into the background and does not matter—for example, when a woman simply enjoys the texture of her clothes or the pleasure of fitting her body into a climbing wall. However, the field constellation can change quickly, and the same activity assumes an explicit gendered dimension—for example, when the female climber competes with men and discovers that her "female-bodied" climbing style is different but as (or more) successful as her male counterparts.[34]
3. As a "pivot" in a field, I can imagine my gender as a focal node in a network, connected to and influenced by a relational system of interconnected elements that are distributed in proximity or distance from the pivot. From an ontological perspective, my gender is a bound and not a free possibility, which means that it depends on the other elements in its relational field. Being gendered is neither my fixed destiny nor my completely free choice, because much of what determines my gender experience is held by the other elements in the constellational field.
4. My gender is "a certain node in the woof of the simultaneous and the successive."[35] It has a spatial and a temporal dimension. Small changes in the field can impact and change the system as a whole. These are the moments of sudden change and surprise in the transcendent field, which we did not see coming.
5. My gender relates to other gendered appearances because it is differentiated from them—in other words, it is part of the diacritical structure of the visible: "We have to pass from the thing (spatial or temporal) as identity, to the thing (spatial or temporal) as difference."[36] Difference is possible not because of separation and opposition, but because of relatedness. In a system difference is essential because no two elements occupy the same place, and it is their diacritical variation, their dehiscence and divergence that allows the whole to be. "What do I bring to the problem of the same and the other? This: that the same be the other than the other, and identity difference of difference."[37] Merleau-Ponty invites us to conceive of differences without contradictions.
6. The idea of a transcendent system allows for openness because there are elements that are not, or not yet, present. There is hope in that the future of my position in the whole can be otherwise than what it is now.

At the end of her critique of Merleau-Ponty's androcentrism, Jeffner Allen tried to think about the promise of the "good dialectic" of the flesh ontology beyond sexism and as the possibility for a new beginning and a possible reality "even though that reality is not wholly achieved at present."[38] She described the hyperdialectic as an "integrative thinking" that points to "open ended wholes" and the possibility for transforming the I—other dualism, which characterizes gender politics, into a genuine "polymorphism":

> There is no longer the interlocked twosome of complementary "neutrality," where one term, women, is always "lacking" unless its contrary, men, is also present. In the wholeness of integrity, no element exists in duplicity, that is in the contradictory doubleness that comes from women being divided against our "self." Movement on the edge of being enables the discovery of a culture constituted in freedom, spontaneity, and surprise. The radical shift of the wild region reveals, as Merleau-Ponty claims, an "identity without super-position," "a difference without contradiction." I see myself in this identity-difference.[39]

EVA-MARIA SIMMS is Adrian van Kaam Professor of Psychology at Duquesne University. She is the author of *The Child in the World: Embodiment, Time, and Language in Early Childhood* (Wayne State University Press, 2008).

NOTES

1. Jeffner Allen, "Through the Wild Region: An Essay in Phenomenological Feminism," *Review of Existential Psychology and Psychiatry* 18, nos. 1, 2, 3 (1983): 241–56.
2. Linda Fisher and Lester Embree, eds., *Feminist Phenomenology* (Dordrecht: Kluwer Academic Publishers, 2000); Iris Marion Young, *On Female Body Experience: "Throwing Like a Girl" and Other Essays* (Oxford: Oxford University Press, 2005).
3. Maurice Merleau-Ponty, *The Visible and the Invisible*, trans. Alphonso Lingis (Evanston, IL: Northwestern University Press, 1968), 114.
4. Allen, "Through the Wild Region."
5. Jacques Taminiaux, "Merleau-Ponty: From Dialectic to Hyperdialectic," *Research in Phenomenology* 10 (1980): 58–76.
6. Ibid., 63.
7. Ibid.
8. Merleau-Ponty, *Visible and the Invisible*, 88.
9. Ibid., 91.
10. Ibid., 93.
11. Ibid., 94.
12. Ibid.
13. Bernhard Waldenfels, "Perception and Structure in Merleau-Ponty," *Research in Phenomenology* 10 (1980): 21–38.
14. Maurice Merleau-Ponty, *The Structure of Behavior*, trans. Alden L. Fisher (1942; Pittsburgh: Duquesne University Press, 1983), 47.
15. Ibid., 206–207.
16. Maurice Merleau-Ponty, *Phenomenology of Perception*, trans. Richard Rojcewicz (Pittsburgh: Unpublished translation, 2009), 20. This refers to the unpublished Rojcewicz

translation, with the first page number as reference. The second page number refers to the Don Landes translation *Phenomenology of Perception*, trans. Donald A. Landes (New York: Routledge, 2012), 4.
 17. Merleau-Ponty, *Visible and the Invisible*, 171.
 18. Ibid.
 19. Ibid., 94; emphasis added.
 20. Ibid., 115n.
 21. Ibid., 114.
 22. Ibid., 114–15.
 23. Ibid., 100.
 24. Ibid.
 25. Ferdinand de Saussure, *Course in General Linguistics* (Peru, IL: Open Court, 1986).
 26. Merleau-Ponty, *The Visible and the Invisible*, 1968, 132.
 27. Ibid., 205.
 28. Ibid., 132.
 29. Ibid., 195.
 30. Ibid., 217.
 31. Ibid., 264.
 32. Ibid., 132.
 33. Ibid., 132–33.
 34. Dianne Chisholm, "Climbing Like a Girl: An Exemplary Adventure in Feminist Phenomenology," *Hypatia* 23, no. 1 (2008): 9–40.
 35. Merleau-Ponty, *Visible and the Invisible*, 132.
 36. Ibid., 195.
 37. Ibid., 264.
 38. Allen, "Through the Wild Region," 252.
 39. Ibid.

BIBLIOGRAPHY

Allen, Jeffner. "Through the Wild Region: An Essay in Phenomenological Feminism." *Review of Existential Psychology and Psychiatry* 18, nos. 1/2/3 (1983): 241–56.
Chisholm, Dianne. "Climbing Like a Girl: An Exemplary Adventure in Feminist Phenomenology." *Hypatia* 23, no. 1 (2008): 9–40.
Fisher, Linda, and Lester Embree, eds. *Feminist Phenomenology*. Dordrecht: Kluwer Academic Publishers, 2000.
Merleau-Ponty, Maurice. *Phenomenology of Perception*. Translated by Richard Rojcewicz. Pittsburgh: Unpublished translation, 2009.
———. *Phenomenology of Perception*. Translated by Donald A. Landes. New York: Routledge, 2012.
———. *The Structure of Behavior*. Translated by Alden L. Fisher. 1942. Pittsburgh: Duquesne University Press, 1983.
———. *The Visible and the Invisible*. Translated by Alphonso Lingis. Evanston, IL: Northwestern University Press, 1968.
Saussure, Ferdinand de. *Course in General Linguistics*. Peru, IL: Open Court, 1986.

Taminiaux, Jacques. "Merleau-Ponty: From Dialectic to Hyperdialectic." *Research in Phenomenology* 10, no. 1 (1980): 58–76.
Waldenfels, Bernhard. "Perception and Structure in Merleau-Ponty." *Research in Phenomenology* 10 (1980): 21–38.
Young, Iris M. *On Female Body Experience: "Throwing Like a Girl" and Other Essays.* Oxford: Oxford University Press, 2005.

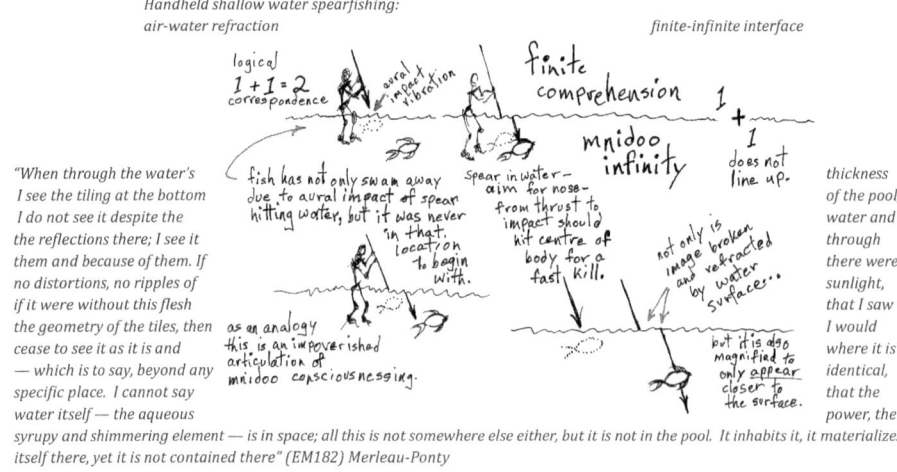

FIG. 9.1. Interdimensional spear fishing (diagram by Dolleen Tisawii'ashii Manning).

9 THE MURMURATION OF BIRDS

An Anishinaabe Ontology of *Mnidoo*-Worlding

DOLLEEN TISAWII'ASHII MANNING

This chapter sketches out precursory notes on the entangled ontology of the North American Algonquian language family, particularly regarding *mnidoo* (spirit/mystery, "potency, potential"),[1] animacy, and other-than-human persons.[2] Since this concept mnidoo is difficult to translate linguistically with all of its intricacies intact, I conduct here a phenomenological—that is, an experientially embodied—translation, which, in my view, is more in keeping with everyday lived-indigeneities.[3] We begin with a schematic drawing and a perplexing annotation on presence and consciousness to be investigated from a number of approaches throughout. These range from the navigational acuity of flocks of birds, to the poetics of Chickasaw Indigenous author Linda Hogan and the phenomenology of Maurice Merleau-Ponty. These vignettes gather and break apart rather like a shoal of fish or a flock of birds—in other words, with an eye for the immediate and a pulse in time with the infinite.

The schematic drawing here (fig. 9.1) assembles the overlapping contour of infinity as expansion seen through the reflection of finitude's recoiling contraction into signification.[4] That is to say, existence is founded for us in the contortion between the limitations of human consciousness (embodied or otherwise) and mnidoo-worlding. The air-water refraction of the here and now bends and breaks images through the encounter of these two mediums. As such, transcendence is gathered into the infinitesimal as the instantaneous, which in return is laboriously concealed by corporeal demands and competing appetites (desirous or affective). This is illustrated in "selfish herd" collective motion theories as "a continuous movement towards the safety of the centre" in efforts to escape predators (theories, in my view, too pragmatic to account for another impetus and other ways of being attuned).⁵ This composition casts an exploratory glimpse toward the interconnected world of the Ojibwe Anishinaabe.⁶ The tremulous dialogue of accessibility and unreachability presents the theory of mnidoo-worlding. The diagram articulates this simultaneous and elsewhere immanence of mnidoo as interfacial coalescence and refracting dissidence, wherein infinite differential microbursts meld to transmit a single fluctuating pulse—a reverberating wave that is invisible to the direct gaze of human consciousness. I undertake mnidoo-worlding to be an unconscious conceding or an interruption of intentions that is embedded over generations. We address, here, differing dimensions and differing ways of being at the same instant (in this essay I focus on finite/infinite mnidoo correspondence).

> To be clear, I speak of differing ways of being at the same time. What follows is a close study of the elusive and faint eruption of mnidoo intimations, leaving aside, for now, brute phenomenal reality. However, mnidoo intangibles and sociality are integrally affective. Consequently, each is impacted by their competing demands. This is particularly evident when mnidoo presence appears to human consciousness only to be dismissed by rationalism as mere coincidence. Problematically, this also insists on a transparency of Indigenous lifeways while continuing to validate intellectualism over other kinds of knowledge. In return, Indigenous ways of knowing have been delegitimized, pathologized, and reduced to obscurantism, or primitive and infantile ineptitude. As a result, the widespread social inequities and patterns of abuse that plague Indigenous communities, due to settler colonialism, evoke paradoxes that appear inconsistent with the mnidoo world that I am proposing here.

Moreover, this palimpsest or "memory/knowing" (as described by Indigenous elders) saturates and imbues.⁷ That is to say, thing-memory subtends human consciousness as opposed to the other way around.⁸ This appreciation—this intimation—is taken up into the unthought givens of what I contend is an Anishinaabe approach.[9] This way of being is conveyed in Ojibwe/Potawatomi as *Nii kina ganaa* ("All my relations/All my relatives"; also implied is "My all/My everything").[10] Between the "my" and the "all" is a reciprocal possession and an interrelational gravity. The ownership is one of responsibility. The "mineness" inheres and indwells with an *everything* that is beyond finite comprehension but to which I am indebted. It is capitalized to acknowledge the profound significance of this coexistent autonomous/oneness structure.

The basic translation of the word "Anishinaabe" is the "original person/being" and it is the identifying term by which the Ojibwe know themselves. In my usage, a second translation "mode of being" or "beingness" always accompanies the first as an originary sedimented resonance.[11] I extend this concept to a condition of being attuned to what is there in the world in a particular way. Though often overlooked, this subtle and oblique comportment is an integral aspect of Anishinaabe philosophies. My mother and formative teacher, Rose Manning Mshkode-bzhikiikwe baa, a first-language Ojibwe speaker, described this as a kind of attentiveness toward what approaches from a distance or what is apprehended from the corner of one's eye (perhaps days or even years in advance). I would add that it quivers (almost imperceptibly) in the convergence of temporal bodies/potencies as they emit, acquiesce, and collapse into one atemporal/instantaneous body while, in another sense, retaining their separate phenomenal materiality. My mother surmised that the closest English term for this dialogue was "intuition." Along with visual acuity, this *intuiting* might also appraise fluctuations in temperature, air pressure, sound distortion, and so on. Yet there are other registers that fall outside of conventionally conceived modes of consciousness, even in a sense that is other to Merleau-Ponty's embodied consciousness—it is a question of accessibility and discernment.

This discreet knowledge-gathering approach informs my engagement with the mnidoo-infused world, as well as the enclosed investigations, since what's out in front is never entirely what or where it appears to be (all things are not only comprised of but are also broached by one another). Forever out on the periphery is where the "real" of mnidoo is most present—that is, just when that amorphous shudder begins to take shape. Since it passes through me, it is never fully and inextricably comprehensible as an object that stands apart from me. Neither does it emerge from my sideways glance turned toward an event, but rather from that unformed place—the periphery of an ocular event placed elsewhere; from *there* it pressures the *here*, while I am attentive but not directly preoccupied with it.

These cursory notes open a conversation between the profoundly interconnective integrity of the Anishinaabe and the "savage mind"—that is, the pre- or non-reflective knowledge gathering of Merleau-Ponty.[12] I elaborate on Ojibwe Anishinaabe ontology through what I term mnidoo-worlding, which takes as its starting place the presumption of a life-world (Husserl's *Lebenswelt*) populated by human and other-than-human persons, "entities/bodies" or, rather, potencies. I bring mnidoo-worlding into dialogue with Merleau-Ponty's chiasmic postulate of an "ahuman lineate."[13] Ojibwe author Basil Johnson asserts that while "Manitous" (also spelled *mnidoog*) are associated with "spirits," the Anishinaabe also hold them in high esteem as *qualities* in the sense of "essence, transcendental, mystical, muse, patron and divine."[14] I bring mnidoo into a philosophical context in order to query this inter(intra) relational stimulus.

Merleau-Ponty describes the conjoining of human corporeality with the world as a "field" that we are taken up into as the interface of an exposed "wound." As such, it is taken for granted and routinely functions as an invisible backdrop that intra-marginally communicates situatedness. Much in the same way, I contend that Anishinaabe philosophies include a gathering-up and a being-there-together with the exception that they also break open onto an interminable and co-responsive permeation. These nonhuman-centered "traditional" or pre-Columbian Anishinaabe ontologies are, in theory, devoid of hierarchy. They strive for interrelational accord amid brutal contemporary forces that compose our complex lived Indigenous realities. The result is a philosophy that resists co-option and concedes to the heterogeneity of being.

I define this murmuration—that is, this concurrent gathering of fluctuating and divergent inflections—as mnidoo-worlding. My use of the term "worlding" brings Heidegger's conceptions of *"In-der-Welt-sein"* (Being-in-the-world) together with Merleau-Ponty's *"être-au-monde"* (being-in-the-world) as a pre-reflective "intra-corporeal" world-adhesion, which I think about through mnidoo ontology.[15] Merleau-Ponty's conception of *possession* makes no inside/outside distinction, since it is the "degree zero of spatiality."[16] It is the immediate experience of being "encrusted" within the world as two sides of the same coin. As such, it is a kind of worlding. To this, I add the ontological presumption of mnidoo immanence to contend that consciousness, and by association agency, arises as an encrusted exchange between animacy, "inanimacy," and immateriality. All of these are mnidoo (energies/potencies/processes) that are *gashka'oode* (entangled) *kina ganaa* (relatives/relations/all/everything).[17] Taken together, each interpenetrates and fluctuates in cascading patterns akin to the murmuration of starlings. Situated thus as a cohesion of particularized differences and a correspondent whole of communal indifferentiation, this theory of entanglement negates the possibility of any absolute indifference. I propose that a kind of autonomy does infiltrate this "reality," not as a bounded locus of knowledge, but as an externally conceived and torn co-responsiveness.

Merleau-Ponty's thesis on somatic consciousness accounts for the "sedimentation" of practices and perception. His approach has significant bearing on my own theory of consciousness as it pertains to Ojibwe ontologies and interconnective Indigenous modes of being. While his later work is situated firmly in a "pre-personal" world, it continues to be inflected by his earlier conclusions on culture and "the social."[18] Unlike mnidoo-worlding, Merleau-Ponty privileges human subjectivity, for, as he contends, "If there really is to be consciousness, if something is to appear to someone, then an enclave, or a Self, must be carved out behind all of our particular thoughts."[19] As such, his theory of consciousness is coexistent with, interdependent on, and, at the same time, restricted to the "living," or in other words, relegated to cognitively perceptual bodies. Moreover, these bodies are ultimately limited to "a Self" and a specific form of cognition (i.e., his own reflective/pre-reflective activities).[20] By identifying consciousness as external to a bounded human subject, and at the same time as internal in terms of immanence (radiating from within as well as from "without"), I carry Merleau-Ponty into the ahuman mnidoo structure that he seems to strive for but cannot reach. I take up his theory of visibility as one sensual example amid an entire field of a worlded-adhesion. This is, as he contends, a world-oriented and a world-conditioned structure, which pleats chiasm with experientially situated knowledge.[21] Even so, I push his thought further in contending that mnidoo-worlding also erodes boundaries while paradoxically instantiating them as discernibles.

My point of departure from Merleau-Ponty might best be understood through his ontology of the flesh, which emphasizes both the space between bodies along with their entwinement. Working alongside his texts, as I extend this pre-Columbian onto-/epistemological Anishinaabe philosophy, I acknowledge that these approaches cannot be entirely extracted one from the other. Stated differently, "categorical abstraction" is insufficient for accessing the "ethno-metaphysical" realities and implications of cultures to which one does not belong.[22] Informed by an Ojibwe mnidoo worldview, my interpretation of Merleau-Ponty's work is "incorporated," and as such, is also imparted with my particular "acquisition" of Anishinaabe knowledge, which can never entirely be cleaved from my being-in-the-world. All the same, I endeavor to convey how his theories overlay, intermingle, and diverge from my own by first attending to his chiasmic ontology of the flesh.

CHIASM AND THE TRANSCENDENCE OF THE BODY/MIND EXCHANGE

For Merleau-Ponty, the reversibility of chiasm transforms through the overlap, where presencing gathers the nullified equation of the foregone and the not yet into a differential seam that is comprised of "a nothingness one can turn over."[23] In this exchange differing entities/bodies are left in their place, albeit transfigured by "the application of the inside and the outside to one another."[24] Unconsciously, or rather, faithfully subtended by world, each body is not only *in* but also *of* the world as a relationally entwined thread.[25] Perceptual experience occurs as a pre-reflection—as a first-order condition—that is invisible to the mind, since it functions on a different dimension. It transcendentally exceeds us as a condition of always already being there and is thus ahead of the second-order operation of reflective cognition/signification. According to Merleau-Ponty, it is that immediacy of experience or corporeal indwelling as a sensible for sensibles, which I can never access due to my being there—at the heart of it. Essentially, I block my own direct gaze of its "presencing" (Heidegger's term) while I am taken up into the encounter. Merleau-Ponty writes:

> There can be no question of describing perception itself as one of the facts thrown up in the world, since we can never fill up, in the picture of the world, that gap which we ourselves are, and by which it comes into existence for someone, since perception is the "flaw" in this "great diamond."[26]

Consequently, this "gap which we ourselves are" is what makes perception a transcendental condition, and makes the present "able to connect up with a past and a future."[27] This lacuna/concealment/continuity, moreover, points to a pre-reflective manner of knowing. Intellection is thereby a second-order operation that is dependent on embodied knowledge as a prerequisite to cognition. The invisibility of transcendence is located in the tangible *model* of sensible bodies and sensibility, since both eclipse and exceed human consciousness, inasmuch as "the sketch of a thing, and the thing is the initial sketch of the world."[28] Merleau-Ponty identifies this reversible transitional structure as "chiasm." His theory makes it possible to understand the world as other than objective truths disentangled and held out as objects for inspection. Instead we are to presume the perspective of "our insertion in the world-as-an-individual" as a means of accessing a pre-personal immediacy with which the "primordial arrangement" of transcendence is entwined "as our inherence in things."[29]

Since the "world is in the field of our experience," we intersubjectively touch upon it through the adhesion of these two outlines that are "superimposed" one onto the other.[30] Getting at this experience through "the look" and things seen, however, requires a tricky reversed reconsideration of how one "incorporates" and is incorporated through a mutual gaze. This liminal space pivots on a shared experience of absence—that is, transcendence—through which sight glides while providing a backdrop for visibles to appear. Merleau-Ponty describes these two dimensions of perception as "obverse and reverse ensembles," conditionally intertwined "abstracts from one sole tissue" of a multidimensional worlded body.[31] The "fission" or negative space between these outlines bonds them together, "each the other side of the other."[32] This co-constituting sameness "in the structural sense" may be enough for Merleau-Ponty.[33] Yet, although it is a point of transition that knits together at the site of contact, the character of the outline as bridge and partition also presents as a line that withholds and divides. It is a line that keeps pace, contours, and frames but, at the same time, withholds the world that it unites with me. Hence "that frontier surface at some distance before me" in some sense also always stands over and against me.[34]

Merleau-Ponty proffers the "two laps" through which chiasm functions as a turnabout.[35] The English translation provided in *The Visible and the Invisible* gives us the "two laps," but in the original it is "*les deux levres*," or "the two lips." Yet, this mistranslation deepens my understanding of their reversible insinuations.[36] I take "laps" to mean overtake and enfold as a continuous circuit. In this interpenetration, each of the two sides is simultaneously implicated as it outstrips the other as with an overlap, whereas, "lips" clearly asserts a demarcation and convergence between two outlines. The term "lips" identifies a border, edge, or brink between bodies (visible or invisible) such as where a rocky cliff face meets its limit to become airborne. It undoubtedly bespeaks of a breach as two surfaces exposed and yet still touch. These plausible translations ("laps" and "lips") present another form of holding and withholding that is indicative of chiasm's reversibility. Such an outline opens onto a complicated network of embodied-worldedness, which is in keeping with conceptions of the mnidoo-worlding that I wrestle with in this chapter. Merleau-Ponty's earlier work articulates this complicated network as a "coexistence" that "must be in each case lived by each person."[37] It is ambiguously perceived as *lived* experience as opposed to a subject/object reflective analysis.

No matter how tight the weave, Merleau-Ponty insists on a discontinuous breach between each intertwining thread. These two lips comprise immersive liminality and division.[38] We might call it a field of resistance that emulates the transcendence of perceptual experience. This spacing ensures that distinct bodies never merge to become an indistinguishable whole, one that might resemble "some huge animal whose organs our bodies would be."[39] Alternately, he proposes that a perceptual "synergy" between "different organisms" is achievable "as soon as we no longer make belongingness to one *same* [human] 'consciousness' the primordial definition of sensibility."[40] To gain a better understanding of sensuality apart from this presumed "sameness," I return to Merleau-Ponty's earlier work in *Phenomenology of Perception*, where he challenges our perceptual faith in accepting "a common situation in which they communicate."[41] In this example, sentience is presupposed as both a human attribute and a shared phenomenon. Yet he wants us to think of consciousness in "the thickness of being,"[42] since, as he observes, "my body is a movement toward the world and because the world is my body's support."[43] However, he does not refute the private thoughts of human consciousness either. We should then understand consciousness to be discontinuous between individual psyches and nevertheless an instance of projecting "this 'single' world" from the background of one's own subjectivity.[44] For Merleau-Ponty, consciousness can only be intersubjectively shared among bodies caught up in the structure of the world.[45] He writes, "The fundamental truth is certainly that 'I think,' but only on condition of understanding by this that 'I belong to myself' in being in the world."[46] As for the question of an other-than-human vital materialism, particularly with respect to inanimate agency, Merleau-Ponty describes this as "an absurd undertaking."[47]

MNIDOO-WORLDING

> Water and air became the same thing, as did water and land.... Birds swam across lakes. It was all one thing. The canoes were our bodies, our skin. We passed through green leaves, wild rice, and rushes.
>
> Linda Hogan, *Solar Storms*

As with Merleau-Ponty, I do not conceive of mnidoo as a massive organism whose parts comprise a unified body, nor do I grapple here with the other-than-human as a distinct "soul/spirit." Rather, mnidoo-worlding/consciousnessing has an autonomous structure, which it imparts in the interspersion of the "my/all" indwelling. As such, mnidoo does indeed merge in the piercing through that fleetingly eradicates my self-holding. Even if the two lips of this seam issue from bodily flesh (human and otherwise), chiasm, it seems, requires a space to cross in staging a conversion. In what follows, I retain Merleau-Ponty's "inherence in things" while redeploying his ontology of the flesh.[48] However, I expand the definition of consciousness beyond human/animal sentience by locating it in the world—a living agential co-responsiveness to the field itself, where the eye first opens.[49] My trajectory introduces another dimension of experience or perhaps a different kind of sensibility, not as an entwined and reversible *of-ness* but instead as a *with-ness*.

Ojibwe Anishinaabe seven directions teachings include north, south, east, west, up, down, and center. Among other applications, they offer a midpoint from which to stake ethical claims no matter how indirect or abstract. They also present another means for approaching mnidoo ontology inasmuch as these intimations are encrusted in countless accessible contemporary Anishinaabe pedagogical models. This shifting cipher does not track geographical coordinates, nor even the globe's contour. Rather, it evokes a three-dimensional swelling of continuous and discontinuous bursting forth that does more than overlap and communicate through this segregated channel, as Merleau-Ponty contends. Undoubtedly, they—this infinite and finite mnidoo outpouring—not only subtend(s) but also coalesce and together bring about the heterogeneity of space, time, and consciousness. But this leap is too great and far too sudden. Nonetheless, how else can I approach except from the "thickness" of my worlded structure, where minuscule universes, so to speak, radiate and converge. From this framework I provisionally consider each mnidoo dimension to harbor a center that intersects and flows through the others. I return here again and again to tease out these complex mnidoo streams, beginning from the center of the self. This is not an anthropocentric retort. Rather, it is the median of my surrender, when I am torn, given over, rendered inoperative and discontinuous. The egoistic "I" offset as "non-I." The reverberation of each microcosm and their perpetual breaking open constitutes an infinite inner horizon. Neither center nor self is limited to the notion of a bounded reality cut off from an outer world. (See fig. 9.2.)

For Merleau-Ponty, an interstice/seam guarantees a holding and a withholding that allow bodies to remain separate amid a co-constituted interchange. I contend that mnidoo/bodies (animate, inanimate, and intangible), in piercing one another, do indeed fuse, in a sense, or in some dimension as an indistinguishable whole. In the example of human consciousness, perhaps this transformation arises in ways that are co-opted by faculties aligned with the natural attitude (thus overlooked as a kind of false consciousness). The linear temporality of mortal consciousness is distinct from an infinite always already (space-time compressed into the instant). Their collision results in the piling up of one upon the other as simultaneity. Yet, material bodies or objective reality remain discrete but are never as discrete as the natural attitude suggests (leastways not as it is defined historically in Western philosophy, especially regarding discourses of animacy and consciousness). Likewise, their interpenetration does not erode disparate attributes, or at least not always and certainly

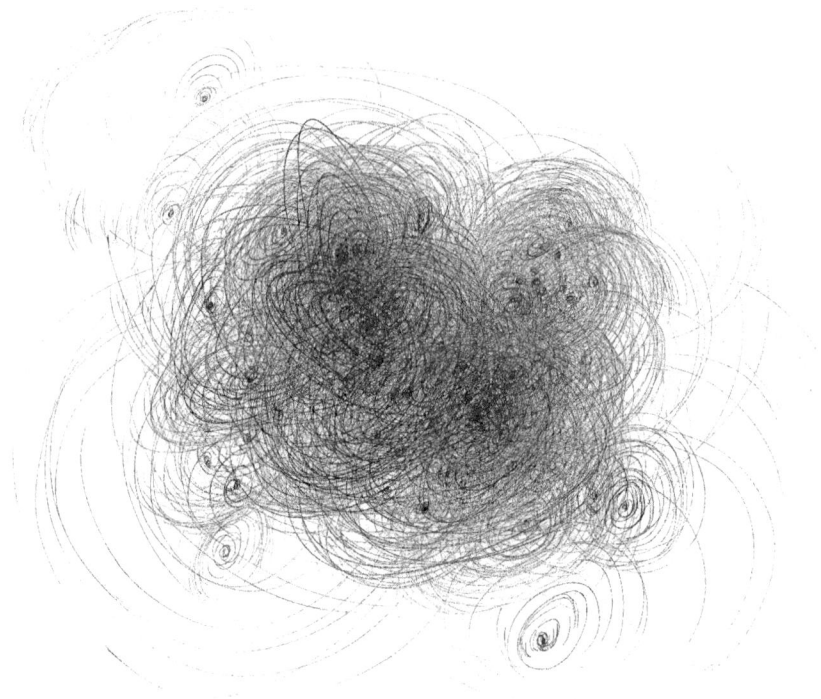

FIG. 9.2. Mnidoo-wave (drawing by Dolleen Tisawii'ashii Manning).

not immediately. Instead, it allows for and even necessitates this discontinuity as a force of continuity. This ceaseless discourse impinges from without as much as from within, implicating mnidoo as a sustaining potency, but not necessarily *life* per se (since mnidoo ontology also challenges conceptions of "life" as it is conventionally understood).

MERLEAU-PONTY: *ÉCART*

Merleau-Ponty's theory of encroachment is conveyed in the overlap between the visible and the invisible, look and sight, seer and things seen, whereby vision is doubled and in reverse sees the seer "installed" and "occupied" in the very depth and interiority of the world that allows vision to arise at all.[50] This edge, these two facing frontiers, are knit together and simultaneously separate. The body-world hence offers up the leaflet of a single adjoining feature, which is perceptual experience itself. Merleau-Ponty writes that this experience unites us directly with the things through its own ontogenesis, by welding to one another the two outlines of which it is made, its two laps [sic]: the sensible mass it is and the mass of the sensible wherein it is born by segregation and upon which, as seer, it remains open.[51]

The French word *écart* describes the paradoxical hinge of bifurcation and entwinement particular to Merleau-Ponty's theory of chiasm. It defines space and surface as a splitting off in every direction while covering over and manifesting bodies that depart and adhere in their pronouncement of difference. Each dimension spreads, diverges, deviates, and separates in a worlded structuration that articulates this complex being-in-the-world adhesion.[52] In a sense, Merleau-Ponty suggests that time and space converge as immediacy through the sensible and the reverse of chiasm's touch. Additionally, I contend that every aspect of existence (not only sentience) knows itself primordially as a thing of the world through the infinite reverberation of mnidoo. That is to say, not as overlap and gap, but as *Nii kina ganaa*—All my relations/All my relatives/My all/My everything—an ownmost immediate knowing.

These infinitely doubled outlines might be said to permeate existence itself in an interrelational dialogue. In my interpretation, infinity and finitude converge as simultaneity, which I argue is experienced as a rupture in the transcendence of perceptual experience. But if transcendence is ruptured, how do we perceive this disruption when transcendence itself exceeds apperception? We might think of it as a flicker, in which indistinguishable static (electromagnetic, visual, or aural), consistent and subtle, gradually fades, reappears suddenly in a hazy coalescence—intermittently seeping through to seize hold without context. Let's consider Merleau-Ponty's concept of the "two outlines" of écart in terms of mnidoo potency conceptualized through the pulsing resonance of bird flight patterns. In a murmuration, a flock of starlings interweave intricate cascading flight patterns (with each correlating to the one next) around land, wind, and other flock formations without ever colliding. A researcher of animal collective behavior describes these patterns as "one of the most impressive examples of organization in the natural world, with flocks of up to 300,000 individuals or more able to coordinate themselves into a cohesive and highly coherent group."[53] From the perceptual faith of the natural attitude, this phenomena might be rationalized as multiple singularities following tangible air currents (perhaps affectively swayed) with each event occurring in space through a sequential unfolding of time.[54] But this conception of the "physiological event," Merleau-Ponty contends, "is but the abstract outline of the perceptual event" with each tackled as objects that stand out in front of consciousness.[55]

166 | *Part 3. The Ontological Future*

Scientists find that perception is the key to starling organization, asking, "What does a bird actually see when it is part of a large flock?" These researchers describe a perceptual analysis in keeping with both mnidoo and Merleau-Pontean ontologies:

> [A single bird's] view out from within a large flock likely would present the vast majority of individuals merely as silhouettes, moving too fast and at too great a distance to be tracked easily or even discriminated from one another. Here the basic visual input to each individual is assumed to be based simply on visual contrast: a dynamic pattern of dark (bird) and light (sky) across the field of vision (although it might be possible to extend this to other swarming species and environmental backgrounds, respectively). This has the appealing feature that it also is the projection that appears on the retina of the bird, which we assume to be its primary sensory input. A typical individual within a very dense flock would see other, overlapping individuals (dark) almost everywhere it looked. Conversely, an isolated individual, detached from the flock, would see only sky (light). The projected view gives direct information on the global state of the flock.[56]

The tension evoked by the spreading inherent to écart in this example points to its capricious status wavering between "sedimentation and spontaneity."[57] The traction engendered by the reverse poles of this fluctuating and paired outline undulates interminably—infinity compressed through the fissure of the absolute present. The internal pressure of holding and withholding exerts a grasp through this seam. A chorus of visible and invisible tangibles emerge, discharge a signature, interpenetrate, co-join, dissipate, emerge—a mnidoo wave that transmits and subtends. Comprised as I am of these mnidoo forces that infinitely exceed me, I incorporate and make sense through the limitation of my cognitive ability to sign and apprehend. Yet, beyond the regions of sight, touch, and their future anticipating, my own rhythmic modulations line up or are ruptured in such a way that the other (my mnidoo ancestors) have shot through me, collapsing distances and bodies (temporal and spatial).[58] I am gathered in your call, in the ache of our being there together—I am awake—suddenly, fleetingly, bitingly, and in the next breath I am alone.

As for chiasm, in order to maintain this "hold" while resisting the returned grasp (so as not to become fully incorporated one into the other), each "dimension" must remain at a distance.[59] Hence, aside from the visible and the invisible dimensions of sensibility, écart emerges, for Merleau-Ponty, as a third possibility for explaining the acute facility of pre-reflective situatedness. He defines écart as the separation necessary for articulation and consciousness "to have a figure on a ground."[60] Despite the series of correspondences between

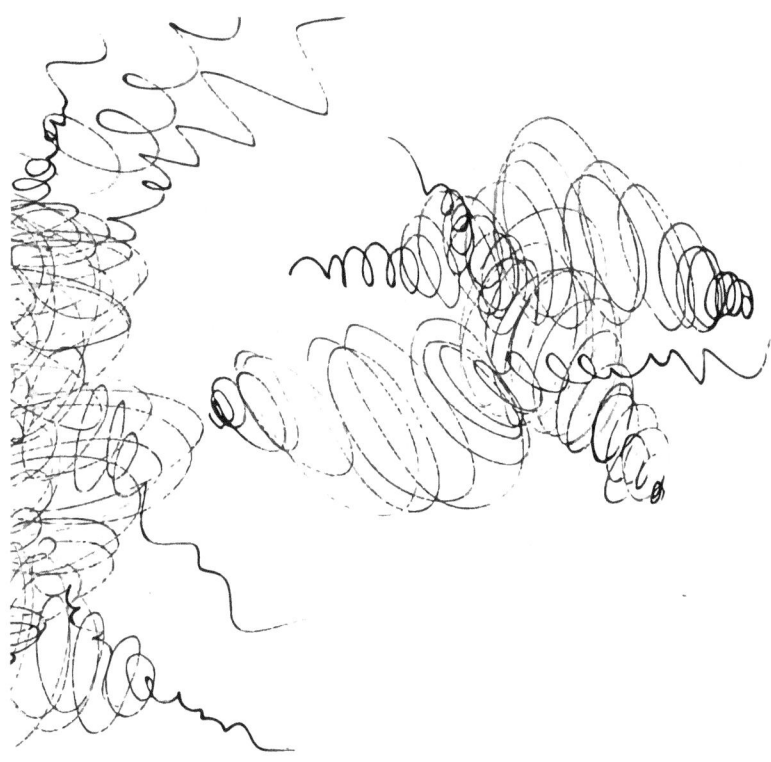

FIG. 9.3. Mnidoo-palpitation: Pulsing, Colliding, Piercing (drawing by Dolleen Tisawii'ashii Manning).

perception and the thing that lines its contour, he contends that there remains a "stroboscopic" interval. Between touch and touching, self and world, cognition stroboscopically/retroactively doubles back to create meaning from perception.[61] In his example of one hand touching the other, the two sensations (of being touched and touching in return) do not collapse into one undifferentiated experience. Rather, consciousness can only attend to either one or the other but is never able to apprehend both distinct senses simultaneously. Even though "the two systems are applied upon one another" as an "encrusted" imprint (and sedimentation of "primordial faith"), Merleau-Ponty insists that "they do not merge into one."[62] Alternately, I propose that, albeit fleeting and fitful, in that very interstice within the rhythm of those spatial distances, human consciousness does indeed break into a unified body of mnidoo correspondence, not as an arrested state but rather as a glancing blow that penetrates, passes through, and deflects, which I articulate as mnidoo-worlding's mode of address. (See fig. 9.3.)

This cascade of infinitesimal explosions resonates immanently and, at times, becomes accessible to the impoverished receptivity of human consciousness (burdened as it is by the obstacle of its own psyche). Starling murmurations are just one example of these resonances. In working through his articulation of an ahuman-world adhesion (a pre-personal somatic-immediacy), Merleau-Ponty finds that he must concede to the breach between one palpitation and the next. He transitions from an emphasis on intersubjective situatedness to chiasmic reversal. To put this in another way, chiasm removes subject/object polarization, while simultaneously counteracting the risk of a totalizing collapse. Yet, the two can be seen to mirror the other as a world structure of the "hold [that] is held."[63]

INTER-DIMENSIONAL THICKENING: FLESH-WORLD/MNIDOO-WORLD

Merleau-Ponty's theory of the stroboscopic describes the instrument of intellection as an intermittent flashing light that makes bodies/objects appear immobile. This cognitive grasping (a flawed revealing) extracts the primordial experience of perception (or at least its receding appearance) from the transcendent (and, hence, ambiguous realm) of its *actual* entwined first-order occurrence/adhesion. This term "stroboscopic" articulates our fluctuating relationship with the visible (perceptual ground for reflective signification) and the invisible (pre-reflective backdrop or embodied knowledge from which cognition arises secondarily).[64] From an Anishinaabe interrelational view, the logic behind écart's stroboscopic interval (doubled as both an intersubjective and a primordial "being-in-the-world") does not leave room for the subtle registry of mnidoo other-than-human encounters. For Merleau-Ponty, to be *of* the world describes an "encroachment" between adjoining tissues. This is despite our capacity to be elsewhere through the insinuation between eye (embodiment) and mind (cognition)—that is, via encrusted anticipation, intersubjective reversal, or reflective imagination. By contrast, the implications for mnidoo entanglement convene as divergent pulsation(s) that are singular, plural, and auto-generative—"spontaneous beings" "made out of nothing."[65] These animate, inanimate, and intangibles converge and inscribe in the proximity of silent masses that absorb and insinuate as they perturb with their relative magnitude. In this sense, every dimension of existence has autonomous agency.[66] If, that is, mnidoo arises not as a cacophony of divergent elements that ignite and splay apart, as with Merleau-Ponty's écart, but instead form a teeming flood—mnidoo potency/potential/process—from which dissidence is considered and taken up differently by each pebble that partakes in a landslide.[67] These varying dimensions might be understood as indifferent or passive and at other times as competitive and active. The interaction of converging spheres breaks other centers open at odd angles. Together they shift and contort to produce tumultuous intersecting waves.[68]

On the other hand, there remains a distillation or an evaporation between finite and infinite dimensions. I am a finite entity (animate or inanimate). I am both breathing and in possession of another finite mode of interconnectivity—that is, human consciousness—one starling entangled in the fluttering murmuration of a multitude. The constituting population of each system is minutely ever more divisible until breaking into the mnidoo potency seen pulsating throughout. This infinite mnidoo consciousness conditions finitude, not merely as a "life-sustaining" interpenetration (as with oxygen molecules that fill our lungs in a shared biological process).[69] But more enigmatically it is an integral fusion that is always already there. We might think of this undifferentiated "consciousnessing" as akin to black matter flowing through us. It allows for other experiences to emerge and challenge the presentation of empirical "truth" (consequently, it is often overwritten by an acute presence to the presentation of objective reality). I am part of this tumultuous unified body. As such I am both finite and infinite: singular, discontinuous, mortal. I am also continuous, immortal, and infinitely divisible. I transpire along two ways of being—finitude and infinitude. The two do not *systematically* line up—in other words, each is askew one from the other. My psyche, or rather my mnidoo-world-self, is overshadowed by my finite concerns. This obstinate human comportment grants neither a sustained direct view nor full access to this other aspect of my existence. Hence, we attend to the sidelong and the circuitous.

MNIDOO WORLD-CONSCIOUSNESS

> *The old world dawning new in me was something like the way a human eye righted what was upside down, turned over an image and saw true.*
> Linda Hogan, *Solar Storms*

The world is consciousness and we human "I's" are mere shimmering reflections, ever receding afterthoughts. Possessed in this way, by world, we are dispossessed of autonomous self and yet also delivered over to an authentic world-self, a mnidoo-self. We do not skillfully master mnidoo. Rather, we arrive to it, through oblique interrelational modes, unconsciously and indirectly glancing with my "side-eye" (to use a phrase from Mona Stonefish). The aim is not to articulate phenomena as they appear to consciousness, but rather to wade into these subtle mnidoo regions in order to momentarily overcome the self (histories and attitudes). Ultimately, ceremonial reflexivity immerses the self in the perceptual field—exceeding subjective projection by rousing instead to this relational entanglement. In slackening my hold of self-possession, an elliptical intimation rushes in as a unified kina and simultaneously as an autonomous dimension of world-self (*nii kina*). Amid an ephemeral encounter, I awaken to *Nii kina ganaa* and gain access as a *thing* profoundly imbued within its transmission. Since conscious awareness is the very obstacle that bends the circuit, as it were, to bypass what is closest to me, this access defies signification, particularly when considered solely from the discontinuous estrangement of finitude. A world-mnidoo-self is not an experience of inert thingly silence, but of ancestors whittling axe handles, diminishing in one sense while increasing in another, consciousness cajoled from the competing and conversing of wood shavings—self and non-self—active, autonomous, *living* materiality. By apparent chance, fleetingly and haphazardly, I stumble into the clarity of mnidoo-consciousness, of which my sense of selfhood is momentarily overridden by a resolute ownmost. Located somewhere in that midpoint as I fumble toward linguistic articulation, I exceed my acquired knowledge and the future-telling anticipation that arises from this "acquisition." This exceeding does indeed entail a merging of consciousness; or a passing through, as with an electric current; or a bursting forth of what is always already there, but is most often suppressed by my reflective prowess.

I take up what Merleau-Ponty defines as an "adhesion" between "one sole body before one sole world" but depart from his pre-personal aim to instead interrogate the slackening of consciousness (i.e., awake, yet inattentive, exhausted, while in some way remaining open).[70] This simultaneity bridges the "gap" or "lacuna" with a second penetration between the linear temporality of mortals and the immediacy of infinity's ubiquitous reach. Hence, in the latter instance I am both heedless and alert, which defies the logical order of finite beings by subtending discontinuity (death or rupture) in the space of delirium and exhaustion. The world suddenly appears and seizes hold of a necessary portion of my cognition.[71] This fissure refocuses my attention in accordance with the things of the world—that is, in keeping with a co-constituted world-relationality that briefly overshadows my own conscious appointment.[72] In that moment, my hold on a particularized self-determining is weakened if not lost altogether.

As much as one dimension is overlapped and drawn into the other, this terminal lip of "acquisition" offers up figure and ground such that "I have the

FIG. 9.4. Mnidoo-memory (drawing by Dolleen Tisawii'ashii Manning).

position of objects through the position of my body, or inversely I have the position of my body through the position of the objects."[73] Taken into the spacing between touch and touching—held and holding to itself—this palimpsest can never be wholly eradicated, remaining instead entangled between one "palpitation" and the next as traces and echoes. Aside from the "encroachment" that serves, as Merleau-Ponty contends, to hold self to self, this seam is inhabited by another dimension that tears through the structure of withholding as a defenseless conceding.[74] Fleetingly and obliquely glimpsed in a bewildering upsurge, the giving over surrenders up authentic self as authentic experience—consciousness divulged before being engulfed again by what Samuel Mallin calls the "technologism" of our time.[75] To clarify, in approaching this sensually registered mnidoo, consciousness overtakes the world. It exceeds itself, is thrown outside of self, and, simultaneously, is seized hold of as a reversed rupture by the things of the world "of which it is also a part."[76] This mnidoo-worlding subtends existence by passing through it. Human consciousness in some sense is also a dimension of this worlding. Mnidoo presencing is the linchpin between interior and exterior horizons, upon which perception stands out from a conflicted and indeterminate terrain. Effaced imprints are commingled—brittle, tender spears shot from a murky void—issuing forth as a faint distraction and at other times as an electrified epiphany. They are atemporal memories covered over by layers of embodied and linguistic symbolic histories. (See fig. 9.4.)

CONCLUSION: SIMULTANEITY AND MNIDOO INDWELLING

> It was this gap in time we entered, and it was a place between worlds. I was under the spell of wilderness, close to what no one had ever been able to call by name. Everything merged and united. There were no sharp distinctions left between darkness and light.
>
> Linda Hogan, *Solar Storms*

Without denying the significance of the double-lined reversibility of chiasm, I contend that with mnidoo-worlding there is another dimension other than the differential reality necessary to uphold finitude's weak grasp. In slackening my hold of the cognitive-linguistic region, I awaken, in some oblique way, to my immersive entanglement with another dimension of myself. That is to say, conscious apprehension does not follow the other "regions of being" but rather is caught up in this disorienting confluence—*Nii kina ganaa* (All my relations/ My all/My world-mnidoo-self). As I am immanently present within this potency, it is not immediately present to my conscious thought. Yet I have access to the other through the collision of time-space as simultaneity. How else do we account for being struck by alarm, for no apparent reason, in response to a loved one's misfortune registered instantly halfway around the world? Or waking from a deep sleep to an empathic summoning from someone, at a distance, unconsciously piercing the veil between us via the heat of a crisis.[77] Entangled exploding microcosms (each aspect retaining a sense of an *isness* and an autonomous *mineness*) collapse time and space into this silent call. We converge as simultaneity. My human consciousness is aroused to this always already unending body to which I am infused. The breach, opened by the call, provides tenuous access to a larger sense of self as mnidoo indwelling. Amid this partially veiled and tremulous experience we pre-reflectively communicate with a mnidoo-world-self as *Nii kina ganaa* (All my relatives/All my relations/My all/ My everything). One's ownmost (mnidoo-self) likewise stands out as a flickering glint against the backdrop of the other.

Mnidoo knowing arrives as a piercing epiphany just as often as a nagging undercurrent, sometimes vague and at others distinct and incontrovertible. It erupts and overturns perceptual experience with a sudden insight. It stirs, pierces, awakens, and draws into contrast that subtle, near imperceptible (perhaps even extrasensory) interiority of one's ownmost. This ownmost exerts a sense of ownership to that part of me that is most familiar. Yet, what is most mine also escapes me when I am taken up into another interiority of alien impulse, leaving me bewildered. I am struck with the monumentality of how it both beguiles and exceeds me. Surely, it is more than I am and, at the same time, all that I am, when I am most at home, lost to myself. This sudden rushing in of what is most mine baffles and defies my reflective veracity. This troubling contour challenges me in subtle ways that I cannot ignore. Just the same, this receding "I" manages to rationalize banal excuses for doing so. Yet I discover here that to arrive at my ownmost requires a break with my reflective concentration, and not of my own volition. This involves a double absorption. Such attentiveness might be pure reflective self-absorption in which presence of mind arises over time through a slow releasing of embodied distractions. It's a withdrawing from world, a loss of my embodied presence. But it's not exactly this, since the experience of my ownmost includes this autonomous self-self (corporeality) and mnidoo-self (a self-communicating receptivity between these finite and infinite dimensions). This term "mnidoo-self" suggests that this oblique communication is somehow made cognizant. It is an infinite mnidoo dimension that operates as its own interlocutor—that is, as both sender and receiver. It exceeds the autonomous/authority of the self-self with the undulation of its own reverberating interiority as mnidoo-world-self presencing (momentarily suppressing the false appearance of subject/object distinctions). This requires the dissolution of ego or self-self. In other words, individualized autonomy is both instantiated and dissolved when I am seized upon by the passing through of a world-positing centrality. Here, any single-dimensional vibration might momentarily take possession or brush by and inadvertently imprint a new fluctuation.[78] Neither slackened nor straining attention inhibits the other; both continue to operate in different ways. In the dispossessed loss of my owness, I awaken to an absolute imperative, or at least to a vague sense of reorientation.

Other-than-human persons—that is, mnidoo ancestors—radiate from every direction as colliding universes. This world-mnidoo interlocution might be understood simply as an exchange (but this is too trivial, too diminutive, too premeditated). Perhaps it collapses into an endlessly undulating body—as a murmuration or a mnidoo-wave—not a unified body stopped up and solidified by harmonious elation, but rather a dialogic body spurred on through permeation and absorption in which resulting tensions rifle out existence and its ontological query. When we attend to mnidoo realities as an object of direct contemplation, it is only by a feeble mind isolated in the construct of an inner world. Hence, in these instances such reflections are cut off from the competing chorus of a world-mnidoo from which thought so often stumbles, unable to discern one dimension of existence from another.[79]

I define this Anishinaabe phenomenology as Ojibwe-*inflected* instead of -specific, because I do not speak on behalf of all Anishinaabeg and the multiple becomings of these divergent philosophers, speakers, and familial dialects. Rather, it represents the small bit that I have been given and in return am responsible to give back. As my mother says, "We only own what we give away."[80] In giving we not only deepen our own knowledge but also enrich our communities and ensure that these Indigenous ways of being attuned are strengthened and revitalized. Moreover, only in conceding to that amorphous something are we gifted with a second sight—that is, with a greater understanding and appreciation of differing ways of thinking, engaging, and being. The theories articulated in this essay oscillate around a specific time and place. In keeping with Anishinaabe comportment, such translations and my arrival to them might be understood as a deeply personal undertaking. Yet, without a doubt this endeavor is mediated through cultural reflections and shared community knowledges that are embedded within my particular being-in-the-world (passed between mnidoo ancestors, past and future, through the infinite and the simultaneous). To be sure, the philosophical structure that I aim for has slipped away in the exchange from lived experience, to thought, to codex, for it lives exclusively with the Anishinaabe—the original people—that is, those marked with a profound integrity as interconnected and co-responsive. As such, this text should not be taken up as a universal model, but rather as a shedding metamorphosis en route to an elsewhere.

Nii kina ganaa.

DOLLEEN TISAWII'ASHII MANNING is a doctoral candidate at the Centre for the Study of Theory and Criticism, the University of Western Ontario, and currently a Visiting Scholar at the Institute for Gender, Sexuality, and Feminist Studies, McGill University.

NOTES

1. "[Scholars] do not know that the word [Manitou/mnidoo] bears other meanings even more fundamental than 'spirit', as such, and/or pertaining to the deities; of a substance, character, nature, essence, quiddity beyond comprehension and therefore beyond explanation, a mystery; supernatural; potency, potential" (11). Basil Johnson, "One Generation from Extinction," in W. H. New, *Native Writers and Canadian Writing* (Vancouver: University of British Columbia Press, 1990).

2. Irving Hallowell coined the term "other-than-human persons" as an English-language translation of the Ojibwe concept mnidoo. Having begun his ethnographic field studies as early as the 1920s, he focused his research "on the Algonkian Indians, especially the Abenaki and Ojibwa Indians of Canada and Wisconsin (Berens River, Lake Winnipeg, Manitoba, and Lac du Flambeau, Wisconsin areas), and the Saulteaux of Berens River." See American Philosophical Society, "Alfred Irving Hallowell Papers," http://www.amphilsoc.org/mole/view?docId=ead/Mss.Ms.Coll.26-ead.xml.

3. It should be noted that although I use the Ojibwe term "mnidoo," similar concepts are shared by Indigenous peoples throughout the Americas. It therefore takes expression in diverse forms. Even among Algonquian language groups there are numerous spellings and interpretations. Elsewhere I explore linguistic translations of key terms such as "Anishinaabe" and "mnidoo" more thoroughly. Hence, other than minimal linguistic definitions, the following is restricted to philosophical inquiries in keeping with my mother's teachings and those from her home territories Kikonaang miinawaa Aazhoodenaang (Kettle and Stoney Point First Nations), and the neighboring Anishinaabe communities in Southwestern Ontario—in particular, Bkejwanong (Walpole Island). The Anishinaabe philosophy in this essay began primarily in conversation with my mother, Rosalie (Elijah) Manning Mshkode-bzhikiikwe baa, Turtle Clan (b 1933–2006), and continues with Elder Mona Stonefish Kahawane, Bear Clan, who generously shares her knowledge as a translator, traditional doctor, traditional knowledge keeper, and cultural advisor, as well as being my aunt. Her teachings, in dialogue with those of my mother, have greatly influenced my thinking. *Chi miigwech*, Mona, for your guidance over the past twenty-eight years. *Chi miigwech* also to my aunt Rita (Sands) Clement Naakwegiizhigokwe, whose more recent friendship and input were essential to the Anishinaabemowin translations in this essay. Thank you both for sharing your considerable expertise as first-language Anishinaabemowin speakers and for helping continue the project begun with my mother to translate the philosophy that resides as much in the people as it does in our language. Also noteworthy is the effort put forth in investigating the intersection of Indigenous and Western philosophy. Not only is this the result of having an Irish father (Murray Alfred Manning, b. 1921–1982), with whom I continue to debate through this interrogation, but it also speaks to my own being-in-the-world as a troubling junction, torn as I am between conflicting and disparate systems of thought and ways of knowing.

4. This sketch does not represent spearfishing in itself. Instead, it articulates our thoroughgoing permeation with mnidoo, as seen through routine acts—that is, without recognizing it in an obvious way. The arrow depicts the direction of the thrust (whereas an actual spear would have three or more prongs). This diagram pronounces how a mnidoo structure of correspondence and discord (or division/difference) is enmeshed without paradox when their variant dimensions are taken together as a fluctuating co-responsiveness.

5. Andrew J. King and David J. T. Sumpter, "Murmurations," *Current Biology* 22, no. 4 (2012): 112–14.

6. Ojibwe is also spelled "Chippewa," "Ojibwa," and "Ojibway." The Ojibwe concepts along with the term "Anishinaabe" itself have mobile meanings, in my explorations. "Anishinaabe" and "Ojibwe" are sometimes used interchangeably. However, my mother understood them as having separate meanings. She reasoned that that is why we call ourselves "Ojibwe Anishinaabe" and not just one or the other. She translated "Anishinaabe" as meaning "a human being/Indian," inscribed with exceptional ethical integrity as the prefix "*anishin*" articulates, whereas the inclusion of the word "Indian," in my understanding, identifies *indigeneity* as the expression of this exceedingly good "way of being" that the Ojibwe identify with. Her translation is consistent with Basil Johnson's "Is That All There Is? Tribal Literature," in *Centering Anishinaabeeg Studies: Understanding the World through Stories* (East Lansing: Michigan State University Press, 2013).

This interpretation implies that other human cultures may not indwell in the same way as Anishinaabe beingness, or that "as a mode of being" the Anishinaabeg carry an element of something that one becomes (as with a moving target we continuously strive to attain), or perhaps grow into, or awaken to what is already there. My mother and I initiated these discussions on translation together when I was in kindergarten in 1974 (after being called a "dirty Indian" at school for the first time that I can recall). The Ojibwe are one philosophical group among many Anishinaabeg who aim at *bimaadiziwin*, "living in a good way" (unconsciously, perhaps, through what Merleau-Ponty describes as sedimentation or embodied social acquisition, as well as consciously). A lengthier translation of "Anishinaabe" is to be in a divine way, so to speak, both by emulating and by being infused with an aspect of this "exceedingly good original (human being—a mnidoo being—that was lowered down." This way of living is also good in the sense of having been ignited, infused with, and open to this *anishin* mnidoo-beingness, "an exceptionally respectful spirit or good way of being together." Anishinaabe is integral to conceptions of an interconnected web of life, coexistence, and "two-way positive" interrelationality. See Richard A. Rhodes, "'We are going to go there': Positive Politeness in Ojibwa," *Multilingua: Journal of Cross-Cultural and Interlanguage Communication* 8, nos. 2–3 (2009). My mother understood the term "Ojibwe" similarly to Mille Lacs Elder Jim Clark, who says that it refers to "a type of Anishinaabe" (cited in Fairbanks). Fairbanks elaborates that these ambiguities likely respect differing interpretations across time, geographical regions, dialects, and personal histories. See Brendan Fairbanks, *Ojibwe Discourse Markers* (Lincoln: University of Nebraska, 2016), 2–4.

Generally, the term "Anishinaabe" refers to members of the Algonquian language group. This includes several different nations, among them the Three Fires Confederacy, comprised of the Ojibwe, Odawa, and Potawatomi. Their particular philosophical teachings are embedded in the many dialects and ways of being (often subtly and indirectly). These philosophical lifeways take reciprocity for granted as an approach that is pervasive in *all* of existence. Despite their differences, these knowledges and ways of interconnecting are shared between the diverse peoples. For this reason, I use the term "Anishinaabe" to acknowledge that these many territories, dialects, and nations have related community-owned teachings and overlapping ethical-political ontologies. These Anishinaabe teachings provide the wellspring of who I am, how I think, and what I write. That said, I take sole responsibility for any missteps that arise from stretching and theorizing the small portion of knowledge that I have been given. I have tried to be specific about the genealogy of my knowledge. I refer here not only to my human teachers but also mnidoo helpers such as my territory, where the land meets the water, and Anishinaabemowin, to acknowledge the magnitude of their influence, and to be accountable for my interpretations. Doubtless I have made plenty of mistakes, particularly since I am not fluent in Anishinaabemowin. However, I was raised in Ojibwe/Potawatomi life philosophies, regardless of the contradictions posed by living in a colonized homeland. Much of this quotidian Anishinaabe knowledge is drawn from personal experience and memory in discussion with my mother. These fragments have then been cross-referenced primarily with Mona Stonefish, along with Rita Sands, and many others community members over the years. This work is driven by the sidelong and its silent stirring—pneuma, mnidoo, breath, spirit—potentiality. Stonefish says, "Gizhe-mnidoo gave the Anishinaabe these gifts" (March 27, 2017, Guelph, Ontario). My mothers have interpreted and relayed these fleeting glimpses to me in multiple gestures—spoken and unspoken.

The deeply interwoven philosophies of North American Algonquian languages require their community-oriented praxis in order to be not only activated (for particular cultural significance) but also continually reactivated in ways that resist uncritical dogmatism. Thus, I approach these Anishinaabe concepts from a variety of directions not to reveal so much as to allude to their outlying complexities and intersecting threads that otherwise threaten to collapse into the frail husk of a disembodied intellectualism. Indigenous knowledge keepers, like my mother and Stonefish, insist that such culturally specific research be conducted with Anishinaabemowin first-language speaking elders (where possible) in a community context (ideally spanning a lifetime). Through attending to our immediate contact with the world—that is, by querying perception itself, as Merleau-Ponty contends—phenomenology similarly emphasizes life knowledge and the world of experience. My phenomenological approach follows the subtle distinctions of an Anishinaabe community-oriented context that apprehends *kina* (all) as community but also as an unending body, which I arrive at through Ojibwe "thing" memory, as in the other-than-human that might be thought of as a pervasive mnidoo vitalism.

7. In a discussion with Haudenosaunee Elder Bruce Elijah (Wolf Clan) about this way of being attuned with the world, in his language he used the term *sadoke* to describe that connection. Elijah is an Onyota'a:ka member of the Oneida Settlement in Southwestern Ontario. Elijah, "Soaring: Indigenous Youth Career Conference," Indspire, London, Ontario, May 5, 2015.

8. Thing-memory resonates somewhat with the concept "blood-memory," which is cited in Indigenous contexts today but was not a familiar part of my childhood vocabulary. I do recall talk of "thing-memory/thing-knowing," spoken about in an implied/indirect manner. "Blood-memory" is a contentious term with an uncertain genealogy and meaning. The intergenerational memory that I conceptualize as a mnidoo interconnectedness between present people, ancestors, descendants, and all of our nonhuman relations *might* be described as blood-memory. In this sense, however, it is understood as the animation of our very blood and cells as mnidoo potencies, with their own agency and way of knowing and communicating. I refer to this phrase cautiously. Blood-memory is controversial for essentializing Indigenous identity as a reduction to blood quantum, a racializing approach instituted by the Indian Act as part of a program of cultural genocide. As Kim Tallbear points out, it problematically conflates Indigenous identity with genetics, which could have deleterious consequences for land claims, self-determination, and resource struggles. See Kim Tallbear, *Native American DNA: Tribal Belonging and the False Promise of Genetic Science* (Minneapolis: University of Minnesota Press, 2013).

9. Even though, as Merleau-Ponty writes, the "experience [*l'épreuve*] of absurdity and that of absolute evidentness are interdependent and even indiscernible," he nonetheless aligns such givenness with the natural attitude. This suggests that all people sensibly gather and arrive at signification in the same way (in a manner, moreover, as it is defined by Western philosophy). This relegates orientation and valuation to the second-order operation of cognitive reflection. Maurice Merleau-Ponty, *Phenomenology of Perception*, trans. Donald A. Landes (London: Routledge, 2012), 309, 201.

10. *Nii kina ganaa* (All my relatives/All my relations) is the term spoken in my home community of Kettle and Stoney Point First Nation; Bkejwanong (Walpole Island) speakers use both *Nii kina ganaa* and *Kina enwemgig* (All the ones I'm related to); people

elsewhere might use *Indinawemaaganidog* (Relatives). The spelling and translation for *Nii kina ganaa* was arrived at in discussion with my mother, Stonefish, and Sands (doing guesswork from oral accounts). However, I was unable to find this dialect of *Nii kina ganaa* in any Ojibwe dictionary. One possible source derives from the mixed Potawatami-Ojibwe ancestry of Kettle and Stoney Point and Bkejwanong. The Potawatami phrasing of *All my relations* is *jage nagonan*. See http://www.kansasheritage.org/PBP/books/dicto/d_frame.html.

11. "Original" in the sense of the always already condition of possibility, which, as Merleau-Ponty suggests, is not only encrusted over a lifetime but also intersubjectively sedimented over generations.

12. Notably, Claude Lévi-Strauss dedicated *The Savage Mind* to Merleau-Ponty. Claude Lévi-Strauss, *The Savage Mind* (Chicago: University of Chicago Press, 1966).

13. Samuel B. Mallin, *Art, Line, Thought* (Dordrecht: Kluwer Academic Publishers, 1996), 264.

14. Basil Johnson, *Manitous: The Spiritual World of the Ojibway* (New York: Harper Collins, 1995), 2.

15. Martin Heidegger, *Being and Time*, trans. John Macquarrie and Edward Robinson (New York: Harper and Row, 1962); Maurice Merleau-Ponty, *The Visible and the Invisible*, trans. Alphonso Lingis (Evanston, IL: Northwestern University Press, 1968), 261.

16. Maurice Merleau-Ponty, "Eye and Mind," trans. Carleton Dallery, in *The Primacy of Perception* (Evanston, IL: Northwestern University Press, 1964), 178.

17. John Nichols and Earl Nyholm, *A Concise Dictionary of Minnesota Ojibwe* (Minneapolis: University of Minnesota Press, 1995), 49.

18. Merleau-Ponty writes, "Through the intermediary of my society, my cultural world, and their horizons—at least a virtual communication with them . . . the social exists silently and as a solicitation." Merleau-Ponty, *Phenomenology of Perception*, 379.

19. Ibid., 421.

20. Ibid.

21. Ibid., xxv, 428.

22. Alfred Irving Hallowell, "Ojibwe Ontology, Behavior, and World View," in *Culture in History*, ed. Stanley Diamond (New York: Columbia University Press, 1960), 20.

23. Merleau-Ponty, *Visible and the Invisible*, 263.

24. Ibid., 264.

25. Merleau-Ponty, *Phenomenology of Perception*, xxiv.

26. Maurice Merleau-Ponty, *Phenomenology of Perception*, trans. Colin Smith (London: Routledge, 2002), 241. (Note: For this particular quote, the Smith translation was required.)

27. Merleau-Ponty, *Visible and the Invisible*, 196.

28. Merleau-Ponty, *Phenomenology of Perception*, trans. Landes, 428.

29. Ibid., 366.

30. Ibid., 428.

31. Merleau-Ponty, *Visible and the Invisible*, 262.

32. Ibid., 142, 263.

33. Ibid., 261.

34. Ibid., 263.

35. Ibid., 136.

36. Maurice Merleau-Ponty, *Le Visible et l'Invisible* (Paris: Gallimard, 1964), 179.

37. Merleau-Ponty, *Phenomenology of Perception*, 373.
38. Merleau-Ponty, *Visible and the Invisible*, 266.
39. Ibid., 142.
40. Ibid., 143; emphasis added.
41. Merleau-Ponty, *Phenomenology of Perception*, 373.
42. Ibid., 202.
43. Ibid., 366.
44. Ibid., 373.
45. Ibid.
46. Ibid., 431.
47. Ibid., 367.
48. Merleau-Ponty, *Phenomenology of Perception*, 366.
49. Not the tangible eye per se, but the adhesion of this "massive sentiment" opening onto the world. Merleau-Ponty, *Visible and the Invisible*, 142. Merleau-Ponty writes, "It can be said that a human is born at the instant when something that was only virtually visible, inside the mother's body, becomes at one and the same time visible for itself and for us." Merleau-Ponty, *Primacy of Perception*, 167–68.
50. Merleau-Ponty, *Visible and the Invisible*, 134.
51. Ibid., 136.
52. Ibid., 197.
53. Daniel J. G. Pearce et al., "Role of Projection in the Control of Bird Flocks," *Proceedings of the National Academy of the Sciences of the United States of America* 111, no. 29 (2014): 10422.
54. For more on this, see Merleau-Ponty, *Visible and the Invisible*, 7.
55. Merleau-Ponty, *Phenomenology of Perception*, 366.
56. Pearce et al., "Role of Projection," 10422.
57. Merleau-Ponty, *Phenomenology of Perception*, 132.
58. Ibid., 428.
59. Merleau-Ponty, *Visible and the Invisible*, 266.
60. Ibid., 197.
61. Ibid., 265.
62. Ibid., 133, 134.
63. Ibid., 266.
64. Merleau-Ponty's theory of the visible and the invisible, as I take it up, is not limited to a discussion on sight and sightlessness, but opens to the invisible primacy of embodied knowledge and our inability to directly access/signify any perceptual experience during its immediate undertaking.
65. Basil Johnson, *Ojibway Heritage* (Toronto: McClelland and Stewart, 1976), 15.
66. I use the weaker argument "in this sense," since mnidoo harbours animacy and inanimacy (holds and withholds as potentiality). This potency runs alongside and saturates affective "intensities," to use Deleuze and Guattari's term, without canceling them out.
67. In *A Thousand Plateaus: Capitalism and Schizophrenia*, Gilles Deleuze and Félix Guattari articulate the "overwhelming" mode of affect through such examples as a swarm of bees that indirectly trigger one another into motion as a shifting assemblage. They describe this as a process of "becoming" in which we are taken up into a "body without organs" through proximal relations. For a longer discussion on this, see

Dolleen Tisawii'ashii Manning, "The Becoming Human of Buffalo Bill," in *Intensities and Lines of Flight: Deleuze/Guattari and the Arts*, ed. Antonio Calcagno, Jim Vernon, and Steve Lofts (London: Rowman and Littlefield, 2014), 187–206. Notably, the term "dissidence" is employed to describe the variance/disagreement inherent to difference. Albeit a necessary friction, I contend in contrast that affect does not overwhelm entirely as a pre-personal process. Rather the material world is *alive*, conscious, and it co-responsively exerts agency. Unhampered by cognition, it/they are not befuddled by the limited capacity of human consciousness. Rather, discernment or the transparency of intellection is itself the opacity that stands in the way of fully accessing the mnidoo-self-world (where so-called lifeless inanimate objects indwell as immediate fully accessing interrelationality).

68. These schematic drawings of colliding spirals (fig. 9.2) and pulsating concentric rings/spheres (fig. 9.3) bring to mind an illustration by Leroy Little Bear (*Revolutions 2012*, Artist Residency, Banff Centre, Alberta 2011). During his presentation on quantum physics and Indigenous knowledge, he scribbled a densely tangled line drawing on the chalkboard to convey the complex entanglement of Indigenous thought systems in contrast to the linear approaches of Western science.

69. See Luce Irigaray, "From *The Forgetting of Air* to *To Be Two*," trans. Heidi Bostic and Stephen Pluháček, in *Feminist Interpretations of Martin Heidegger*, ed. Nancy J. Holland and Patricia Huntington (University Park: Pennsylvania State University Press, 2001).

70. Merleau-Ponty, *Visible and the Invisible*, 142.

71. Seizes hold perhaps through Merleau-Ponty's three pre-linguistic regions—motility, social, and perceptual. See Mallin, *Art, Line, Thought*, 1996, 275.

72. We leave aside the question of oneiric dreaming for a future essay.

73. Merleau-Ponty, *Phenomenology of Perception*, 366.

74. Merleau-Ponty, *Visible and the Invisible*, 202.

75. Mallin, *Art, Line, Thought*, 281.

76. Merleau-Ponty, *Visible and the Invisible*, 133.

77. Why, then, do we so often not hear the cry? Why do we not tune in to strangers or natural disasters when they quake? Tackling these questions through what Merleau-Ponty defines as "intellectualism" would surely carry us away into the rabbit hole. I have attempted to broach some of these inconsistencies through the finite limitations of human consciousness pitted against an infinite world-consciousnessing. But more than that is too complicated for this short essay. The simple answer would be that I am not so certain that in some sense we are not already there, but that it is concealed from our immediate and sustained grasp due to a lack of attentiveness.

78. "Self-self" refers to bounded intentional human consciousness; "mnidoo-self" is an orienting but indeterminate intuiting that exceeds a personalized centeredness, whereas "mnidoo-world-self" (synonymous to world-mnidoo) courses through and suffuses everything—the *All*—to which I am grounded, interdependent, and coexistent. These terms are not only insufficient placeholders but also misleading, since they are neither states of mind nor separate entities.

79. This includes imaginary representations and empirical or tangible facticity, each equally valid and interdependent dimensions.

80. This is a well-known saying among the Ojibwe of Southwestern Ontario.

BIBLIOGRAPHY

American Philosophical Society. *Alfred Irving Hallowell Papers, 1892–1981*, Mss. MS Coll. 26. http://www.amphilsoc.org/mole/view?docId=ead/Mss.Ms.Coll.26-ead.xml.

Deleuze, Gilles, and Félix Guattari. *A Thousand Plateaus: Capitalism and Schizophrenia*. Translated by Brian Massumi. Minneapolis: University of Minnesota Press, 1987.

Fairbanks, Brendan. *Ojibwe Discourse Markers*. Lincoln: University of Nebraska, 2016.

Hallowell, A. Irving. "Ojibwe Ontology, Behavior, and World View." In *Culture in History*, edited by Stanley Diamond, 17–49. New York: Columbia University Press, 1960.

Heidegger, Martin. *Being and Time*. Translated by John Macquarrie and Edward Robinson. New York: Harper and Row, 1962.

Hogan, Linda. *Solar Storms: A Novel*. New York: Simon and Schuster, 1995.

Irigaray, Luce. "From *The Forgetting of Air* to *To Be Two*." Translated by Heidi Bostic and Stephen Pluháček. In *Feminist Interpretations of Martin Heidegger*, edited by Nancy J. Holland and Patricia Huntington, 309–315. University Park: Pennsylvania State University Press, 2001.

Johnson, Basil. "Is That All There Is? Tribal Literature." In *Centering Anishinaabeg Studies: Understanding the World through Stories*, edited by Jill Doerfler, Niigaanwewidam James Sinclair, and Heidi Kiiwetinepinesiik Stark, 3–12. East Lansing: Michigan State University Press, 2013.

———. *Manitous: The Spiritual World of the Ojibway*. New York: Harper Collins, 1995.

———. *Ojibway Heritage*. Toronto: McClelland and Stewart, 1976.

———. "One Generation from Extinction." In W. H. New, *Native Writers and Canadian Writing*. 10–15. Vancouver: University of British Columbia Press, 1990.

King, Andrew J., and David J. T. Sumpter. "Murmurations." *Current Biology* 22, no. 4 (2012): 112–14.

Lévi-Strauss, Claude. *The Savage Mind*. Chicago: University of Chicago Press, 1966. Originally published as *La Pensée Sauvage*. Paris: Pion, 1962.

Mallin, Samuel B. *Art, Line, Thought*. Dordrecht: Kluwer Academic Publishers, 1996.

Manning, Dolleen Tisawii'ashii. "The Becoming Human of Buffalo Bill." In *Intensities and Lines of Flight: Deleuze/Guattari and the Arts*, edited by Antonio Calcagno, Jim Vernon, and Steve Lofts, 187–206. London: Rowman and Littlefield, 2014.

Merleau-Ponty, Maurice. "Eye and Mind." Translated by Carleton Dallery. In *The Primacy of Perception*, edited by James M. Edie, 159–90. Evanston, IL: Northwestern University Press, 1964.

———. *Phenomenology of Perception*. Translated by Donald A. Landes. London: Routledge, 2012.

———. *Phenomenology of Perception*. Translated by Colin Smith. London: Routledge, 2002.

———. *The Visible and the Invisible*. Translated by Alphonso Lingis. Evanston, IL: Northwestern University Press, 1968. Originally published as *Le Visible et l'invisible*. Paris: Gallimard, 1964.

Nichols, John, and Earl Nyholm. *A Concise Dictionary of Minnesota Ojibwe*. Minneapolis: University of Minnesota Press, 1995.

Pearce, Daniel J. G., Adam M. Miller, George Rowlands, and Matthew S. Turner. "Role of Projection in the Control of Bird Flocks." *Proceedings of the National Academy of the Sciences of the United States of America* 111, no. 29 (2014): 10422–26.

Rhodes, Richard A. *Eastern Ojibwa-Chippewa-Ottawa Dictionary.* Vol. 3. New York: Mouton Publishers, 1985.

———. "'We are going to go there': Positive Politeness in Ojibwa." *Multilingua: Journal of Cross-Cultural and Interlanguage Communication* 8, nos. 2–3 (1989): 249–58.

Tallbear, Kim. *Native American DNA: Tribal Belonging and the False Promise of Genetic Science.* Minneapolis: University of Minnesota Press, 2013.

Valentine, Randy. *Nishnaabemwin Reference Grammar.* Toronto: University of Toronto Press, 2001. 80.

10 TRANS-SUBJECTIVITY/ TRANS-OBJECTIVITY

CHRISTINE DAIGLE

My work, whether it is grounded in Nietzsche, Sartre, Beauvoir, or others, is informed by a desire to understand the human being's presence in the world and seek to establish grounds for an ethics of flourishing. However, an ethical theory can be successful only if it is grounded in an adequate theory of subjectivity. Like many other feminist critics, I fail to be convinced by traditional rationalistic philosophy that paints a portrait of the relation between individual and world as straightforward and easily conceived. Instead I draw on the work of existentialists and phenomenologists, as well as structuralists and post-structuralists, some with feminist leanings, some not, for their attempt to come to terms with what is, after all, a messy relation between human and world. In this context, investigating the "nature" of the human agent, the "being for whom being is in question," as Martin Heidegger would have it, becomes imperative. In opposition to René Descartes's "thinking substance" that encounters the material world in a dualistic setting—wherein the encounter is often conceived of in terms of a confrontation—existentialists and phenomenologists uncover a being that is an embodied intentional consciousness entangled with the world. Their take on the subject is that there is much more to it than mere rational thinking.

Thinking with Friedrich Nietzsche, I like to consider the human being as a "subjective multiplicity."[1] The human being is a manifold that both makes itself through its experiences and is shaped by these experiences. However, I am not proposing a Nietzschean view of subjectivity. My approach is rather irreverent; instead I am attempting to develop a view of subjectivity, or what it is to be an agent, that borrows and blends together the various concepts I find interesting or potentially helpful in the philosophers and theorists I read. So while this essay will explore the views of a number of philosophers, this exploration will be selective and will take the form of a flirt. My analysis has no exegetical aims or pretentions. To put it another way: I conceive of myself as Michel de Montaigne's bee that collects nectar from different flowers and eventually produces the honey that is its own, which is his analogy for the pupil he desires.[2] What will emerge out of my own nectar collection is a view of the human being as trans-subjective and trans-objective—that is, a proposal for a new feminist phenomenological ontology.

The phenomenological ontology I begin to elaborate in this essay is a weak ontology in Stephen K. White's sense. In his book *Sustaining Affirmation*, White distinguishes between foundationalist strong traditional ontologies and those ontologies that are non-foundationalist and yet wish to retain some features of strong ontologies, such as those emerging as a result of the deconstructive and critical work done by thinkers like Michel Foucault, Jacques Derrida, and Jean-François Lyotard. (One might want to add to this list the array of feminist critiques aimed at traditional ontologies.) White explains that weak ontologies present "deep reconceptualizations of human being in relation to its world. More specifically, human being is presented as in some way 'stickier' than in prevailing modern conceptualizations."[3] And further, he indicates that weak ontologies "respond to two pressing concerns. First, there is the acceptance of the idea that all fundamental conceptualizations of the self, other and world are contestable. Second, there is the sense that such conceptualizations are nevertheless necessary or unavoidable for an adequately reflective ethical and political life."[4] I share these concerns, and my proposals in this essay constitute a weak ontology.

VARIOUS THEORETICAL VIEWS

Given the possibilities it provides to rethink the traditional notion of subjectivity qua rational, I take Simone de Beauvoir's philosophy as my starting point. I focus not only on the feminist phenomenology she presents in *The Second Sex* but also on the notion of ambiguity that she develops in earlier works, such as "Pyrrhus and Cinéas" and *The Ethics of Ambiguity*. In her work, Beauvoir is preoccupied with the question of intersubjectivity and ethics. Her ethical concern is also a political one because of the patterns of oppression she uncovers and the related problem of liberation. As she sees it, we have to work toward our liberation as well as the liberation of others in order to make possible the flourishing of individuals. This claim stems from her view of the human being as fundamentally ambiguous. She emphasizes the anchoring of consciousness in the body and in the world as situated. We cannot be conceived as separate, either from our own body, our own situation in the world, or other people. This relationality is constitutive of who we are. This belief leads Beauvoir to analyze the oppression that women face and that is constitutive of their being in a novel manner. The groundbreaking argument of *The Second Sex* is that female human beings have been made into women because the patriarchal world in which they live permeates them and, consequently, they have interiorized their own oppression. Beauvoir's argument is made possible by the way she conceives consciousness.

It is because subjectivity remains free while being oppressed—which is one aspect of ambiguity for Beauvoir—that it is possible for women to liberate themselves from patriarchal oppression. Ambiguity is a manifold concept in Beauvoir. It points to the fact that the human being is subject *and* object, mind *and* body, being for-itself *and* being with-others, immanence *and* transcendence, free *and* situated (having to make oneself free), free *and* tied to others' freedoms, and an unfolding project (it is what it is not *and* it is not what it is).[5] She defines the human being as an embodied intentional consciousness *in* the world and *with* others. In "Pyrrhus and Cinéas," she says, "A man is freedom and facticity at the same time. He is free, but not with that abstract freedom posited by the Stoics; he is free in situation."[6] Her 1945 review of Maurice Merleau-Ponty's *Phenomenology of Perception* for *Les Temps modernes* leads her to add another dimension to the ambiguity she has described. She is very positive about Merleau-Ponty's work and, in particular, praises the understanding of consciousness as embodied and as a fold. Merleau-Ponty explains, "I am not, to recall Hegel's phrase, 'a hole in being,' but rather a hollow, or a fold that was made and that can be unmade."[7] The body is our anchor in the world, our location in the world, where consciousness as a fold can constitute itself by perceiving things, others, and itself. As a fold, consciousness shapes and is being shaped by the world. As Dorothea Olkowski puts it, "Merleau-Ponty's particular view of this [the situatedness of human beings] is that a being-in-situation is an embodied, perceptual being."[8] Perception is at the crux of our being-in-the-world, and Merleau-Ponty insists that there is no radical split between subject and object, perceiver and perceived; rather, they are intertwined. The perceiving subject is not a container in which the object of perception is collected; rather, the object lets itself be enfolded by the perceiving consciousness, thereby constituting it and being constituted by it. The views offered by Merleau-Ponty in his work all appeal to Beauvoir.[9]

Another important dimension of ambiguity is elaborated in *The Second Sex*. As embodied consciousness and as a body that is sexed, one is necessarily sexed. In the "Biological Data" chapter of the book, Beauvoir introduces a distinction between the biological body and the social body and argues that sexual differences are meaningful only in the social realm.[10] In *The Ethics of Ambiguity* she writes, "The body itself is not a brute fact. It expresses our relationship to the world [but] it *determines* no behavior."[11] She reiterates this view in *The Second Sex*, this time emphasizing the sexed aspect of being and how it is constitutive of beings. She says, "Because the body is the instrument of our hold on the world, the world appears different to us depending on how it is grasped, which explains why we have studied these [biological] data so deeply; they are one of the keys that enable us to understand woman." However, she continues, "we refuse the idea that they form a fixed destiny for her."[12] The body of the human being is not a thing; it is a situation; "it is our grasp on the world and the outline for our projects."[13]

In her *Volatile Bodies*, Elizabeth Grosz thinks with and beyond Beauvoir and addresses the way the individual lives in the world. She discusses the notions of porosity and liquidity. As she puts it, "The body is a most peculiar 'thing,' for it is never quite reducible to being merely a thing: nor does it ever quite manage to rise above the status of thing. Thus it is both a thing and a nonthing."[14] She illustrates this by using the Möbius strip as a model for the body. It is a "model which shows that while there are disparate 'things' being related [mind and body], they have the capacity to twist one into the other."[15] For Grosz the body is a borderline concept, a threshold, a hinge. It is a porous and volatile being, because it is always "in the making." This notion of porosity is one I wish to use to explain how consciousness as fold can be constituted by what it enfolds. I wish to speak of a porous fold. I am not convinced that Grosz provides us with the tools to understand the nature and mechanics of this model of the mind/body relation. Dealing with it on its own is not sufficient. That is why I take this metaphor in a different direction.

Rosi Braidotti's Nietzschean/Deleuzian concept of nomadism—which also takes its roots in her understanding of Beauvoir's notion of ambiguity[16]—can be articulated with this view of the porous fold. Braidotti explains, "The nomadic consciousness . . . aims to rethink the unity of the subject, without reference to humanistic beliefs, without dualistic oppositions, linking instead body and mind in a new set of intensive and often intransitive transitions."[17] Nomadism is "an acute awareness of the nonfixity of boundaries. It is the intense desire to go on trespassing, transgressing."[18] While Braidotti's emphasis is on the worldliness and historicity of consciousness, it leads her to posit a fluid and hybrid subject for her nomadic ethics. Nomadic subjects are in transit because they are constantly becoming and necessarily permeated by their experiences.

This permeation is why Braidotti insists on the notion of fluidity. The view I will elaborate in what follows offers an ontological foundation upon which to ground such a notion.

Grosz's and Braidotti's dealings with the notion of subjectivity and agency are intensive critiques of any dualistic understanding of ourselves. They go further than Beauvoir in dismissing this dualism, pushing the notion of ambiguity to its extreme by emphasizing flux and becoming. While this may or may not lead to the dismissal of the self and agency, I do not want to go that far. I use Braidotti's concept for my own purposes, given that I am interested in conceiving of the human agent as something that is in a "process" of shaping itself and being shaped. In this regard the self may be understood as an ambiguous field of tensions, in between the act of constitution and self-constitution. I use Grosz's notion of fluidity in an attempt to capture what I see as a self that is continuous from one moment to the other: the self is both identical and yet different. It fluctuates and morphs from one moment to the other, from one experience to the other, prompted to morph by the very experiences it undergoes: the experiences of being with-others and being in the presence of the world and objects is deeply transformative, since the subject is fluid. There is both self-constitution occurring as a result of one's relation to oneself, but there is also a great deal of constitution that is done to the subject to which the subject may or may not relate. I will discuss this point below.

The views presented by Beauvoir, Grosz, and Braidotti emphasize, each to a different degree, the fact that we are worldly intersubjective beings, beings that are intermingled with others and with the world. But they tend to underemphasize the very material aspect of the world, as did Beauvoir when she insisted that rather than being a "thing," the body is a "situation." Thus I find it important to look at the views of material feminists and posthumanists such as Nancy Tuana, Karen Barad, and Stacy Alaimo. Alaimo conceives of the human being as transcorporeal and explains, "The human is always the very stuff of the messy, contingent, emergent mix of the material world."[19] She embraces Tuana's view of viscous porosity, which is connected to interactionism. Tuana explains, "Interactionism posits 'a world of complex phenomena in dynamic relationality.'"[20] Further, she defines "viscous porosity" in the following manner:

> *Viscosity* is neither fluid nor solid, but intermediate between them. Attention to the *porosity* of interactions helps to undermine the notion that distinctions, as important as they might be in particular contexts, signify a natural or unchanging boundary, a natural kind. At the same time, "viscosity" retains an emphasis on resistance to changing form, thereby a more helpful image than

"fluidity," which is too likely to promote a notion of open possibilities and to overlook sites of resistance and opposition or attention to the complex ways in which material agency is often involved in interactions, including, but not limited to, human agency.[21]

Insisting on viscosity, Tuana offers an implicit critique of the views of Grosz and Braidotti. All three views challenge the notion of boundaries and fixity, but Tuana's view incorporates considerations about resistance that grounds her view in the very materiality of our beings in a way unacknowledged by Grosz and Braidotti. As Tuana puts it, "There is a viscous porosity of flesh—my flesh and the flesh of the world. This porosity is a hinge through which we are of and in the world."[22] That hinge, if we follow Alaimo, is transcorporeal, or perhaps even transmaterial.

Alaimo's posthumanist stance is also influenced by Barad's proposals. Barad proposes that there are material discursive forces—sometimes mislabeled as social, cultural, and so forth—that play a role in processes of materialization. She says, "What is needed is a robust account of the materialization of all bodies—'human' and 'nonhuman'—and the material-discursive practices by which their differential constitutions are marked."[23] In Barad's view it is through processes of intra-actions that separate and determinate bodies emerge: intra-action generates agential separability. Further, "Reality is not composed of things-in-themselves or things-behind-phenomena but 'things'-in-phenomena. The world *is* intra-activity in its differential mattering."[24] It is a dynamic state of becoming, and in this context, "Agency is not an attribute but the ongoing reconfigurings of the world."[25] This, however, amounts to an elimination of the subjective aspect of our beings that I am not willing to accept.

While I am willing to consider that "matter is a stabilizing and destabilizing process of iterative intra-activity,"[26] I am not willing to eliminate human agency and the subjective experience of being a self. As I see it, we experience ourselves as subjects and as agents, and this consciousness of ourselves as such, the fact that we relate to ourselves—and others—as agents and subjects, unveils a truth about the existence of this consciousness and agency. Despite my criticism of the views mentioned above on that count, I find Barad's and Alaimo's views helpful to understand and emphasize that there is a material aspect of our being that is constitutive of who and what we are, an aspect that we tend to obscure. Without embracing a materialist ontology like the one they propose, I offer that an ontology must take into account our material being.

Taking into consideration the views of Bruno Latour and Foucault may help flesh out the weightiness of our worldliness in a different way. I should note, however, that I do not think that structuralism and posthumanism are mutually exclusive either. Rather, I see them as complementing one another. In his actor-network theory, Latour introduces the notion of interobjectivity and speaks of objects as *doing* something, they are *actants*—that is to say, subjects of action.[27] They are agents in the same way that we conceive of humans as agents. In the social world, there are various networks constituted by these actants. This is the realm of the interobjective, which is as important as the realm of the inter-subjective for Latour. Human subjects interact within a certain frame that is composed of nonhuman-actors—the interobjective.[28] One can say that the social world is flat and inhabited by various entities that are on the same plane, regardless of their different natures.[29] Emphasis is thus placed on the ontological equality of beings: all are in the world and present to one another and to the world, regardless of whether they are subjects or objects, animate and living or not (a plant or a concrete building), simple or complex (a rock or a corporation). However, if we take Foucault's analyses into consideration, for example, as well as various feminist analyses, we can posit that this flatness is merely ontological. I would claim that ontology, insofar as it concerns itself with defining being and describing what it means to say of a thing that it is, is flat. To say that beings are and that they are as actants is not to say that they are engaged in power relations. Structures of power exist only because human beings attribute meaning and interpretations to things that embed power and power relations in them. Thus, the phenomenal realm, the realm of lived experience is never flat.

Foucault's discussion of power, structures, and self-constitution evolved greatly throughout his career. However, some core ideas endure, such as that of self-constitution vis-à-vis power. I take the following as an indication of that. Speaking of the relation of the subject to power, Foucault says, "It is a form of power which makes individuals subjects,"[30] and again, "Every power relationship implies, at least in potentia, a strategy of struggle, in which the two forces are not superimposed, do not lose their specific nature, or do not finally become confused."[31] I take this to mean that there is mutual constitution of subject and power. Given the different subjects constituted by power and their ensuing different relationships to power, and co-constitution, the ontological realm is anything but flat for Foucault. Relating this to Latour's proposals, one may say that in the realm of lived experience, the phenomenal realm, the actions of actants weigh more or less depending on their power and the power relations in place. Therefore, the realm of the interobjective is no more flat than the realm of the intersubjective.

To recapitulate, I wish to revisit the notion of intentional embodied consciousness as a fold. As a fold, consciousness enfolds what it encounters, shaping it as it encounters it and shaping itself by the same token. I consider it essential to understand consciousness as a fold to be porous and viscous. Doing so strengthens the view of embodied consciousness as a fold. Indeed, taking embodied consciousness to be a porous fold of being that unfolds—that makes itself—yields interesting results. Porosity points to how consciousness can be shaped by its encounter with things and others. If things "enter the fold," or are "enfolded" within consciousness, then consciousness *is* other if the fold is itself porous, thus eliminating any dualistic remnants there might be to the notion of embodied consciousness. The being of consciousness *is* the act of enfolding. Consciousness as porous viscous fold enfolds and unfolds in the realms of the intersubjective and the interobjective and navigates various fields of tensions.

TRANS((SUBJ)(OBJ))ECTIVITY

Because we are ambiguous beings, we are both subjects and objects, and as such, we participate in both realms of intersubjectivity and interobjectivity, not alternatively but concomitantly. As I explained, as an ambiguous intentional consciousness that is a porous fold, human subjectivity shapes and is shaped by its interactions, not only with other human subjectivities but also with the world as a whole and in its parts. The human being is caught in a web of inter-subject-object-ivity, what I wish to call inter((subj)(obj))ectivity. It is both caught in this web and it is itself this ambiguous web. I think, however, that it is best to refer to it as *trans*((subj)(obj))ectivity. "Inter" really means "between," "among," while "trans" means "across," "beyond," or "into a different state." The prefix "trans" thus better captures what I wish to offer in my reevaluation of the notion of subjectivity. I also take Alaimo's point about "trans" seriously. She says, "*Trans* indicates movement across different sites," and then she explains that transcorporeality "opens up a mobile space that acknowledges the often unpredictable and unwanted actions of human bodies, nonhuman creatures, ecological systems, chemical agents, and other actors."[32] The way I conceive of trans((subj)(obj))ectivity, there is indeed this kind of mobility embedded in our being and in our (self-)constitution.

I believe that such an understanding provides a better theoretical framework of how subjectivity both constitutes itself and is constituted. My proposal for a feminist phenomenological ontology of trans((subj)(obj))ectivity explains why we experience the world and ourselves as we do: as fragmented beings whose fragments coalesce to form our being. The following metaphor, used by Nietzsche, seems to capture well what I am proposing: "With every moment of our lives some of the polyp-arms of our being grow and others dry up, depending on the nourishment that the moment does or does not supply. . . . all our experiences are, in this sense, types of nourishment."[33] This is an apt metaphor if we understand the polyp to be a porous being. I offer that we are such polyps, individually and socially, trans-subjectively and trans-objectively. We are trans((subj)(obj)ective beings.

CONSTITUTING THE TRANS((SUBJ)(OBJ)ECTIVE BEING: TRAUMA, EXTREME EXPERIENCES, AND EVERYDAY SELF-CONSTITUTION

The renewed phenomenological-ontological view of the human being that I offer provides a better way to understand how trauma and extreme experiences affect individuals in their core. Contrary to what some may think, trauma is not merely mnemonic, nor is it only physical or psychological. It is profoundly constitutive of the beings that we are. It is the fabric of our existence.

To illustrate this, I wish to analyze the lyrics of an intriguing song by Quebec singer Jean Leloup. The song is titled "Lucie," and the lyrics tell the story of a young girl who hires a man to kill her family. In the compact disk booklet, Leloup explains that the inspiration for the song came from having seen a girl of eleven or twelve years old sitting at a garage sale in the middle of a driveway with her bicycle and dolls. She was all scruffy and dirty, as were her parents, who were sitting on each side of her, both appearing to be drunk and violent. Her father looked particularly vicious. That scene lead Leloup to think that their family life must have been horrible, and he writes, "It was evident that she wanted to burn these ignoble parents."[34] In the song, Lucie hires a killer and promises to pay him with her virginity. The man kills the family by lighting the house on fire while Lucie waits in the shed. She pays him off as promised. The song ends with these words:

> And Lucie has become a killer
> She has fun and she travels
> She has received a small inheritance

The whole song is sung by a chorus of two or three predominantly female voices, but then a single male voice, sounding slightly deranged, sings:

> I will age right beside you
> I will age with you
> I will age in your arms
> I will age right by you
> I will age right beside you

I will age right inside you
I will rot inside you
And I will be you. . .
I am an outlaw!³⁵

These lyrics illustrate well the effect of the trans-subjective and the trans-objective. No matter how much fun she has or how much she travels, Lucie is now the person who has had her whole family killed. She is the person who paid off the killer with her body. The sexual organ of the killer has penetrated Lucie, not merely once at the time of payment, but forever. He is inside her; he is her. The sexual relation qua payment, the intermingling of bodies, but also of deeds, are all illustrated by these lyrics. As a trans((subj)(obj))ective being, Lucie is ontologically transformed by the deed she commissioned as well as by her mode of payment. She has become a killer despite the fact that she did not light the house on fire herself.

    Another example will illuminate this in a slightly different way. In a famous television show in Quebec, *Tout le monde en parle*, Karl Zero, the biographer of Canadian murderer Luka Rocco Magnotta, was interviewed on March 10, 2013. A few Quebec filmmakers were also present (Podz, Kim Nguyen, Xavier Dolan, and Rafaël Ouellet) as well as a popular stand-up comic, Laurent Paquin. Paquin and Zero discussed the video that Magnotta put online with the title "1 Lunatic 1 Icepick," his recording of the torture, murder, dismembering, and rape of Chinese student Lin Jun.³⁶ The biographer explained he had to watch it as part of his research for the book he wrote. Paquin expressed his surprise at how detached Zero seemed to be, while people who had seen the video had told Paquin they should never have watched it. Zero explained that his job revolved around such news items all the time. One of the filmmakers present, Podz, intervened and said, "This is not just any news item, this video is really peculiar. We can talk about it but it is contributing to what Magnotta wanted to achieve."³⁷ This was a very interesting and telling moment. The malaise was real for Podz, as it was for others on the set. He began by saying, "I have seen it and I have really regretted it, watching it." His body language told the story of how deeply transformative watching the video had been. Even though Zero posed as rather blasé about the experience of watching the video, it was evident from his body language while listening to Podz that he had been as deeply transformed by the viewing.

    Researching this example and seeking to view this interview again, I used Google to see if I could find it online. In order to search for it, I included "Magnotta video" among my search keywords. At this point I became quite self-conscious of my search; I was very much aware of the risk of clicking on the wrong link and actually seeing Magnotta's video, which I *did not* see nor did I want to see. I have never read link descriptions so carefully before clicking on them as I did that day. I was horrified to see that the video made by Magnotta was still online and available, making the risk of viewing it an immanently present danger.[38] The point I wish to make is that as a trans((subj)(obj))ective being, the filmmaker and the biographer (as well as anyone else who has watched this video) took part in the deed. As spectators, the trans((subj)(obj))ective beings Podz and Zero had the experience of watching someone being tortured, killed, raped, and dismembered. To push the Nietzschean polyp metaphor, their beings now have an arm that has been nourished by this experience. They have been transpierced by the deed and have, willy-nilly, incorporated the deed into their very being. The tangible malaise on the television set, which was palpable during the discussion, made visible this transformative constitution of their selves as thereafter complicit in the deed they viewed.[39]

These examples are admittedly extreme. Thankfully, Lucies are rare, as are Magnottas. As a trans((subj)(obj))ective being, Lucie is radically transformed ontologically. As a trans((subj)(obj))ective being, the filmmaker Podz and the biographer Zero cannot help but be ontologically transformed by having viewed the video.

Extreme or traumatic experiences do a good job of illustrating the process of transformation that a trans((subj)(obj))ective being undergoes, but it should be pointed out that this process of ontological/phenomenological transformation happens for all human beings at all times. It is happening to and through us now. As trans((subj)(obj)ective beings, we are not only constituted by ourselves and others in direct interrelations; we are also constituted in a fundamental way by the social imaginaries and grand narratives that permeate our lives. Conceiving of human beings as in the way I propose helps to understand how rational human beings can see their behavior transformed and shaped by non-rational beliefs and discourses. One contemporary example is the culture of fear that has emerged out of the events of 9/11. The "war on terror" has launched a narrative of fear toward the cultural, ethnic, and religious other that has demonized Middle Eastern individuals in an unprecedented way. Our Western social imaginaries have been transformed through the repeated impact of politicians' and senior military officers' discourses, newscasts, popular cinema, and television series such as *24* and *Homeland*. We are all affected by these narratives, whether we are "enlightened" or not. Our behavior and our response to our environment and world is shaped by narratives, regardless of whether they are grand or personal. Our intimate relations with others, and the narratives these relations build for us and by us, are also constitutive of who we are: the narratives we inherit from our parents, those we acquire with our spouses, and those we create with our children. These are all constitutive of the trans((subj)(obj))ective beings we are along with the social imaginaries and grand narratives that permeate our lives.[40]

To conclude, I would like to add some considerations on linguistic expression and temporality. For each "individual"—this has become the ultimate misnomer now—experiences are had as an ambiguous multiplicity. Various elements of the experience are incorporated and become part of our being. This is how the trans((subj)(obj))ective being is constituted. At a surface level, one may be able to express and articulate the experiences undergone. Given that a large part of experiences are had at a pre-reflective, pre-linguistic level, however, many of these experiences will resist linguistic expression. Yet the impossibility of putting them into words, so to speak, is no indication that they are less impactful in the constitution of our beings. These aspects of our experiences may even have more bearing for our self-constitution. Victims of traumatic experiences, for example, may opt for silence as a coping strategy, refusing to articulate the trauma linguistically for fear of making it more tangible, more powerful and overwhelming. Nonetheless, the constitutive effect of the trauma is still operative. The verbalization of it, which on the surface may seem to be a better strategy for the victim of trauma, cannot evacuate the trauma and its constitutive effect. As I have indicated above, trauma is much more and most of it is ineffable and yet operative on the self-constitution of our being.

However, the question may arise, "Is it not the case that the polyp-arms grow and wither?" Our being always grows in the sense that our being always incorporates new experiences as the trans((subj)(obj))ective being it is. The withering that happens may be a flickering away from reflective consciousness due to a temporal lapse (the experience does not endure temporally) or other mechanisms at work, such as forgetting, withering in the past. But the withering has to do with the current lived experience, not with the being as it has been constituted. Trauma victims who have managed to repress their memories of the traumatic events, sometimes quite successfully, can see them reemerge quite vividly and unexpectedly after long periods of "forgetting." This is because the experience is always there; it is part of the being, waiting to be revived reflectively but always constitutive of the being we are. Again, trauma helps to show what in fact is the case for any constitution of the self. All experiences, traumatic, extreme, or mundane and everyday, are constitutive of our being.

These considerations are important ethically in that they multiply our responsibility toward ourselves and others. "Do not do unto others what you would not like done unto you." Indeed, the doing unto another is a doing unto one. What a trans((subj)(obj))ective being does to another is not circumscribed in time and space, but it is an everlasting deed. It is constitutive of one's being as both trans-subjective and trans-objective, that of the doer and of the other. A being's deed is one that is not limited to itself by virtue of the fact that they are trans-subjective beings. Conceiving of the human being as I propose to do entails undertaking important reflections with regard to ethical and political responsibility. Moving beyond the critique of received, unsatisfying dualistic and rationalistic notions of the human, my phenomenological-ontological view of the human being as trans((subj)(obj))ective being allows us to understand why these received views fail, but it also allows us to engage in a reconceptualization of ethical and political relations by positing us as fundamentally relational beings.[41] I see this as one of the many future directions feminist phenomenology will take.

CHRISTINE DAIGLE is Chancellor's Chair for Research Excellence and Professor of Philosophy at Brock University. She is the author of *Jean-Paul Sartre* and editor (with Élodie Boublil) of *Nietzsche and Phenomenology: Power, Life, Subjectivity* (Indiana University Press, 2013), and (with Jacob Golomb) of *Beauvoir and Sartre: The Riddle of Influence* (Indiana University Press, 2009).

NOTES

1. Friedrich Nietzsche, *Beyond Good and Evil*, trans. Walter Kaufmann (New York: Vintage, 1989), section 12.

2. Michel de Montaigne, *Michel de Montaigne: Essays*, trans. J. M. Cohen (London: Penguin, 1993), 56. In his essay "On the Education of Children," Montaigne says, "The bees steal from this flower and that, but afterwards turn their pilferings into honey, which is their own; it is thyme and marjoram no longer. So the pupil will transform and fuse together the passages that he borrows from others, to make of them something entirely his own, that is to say, his own judgment. His education, his labour, and his study have no other aim but to form this."

3. Stephen K. White, *Sustaining Affirmation* (Princeton, NJ: Princeton University Press, 2000), 5.

4. Ibid., 8.

5. This is a phrase used by Jean-Paul Sartre in his *Being and Nothingness*. It is meant to capture his view that the human being is constantly making itself through his deeds and that one cannot arrive at the being of an individual while this one is still alive and unfolding as an existential project.

6. Simone de Beauvoir, "Pyrrhus and Cinéas," in *Philosophical Writings*, ed. Margaret A. Simons (Urbana: University of Illinois Press, 2004), 124.

7. Maurice Merleau-Ponty, *Phenomenology of Perception*, trans. Donald Landes (New York: Routledge, 2012), 223.

8. Dorothea Olkowski, "Introduction: The Situated Subject," in *Feminist Interpretations of Merleau-Ponty*, ed. Dorothea Olkowski and Gail Weiss (University Park: Pennsylvania State University, 2006), 3.

9. Beauvoir presents views that are similar to those of Merleau-Ponty. It is difficult to determine a straight line of influence from Merleau-Ponty to Beauvoir or from Beauvoir to Merleau-Ponty, for that matter. It could very well be that, as in the case of the question of influence between Beauvoir and Sartre, in this case too there is an intermingling of influence.

10. The original title of this chapter is "Les données de la biologie." Translating "données" as "data" in both the Parshley and the Borde/Malovany-Chevallier translations serves to erase an important connotation of the original French: something that is *donné* is a given. The chapter title could thus be understood to refer to both the data and the givens of biology.

11. Simone de Beauvoir, *The Ethics of Ambiguity*. Translated by Bernard Frechtman. (New York: Citadel Press, 1976), 41.

12. Simone de Beauvoir, *The Second Sex*. Translated by Constance Borde and Sheila Malovany-Chevallier. (New York: Vintage Books, 2011), 44.

13. Ibid., 46.

14. Elizabeth Grosz, *Volatile Bodies: Toward a Corporeal Feminism* (Bloomington: Indiana University Press, 1994), xi.

15. Ibid., 209–10.

16. Rosi Braidotti, *The Posthuman* (Cambridge, UK: Polity Press, 2013), 13–54. In her recent book, Braidotti has explained how Beauvoir's work inspired her own.

17. Rosi Braidotti, *Nomadic Subjects: Embodiment and Sexual Difference in Contemporary Feminist Theory* (New York: Columbia University Press, 1994), 31.

18. Ibid., 26.

19. Stacy Alaimo, *Bodily Natures: Science, Environment, and the Material Self* (Bloomington: Indiana University Press, 2010), 11.

20. Nancy Tuana, "Viscous Porosity: Witnessing Katrina," in *Material Feminisms*, ed. Stacy Alaimo and Susan Hekman (Bloomington: Indiana University Press, 2008), 191.

21. Ibid., 194; emphasis in original.

22. Ibid., 199.

23. Karen Barad, "Posthumanist Performativity: Toward an Understanding of How Matter Comes to Matter," *Signs* 28, no. 3 (2003): 810.

24. Ibid., 817.

25. Ibid., 818.

26. Ibid., 822.

27. Bruno Latour, "Une Sociologie sans objet? Remarques sur l'interobjectivité," in *Objets et mémoires*, ed. Octave Debary and Laurier Turgeon (Quebec: Les Presses de l'Université Laval, 2007), 49. Latour says, "Les objets font quelque chose, ils ne sont pas seulement les écrans ou les rétroprojecteurs de notre vie sociale."

28. Ibid., 52. Latour explains that "chez les humains, l'interaction est le plus souvent localisée, cadrée, tenue. Par quoi? Par le cadre justement, constitué d'acteurs qui ne sont pas humains."

29. Michel Grossetti, "Les limites de la symétrie," *SociologieS* (October 22, 2007), http://sociologies.revues.org/index712. Grossetti suggests this view. In the essay, he argues that while Latour includes objects in social relations and holds that relations be-

tween humans and nonhuman objects are on the same plane and of the same "quality" as those between humans, this is not the case. Empathy and reciprocity cannot emerge from a relation between humans and non-objects. This is the limit that Grossetti sees to the symmetry he finds in Latour's theory.

30. Michel Foucault, "Afterword: The Subject and Power," in *Michel Foucault: Beyond Structuralism and Hermeneutics*, ed. Hubert L. Dreyfus and Paul Rabinow (Chicago: University of Chicago Press, 1983), 212.

31. Ibid., 225.

32. Alaimo, *Bodily Natures*, 2.

33. Friedrich Nietzsche, *Daybreak: Thoughts on the Prejudices of Morality*, trans. R. J. Hollingdale (Cambridge, UK: Cambridge University Press, 1997), section 119. A polyp is a relatively simple marine creature that does not have a brain and therefore is understood not to have consciousness. It is basically a digestive tube that ingests, digests, and secretes the food that its arms grab for it. However, there is no way to know whether it experiences itself as conscious in any way, just as it is impossible to conceive in what way any nonhuman being or even severely disabled human being may be conscious. That said, even if it were true that it has no consciousness, I still think that the polyp can serve as an apt metaphor. Indeed, as a "digestive" being, the polyp's being is affected by what it takes in from its environment. It is shaped by what comes its way and what it absorbs. The same can be said to a certain extent of the consciousness of human beings as porous fold. However, I do not wish to go as far as to say that we are entirely constituted by what enters our fold.

34. Jean Leloup, "Lucie," *Mille Excuses Milady*, Grosse Boîte et Roi Ponpon, 2009. My translation of "Elle avait envie de leur cramer la gueule, à ses parents ivrognes, ça se voyait."

35. Ibid. My translation of the following:

> A l'a du fun pis a voyage
> A l'a eu un p'tit héritage,
> . . .
> Je vieillirai tout contre toi
> Je vieillirai auprès de toi
> Je vieillirai dedans tes bras
> Je vieillirai tout près de toi
> Je vieillirai tout CONTRE toi!
> Je vieillirai au FOND de toi!
> Je POURRIRAI tout dedans toi!
> Et je serai TOI!!!
> . . .
> Je suis un HORS-LA-LOI!

36. Following a worldwide manhunt, Magnotta was arrested in Berlin on June 4, 2012. He stood trial for first-degree murder in the fall of 2014 and was declared guilty of first-degree murder with premeditation on December 23, 2014.

37. *Tout le monde en parle*, TV, Avanti Ciné Vidéo, March 10, 2013.

38. I find it quite distressing that the video is still available online. Equally distressing is the fact that Magnotta is said to have received and responded to "fan mail" in prison while awaiting his trial.

39. This might explain why such violent and gory videos attract viewers. The viewing may serve, in some cases, as an ersatz for the actual deed. This is troubling in that it unveils some inner leaning toward either witnessing or engaging in violence that we thought we had moved away from in our so-called civilized Western societies. One need only think of the violent public executions that were attended en masse in past centuries.

40. I think this view differs from the notion of lived body that we find in Merleau-Ponty and Beauvoir in that their notion still focuses on consciousness in a way that the trans((subj)(obj))ective being does not. This being engages in self-constitution but is also equally, and perhaps even more, constituted in ways that escape consciousness. Thus I think that it constitutes an extension of the lived body.

41. My view, however, goes beyond the notions proposed by Seyla Benhabib and Adriana Cavarero, respectively, the situated self and the relational self. While they focus on what I have called the trans-subjective aspect of our being, they do not address and incorporate, as I do, the trans-objective aspect. See Seyla Benhabib, *Situating the Self: Gender, Community, and Postmodernism in Contemporary Ethics* (New York: Routledge, 1992); and Adriana Cavarero, *Relating Narratives: Storytelling and Selfhood*, trans. Paul A. Kottman (London: Routledge, 2000).

BIBLIOGRAPHY

Alaimo, Stacy. *Bodily Natures: Science, Environment, and the Material Self*. Bloomington: Indiana University Press, 2010.

Barad, Karen. "Posthumanist Performativity: Toward an Understanding of How Matter Comes to Matter." *Signs* 28, no. 3 (2003): 801–831.

Beauvoir, Simone de. *The Ethics of Ambiguity*. Translated by Bernard Frechtman. New York: Citadel Press, 1976.

———. "Pyrrhus and Cinéas." In *Philosophical Writings*, edited by Margaret A. Simons, 89–149. Urbana: University of Illinois Press, 2004.

———. *The Second Sex*. Translated by Constance Borde and Sheila Malovany-Chevallier. New York: Vintage Books, 2011.

Benhabib, Seyla. *Situating the Self. Gender, Community, and Postmodernism in Contemporary Ethics*. New York: Routledge, 1992.

Braidotti, Rosi. *Nomadic Subjects: Embodiment and Sexual Difference in Contemporary Feminist Theory*. New York: Columbia University Press, 1994.

———. *The Posthuman*. Cambridge, UK: Polity Press, 2013.

Cavarero, Adriana. *Relating Narratives: Storytelling and Selfhood*. Translated and with an introduction by Paul A. Kottman. London: Routledge, 2000.

Foucault, Michel. "Afterword: The Subject and Power." In *Michel Foucault: Beyond Structuralism and Hermeneutics*, edited by Hubert L. Dreyfus and Paul Rabinow, 208–226. Chicago: University of Chicago Press, 1983.

Grossetti, Michel. "Les limites de la symétrie." *SociologieS* (October 22, 2007). http://sociologies.revues.org/index712.

Grosz, Elizabeth. *Volatile Bodies: Toward a Corporeal Feminism*. Bloomington: Indiana University Press, 1994.

Latour, Bruno. "Une Sociologie sans objet? Remarques sur l'interobjectivité." In *Objets et mémoires*, edited by Octave Debary and Laurier Turgeon, 37–58. Québec: Les Presses de l'Université Laval, 2007.
Leloup, Jean. "Lucie." *Mille Excuses Milady*. Grosse Boîte et Roi Ponpon. 2009.
Merleau-Ponty, Maurice. *Phenomenology of Perception*. Translated by Donald Landes. New York: Routledge, 2012.
Montaigne, Michel de. *Michel de Montaigne: Essays*. Translated by J. M. Cohen. London: Penguin, 1993.
Nietzsche, Friedrich. *Beyond Good and Evil*. Translated by Walter Kaufmann. New York: Vintage, 1989.
———. *Daybreak: Thoughts on the Prejudices of Morality*. Translated by R. J. Hollingdale. Cambridge, UK: Cambridge University Press, 1997.
Olkowski, Dorothea E. "Introduction: The Situated Subject." In *Feminist Interpretations of Merleau-Ponty*, edited by Dorothea Olkowski and Gail Weiss, 1–24. University Park: Pennsylvania State University Press, 2006.
Tuana, Nancy. "Viscous Porosity: Witnessing Katrina." In *Material Feminisms*, edited by Stacy Alaimo and Susan Hekman, 188–213. Bloomington: Indiana University Press, 2008.
White, Stephen K. *Sustaining Affirmation*. Princeton, NJ: Princeton University Press, 2000.

PART 4
OUR FUTURE BODY IMAGES

11 THE "NORMAL ABNORMALITIES" OF DISABILITY AND AGING

Merleau-Ponty and Beauvoir

GAIL WEISS

INTRODUCTION

Two of the most slippery yet well-established divisions that have traditionally distinguished human beings from one another are age and disability, respectively. With respect to the former, even a cursory examination of different cultures and different historical time periods reveals how widely societies vary in their identifications of youth, middle age, and old age, much less in the roles and responsibilities that are deemed appropriate for each period of life. This cultural and historical variability is clearly due to many complex factors, chief among them being the average life expectancy for a particular group of people and the specific habitus (to use Pierre Bourdieu's language) that is operative within a given community.[1] With respect to disability, it is also evident that a mental or physical condition that would lead a person or group of people to be regarded as disabled in one society has not always led to a similar identification in another society. What interests me particularly is not the cultural and historical variability that has produced different understandings of when and how one is considered to be young, middle-aged, elderly, or disabled (though these are fascinating in their own right), but the different types of treatment, both medical and non-medical, that have resulted from and been "justified" by these identificatory labels. The ambivalent responses individuals themselves have had to the somatic differences that mark them as being more "like" or "unlike" other individuals are also extremely relevant in this context, since our relations to our own bodies are inevitably mediated by how other people respond to them.

As disability theorists such as Rosemarie Garland-Thomson have shown, possessing an unusual or "extraordinary" body has not infrequently led that person to be viewed as having special powers that ordinary people lack.[2] Whether these special powers are viewed as a serious threat to the community that needs to be eliminated (as was the case with women identified as "witches" in Puritan communities in the colonial United States) or as a boon that could benefit the community (such as bringing good luck or, like Sophocles's blind Tiresias, as leading their possessor to have prophetic powers), the point is that those people who defy dominant perceptual norms more often than not are socially, symbolically, and politically separated from their "normal" counterparts.[3] In the most troubling cases, these "abnormal" individuals have even been seen as transgressing the boundary of the human altogether and, all too frequently, their dehumanization has been intensified and reinforced by their inhumane treatment at the hands of their allegedly more civilized human counterparts (without, it should be added, the latter's own humanity being placed in question). The Nazis, as we know, had this process down to a science and used the desperate responses of the people they starved, tortured, and targeted for death as "proof" of the latter's subhuman status.

Although history is replete with examples of individuals who were sometimes celebrated but more often punished for failing to embody (whether voluntarily or involuntarily) the reigning perceptual norms of their community, either by exceeding them (e.g., by exhibiting both masculine and feminine traits or unusual intelligence) or by falling short of them (e.g., lacking limbs or lacking sanity, etc.), it is far more common to find conflicting or ambivalent attitudes toward those people who are deemed to be significantly different from other members of their community. Following both Mary Douglas and Julia Kristeva, I argue that this ambivalence must not be understood simply as an ambivalence toward those who do not express the behavior or bodies associated with "normal" human beings but rather as an ambivalence toward the corporeal variability that exists within the human realm, and an accompanying fear that one will be "infected" with the abject, boundary-defying status of the radically Other.[4]

Kristeva maintains that human beings project the status of abject other onto other people in order to avoid confronting the troubling evidence of our own bodily vulnerabilities, and she associates the latter with the fluidity and instability that defines the vicissitudes of corporeal existence, including our dependence on other bodies to sustain our own.[5] This same strategy of abjectification, I suggest, is powerfully revealed in many people's negative attitudes toward elderly people and old age. And, as Robert Murphy and other disability scholars have shown, a similar pattern of response also characterizes many people's encounters with, and antipathy toward, disabled individuals' bodies.[6]

In his powerful autobiography, *The Body Silent: An Anthropologist Embarks on the Most Challenging Journey of his Life: Into the World of the Disabled*, Murphy argues that people with physical or cognitive impairments suffer from what Erving Goffman calls a "stigmatized" or "contaminated" identity whereby their disability comes to "trump" all other aspects of who they are, including their race, gender, social class, and profession.[7] Writing within a US context, Murphy asserts that people with disabilities are regarded as "subverters" of the American dream, their very presence serving as a stark and terrifying reminder that "the society they live in is shot through with inequity and suffering," and that the disability of another could, through a sudden accident or illness, just as easily become one's own.[8] Avoiding close encounters with people with non-normative bodies thus becomes a management strategy on the part of able-bodied people to keep this "fearsome possibility" at bay.

The fact that it is impossible, despite the promises of plastic and cosmetic surgeons, to avoid experiencing the corporeal and psychic effects of aging as long as one is alive (even though these effects are registered in as many different ways as there are people who experience them), suggests that the ambivalent responses that often characterize individual responses to "extraordinary" bodies are not produced by those bodies alone, but rather can and often do arise in the relationships that "ordinary" people sustain with their own bodies, especially when confronted with the undeniable reality of their own corporeal vulnerabilities. Indeed, aging is a paradigmatic case of an experience that is at once understood because of its universality to be quintessentially normal and yet, as Simone de Beauvoir persuasively demonstrates, is nonetheless experienced as a corporeal violation of sorts.[9] This sense of violation arises not merely from a feeling that my formerly youthful body is "betraying" me because I can no longer do, or can only with difficulty do, some of the things I once did quite easily, but, I maintain, is also a violation of the perceptual norms that are founded, not upon a realistic assessment of the body's changing capacities as it ages, but rather upon an idealized, static, youthful body image that makes the aging body a site of fear and disgust for oneself and for others.[10]

AMBIVALENCES OF AGING AND DISABILITY

As Beauvoir succinctly observes in *The Coming of Age*, "What is so disconcerting about old age is that normally it is an abnormal condition."[11] While it may seem strange to claim that a universal experience such as aging is "normally" regarded by elderly and non-elderly people alike as an "abnormal condition," Beauvoir has already revealed a similar phenomenological anomaly in *The*

Second Sex—namely, the fact that women's bodies also have been viewed as "abnormal" especially when compared to the normative standards established by men's bodies.[12] In what follows, I will focus closely on this paradoxical notion of a "normal abnormality" in order to show how it is utilized critically by Beauvoir and Maurice Merleau-Ponty (though the latter never uses this exact term) with respect to aging and disability, respectively, to deconstruct traditional understandings of the normal/abnormal binary. More specifically, by challenging the view that aged or disabled bodies are abnormal or irremediably deficient, I argue that both authors offer us valuable lessons on how to dismantle oppressive perceptual norms that privilege some bodies at the expense of others.

Following the approach she uses in *The Second Sex*, in *The Coming of Age* Beauvoir deftly interweaves insights from diverse fields, including phenomenology, cultural anthropology, economics, medicine, and psychoanalysis, providing her readers with a rich description of how old age is experienced by elderly men and women themselves as well as by those who are still young or middle-aged. Although aging is itself a natural temporal process that is corporeally enacted within every animate organism from one moment to the next, it is clear, as noted earlier, that there is a great deal of variety in how human beings experience this universal phenomenon, and, as Beauvoir amply demonstrates, there is also a great deal of variety in how different societies have historically viewed their aging populations.[13] Regardless of exactly *when* or even *why* an individual is considered to be old within a given society, she repeatedly emphasizes that old age is a phenomenon that generates tremendous ambivalence on the part of the elderly and non-elderly alike. Indeed, since we all age as long as we are alive, it is difficult, unless one is seriously cognitively impaired, to distance oneself completely from the recognition that even if one is currently young, one will also become old unless one's life is cut short by illness, accident, crime, or some other misfortune.

What renders the normal process of aging "an abnormal condition," for Beauvoir, is due not to dramatic differences in the experience of aging but rather to what I would call "pre-perceptions" (as distinguished from "preconceptions") that discount and devalue the vulnerable bodies and unique temporal perspectives of elderly people. While a preconception is ordinarily taken to be a *mental* attitude or belief that prescribes, in advance, how an individual might understand or evaluate a particular situation, I am using the term "pre-perception" to refer to a process that primarily takes place on a perceptual, corporeal level rather than a conceptual level. Pre-perceptions certainly can be and often are accompanied by preconceptions, but the former, unlike the latter, do not require a specific cognitive component in order to play an influential, albeit largely unthematized, role in how we react to people, places, and things. Perceptual norms, I suggest, wield their primary influence at the level of pre-perceptions.

As she earlier observed in response to the common antipathy felt toward women's bodies that is described in so much depth in *The Second Sex*, Beauvoir maintains in *The Coming of Age* that the "abnormality" of old age is not due to anything inherently pernicious about elderly bodies or about the aging process itself, but rather to widespread, persistent, and ill-founded societal prejudices against the elderly, who "are looked upon as an inferior species."[14] Yet, the cost of radically dis-identifying with those who are old or even those who are sick or disabled is that we will inevitably experience one or more of these conditions in our lifetime, and when we do, we will have deprived ourselves of important resources that are available to understand these experiences in a non-alienating fashion. By exploring the "normal abnormalities" of disability and aging, I argue, we can pose important challenges to accepted understandings of normalcy insofar as they exclude the daily experiences of so many elderly and disabled people in the world today. My specific aim is not only to show that Beauvoir's and Merleau-Ponty's perspectives on aging and disability, respectively, are mutually illuminating in this regard but also to make the case that the phenomenological method they utilize offers largely untapped and unacknowledged resources for future research in critical gerontology, disability studies, and other fields, such as queer theory and the study of intersexuality, that focus on non-normative bodies.

Given global advances in medical technology that have vastly increased the number of elderly people in the world, many of whom are living with multiple disabilities, and given the fact that social, political, and economic discrimination against both elderly and disabled people seems to be continuing unabated despite greater media attention being paid to these overlapping (but not identical) populations, it seems urgent that philosophers directly address these angst-ridden dimensions of human experience. Phenomenology seems like an obvious place to start, since its main task is to describe lived experience, and old age and disability are indeed lived experiences for millions and millions of people in the world today (not to mention the elderly and disabled people who lived in the past or those who will live in the future). And, since both Beauvoir and Merleau-Ponty offer us many rich insights regarding aging and disability that have often been ignored in favor of more popular themes they take up and address, it seems like it is high time to return to their work in order to see how it can be productively utilized to combat the deleterious stigmatization of elderly and disabled individuals and communities. I will start by turning to Beauvoir's discussion of the sense of alterity, which, she claims, frequently accompanies an individual's personal experience of the aging process.

THE OTHER WITHIN AND THE OTHER WITHOUT

Beauvoir observes that as we age it is common to feel that "it is the Other within us who is old," and for this reason, she suggests, "it is natural that the revelation of our age should come to us from outside—from others."[15] In these short lines, she indicates not one, but two ways in which the Other mediates an individual's experience of the aging process. First, she identifies an experience of alterity at the heart of subjectivity—an Other, to be precise—who presumably registers the corporeal effects of the aging process while the "I" escapes unscathed.[16] This Other who grows old while I continue to live and love in the endless present of the cogito is the product of complex processes of projection and introjection: I project onto this Other the undesirable aspects of the aging process, including a growing sense of corporeal vulnerability, to preserve, it would seem, the agelessness of the self. And yet, unlike the classic psychoanalytic model of projection, the Other who becomes the abject recipient of my corporeal insecurities is not out in the world but an intimate with whom I uneasily share the same psychic and perceptual space! This schizoid experience, moreover, is not, for Beauvoir, at all extraordinary or pathological, but rather is proffered as an account of how aging is (or, more accurately, fails to be) experienced by the "normal" subject. Thus, she seems to be suggesting, there is an alienating dimension that lies at the heart of the aging process that is distinct from, yet compounded by, the very real societal prejudices against elderly people that are exhibited in the majority of known cultures.[17]

This primary schism between self and Other that plays out within one and the same individual can be understood as an ineradicable tension between the continuity of consciousness as well as our embodied experience more generally, on the one hand, and the apparent *discontinuities* in that experience that separate my younger body and its appearance and capabilities from my older one, on the other hand. Not surprisingly, the discontinuities that the aging process introduces into an individual's experience are most often described temporally—that is, in terms of the body *before* it became old and the body *after* the onset of old age—and this before and after is marked by the undeniable evidence of the body itself: the appearance of wrinkles where once there were none, the loss (or even sudden growth) of hair, the onset of menopause for women (though this often happens to women in contemporary societies before they are considered to be old, menopause nonetheless has functioned both symbolically and literally as a turning point in life that marks one as aged), the increased risk of prostate cancer and increased frequency of urination experienced by older men, the appearance of age spots on the skin, and so on. Many of these bodily changes are readily visible by others, who often notice them before we do (especially people who haven't seen us for a long time), and this leads us to the second influence of the Other that Beauvoir invokes that mediates my experience of aging. It comes not from the Other within, who, I am claiming, is a dual product of projection and introjection, but from the outside—that is, from my actual interactions with others who are directly confronted with the tangible evidence of how my appearance has changed over time.

Both Merleau-Ponty and Jean-Paul Sartre would account for the "naturalness" of others recognizing my aging before I do as due to the fact that other people enjoy a perspective on my lived body that I do not share. Even when I am looking into a reflective surface, I am unable to view myself acting through the eyes of the other, because the self-referentiality or reflexivity of the act of gazing at my own reflection prevents me from seeing myself at the same time engaged in the larger world of my concern.[18] Though she maintains that it is natural for the Other to bear witness to our aging and for our own understanding of how we have aged to be mediated by the Other, what Beauvoir identifies as *unnatural* is the extremely negative form this recognition on the part of the Other (and derivatively on the part of the individual herself) most frequently takes. For if aging is itself a natural process that no one can escape, the vilification not only of the experience of old age but, more importantly, of elderly people themselves (who seem to be irrationally blamed for having the bad taste not only to get old but also to show their age publicly in their appearance and behavior) is clearly against the self-interest of each of us to the extent that we aspire to live a long life.

NORMALIZING THE ABNORMAL

Beauvoir claims that "by the way in which a society behaves toward its old people it uncovers the naked, and often carefully hidden, truth about its real principles and aims," thereby suggesting that rather than viewing the ill treatment of elderly people as a kind of "collateral damage" that occurs because a society has more pressing concerns to focus on, its treatment of its elderly population reveals the values that society holds (and fails to hold) dear.[19] What Beauvoir is asserting, then, is that something that might appear to be a more marginal concern (namely, how a society comports itself toward its aging population in both word and deed) can actually give us important clues as to how the entire society operates. Reading this passage, I am struck by how much it resonates with Merleau-Ponty's insistence in *Phenomenology of Perception* that allegedly abnormal human beings such as Schneider, a World War I veteran who suffered brain damage when shrapnel pierced his skull in combat, or amputees who have experienced motor and body image disturbances, or aphasiacs who have partially lost the power of expressive speech, must not be regarded as a species apart from the "normal" individual.[20] Instead, what Merleau-Ponty seems to be implying by so frequently invoking such non-normative examples is that people who experience intellectual and motor disturbances enable us to arrive at a better understanding of what perceptual norms are and how they habitually function on a pre-perceptual level.[21]

Like Sigmund Freud before them, Merleau-Ponty and Beauvoir portray the differences between what is considered normal and what is considered abnormal not as an absolute divide but as a continuum. The elderly man with Alzheimer's disease, for instance, has his own unique way of living time: his inability to recall both major and minor events in his past does not leave gaps in his world, even though, as with Schneider, it may result in future and past becoming "for him nothing but the 'shriveled up' continuations of the present."[22] While for the "normal" person, the experiences of Schneider and the elderly Alzheimer's patient may seem impoverished because they have very restricted access to the past and future horizons, according to which, in Merleau-Ponty's words, "the normal person *reckons with* the possible," he suggests that both individuals continue to inhabit space and time in meaningful ways even if the significance they attribute to their respective experience is markedly different from what the "normal" person attributes to it.[23]

More specifically, even if "the normal person *reckons with* the possible, which thus acquires a sort of actuality without leaving behind its place as a possibility," and Schneider now lacks this ability, this doesn't mean that Schneider's world is incomplete, since, as Merleau-Ponty observes, he still possesses a perceptual field, albeit one that has lost the plasticity that characterizes the "normal" human subject's ability to integrate past memories and future anticipations into her present perceptual experience.[24] Despite his own controversial descriptions of Schneider's alleged sexual deficiencies, it is evident that Merleau-Ponty rejects pathologizing interpretations of Schneider's experience that would render him an object of pity. Indeed, one of the striking features of Schneider's injuries is that they seem to inoculate him against any negative feelings concerning his own changed situation, since it seems he now lacks the reflective capacity to compare his prior non-disabled experience to his current situation. Schneider, at least as Merleau-Ponty describes him, lives wholly in the present moment. He does not bemoan the capacities he once possessed but manages to live a meaningful human life, concretely engaged in the world of his concern. And, I would suggest, this is one of the crucial lessons that Schneider can teach us, a lesson echoed over and over again by contemporary disability activists and scholars—namely, that we must never fail to recognize and respect the chiasm that separates how an individual actually lives her life and how another person might perceive her existence even as we acknowledge that the one perspective is always already informed by the other.

Merleau-Ponty's own refusal to bemoan Schneider's fate comes across clearly when he asserts, "Disorders that are properly intellectual—those of judgment and of signification—will not be able to be considered as ultimate deficiencies."[25] This is a striking claim and, I believe, it has yet to receive its due. While contemporary disability studies scholars have made similar claims, observing that disabilities tend to be experienced as deficiencies more by the able-bodied than by disabled individuals themselves (except insofar as these latter are dis-abled by the negative stereotypes associated with their particular manner of living in the world as well as the obstacles the built environment poses to their full participation in it), Merleau-Ponty's name does not appear very often within the burgeoning literature in this exciting interdisciplinary field. And, I would argue, the promise of his work for the important political project of resignifying disability from a culturally stigmatized phenomenon to a source of valuable existential insights that can enrich our collective understanding of what it means to be human, is far from being realized.

A central aim of my discussion, as noted earlier, is to show how Beauvoir's analyses of aging and Merleau-Ponty's analyses of disability from both first- and third-person perspectives together demonstrate that what can and should be normal phenomena are rendered abnormal because they violate unarticulated and unrealistic perceptual (and conceptual) norms that prevent us from recognizing and appreciating the unique perspectives offered by elderly and disabled people, respectively. As people continue to live longer with illnesses and disabilities that would have killed their parents a generation earlier, it is evident that there is an urgent need to transform the lived experience of both aging and disability so that they can be seen as opening up new possibilities rather than just closing off old ones. What Beauvoir's and Merleau-Ponty's respective work suggests, I am claiming, is that changing our attitudes toward elderly and disabled people does not mean denying the distinctive corporeal and psychical qualities associated with advanced age or with a particular disability, or even the "othering" and often painful dimensions of these lived experiences.

Rather, such change involves deconstructing limiting perceptual norms by expanding our available horizons of meaning to include the perspectives of those who have been excluded by them. Taken together, their work reminds us that old age and disability are ordinary *human* experiences and that the dehumanization of those who experience them diminishes us all.[26]

Merleau-Ponty, in particular, seems to offer us two different strategies for accomplishing what I call the "normalization of the abnormal." The first approach, which I have just discussed, is to show us that an experience that appears to be very abnormal (such as Schneider's inability to engage in abstract thinking, or the amputee's visceral experience of pain in a limb that is no longer attached to her body) is only abnormal if I approach it from the outside, from a detached perspective in which I view this experience or behavior as radically Other than how *I myself* would behave in a similar situation. This absolute division between a first-person and a third-person perspective leaves us with two incommensurable points of view; in the case of Schneider, his world makes sense to him but appears quite deficient to others. By emphasizing that Schneider is able to live coherently in the world of his concern, Merleau-Ponty reframes the issue so that lived experience indeed has the last word rather than dubious projections of how I think I would feel if I had an experience I have never had. The danger of giving final authority to an Other's view "from the outside" is amply demonstrated by the great statistical discrepancy between the vast number of non-paralyzed people who claim they would commit suicide before they would live as a para- or quadriplegic and the very small number of paralyzed people who have actually resorted to suicide to escape their allegedly "unlivable" existence.

The second strategy Merleau-Ponty deploys to normalize the abnormal is to argue that even "normal" subjects bear witness on a daily basis to the body's miraculous ability to "incorporate the most surprising of phenomena."[27] Through his rapid-fire series of examples of objects as diverse as a typist's keys, the feather in a woman's hat, and a blind man's cane, Merleau-Ponty subtly suggests that we should not see the blind man's resourcefulness with his cane as a unique quality developed in a compensatory way, an inferior, albeit necessary substitute for the eyesight he no longer enjoys or never did enjoy. Rather, by placing the cane on a par with the typist's keys and the feather in the woman's hat, Merleau-Ponty suggests that they all equally reveal the human capacity to utilize even the most mundane resources that are at our disposal to exceed the borders of our skin and to open up new intercorporeal possibilities for engagement in the world.

Although Merleau-Ponty describes this process as an almost seamless extension of our bodies into other objects that serve as new prosthetic devices (new fleshly possibilities) for palpating the world, this "miraculous" capacity can be seen as readily as an act of bodily incorporation whereby we take objects in the world into our body, making their properties our own. For Merleau-Ponty this dynamic two-way movement is possible only because:

> I am not in space and in time, nor do I think space and time; rather, I am of space and of time; my body fits itself to them and embraces them. The scope of this hold measures the scope of my existence; however, it can never in any case be total. The space and time that I inhabit are always surrounded by indeterminate horizons that contain other points of view. The synthesis of time, like that of space, is always to be started over again.[28]

The cautionary note Merleau-Ponty strikes here is important, for some spaces and some times will inevitably remain inaccessible to my bodily explorations. Or, as Elizabeth Grosz notes in *Volatile Bodies*, even as old corporeal barriers are continuously broken, there are still some things that human bodies can't do.[29] Not everything is possible. If it were, the differences between my own experiences and those of others would be in danger of being erased altogether. The other points of view that Merleau-Ponty reminds us of include not only perspectives that I am unaware of or that I am aware of but have not *chosen* to adopt, but also perspectives that I *cannot* adopt because they require unique corporeal syntheses of time and space that I may not be able to perform. This means that even though the similarities among human bodies (e.g., on a physiological level) may guarantee a great deal of overlap in the temporal and spatial syntheses we enact on a daily basis and, therefore, on the construction of perceptual norms that arise in and through their repetition, insofar as no two bodies are alike, there will always be important differences in how (and whether) certain syntheses are performed, and thus, the perceptual norms that human beings develop will vary as well. However, given that perceptual norms are not constituted solely through an individual's idiosyncratic temporal and spatial syntheses but reflect broader cultural standards and expectations, as noted earlier, the norms that are developed and that operate at the level of pre-perceptions often fail to do justice to the full spectrum of bodily possibilities available.

CONCLUSION: CHALLENGING PERCEPTUAL NORMS

The project of challenging oppressive perceptual norms that perpetuate negative judgments regarding people who can no longer do things the same way that other people do, or who never could do them to begin with, necessitates a discussion of habit, for perceptual norms themselves arise directly out of habitual "syntheses" of space and time, the "miraculous" yet mundane intercorporeal activities through which my body "lends itself to the world" and the world lends itself to my body. If, as Merleau-Ponty tells us, habits express "the power we have of dilating our being in the world," if the development of new habits transforms both our body images and our relationship with the world as we incorporate new objects, skills, and activities into our daily lives, shaping our identities in the process, then this is true not only for "normal" human beings whose habits we find familiar and reassuring but also for allegedly abnormal subjects such as Schneider or other disabled or elderly people who have found their own unique ways of navigating the world and making it habitable.[30] "Habit," Beauvoir asserts,

> is the past in so far as we do not re-present it but live it in the shape of attitudes and forms of behavior; it is the mass of acquired reactions and automatic reflexes that allow us to walk, speak, write, etc. In a normal old age they do not deteriorate; indeed, their role increases, since they are made to help in the establishment of a routine.... A principle of economy is operative in routine, and active people of all ages take it into account.[31]

Regarding the inevitable bodily changes (including the loss of previous abilities) that accompany old age and the alterations in routine they may require, Beauvoir observes that "very often the burden of the body counts for less than the attitude that is adopted towards it."[32] While bodily infirmities are indeed real and can't be denied, the point that needs to be acknowledged, following both Merleau-Ponty and Beauvoir, is that even as one perceptual norm becomes unrealizable for an individual through age, illness, or accident, another one can (and even must) be developed. It may be unusual or appear strange to the "normal" subject, but it, too, is the product of the "miraculous" syntheses of space and time that all bodies enact as long as they live.

By calling our attention to them, both Merleau-Ponty and Beauvoir challenge us to refuse the oppressive perceptual norms that so powerfully and yet almost invisibly reinforce an understanding of both disabled and elderly people as lacking or deficient. These norms, by definition, are based on the experience of the "normal" subject, and yet, as Merleau-Ponty has shown, the "abnormal" subject also normalizes her world, in a way that makes sense to her even if it doesn't make sense to others. By opening ourselves up to the possibility that there are new ways of synthesizing space and time that a disabled or elderly person can enact that we may never be able to realize, we have the capacity, both individually and collectively, to transform our very understanding of what counts as a perceptual norm and therefore what counts as a "normal" existence. For, if a normal subject is someone who is immune to the effects of aging and to the possibility of experiencing profound bodily alterations in appearance and function, then the normal subject is himself (and it is almost always a "he," is it not?) a chimera who preserves his normalcy by refusing to acknowledge the bodily vulnerabilities without which he would have no access to the wonders of the world.

GAIL WEISS is Professor of Philosophy at George Washington University and also the General Secretary of the International Merleau-Ponty Circle. She is the author of *Refiguring the Ordinary* (Indiana University Press, 2008) and *Body Images: Embodiment as Intercorporeality* (Routledge Press, 1999). In addition she is the editor of several volumes on Merleau-Ponty and embodiment and is currently completing a monograph on existential ambiguities in Beauvoir and Merleau-Ponty.

NOTES

I am grateful to the editors of this volume, Helen Fielding and Dorothea Olkowski, for their insightful comments on an earlier version of this chapter and especially for their invitation to expand my discussion of both perceptual norms and pre-perceptions. I am also grateful for the invaluable feedback I received when I presented this paper at several international conferences including the International Merleau-Ponty Circle whose members were its original audience and who never fail to stimulate my thought.

    1. Pierre Bourdieu, *The Logic of Practice*, trans. Richard Nice (Stanford, CA: Stanford University Press, 1990).

    2. Rosemarie Garland-Thomson, *Extraordinary Bodies: Figuring Physical Disability in American Culture and Literature* (New York: Columbia University Press, 1997).

    3. By "perceptual norms" I am referring to socially constructed standards that define what counts as a "normal" body—bodily appearance, bodily comportment, bodily gestures, and so on—in an individual's daily interactions with other people. These standards are clearly culturally variable and often operate implicitly in daily life. The infamous "I know it when I see it" test is probably the most apt characterization of how these norms function, since, although they can be difficult to articulate with precision, they are nonetheless rigorously applied in our everyday encounters, most notably in the often hasty judgments we make about other people on the basis of how well or poorly their bodies and behavior fit the reigning perceptual norms. It should be pointed out, however, that although vision (if one is sighted) can and does tend to play the dominant role in the assessment of whether a person upholds or appears to transgress these corporeal norms, perceptual norms are not restricted to the visual realm but can be violated along auditory and olfactory dimensions, such as when a person is perceived as being too loud or as smelling badly.

    4. Mary Douglas, *Purity and Danger: An Analysis of the Concepts of Pollution and Taboo* (London: Routledge, 1992).

5. For an in-depth discussion of her understanding of abjection, see Julia Kristeva, *Powers of Horror: An Essay on Abjection*, trans. Leon S. Roudiez (New York: Columbia University Press, 1982).

6. Robert Murphy, *The Body Silent: An Anthropologist Embarks on the Most Challenging Journey of His Life: Into the World of the Disabled* (New York: W. W. Norton, 1990).

7. Erving Goffman, *Stigma: Notes on the Management of Spoiled Identity* (Englewood Cliffs, NJ: Prentice-Hall, 1963).

8. Murphy, *Body Silent*, 117.

9. Simone de Beauvoir, *The Coming of Age*, trans. Patrick O'Brian (New York: W. W. Norton and Company,1996).

10. For an account of the powerful effects of the body image ideals that circulate in any given culture, which reflect and reinforce the gendered standards of beauty that function as perceptual norms, see Gail Weiss, *Body Images: Embodiment as Intercorporeality* (New York: Routledge, 1999).

11. Beauvoir, *Coming of Age*, 285.

12. Simone de Beauvoir, *The Second Sex*, trans. Constance Borde and Sheila Malovany-Chevallier (New York: Alfred A. Knopf, 2010).

13. Beauvoir, *Coming of Age*, 1996.

14. Ibid., 286.

15. Ibid., 288.

16. Oscar Wilde brilliantly incarnates this Other and the abject horror of its presence in *The Picture of Dorian Gray*, in the form of a portrait that registers not only the title character's age but also his moral decline—that is, the corruption of his character as well as the temporal "corruption" of his youthful beauty. For a detailed discussion of the peculiar narcissism exemplified by Dorian's murderous relationship with his portrait, see Gail Weiss, "The Myth of Woman Meets the Myth of Old Age: An Alienating Encounter with the Aging Female Body," in *Simone de Beauvoir's Philosophy of Age: Gender, Ethics, and Time*, ed. Silvia Stoller, 47–64 (Berlin: Walter de Gruyter, 2014).

17. Indeed, Beauvoir argues that even in societies that publicly venerate their elderly members and in which the elderly wield a great deal of social, political, and familial power, elderly people are nonetheless a source of resentment not only because they are usually unable to work as hard as their younger counterparts and may require a great deal of care, but also because they can be seen as usurping valuable resources (including marriageable women) that would otherwise go to the society's younger members.

18. Jean Paul Sartre, *Being and Nothingness*, trans. Hazel E. Barnes (New York: Washington Square Press, 1984).

19. Beauvoir, *Coming of Age*, 87.

20. Maurice Merleau-Ponty, *Phenomenology of Perception*, trans. Donald A. Landes (London: Routledge, 2012).

21. Though I am unable to develop this point further here, I would also argue that Merleau-Ponty's early observations regarding people with disabilities and Beauvoir's later insights regarding elderly people offer us new ways of thinking about the roles of time and memory in the constitution of the self.

22. Merleau-Ponty, *Phenomenology of Perception*, 137.

23. Ibid., 112.

24. Ibid.

25. Ibid., 135.

26. This is not to suggest that nonhuman creatures do not also experience old age and disability, since they obviously do. However, if we cannot respect our fellow human beings who live these conditions, then it is unclear to me how we are going to be able to do this for animals!

27. Merleau-Ponty, *Phenomenology of Perception*, lxxiv.

28. Ibid., 141.

29. Elizabeth Grosz, *Volatile Bodies: Toward a Corporeal Feminism* (Bloomington: Indiana University Press, 1991).

30. Merleau-Ponty, *Phenomenology of Perception*, 145. A possible exception here is a psychotic person who may be unable to form habits and for whom the world may indeed seem chaotic and uninhabitable. Indeed, the inability to develop relatively stable perceptual norms is, I would argue, one of the reasons why such an individual may be unable to live in the world in a coherent way.

31. Beauvoir, *Coming of Age*, 466.

32. Ibid., 302.

BIBLIOGRAPHY

Beauvoir, Simone de. *The Coming of Age*. Translated by Patrick O'Brian. New York: W. W. Norton, 1996.

———. *The Second Sex*. Translated by Constance Borde and Sheila Malovany-Chevallier. New York: Alfred A. Knopf, 2010.

Bourdieu, Pierre. *The Logic of Practice*. Translated by Richard Nice. Stanford, CA: Stanford University Press, 1990.

Douglas, Mary. *Purity and Danger: An Analysis of the Concepts of Pollution and Taboo*. London: Routledge, 1992.

Garland-Thomson, Rosemarie. *Extraordinary Bodies: Figuring Physical Disability in American Culture and Literature*. New York: Columbia University Press, 1997.

Goffman, Erving. *Stigma: Notes on the Management of Spoiled Identity*. Englewood Cliffs, NJ: Prentice-Hall, 1963.

Grosz, Elizabeth. *Volatile Bodies: Toward a Corporeal Feminism*. Bloomington: Indiana University Press, 1991.

Kristeva, Julia. *Powers of Horror: An Essay on Abjection*. Translated by Leon S. Roudiez. New York: Columbia University Press, 1982.

Merleau-Ponty, Maurice. *Phenomenology of Perception*. Translated by Donald A. Landes. London: Routledge, 2012.

Murphy, Robert. *The Body Silent: An Anthropologist Embarks on the Most Challenging Journey of his Life: Into the World of the Disabled*. New York: W. W. Norton, 1990.

Sartre, Jean-Paul. *Being and Nothingness*. Translated by Hazel E. Barnes. New York: Washington Square Press, 1984.

Weiss, Gail. *Body Images: Embodiment as Intercorporeality*. New York: Routledge, 1999.

———. "The Myth of Woman Meets the Myth of Old Age: An Alienating Encounter with the Aging Female Body." In *Simone de Beauvoir's Philosophy of Age: Gender, Ethics, and Time*, edited by Silva Stoller, 47–64. Berlin: Walter de Gruyter, 2014.

Wilde, Oscar. *The Picture of Dorian Gray*. New York: Modern Library, 1992.

12 THE TRANSHUMAN PARADIGM AND THE MEANING OF LIFE

CHRISTINA SCHÜES

REPRODUCTIVE AND TRANSPLANTATION medicine, genetics and molecular biology provide the means for intervening in the body and for interchanging living tissues, organs, or other body materials between human beings. Examples include organ or stem cell transplantations, the genetic determination of embryos in reproductive genetics, or receptor-specific psychopharmaceuticals. However, biotechnological interventions not only aim at the materiality and functionality of the human body, but they also transform the familial and social relations among humans. This means that biotechnologies can be profound interventions into human experiences and lives. The paradigmatic profoundness of these technologies of the later twentieth and early twenty-first centuries is just as deep as other epoch-making historical changes of moral and legal orders, scientific knowledge, and day-to-day practices. Although phenomenology allows us to address the meaning of experiences, in order to address the meaning of experiences made in light of these paradigm shifts in medicine, biology, and techno-sciences, phenomenology must be transformed into a *feminist bio-phenomenology*.

I believe that a bio-phenomenological exploration can be developed out of two already existing discourses: first, a phenomenological approach that investigates the constitution of meaning by acknowledging the embodiment of the self, a generative dimension, and relational experiences; and, second, by reference to bioethics, which already addresses themes such as transplantation practices or genetic diagnostics.

Taking my cue from Hannah Arendt, who dismantles the metaphysical belief of a two-world theory of being and appearance, I will argue that the meaning of life is not distinct from or presupposed by the experiences of life.[1] Hence, a phenomenological perspective about the meaning of life focuses on the *experiences* of life. The meaning that is given to life hinges upon *how* life is experienced. Experiences that give life meaning are most of all experiences of human relationships, of emotions and events with others who are close to us or who affect us in some way. Concrete lived life receives its meaning through experiences with others. Life can be meaningful or meaningless, and experiences can be good or bad.[2] Our experiences of life can be more or less intensive, and they can be qualitatively more or less happy or sad, depressing or joyful; thus, life is given its meaning by our experiences of relations. Experiences of life always and necessarily take place in human relations, in a social world, and in space and time—I take this to be the "apriority of existence."[3]

An understanding of relational experiences in the context of biotechnological practices needs a thorough investigation of its presuppositions, and they are to be found—as I hope to show in this essay—in bio-phenomenology. What sorts of experiences are important for the meaning of life? How does life gain or lose meaning? How is the concrete meaning of life influenced by such new biotechnological practices? If experiences take place through relations, and if these human relations are medically and technologically determined and characterized by, for instance, blood compatibility (in the case of bone marrow transplantation) or genetic knowledge (in the case of predictive medicine), then questions arise as to how this knowledge about and intervention in biological life may give new interpretations of the relations between men and women, among family members, or with strangers (whose blood is compatible or who share body material, such as bone marrow or an organ). Thus, perhaps not only the happy and tragic events we share with our close ones but also the knowledge about their biological lives shapes our biographical relations with others and social structures. And this relational and structural realm grounds our experiences. Biotechnology and biography might enter into an intimate relation that calls for a new approach to understanding. Bio-phenomenology has the task of elucidating such different meaning dimensions, each belonging to its own discipline, yet without privileging any one of these approaches. Bio-phenomenology acknowledges that biotechnological practices are already implemented in human life and experience. Hence, it investigates how they become meaningful within human relations and everyday life.

In this essay, I will proceed by first presenting the paradigm changes that have given rise to what I call a bio-phenomenology; second, I will draw upon bioethics, its rise and its blind spots. Third, I will address a prospective concept of phenomenology as bio-phenomenology. I will illustrate this turn to bio-phenomenology with the examples of organ transplantation and the creation of so-called savior siblings.

SCIENCE HISTORY AND A PARADIGM CHANGE

The history of science and its social context is marked by specific paradigm changes, which often can be recognized only in retrospect.[4] These paradigm changes concern humankind's relation to nature and technology, how scientific practices are embedded in society, and how they structure and form experience. I take paradigm changes to mark a shift in experiences in which new ways of thinking and understanding are introduced yet the "old" technologies of the previous period may still be—at least to an extent—utilized as a matter of course.

Bernhard Waldenfels argues that since the twentieth century we have lived in a "hypermodernism," which has to an extent left modernity behind.[5] Modernism and its dualisms have not been overcome; instead its dualistic oppositions are "neutralized" by way of an interplay between the artificial and the natural. The integration of technology into nature (antiquity) and the control of nature by technology (modernism) are now followed by an "unleashing of technology."[6] This form of operation has its predecessor in Immanuel Kant's concept of the self-organization of life, which shows that teleology makes sense only if the parts of a system are simultaneously means and ends.[7] The Nietzschean concept of "self-creation" and Humberto Maturana's "autopoiesis" are examples of a phenomenon that cannot be described by any cause-and-effect schema: the *liveliness of life*. Yet the fascination with creating and reorganizing life remains a scientific project that also influences clinical research, as, for instance, in gene therapy. The promises of gene therapy or genetic enhancement are compelling—once we fully understand the functions of life, perhaps even the functions of cells, we can use living material for therapeutic or enhancement purposes. Hence, technology and biology are joined in an interplay—that is, life (*bios*) is interpreted technologically and, even more so, technology is understood biologically. Technology becomes part of a regime of revitalization and exerts its fascination as the *liveliness of technology*. This is the ambition of the twentieth and twenty-first centuries.

When technology is implanted into the human body in order to maintain or enhance human capacities, then one goal of such an intervention is that the patient can pursue his or her life by integrating technology in the best way possible. Waldenfels calls the integration of technology or even its intervention into our experience without being recognized in the experience itself "phenomenotechnology."[8] Technology and the living body merge into a single unity while even reflective consciousness cannot detect a bodily difference in the experience. Two examples of phenomenotechnology are the prosthetic integration of a cochlear implant into the ear as part of hearing, and the pharmaceutical stabilization of "normal" behavior with mood-stimulating drugs.[9] If hypermodern technologies intervene in experiences, and if such interventions are not intended as an attempt to control experience, then we must ask about the relation of what intervenes and of that in which it intervenes. If the difference between what intervenes and that in which it intervenes can no longer be detected, then "the intervention (*Eingriff*) is transformed into an invasion (*Übergriff*) of the technology."[10] With the reference to the notion of phenomenotechnology, Waldenfels is concerned with the interface between technology and phenomenology. He observes that technology, including biotechnology, affects the foundation of our experience insofar as it is an "acting" technology and not simply a means or a tool.[11] Hypermodernism refers to aspects of acting technology and the transgression of technology in nature, of technology and phenomenology, and hence to experiences in which technology may already be (unnoticeable or habitually) interwoven. These are threads that run through the different senses of what I call the *transhuman paradigm*. What does the transhuman paradigm mean for life? What does it mean for our experiences and relations?

I would like to distinguish three different meanings of the notion "transhuman" in the context of biomedicine and biotechnology: enhancement, posthumanism, and the transplantation of body material. The three different understandings refer to different transhuman practices. First, the paradigm of the transhuman, used in the sense of transcending humankind's capacities, confronts us with medical, technical, and biological possibilities and fantasies that provoke us to ask questions about life. As Michel Foucault observed, we make life, not death.[12] Death is no longer a part of life and has come to be regarded as a failure of medicine. The possibility and practice of the enhancement of human capacities—whether they are real or fictional—has led to controversial discussions in philosophy and in social and cultural sciences.[13] One aspect of these discussions is that medicine aims at curing, "normalizing," or enhancing human beings. Yet, the distinctions among therapy, "normalization," and enhancement are not clearly defined and lead to conflicting discussions.

In any case, biotechnological interventions for enhancement aim at the materiality of the human body in order to enhance its capacities or functions. Such interventions lead, among others, to a tendency to medicalize social problems.[14] A result is that not only individual aspects of the human personality are associated with the somatic dimension of biomedicine. Social and environmental factors, biographical experiences, or socioeconomic conditions are still taken to be influential for the self and human relations, but such influences are more and more often described in terms of the functions of receptors, genetic dispositions, enzymes, neurotransmitters, and so on, and hence with references to neuroscience, genetics, or biotechnology. Thus, personality is considered to be biologically modified, or self-managed, as, for instance, when learning becomes a question of biology.

Second, the term "transhuman" is used in the sense of posthuman. The idea is that by blurring the distinction between human and nonhuman and transcending humankind, even the question of what is human becomes absurd. The progress of bio- and nanotechnology will lead to an epoch of posthuman creatures.[15] (A discussion of this thesis is beyond the scope of this essay.)

Third, the notion of the "transhuman" can be taken in the sense of *transplanting* living body material from one human body to another. The prefix "trans" means that something is taken "across" from one "side" to another, as in "translation," "transmission," and "transplantation." During the last decades, the number of transplantations has considerably increased. From a medical perspective, more and more dysfunctions, such as organ failures, diseases of the immune system, different forms of leukemia, or injuries due to accidents, can be cured by transplanting and replacing the broken part of the sick body with functional parts from a healthy body. The living therapeutic material is expected to grow within its new environment and help improve the life quality of the patient. The exploration and understanding of such experiences go beyond a medical perspective and need a hermeneutic-phenomenological interpretative approach.

These kinds of medical and biological possibilities and practices result in very specific experiences for the donor and the receiver of the donated body part as well as for the families involved. The idea that a human body can become a pharmaceutical tool for another individual provokes quite ambiguous feelings, and it has the potential to change social relations and power structures. Yet society is always the normative and evaluative context of these medical possibilities and transplantation practices. Even though ideally the new living organ or the new living blood stem cells are not felt as such in the body of the receiver, the experiences and hence the meaning of life may still be constituted differently. A successful transplantation is often seen as a rebirth, because a life has been saved. But is it just about biological life? Receivers of organs or bone marrow report that they often think about their donors, how they lived and died, and whether or how they are related to them.[16] Thus, we need a methodological approach that addresses the realm of phenomena that concern intercorporeal relations and body exchanges in transplantation practices as a transhuman practice.

Therefore, when we look at transhuman practices, such as transplantation medicine, reproductive genetics, or enhancement technologies, we see a story not only of success but also of radical changes for society and its norms, along with a challenging rearrangement of human relations. Reproductive genetics, for instance, is restructuring natality (what it means to be born from somebody) and generativity (what it means to be related between generations);[17] these are challenges to our understanding in general but also to biopolitical and bioethical discussions specifically. Hence, we need a methodological approach that adequately addresses these epistemological and ethical questions. In the next section I briefly introduce some main threads in bioethics that thematically discuss biotechnology and biomedicine, and then I turn to an exploration of bio-phenomenology.

BIOETHICS

Bioethics has become a heterogeneous field of expertise. Mainstream bioethical approaches are mostly either Aristotelian (the notion of a "good life"), deontological (the concept of duty), casuistic (case-by-case reasoning), or practical (guidelines of principles for the physician).[18] Most approaches follow an individualistic concept of ethics by emphasizing the right of the individual to autonomy, principles of beneficence—for example, acting in the best interest of the other—or a concept of justice based on fairness and equality. Feminist bioethics has thematically enlarged the field of themes with regard to, for instance, the nurturing role of women, underrepresentation of women in medical research, or stigmatization of disability.[19] And it has methodically introduced relational perspectives showing that individual choices already reflect the opportunities made available and desirable in society.[20] The idea that context-sensitivity and narrative perspectives are needed for ethical reflection and theorizing has led to a trend in empirical studies.[21] However, empirical approaches alone are inadequate to address the changes that arise within the paradigm of the transhuman; they remain naïve concerning a critical reconstruction of underlying normative structures of meaning and the power relations that constitute how experiences can be made. Even though they express a first-person perspective, they are inadequate because they address only issues that emerge in interviews or are expressed by behavior. To this extent, I regard them as a kind of positivism.

Bioethics needs to be completed epistemologically by phenomenological research. Medicine intervenes into the body and its functions. But it doesn't intervene only in the biological body. "I have a body and I am my body," as Maurice Merleau-Ponty pointedly expresses it.[22] Most bioethical positions fail to sufficiently differentiate between different aspects of the body, such as the biological body, the material body, and the lived body; the semantic and symbolic dimensions of the body; the body whose borders are crossed; and concepts of bodily and personal integrity. Little work has been done about how relations among human beings, such as power relations, familial relations, and gender relations, change with new medical and technological practices. Often questions about the meaning of life are discussed in reference to illness experiences or quality of life, but less in terms of how experiences of the lived life are made possible and how these experiences are changed through medical interventions. Such a critical reconstruction of meaning constitution is the task of bio-phenomenology.

BIOTECHNOLOGY AND BIO-PHENOMENOLOGY

Biotechnologies touch upon basic conditions and structures, modes and kinds of experiences; therefore, phenomenology is needed for their exploration. If it is true that biotechnology is under the paradigm of the transhuman, and if phenomenology is structured and moved by the intertwining of "theme" and "method," then we need a turn to a particular kind of phenomenology, one that I call "bio-phenomenology."

How does biotechnology restructure experience? This is a general question that can be directed to each sector of biotechnology. With regard to assisted reproductive technologies and intergenerational applications of genetics, the question would be more precisely: How do biotechnological reprogenetic interventions change the conditions and possibilities, the modes and kinds of experiences? How do they change interpersonal, familial, and intergenerational relations? Experiences are bodily embedded and they are made in relations; if biotechnology changes bodily and human relations, then it also changes the possibilities and conditions of our experiences and the meaning of life that is given through relational experiences. For instance, a life donation of a kidney or a refusal of such between two persons who are a couple will certainly also change their relation to each other and give their lives—their concrete lives, their bodily lives, indeed life in general—a "new" meaning.

The idea to combine "bio" with "phenomenology" emerges out of the belief that the theme guides the method and that medicine, biology, and the technosciences do not adequately reflect upon the meaning they generate with their models of life.[23] Bio-phenomenology has the task of clarifying the many voices of these different disciplines, each with their own style of thinking, without claiming to translate these approaches into a single "proper one." Bio-phenomenology does not try to understand science in the sense of Gaston Bachelard—namely, as one's own region or as one's own concrete form of life; neither does it follow Husserl, who tried to reconnect, at least in some aspects, science to the everyday lifeworld. Rather, bio-phenomenology confirms that medical and bio sciences are already implemented in everyday life; therefore, it tries to investigate how certain transhuman practices are experiences and become meaningful in everyday life. Furthermore, phenomenological investigation shows that both the general and the concrete meaning of life, as pointed out above, have an important role in understanding life and in living one's life.

If it is true that certain technologies reshape relations and generative structures, then we need a method of exploration and understanding that appropriately reflects the meanings involved. These meanings have to do with the concept of "bio."[24] For a phenomenological exploration I prefer the term "bio" to "life," first because life-phenomenology is already an established discourse associated with themes of the self-appearance of transcendental subjectivity, as inspired by authors such as Maine de Biran, Henry Bergson, or Michel Henry, and as presently advocated by Jean-Luc Marion and Rolf Kühn.[25] Second, the term and prefix "bio" is already established in the scientific realm by way of disciplines such as bioethics, biotechnology, and biology. And, third, its use in the concept of biography does justice to the concern for the meaning-giving procedures of an individual's life. Therefore, briefly put, I think the name "bio-phenomenology" best illuminates the balancing act between biology and biography, between forms of science and the conditions of possible experiences and its meaning constitution.

Bio-phenomenology provides an appropriate approach to investigating the underlying dimensions of meaning and the structures of experiences, which concern the biotechnological, medical, and reprogenetic practices in the transhuman paradigm. Bio-phenomenology involves, like classical phenomenological themes such as experience, *the body, human relations,* and *generative structures*, but it focuses in particular on the different meanings of life that are involved in reshaping human relations and practices on the basis of medicine and biotechnology. Each practice of reproductive or transplantation medicine, genetics or molecular biology always involves more than one individual. Hence, the reference to individual experiences is not sufficient for understanding the meaning-dimensions of life, the social relations, and how people are affected in different ways. For instance, a genetic testing of one individual also detects some of the existential dispositions of her (biologically related) relatives and even those of the next generation—with or without their knowledge. What does that mean for the family relations? Do they need to be informed? Shall the knowledge be kept secret? What are the concerns about the relation itself? Do we experience "life" with other people differently on the basis of genetic knowledge? This small example shows that these and many more questions and their meanings are part of the questioning of a bio-phenomenology that is generally concerned with the different dimensions of the question "what is the meaning of life?" in the context of the new bio-technologies.

Experiences are the starting point of phenomenological analysis.[26] Superficially this could be understood as simply doing some empirical groundwork in order to describe them. However, this is not the task of phenomenology. Phenomenology as done by Edmund Husserl or Maurice Merleau-Ponty takes experience as a theme and not just as access to knowledge. Not as an empirical study but as a theory of experiences, phenomenology searches for the conditions and modes of experiences by following the guiding questions of how experiences are made possible, how they can be understood, and how they could have been constituted. Each "consciousness of something" has "an intentional *horizon of reference* to potentialities of consciousness that belong to the process itself."[27] The idea of the structure of reference, which is essential to intentionality, and the concepts of a bodily and mundane self are special to phenomenology in the line of Husserl but also Merleau-Ponty. How experiences occur to us has to do with, for instance, the various conditions that influence us, with the modes of our relations and the pre-understanding of what is "normal."

The difference between a phenomenological investigation of experiences and empirical work can best be explained by reference to the idea of the transcendental. Phenomenology is a transcendental method because it inquires into both the structures of intentionality of the person who has an experience and the possibility of the conditions for having a particular experience.[28] Thus, if possibilities change, then the conditions for the constitution of a particular experience shift as well. It is the task of phenomenology to investigate how experiences are made possible and also how certain "things" in life actually withdraw from experience (as, for instance, one's own birth). Phenomenology asks about the structural and relational prerequisites and the concealed cultural or social meanings of our experiences and relations. The meaning of life is co-constituted.

Merleau-Ponty opens up a "third way" between empiricism and rationalism and places the body-subject as being *in* the world and *toward* the world. His phenomenology of the body develops a way of thinking about an embodied and worldly self. The distinction between the lived body (*corps propre*) and the objective body is essential to understanding the underlying meanings and structures of the experiences concerning transplantation practices. Any interventions into the body touch the lived body and thereby also the self. The embodiment of the self and relations is fundamental to experiences. Experiences give meaning to life and are made by embodied selves within relations in the world and toward the world. This embodied and positional self rests in the primacy of relatedness among human beings and the variety of their practices. The relationships among human beings can be seen in the light of the possibility of a co-constitution, or relational constitution, of experiences. Hence, transhuman practice touches not only the lived body and the self but also human relations in and toward the world.

Phenomenology needs to turn to a feminist bio-phenomenology in order to address the meaning of experiences made in light of these paradigm shifts in medicine, biology, and techno-sciences. The developments and practices of the new biotechnologies concern the human condition, societal relations, individuals, and their experiences; hence they concern the basic philosophical question, What is the meaning of life? or, more concretely, What is the meaning of *my* life? This very personal question refers to the experiences a person makes within the relations and social structures in which she lives. Human relations are always socially and normatively determined as well as influenced by explicit or implicit power structures and beliefs about values. Accordingly, any approach we use cannot do without a turn to feminist theory, whose central task is to reveal epistemic blind spots; underlying normative beliefs about relations, the body, or gender roles; and hidden, perhaps unjust, social structures. With feminist phenomenology I give preference to a relational perspective that situates the embodiment and relatedness of humans as prior to their individualism. Hence, a phenomenology that would address the meaning of life in light of scientific understandings and the experiences brought about by them must not only turn to a *bio*-phenomenology but explicitly to a critical and *feminist* bio-phenomenology.

Human relations, the temporality of human existence, and the varied dimensions of meaning in practice are based on the *conditio humana* such as natality and mortality, life, world, embodiment, gender, vulnerability, and relatedness.[29] All of these aspects are structurally meaningful for life and relevant for bio-phenomenology. If, for instance, medicine could make human beings less vulnerable or even invulnerable, then, for instance, the possibility of experiencing fear or pain would diminish and reduce interpersonal relations of empathy and care. Or if humans were created out of laboratories and not born from a mother, then the questions about one's own life would start with the biographical narratives that include clinics and physicians, and perhaps not parents, as well as presumably one's self-situatedness in the world. Accordingly, the understanding of generations would be different.

Vitalization, the combination and growing of life material, the "living life," becomes the question and concern of experiences and human relations. Vitalization becomes an issue in life if material is transplanted in order to rescue life and if transplanted organs live and function in their new environment. As body-gift relationships in transplantation practices or enhancement technologies, biotechnologies are encroached into lived experiences and cannot be traced back to direct insight or bodily sensation. Yet they concern self-understanding, generative and social relations, the biological and biographical life, material and ethical aspects, and the future of individuals and society (and even future generations).

Today's biotechnological, political, and ethical concerns do not just confront human beings with technology. Biotechnology restrains "life" on more dimensions than just the biological one, insofar as it is capable of reorganizing life, by replacing nonfunctional parts of living organisms with new ones or by controlling whether a living organism, such as an embryo, shall be kept alive and have its biography. As a result, bio-phenomenology is confronted with several research questions, such as, How does biotechnology intervene into the liveliness of the body and, thereby, lived life as it is experienced? How does transplantation change experiences of relations, the relations themselves, and hence the experiences? How does the possibility to enhance human capacities change social norms or social relations among humans? These are questions that can be answered only by reference to the underlying meaning structure of experiences and by the investigation into the possibility of their conditions. They are asked in reference to the guiding question, What is the meaning of life? or, more precisely, How could the meaning of life have been constituted?

The following two examples of transhuman practices concern biotechnology's therapeutic success in curing different kinds of organ failure, leukemia, or blood diseases. The examples of organ transplantation and the creation of savior siblings refer to the third understanding of the transhuman practice. The first example refers to the aspect of transcorporeality and the second to the phenomenon of inscribing a duty into the materiality of a "body" by birth. Both examples show that bio-phenomenology has the task of exploring the meaning dimensions of life—that is, the constitution of the body, the interrelation between the biological and biographical, the medically inspired new relation between human beings, and the phenomenon of bodily life-gift giving.

The Gift of Life I: Organ Transplantation

Since the 1980s, organ transplantation has become a common practice. The organ donor is construed as an altruistic person who has planned to give her organs, such as a kidney or a part of the liver, or who is declared dead and available as a "gift of life."[30] The decision and experience of giving and receiving is grounded in the semantics of the gift. In a contemporary medical perspective, bodies are seen and understood as potentially divisible and shareable and hence as potential "therapeutic tools" for other human beings.[31] Thus, transplantation medicine enables the sharing of body parts or tissue across the corporeal border, across social and national borders; it has opened up a completely new realm of questions and fantasies concerning our self-understanding, our bodies, death, and decision making about ourselves, our children, and beloved family members: Do I have to give my kidney for a sick family member? Does a person who receives a heart participate in the emotional life the donor once had? If I *have* a body and if I *am* my body, as Merleau-Ponty says, what about myself do I give away with my organ?

Marcel Mauss's semantic of the gift insightfully depicts the gift-giving bond between the gift giver and the receiver, gift exchange, and social relations.[32] A gift received has to be recompensed. How is a gift part of exchange? Can an organ be taken, received, and given just like a gift? What follows from this? What sort of morality and economy is at work in an organ "gift relationship"? Generally, gifts are given voluntarily or under obligation; according to Mauss, what is important is to "show respect to each other."[33] One gives of oneself in giving, and if one gives of oneself, it is that one owes oneself to others, oneself, and one's property. One remains concerned about the well-being of the other to whom one belongs because of the giving. Giving and receiving gifts is a practice that involves a system of respect. In Mauss's "gift economy" there is a spiritual force inherent in a gift from the person who gave it, and this force can be transmitted and passed on to the next person.[34] The bond that is initiated and reinforced by the gift is thus morally and spiritually grounded.

How big are the differences between a gift—say, jewelry—and the gift of an organ? How big are the differences for the meaning of experience? I will highlight a few of these differences in order to show what sorts of questions can be posed in a bio-phenomenological exploration. Even though medical practice puts forward the idea that organ transplantation only means improving or rescuing the body's function, phenomenologically speaking an organ is not regarded as only a thing; the person to whom it belongs, the lived body, and the functional object are intertwined. Therefore, for the receiver of an organ a transplantation has the connotation that she will also receive part of the life story, culture, and social belonging from the organ donor. The organ, the gift of life, or in the term of Merleau-Ponty's later works, the "flesh," creates a new bond, an intercorporeality, between the giver and the receiver.[35] This bond seems morally, physically, spiritually, biologically, biographically initiated by another person just as if Mauss's concept of "gift economy" holds true for organ gifts as well.[36] As a result, it is not always easy for the receiver to emotionally incorporate a new organ. The "spiritual force" Mauss was talking about seems to be attached to the organ gift (at least for some receivers). Thus, when children are involved, both families need time to adapt their biographical and family narratives to the new situation. It is not just the biological body that needs to adapt to the new organ.

The relation between the donor and the receiver is asymmetrical: "The one who receives a gift can turn into a person who feels overwhelmed by the obligation to give something in return."[37] Normally, not to do anything is a sign of ingratitude and can be taken as a sign that a gift "had been given wrongly" (wrong gift, bad taste, wrong person, misperception of the relation). An organ is different. Often the people involved do not know each other; in most countries anonymity is preserved in order to make sure that no pressure is exerted.[38] But not to give any thanks seems wrong. Yet, a gift of life is too much to be able to give thanks for. A *proper* response to a gift of life is impossible; a proper *response* is impossible, but it is still necessary for the receiver and for the donor, if alive, or for the family of the donor if not. The experiences remain ambivalent because of the inherent meaning structure of the transplantation body practice.

The Gift of Life II: A Savior Sibling

For about forty years, blood stem cell transplantations have been possible as a therapy to cure patients with leukemia and other diseases of the immune or blood system. In this example, I discuss bone marrow transplantation with children. In the case of siblings, parents have to make a decision about a non-indicated medical intervention in their healthy child in order to cure the sick one. I am not discussing here the problems parents face in a conflict of this nature and in surrogate decision making.[39] Rather, I am interested in the problem that occurs when a child is sick and would benefit from an allogeneic bone marrow transplant but no donor, neither an adult nor a sibling, is available.

Recent developments in medical technology now enable parents to choose a specific child's body in order to have matching body material for their sick son or daughter. This has the effect that savior siblings are made and born with a task: the task of rescuing a sick sibling; this means they are born to be a donor and they are a gift *to* someone—a gift of life. In the year 2000 the first so-called savior sibling was selected as a result of in vitro fertilization (IVF) and pre-implantation genetic diagnosis/human leukocyte antigen (PGD/HLA) screening. The infant is born to donate blood stem cells for a sister or brother suffering from life-threatening illnesses of the immune system, such as leukemia or Fanconi anemia. Being born as a savior child means serving as a therapeutic tool—the child is a *bébé-médicament*—for the benefit of another sick child.[40] The practice of creating savior siblings presupposes not only medical technologies such as genetic diagnostic or transplantation technologies but also certain anthropological and ethical views about body sharing, the meaning of life, transcorporeal gift relationships, and being conceived and born under certain conditions, such as, for instance, a precise genetics diagnostic selection process for someone else's benefit. The prenatal history of a donor child includes a selection procedure of corporeal criteria according to the body of the sick sibling and the possible rejection if there is no HLA match. The child is alive only because of certain physical criteria; the condition of its existence is to have a body that is selected according to its benefit for someone else. Thus, the (first) meaning of the savior sibling's life is to be a therapeutic tool that can be shared and taken as a gift. This has conceptual consequences about the meaning of birth and the meaning of life for the child and the family involved. The donor child's birth takes place under the material and physical condition of being a (lifelong) corporeal gift for a sick child.

My point is not to morally judge whether or not it should be allowed or forbidden to create savior siblings. I understand that parents with a child who is ill with leukemia are emotionally caught up, so when it concerns the survival of their beloved daughter or son, they will take advantage of every possibility offered them.[41] My questions concern the bio-phenomenological prerequisites and an understanding of the concept of being born as a corporeal gift for somebody else. In the following section I will discuss two questions:(1) What is the meaning of life, the existential sense of the bodily traces of a child who is born to be a donor? And, (2), what is the nature of that child's relation to his or her family—to her sibling(s) or parents?

THE MEANING OF LIFE, THE BODY, AND BODILY TRACES

In order to understand the concept of the meaning of life and the concept of the body, I will begin by looking at the dualist conception of the body and then ask about the aspect of the lived body and its bodily traces. First, it is important to point out that the medical, social, and cultural practices that justify the creating and using of a savior sibling require a dualist conception of the human being.

Medical biological bodies are seen as divisible; ethical and medical discourses hold that the person or the self remains untouched from medical interventions into the physical body. This view from outside construes the concept of the self as devoid of its embodiment. Thinking of a body as a therapeutic tool could mean disassociating it from its mental, emotional, and personal integrity. This disassociation is necessary if the parents and society are to legitimize such use of savior siblings, and it becomes understandable should the transplantation fail. Without such dualistic thinking, we could say that "the child" is a failure or "its life had not been necessary." Would the parents, who were trying to do everything for the sake of their sick child, then be resentful toward their savior child if it was he or she as a person who had failed to do the job? If it was just the body, or even more correctly, if it was just the recombination of cells that did not function as a therapeutic tool, then at least the child is not to be blamed (subconsciously).

From a Merleau-Pontean approach, the legitimization of stem cell donation involves an abstraction between the materiality of the transplanted body cells and the person. But, following Merleau-Ponty, the donor child is (also) a lived body. Human beings have their bodies and are their bodies insofar as their bodies are the medium toward the world and their anchorage in the world. If a child is born to be a donor, then, first, she has been through all the procedures of in vitro fertilization, preimplantation diagnosis, and all of the other prenatal, perinatal, and postnatal controls. Thus, the growing lived body has been under permanent medical control until the subsequent transplantation.

As Merleau-Ponty explains, "Because I am swept along into personal existence by a time that I do not constitute, all of my perceptions appear perspectivally against a background of nature. While I am perceiving—and even without any knowledge of the organic conditions of my perception—I am conscious of integrating detracted and dispersed 'consciousnesses,' namely, vision, hearing and touch, along with their fields, which are anterior to and remain foreign to my personal life."[42] In other words, I will never remember my organic condition, but I will always be captivated by it and develop my personal history using my imagination just as if I see "some footprints in the sand."[43] They initiate and inspire personal stories—that is, my life story—about them.

When I speak about traces, I mean the hidden and silent traces that were laid down by some event or experience and were immediately forgotten or never recognized as such. Silent traces are also forgotten traces, but they are nevertheless the bases for a personal history and a relation with and in the world. The traces remain in the body; they may be felt or never felt; perhaps they remain silent forever, or only until her sibling has health problems.[44] Such traces, however, are part of the meaning of the life the donor child will live.

THE RELATIONS: BEING A GIFT AND HAVING THIS TASK

The duty to donate is inscribed into the lived body, into the person. Part of the body history is that the child had been created in order to be a donor; biology and biography are intertwined. The donor's history includes stories about hospitals, about tests and sedations. It also refers to being the gift of life to a sick sibling in need and being never able to recompense it. If the savior sibling would (or could) refuse to make the donation, then she would be burdened with guilt at not having prevented the death of her sibling, a death, however, that was actually caused by a disease and is only her "responsibility" because of her birth and her body material.[45] Furthermore, if she had the wish to donate her body tissue, then this wish would actually be without meaning, because she was already born to be a donor. Is the meaning of her life to be a gift to her sick sister or brother?

The history of medicine and biotechnology is one of progress and success; it turns the body into material "flesh" and into information that can be disseminated and shared. But there is also a dark side. The threat of the instrumentalization of human beings is systematically built into a technology that is used to enhance human capacity for the end of either something or someone else, such as the economic system or for a person with an illness.[46] Hence, the threat of instrumentalization is not inherent in technology per se. Technology is already intertwined with human beings, but when technology is used as a tool for intervention and for body sharing, then this may lead to the instrumentalization of human beings. Thus, in order to further understand these power structures, social constellations, and generative relations, which are reconstructed by the use and the imagination of the use of certain technologies and which ground our experiences of the meaning of life in times of the transhuman paradigm, we need research in bio-phenomenology.

HOW IS THE MEANING OF LIFE CONSTITUTED?

The concrete lived life receives its meaning through experiences. When the human condition—its relations, embodiment, or generative structure—are transformed by biotechnological or medical interventions, then this also has an effect on the conditions of the possibility of experiences. Certain modes of human relations, such as creating matching bodies for the therapeutic benefit of someone sick, may include the instrumentalization of a person, and technology may help to constitute such relations.

Accordingly, if experiences can make life more or less meaningful, and if life can be more or less meaningful then, as Frédéric Worms also argues, life cannot be understood as a "thing," an "absolute value" or "objective fact."[47] Rather, the dimensions of life are intermingled, the general with the concrete, the biological with the biographical.[48] By pointing to such interconnectedness, we can draw upon the meaning that lies in every life, in every story, and in every concrete "human drama."[49] Such an approach requires a critical stance against unfounded abstraction, generalization, or the homogenization of life, and it argues for the acknowledgment of the meaning of human experiences and their relations (yet without getting stuck in a bold empiricism).

We always participate in our organic life; therefore, biology influences biography. Before the transhuman paradigm, biology exercised its influence in an anonymous sense insofar as one used biology to describe certain general characteristics or one used evolutionary theories or ecological programs in an attempt to intervene into life. Of course, some of these "descriptions" were not harmless; they led to exclusion or even to euthanasia. General lines of life or death, of inclusion or exclusion, were drawn brutally—and they still exist. However, under the transhuman paradigm, "life" and "living material" itself are isolated and used to personally enhance others or to be shared transcorporeally. The DNA understood as the "book of life" intertwines biology and biography; the ascription of blood markers and body disposition implies norms and duties. Ethical duties are inscribed into the living material of the body. The individual concrete meaning of life is embedded in relations with other people. Which kinds of relations do I have with others in times of enhancement, posthumanist fantasies, and transplantation practices?

In the introduction to this essay I thematized the idea that experience is intimately connected with the meaning of life. Bio-phenomenology can address this theme. The conditions for certain concrete experiences are taken to be more or less meaningful for one's own life. When people think about the meaning of life, they usually think about their relations with friends and family, about relations of love, care, or closeness. If relations are created or transformed by biological or other scientific conditions, then experiences are certainly not lost, but the answer to the question of how the meaning of life is constituted changes.[50]

CHRISTINA SCHÜES is Professor of Philosophy in the Institute for the History of Medicine and Science Studies at the University of Lübeck, and Adjunct Professor of Philosophy in the Institute for Philosophy and Art Sciences at the Leuphana University, Lüneburg. She is editor (with Dorothea E. Olkowski and Helen A. Fielding) of *Time in Feminist Phenomenology* (Indiana University Press, 2011).

NOTES

1. Hannah Arendt, *The Life of the Mind* (San Diego: Harcourt Brace Jovanovich, 1978), 19.
2. Susan Wolf, "Happiness and Meaning: Two Aspects of a Good Life," *Social Philosophy and Policy* 14, no. 1 (1997): 207–225.
3. Christina Schües, *Philosophie des Geborenseins* (Freiburg: Alber, 2008), 320.
4. The notion of paradigm change is not taken in a Kuhnian sense of an absolute change. See Thomas Kuhn, *The Structure of Scientific Revolutions* (Chicago: University of Chicago Press, 1962).
5. Bernhard Waldenfels, *Bruchlinien der Erfahrung, Phänomenologie, Psychoanalyse, Phänomenotechnik* (Frankfurt: Suhrkamp, 2002), 370.
6. Ibid., 379.
7. Immanuel Kant, *Werkausgabe Band X: Kritik der Urteilskraft*, ed. Wilhelm Weischedel (Frankfurt: Suhrkamp, 1968), B292.
8. Waldenfels uses the notion of "phenomenotechnique" for describing experiences; Bachelard intended, rather, to describe scientific formations. See Waldenfels, *Bruchlinien der Erfahrung*, 375; and Hans-Jörg Rheinberger, "Gaston Bachelard and the Notion of 'Phenomenotechnik," *Perspectives on Science* 13, no. 3 (1969): 320. Bachelard refers to the notion of "phenomenotechnique" with the idea that "nothing is given. Everything is constructed," therefore, "phenomenotechnology extends phenomenology." Gaston Bachelard, *La formation de l'esprit scientifique*, 6th ed. (Paris: Vrin, 1969), 14, 61.
9. The cochlear implant is to be distinguished from a hearing aid insofar as the latter can be turned on and off and function as an instrument that one may, however, forget. The question here is not whether such interventions are judged as good or bad.
10. Waldenfels, *Bruchlinien der Erfahrung*, 362.
11. The integration of technology, particular medicine, or drugs had been done throughout all paradigms. Now the tendency seems to be that biomedicine and biotechnology interact with the body on their own—for example, implanted cells have a life of their own.
12. "One might say that the ancient right to *take* life or *let* live was replaced by a power to *foster* life or *disallow* it to the point of death." Michel Foucault, "Right of Death and Power over Life," from *The History of Sexuality*, vol. 1, in *The Foucault Reader*, ed. Paul Rabinow (New York: Pantheon, 1984), 261. And sometimes we make life that destroys life.
13. President's Council on Bioethics, *Beyond Therapy: Biotechnology and the Pursuit of Happiness* (New York: Dana Press, 2003); Max Mehlmann, *The Price of Perfection: Individualism and Society in the Era of Biomedical Enhancement* (Baltimore: Johns Hopkins University Press, 2009); Erik Parens, ed., *Enhancing Human Traits: Ethical and Social Implications* (Washington, DC: Georgetown University Press, 1998); Christina Schües, "Improving Deficiencies? Historical, Anthropological, and Ethical Aspects of the Human Enhancement Debate," in *The Human Enhancement Debate and Disability*, ed. Miriam Eilers, Katrin Grüber, and Christoph Rehmann-Sutter (Basingstoke: Palgrave Macmillan, 2014).
14. Between 1990 and 2000 the sales figures of psychoactive drugs increased by about 125 percent in Europe and 600 percent in the United States; this amounts to an increase of about 40 percent in Europe and of about 70 percent in the United States relative to the

standard doses. See Nicolas Rose, "Neurochemical Selves," in *Society: Social Science and Modern Society* 41, no. 1 (2003): 47.

15. Stefan Herbrechter, *Posthumanismus. Eine kritische Einführung*. (Darmstadt: Wissenschaftliche Buchgesellschaft, 2009); Katherine N. Hayles, *My Mother Was a Computer: Digital Subjects and Literary Texts* (Chicago: University of Chicago Press, 2005).

16. Vera Kalizkus, *Dein Tod, mein Leben, Warum wir Organspenden richtig finden und trotzdem davor zurückschrecken* (Frankfurt: Suhrkamp, 2009); Aslihan Sanal, *New Organs within Us: Transplants and the Moral Economy* (Durham, NC: Duke University Press, 2011).

17. Schües, *Philosophie des Geborenseins*; Christina Schües, "'The Meaning of Natality'—'Doğumluluğun Anlami,'" in *Metafizik ve Politika—Metaphysics and Politics: Martin Heidegger & Hannah Arendt*, ed. S. Yazicioğlu Öge, Ö. Sözer, and F. Tomkinson (Istanbul: Boğaziçi University Press, 2002), 181–223.

18. These can be found in standard textbooks—for instance, see Tom L. Beauchamp and James F. Childress, *Principles of Biomedical Ethics*, 6th ed. (Oxford: Oxford University Press, 2008). Empirical research methods, such as semi-structured interviews and grounded theory, are used to provide insight into how such principles are actually used in concrete decision-making processes. See Katie Page, "The Four Principles: Can They Be Measured and Do They Predict Ethical Decision Making?" *BMC Medical Ethics* 13, no. 10 (2012).

19. As an overview, see Anne Donchin, "Feminist Bioethics," in *Stanford Encyclopedia of Philosophy*, online, 2009.

20. Susan Sherwin, "Whither Bioethics? How Feminism Can Help Reorient Bioethics," *International Journal of Feminist Approaches to Bioethics* 1, no. 1 (2008): 14.

21. Sabine Salloch, Jan Schildmann, and Jochen Vollmann, "Empirical Research in Medical Ethics: How Conceptual Accounts on Normative-Empirical Collaboration May Improve Research Practice," *BMC Medical Ethics* 13, no. 5 (2012); Christoph Rehmann-Sutter, Rouven Porz, Jackie L. Scully, "How to Relate the Empirical to the Normative: Towards a Phenomenologically Informed Hermeneutic Approach to Bioethics," *Cambridge Quarterly of Healthcare Ethics* 21 (2012): 436–47; Jackie Leach Scully, Laurel Baldwin-Ragaven, Petya Fitzpatrick, eds., *Feminist Bioethics: At the Center, on the Margins* (Baltimore: Johns Hopkins University Press, 2010); Donchin, "Feminist Bioethics."

22. Maurice Merleau-Ponty, *Phenomenology of Perception*, trans. Donald A. Landes (New York: Routledge, 2012). Phenomenology has increasingly become a valuable approach for several researchers in the social sciences who approach medical or bioethical practice. However, in that field, for the most part, phenomenology is just seen as a first-person perspective or as a descriptive and narrative method that can be applied to a theme, such as medicine. Even though I find it very important to recognize the first-person perspective or create context-sensitive description, such approaches remain on the level of what Husserl would call "psychological phenomenology" (Ideas I). Good examples are Havi Carel, "Phenomenology and Its Application in Medicine," *Theoretical Medicine and Bioethics* 32, no. 1 (2011); Havi Carel, *Illness* (Durham, NC: Acumen, 2008); Fredrik Svenaeus, "What Is Phenomenology of Medicine? Embodiment, Illness and Being-in-the-World," in *Health, Illness and Disease: Philosophical Essays*, ed. Havi Carel and Rachel Cooper (Durham, NC: Acumen, 2013), 97–111; Linda Finlay, "Debating Phenomenological Research Methods," *Phenomenology and Practice* 3, no. 1 (2009): 6–25.

23. Rehmann-Sutter argues that even though he agrees that the language of molecular genetics does not address the lived life, it does not follow that the molecular biologist cannot be more hermeneutical: "Describing and (thereby necessarily interpreting) development means positing ourselves in a morally relevant way with regard to the living entities we describe." See Christoph Rehmann-Sutter, "Poiesis and Praxis: Two Modes of Understanding Development," in *Genes in Development: Re-reading the Molecular Paradigm*, ed. Eva M. Neumann-Held and Christoph Rehmann-Sutter (Durham, NC: Duke University Press, 2006), 314. Yet even though some persons might have the knowledge in different discourses, there still might be the problem of translation. The fact that we are biological creatures and that we participate in organic life and in everyday life in the world does not mean that we are able to hermeneutically make the transfer from one realm of description to the other. The language and understanding of biology and everyday life may marginally overlap, but being a member of one of the two categories does not mean at all that one can talk about both categories—for example, drinking water and its taste is not well captured by the chemical formula of water. Being knowledgeable in both discourses can help to switch languages. But a shift of meaning cannot be overcome.

24. The Greek term *bíos* is used in several ways in ancient philosophy to describe the life of humans who nevertheless also remain to be a *zóon logon echon* (*zoë* means physical life, often used for plants). The complex concept of the human being develops because of the human's situatedness between the sphere of immanence and transcendence, the mundane and divine.

25. Life phenomenology searches for the self-appearance of being, for the pure immanence of life, a life in which the ego is completely by itself, pure of subjectivity, free of any otherness and contingency. The move from the transcendental reality of the world or from any existential experience of the body to the immanence of life is meant to access an original sphere in which all transcendence (for example, experience, otherness) arises. Life does not mean in this conception any vitalistic or biological notion of life; rather, it means "life in the first person." See Michel Henry, *Philosophy and Phenomenology of the Body*, trans. Girard Etzkorn (New York: Springer, 1975), 272.

26. Merleau-Ponty, *Phenomenology of Perception*, xxxv. In this aspect his position resembles Husserl's.

27. Edmund Husserl, *Cartesian Meditations: An Introduction to Phenomenology*, 6th ed., trans. Dorion Cairns (The Hague: Martinus Nijhoff Publishers, 1977), section 19; translator's emphasis.

28. The notion of "transcendental" here differs from the Kantian use. Kant asks for the condition of the possibility of cognition; Husserl investigates the structures of intentionality in light of the question of the possibility of the condition for a particular experience.

29. Schües, *Philosophie des Geborenseins*; Schües, "'Meaning of Natality.'"

30. "Transplantation has been defined by the medical profession and society at large as a 'gift of life' since the first human organ grafts were performed." Renée Fox and Judith Swazey, *Spare Parts: Organ Replacement in American Society* (New York: Oxford University Press, 1992).

31. Linda F. Hogle, "Transforming 'Body Parts' into Therapeutic Tools: A Report from Germany," *Medical Anthropology Quarterly* 10, no. 4 (1996): 675–82; Margaret Lock, "Human Body Parts as Therapeutic Tools: Contradictory Discourses and Transformed Subjectivities," *Qualitative Health Research* 12, no. 10 (2002).

32. Marcel Mauss, *The Gift: Forms and Functions of Exchange in Archaic Societies* (New York: Norton Library, 1967).

33. Ibid., 4.

34. Spiritual power is named *hau* in Maori, language of the Indigenous population of New Zealand. The term "economy" refers to a system of exchange. The gift has a certain power over the receiver. Therefore, for Mauss, even the relation of exchanging gifts establishes a gift economy. Mauss, *The Gift*, 1967.

35. Maurice Merleau-Ponty, *The Visible and the Invisible*, trans. Alphonso Lingis (Evanston, IL: Northwestern University Press, 1964).

36. Kalizkus, *Dein Tod, mein Leben*; Sanal, *New Organs within Us*.

37. Paul Ricoeur, *The Course of Recognition*, trans. David Pellauer (Cambridge, MA: Harvard University Press, 2005), 240, 231. "How to respond to a gift?" "The gift in return comes in the wake of the generosity of the first gift." See also Mona Motakef, *Körper Gabe. Ambivalente Ökonomien der Organspende* (Bielefeld: Transcript Verlag, 2011).

38. For example, out of expectation of special gratitude on the one side, or out of revenge if the organ does not function properly on the other side.

39. For an ethical discussion on pediatric blood stem cell transplantation, see Christina Schües and Christoph Rehmann-Sutter, "Has a Child a Duty to Donate Hematopoietic Stem Cells to a Sibling?," in *Ethics and Oncology: Therapy, Care, Research*, ed. Monika Bobbert, Beate Hermann, and Wolfgang U. Eckart (Freiburg: Alber, 2015).

40. Patricia Baetens et al., "HLA-Matched Embryos Selected for Siblings Requiring Haematopoietic Stem Cell Transplantation: A Psychological Perspective," *Reproductive BioMedicine* Online 10 (2005): 154–63; Beth Whitehouse, *The Match: "Savior Siblings" and One Family's Battle to Heal Their Daughter* (Boston: Beacon, 2011).

41. See also the essay by Tjeerd Tymstra, who discusses insightfully the problem of stopping a therapeutic path because one might regret later not having done *everything*. Her essay has the telling title "The Imperative Character of Medical Technology and the Meaning of 'Anticipated Decision Regret.'"

42. Merleau-Ponty, *Phenomenology of Perception*, 362.

43. Ibid., 363.

44. The empirical research on children who were born as savior siblings has not yet been carried out, but it could make use of these insights.

45. Practically this point does not arise. Usually, savior siblings are too young to refuse.

46. Apparently, the evaluation of instrumentalization does not necessarily lead to the judgment that one should never agree to the instrumentalization of oneself and one's body.

47. Frédéric Worms, "Qu'est-ce qui est vital?," *Bulletin de la Société française de Philosophie* 101, no. 2 (2007): 9, 15.

48. Frédéric Worms, "La vie qui unit et qui sépare? La question philosophique du sens de la vie aujourd'hui." *Kairos* 23 (2004): 213, 218. See also the newly rewritten essay by the same author and the similar title, *La vie qui unit et qui sépare* (Paris: Payot, 2013).

49. Merleau-Ponty, *Phenomenology of Perception*, 134; Schües, *Philosophie des Geborenseins*, 344; Worms, "La vie qui unit et qui sépare?," 35. All authors refer to the notion of drama in its etymological sense without Romantic overtone and in reference to Georges Politzer, *Critique des fondement de la psychologie* (Paris: Rieder, 1929), 23.

50. I am very grateful for helpful comments made by Pascal Delhom, Helen Fielding, Dorothea Olkowski, and Christoph Rehmann-Sutter.

BIBLIOGRAPHY

Arendt, Hannah. *The Life of the Mind*. One-Volume Edition. San Diego: Harcourt Brace Jovanovich, 1978.
Bachelard, Gaston. *La formation de l'esprit scientifique*. 6th ed. Paris: Vrin, 1969.
Badmington, Neil, ed. *Posthumanism: Reader in Cultural Criticism*. Houndmills: Palgrave, 2000.
Beauchamp, Tom L., and James F. Childress. *Principles of Biomedical Ethics*. 6th ed. Oxford: Oxford University Press, 2008.
Baetens, Patricia, Hilde Van de Velde, Michel Camus, Guido Pennings, Andre Van Steirteghem, Paul Devroey, and Ingeborg Liebaers. "HLA-Matched Embryos Selected for Siblings Requiring Haematopoietic Stem Cell Transplantation: A Psychological Perspective." *Reproductive BioMedicine Online* 10 (2005): 154–63.
Carel, Havi. *Illness*. Durham, NC: Acumen, 2008.
———. "Phenomenology and Its Application in Medicine." *Theoretical Medicine and Bioethics* 32, no. 1 (2011): 33–46
Donchin, Anne. "Feminist Bioethics." In *Stanford Encyclopedia of Philosophy*. Article published Summer 2009. http://plato.stanford.edu/entries/feminist-bioethics.
Finlay, Linda. "Debating Phenomenological Research Methods." *Phenomenology and Practice* 3, no. 1 (2009): 6–25.
Foucault, Michel. "Bio-power." In *The Foucault Reader*, edited by Paul Rabinow, 257–90. New York: Pantheon, 1984.
———. "Right of Death and Power over Life," from *The History of Sexuality*, Vol. 1. In *The Foucault Reader*, edited by Paul Rabinow, 258–72. New York: Pantheon, 1984.
Fox, Renée, and Judith Swazey. *Spare Parts: Organ Replacement in American Society*. New York: Oxford University Press, 1992.
Hayles, N. Katherine. *My Mother Was a Computer: Digital Subjects and Literary Texts*. Chicago: University of Chicago Press, 2005.
Henry, Michel. *Philosophy and Phenomenology of the Body*. Translated by Girard Etzkorn. New York: Springer, 1975.
Herbrechter, Stefan. *Posthumanismus. Eine kritische Einführung*. Darmstadt: Wissenschaftliche Buchgesellschaft, 2009.
Hogle, Linda F. "Transforming 'Body Parts' into Therapeutic Tools: A Report from Germany." *Medical Anthropology Quarterly* 10, no. 4 (1996): 675–82.
Husserl, Edmund. *Cartesian Meditations: An Introduction to Phenomenology*. 6th ed. Translated by Dorion Cairns. The Hague: Martinus Nijhoff Publishers, 1977.
———. *Ideas: General Introduction to Pure Phenomenology*. Translated by W. R. Boyce Gibson. London: Collier Macmillan, 1962.
Kalizkus, Vera. *Dein Tod, mein Leben. Warum wir Organspenden richtig finden und trotzdem davor zurückschrecken*. Frankfurt: Suhrkamp, 2009.
Kant, Immanuel. *Werkausgabe Band X. Kritik der Urteilskraft*. Edited by Wilhelm Weischedel. Frankfurt: Suhrkamp, 1968.
Kuhn, Thomas. *The Structure of Scientific Revolutions*. Chicago: University of Chicago Press, 1962.
Lock, Margaret. "Human Body Parts as Therapeutic Tools: Contradictory Discourses and Transformed Subjectivities." *Qualitative Health Research* 12, no. 10 (2002): 1406–18.

Mauss, Marcel. *The Gift: Forms and Functions of Exchange in Archaic Societies*. New York: Norton Library, 1967.
Mehlmann, Max. *The Price of Perfection: Individualism and Society in the Era of Biomedical Enhancement*. Baltimore: Johns Hopkins University Press, 2009.
Merleau-Ponty, Maurice. *Phenomenology of Perception*. Translated by Donald A. Landes. New York: Routledge, 2012.
———. *The Visible and the Invisible*. Translated by Alphonso Lingis. Evanston, IL: Northwestern University Press, 1964.
Motakef, Mona. *Körper Gabe. Ambivalente Ökonomien der Organspende*. Bielefeld: Transcript Verlag, 2011.
Page, Katie. "The Four Principles: Can They Be Measured and Do They Predict Ethical Decision Making?" *BMC Medical Ethics* 13, no. 10 (2012). DOI: 10.1186/1472-6939-13-10.
Parens, Erik, ed. *Enhancing Human Traits: Ethical and Social Implications*. Washington, DC: Georgetown University Press, 1998.
Politzer, Georges. *Critique des fondement de la psychologie*. Paris: Rieder, 1929.
President's Council on Bioethics. *Beyond Therapy: Biotechnology and the Pursuit of Happiness*. New York: Dana Press, 2003.
Rehmann-Sutter, Christoph. "Poiesis and Praxis: Two Modes of Understanding Development." In *Genes in Development: Re-reading the Molecular Paradigm*, edited by Eva M. Neumann-Held and Christoph Rehmann-Sutter, 313–34. Durham, NC: Duke University Press, 2006.
Rehmann-Sutter, Christoph, Rouven Porz, and Jackie L. Scully. "How to Relate the Empirical to the Normative: Towards a Phenomenologically Informed Hermeneutic Approach to Bioethics." *Cambridge Quarterly of Healthcare Ethics* 21 (2012): 436–47.
Rheinberger, Hans-Jörg. "Gaston Bachelard and the Notion of 'Phenomenotechnique.'" *Perspectives on Science* 13, no. 3 (2005): 313–28.
Ricoeur, Paul. *The Course of Recognition*. Translated by David Pellauer. Cambridge, MA: Harvard University Press, 2005.
Rose, Nicolas. "Neurochemical Selves." In *Society: Social Science and Modern Society* 41, no. 1 (2003): 46–59.
Salloch, Sabine, Jan Schildmann, and Jochen Vollmann. "Empirical Research in Medical Ethics: How Conceptual Accounts on Normative-Empirical Collaboration May Improve Research Practice." *BMC Medical Ethics* 13, no. 5 (2012). https://bmcmedethics.biomedcentral.com/articles/10.1186/1472-6939-13-5.
Sanal, Aslihan. *New Organs within Us: Transplants and the Moral Economy*. Durham, NC: Duke University Press, 2011.
Schües, Christina. "Improving Deficiencies? Historical, Anthropological, and Ethical Aspects of the Human Enhancement Debate." In *The Human Enhancement Debate and Disability*, edited by Miriam Eilers, Katrin Grüber, and Christoph Rehmann-Sutter, 38–63. Basingstoke: Palgrave Macmillan, 2014.
———. "'The Meaning of Natality'—'Doğumluluğun Anlami.'" In *Metafizik ve Politika—Metaphysics and Politics: Martin Heidegger & Hannah Arendt*, edited by S. Yazicioğlu Öge, Ö. Sözer, and F. Tomkinson, 181–223. Istanbul: Boğaziçi University Press, 2002.
———. *Philosophie des Geborenseins*. Freiburg: Alber, 2008.
Schües, Christina, and Christoph Rehmann-Sutter. "Has a Child a Duty to Donate Hematopoietic Stem Cells to a Sibling?" In *Ethics and Oncology: Therapy, Care,*

Research, edited by Monika Bobbert, Beate Herrmann, and Wolfgang U. Eckart, 81–100. Freiburg: Alber, 2015.

Scully, Jackie Leach, Laurel Baldwin-Ragaven, and Petya Fitzpatrick, eds. *Feminist Bioethics: At the Center, on the Margins*. Baltimore: Johns Hopkins University Press, 2010.

Sherwin, Susan. "Whither Bioethics? How Feminism Can Help Reorient Bioethics." *International Journal of Feminist Approaches to Bioethics* 1, no. 1 (2008): 7–27.

Svenaeus, Fredrik. "What Is Phenomenology of Medicine? Embodiment, Illness and Being-in-the-World." In *Health, Illness and Disease: Philosophical Essays*, edited by Havi Carel and Rachel Cooper, 97–111. Durham, NC: Acumen, 2013.

Tymstra, Tjeerd. "The Imperative Character of Medical Technology and the Meaning of 'Anticipated Decision Regret.'" *International Journal of Technology Assessment in Health Care* 5 (1989): 207–213.

Waldenfels, Bernhard. *Bruchlinien der Erfahrung. Phänomenologie, Psychoanalyse, Phänomenotechnik*. Frankfurt: Suhrkamp, 2002.

Whitehouse, Beth. *The Match: "Savior Siblings" and One Family's Battle to Heal Their Daughter*. Boston: Beacon, 2011.

Wolf, Susan. "Happiness and Meaning: Two Aspects of a Good Life." *Social Philosophy and Policy* 14, no. 1 (1997): 207–225.

Worms, Frédéric. "La vie qui unit et qui sépare? La question philosophique du sens de la vie aujourd'hui." *Kairos* 23 (2004): 211–28.

———. "Qu'est-ce qui est vital?" *Bulletin de la Société française de Philosophie* 101, no. 2 (2007): 1–28.

———. *La vie qui unit et qui sépare*. Paris: Payot, 2013.

Zeiler, Kristin, and Lisa Folkmarson Käll. *Feminist Phenomenology of Medicine*. Albany: State University of New York Press, 2014.

13 THE SECOND-PERSON PERSPECTIVE IN NARRATIVE PHENOMENOLOGY

ANNEMIE HALSEMA AND JENNY SLATMAN

INTRODUCTION

> INTERVIEWER: Well, we were talking about saying good-bye to your breast...
> RESPONSE: Yes. No, perhaps, well, I have been standing before the mirror once or twice saying to my husband, "Look, soon I will be flat." Yes, but apart from that, no, not really, no. No, but I did imagine what it would be like to be flat. (Kathy)

What is it that happens in interviews that aim at exploring people's lived experiences? In a recently conducted empirical study, we interviewed women just after they were surgically treated for breast cancer.[1] In these interviews we focused on how they gave meaning to bodily changes and to their scars, thus employing a phenomenological approach. Phenomenology is mostly seen as an investigation of the first-person perspective, because it seeks to make explicit the process of world-disclosure.[2] Because of its sensitivity to the way patients experience their illnesses, phenomenology has been developed as a research method in its own right that is increasingly used in the field of health, illness, and quality-of-life research.[3] It has been embraced readily by health and nursing studies that seek to develop a more humanistic approach to care, and it fits well within the current move to provide more "patient-centered care."[4] Since a phenomenological approach starts from the position of the patients in their lifeworld instead of treating them as isolated individuals, it can help to reduce the risk of patient-centered care deteriorating into "consumer-driven care."[5]

We believe, however, that phenomenology should not just concentrate upon the first-person perspective but should also consider the second-person perspective. As can be seen in the above dialogue, in giving meaning to their stories in a narrative way, interviewees do not necessarily talk spontaneously, and narrating can involve searching for words and ambivalent sayings. The interviewer plays a maieutic role in this process. In this essay we explore this second-person perspective of the interviewer, which is significant for revealing experiences from a first-person perspective. We will do so while drawing on the in-depth interviews we conducted with nineteen women who had undergone breast amputation or lumpectomy. Rather than analyze the content of these interviews, we will instead provide a reflection on our own research practice.[6]

In this essay we explore how sense-making comes about in the practice of research interviewing. We scrutinize the process of wording experience, thereby concentrating upon the role of the interviewer. What we would like to show is that the interviewer—far from being a neutral researcher (as if that were at all possible)—is central because her presence and interest (and sometimes pretended ignorance) invite respondents to talk about and make sense of their experiences.[7] Hence, the interviewer adopts a second-person perspective while being engaged in a dialogue with another person. In reflecting upon the interviews, we came to realize that the interviewer facilitates the process of sense-making for those interviewed. Bringing to the fore this second-person perspective helps us to argue that phenomenological research in health and medicine should not be seen as an investigation into how patients think and feel about things as opposed to the perspective of the medical professional. We indeed believe that the medical perspective does not necessarily entail a third-person perspective—that is, a detached, neutral perspective. Sense-making is not the work of an individual, but takes place in joint narrative work. We therefore think that our analysis can also contribute to a further understanding of so-called narrative medicine. Narrative medicine argues for the importance and relevance of narrative training in reading and writing for health-care professionals, because there are healing effects for patients in giving voice to what they endure and in being able to frame and give meaning to their illnesses.[8] But until now, little to no attention has been paid to the role of the medical professional as interlocutor. Our analysis of research interviewing as narrative practice may thus also be useful for the narrative practice in patient-physician encounters.

INTERVIEWS AS NARRATIVE PRACTICES

In order to clarify the setup of the specific narrative practice in research interviewing, we first provide a brief description of our research design. The central question was how women who have undergone breast surgery—both breast amputation and breast saving—habituate to their altered bodies. Since our aim was to capture the process in its temporal development, we initially chose to enroll participants who would keep diaries over a longer period of time. During the recruitment period, however, it appeared that most women were rather reluctant to write about their experiences. Therefore we decided to change our data collection plan and replaced diary keeping with multiple in-depth interviews. In total we recruited nineteen women (breast amputation, N = 10; breast saving, N = 9). Each woman had either two or three interviews. In addition to the interviews, two women kept a diary for us (another woman also kept a diary but only for herself). Only one of these two women kept her diary conscientiously, almost daily, over a period of about eight months and decided to continue to do so (just for herself) after the concluding interview.

All interviews started with the open question: "From the information I have, I know that you were surgically treated for breast cancer *xx* weeks ago. Can you tell me in your own words what happened?" The interviews were subsequently structured by taking into account the following topics: options and choices for treatment; experience and perception of one's body after treatment; change and continuity in daily activities and habits; role of partner, family, friends, fellow sufferers, and medical professionals in the process. Also, all respondents were explicitly asked to describe their normal routines of care for their bodies (including dressing habits, use of cosmetics, sports and leisure habits, bathing and sauna habits) and to describe whether they endorsed a certain ideal of feminine embodiment.

We refer to our analysis as exploring "close to the skin" in the sense of employing a meticulous analysis and in this analysis touching upon the patient's body as well as her relations with others. There was one surprising outcome from this form of exploration and analysis that involved asking respondents about their experiences in such a way that intimate and sometimes emotional issues were neither circumvented nor avoided: the interviewer, not always knowingly, encouraged interviewees to reflect on their experiences, to the extent that sometimes the interviewees became aware of certain thoughts and ideas that until then they had not reflected upon. After the oral accounts had been transcribed verbatim and we were reading and analyzing them, we recognized rather quickly that putting one's experience into language, finding words for events, also has a formative character.

THEORETICAL FRAMEWORK

To explain how language is co-creative of experience, we have interpreted the interviews through the work of Paul Ricoeur. We believe that the distinction between mimesis[1], mimesis[2], and mimesis[3] that he makes in *Time and Narrative* helps us to understand how respondents in the first person made sense of their illness and recovery, and how this was not only received but also called up by the second person, the interviewer. After the interviews, the process of analysis began. We discuss that process here in terms of the notions of "text" and "discourse" that Ricoeur develops in *From Text to Action*.

It is particularly through narrative that we make events into "our own." The women who were diagnosed with breast cancer had gone through a series of events they did not choose. By telling about these events, they humanized them; they gave sense to them and put them into a meaningful order. In appropriating time, and giving specific meaning to what happens, narratives humanize time.[9] In the interviews the respondents put into their own words what happened to them from the moment they were diagnosed with breast cancer, including how they were diagnosed, how they experienced further treatment, and how those around them responded. These narratives can be considered as first-order sense-making of the events in which they were engaged.

The respondents created a coherent narrative out of the heterogeneous events that happened to them. Doing so is possible on the basis of what Ricoeur calls mimesis[1], which implies that human action is prefigured in a narrative sense. The field of human action is already structured in such a way that it can be captured in a narrative. Actions have beginnings and endings; we can answer questions about them, such as "what," "who," "why," "with whom," "how," and they are symbolically mediated—that is, within specific contexts actions receive their meaning and can be evaluated. Mimesis[1], or *prefiguration*, refers to this pre-understanding of human action with which one beholds the world. As Rita Charon explains in *Narrative Medicine*, "The beholder brings to that which is beheld categories of thought—in semantics, symbols, and temporality—that endow the perceived with the *potential* that meaning may emerge from it, and even more fundamentally, that understandable event or action can be configured from it."[10] It is posited on a shared realization of what might deliver meaning.

When this pre-understanding of action is put into words, Ricoeur speaks of mimesis[2], or *configuration*. This is the level of the interviews themselves, the oral interactions between interviewee and interviewer. Mimesis here refers to the act of narrative plotting (or emplotment), in which events are converted into something tellable or representable. Form is conferred onto experience, which makes it receivable. The diverse elements of a situation are brought into an imaginative order in just the same way as the plot of a story orders events. Emplotment configures heterogeneous elements such as events and agents and renders those elements meaningful as part of a larger whole in which each takes a place in the network that constitutes the narrative's response to the first open question asked in the interviews: "Can you tell me what happened? The whole trajectory?"

In the interviews, apart from the act of configuration, telling one's story, mimesis³, is also a concern. Mimesis³, or *refiguration*, refers to the consequences for the reader of receiving what another composes. While reading and analyzing the transcribed interviews, we researchers "refigurate" the data and thus perform mimesis³. The traversal of mimesis receives its fulfillment in the reader. It marks the intersection of the world of the text and the world of the reader.[11]

Apart from the three forms of mimesis, which are both sequential and simultaneous, Ricoeur's distinction between "discourse" and "text" is also relevant for the analysis of what happens in the interviews. While discourse is closer to oral exchange and relates to the situation in which it is spoken, text is closer to written accounts. In discourse "reference is determined by the ability to point to a reality common to the interlocutors."[12] Discourse takes place here and now, which facilitates mutual understanding because both interlocutors are engaged in a common reality. Text, however, does not have this relation with the common situation in which both interlocutors are present. In what follows, we also examine the difference between listening to the interviews and reading them—in other words, between the interviews as discourse and as text.

ANALYZING "CLOSE TO THE SKIN"

We consider the interviews as narrative practices in which the women have told the interviewer about what happened to them and what they experienced. The interviewer in this process functions as a second person who, as addressee, listens to the interviewee and receives her oral account, but who also activates the process of recounting the experiences. In this section, on the basis of the interviews, we discuss the role of the second person, the interviewer, by distinguishing three different ways in which the dialogue between interviewer and interviewee brought about lived experience:[13] (1) While posing a rather unusual question—that is, the question of whether respondents had explicitly performed some kind of farewell ritual before surgery—some women retrospectively configured an account of a certain action or performance they had not yet recognized as a farewell ritual. (2) In the course of the interviews, interviewees sometimes said they had not yet thought about certain issues but all the same started talking about them and, while talking, constituted coherent accounts. (3) One respondent who kept a diary constituted a secondary reflection on what she had said during the interviews. What follows in this section are examples of these three aspects. In the next section, they will be analyzed with the help of the Ricoeurian concepts developed above.

Invitation to Respond to a Somewhat Unusual Question

One question addressed in all the interviews was the question of parting from one's "old" body before the surgery. Most frequently the respondents did not address the issue spontaneously. The majority of the respondents said they had not performed such a ritual, they had not thought about performing one, nor had they felt any need to do so. Moreover, in hindsight, they did not regret not having done so. Only one respondent (Simone) spontaneously recounted the benefits she had received from an explicit farewell ritual she had performed. However, in her case the ritual had not been her own idea; she had not thought about it herself. It was her niece (who is a therapist) who had suggested it to her. Because the very idea of this ritual is not at the foreground in breast cancer consultation and information, the issue was introduced by the interviewer, who mentioned that it might involve a bit of an odd and unusual question:

> INTERVIEWER: And I have another question that I usually ask, uh, a bit odd perhaps, but did you say farewell to your breast?

For Simone the ritual and especially talking about the signification of her breast was very important. It gave her a grip on the situation, and she wanted everyone to know about it.

> SIMONE: And I do find it so important that everyone knows about it, it has meant so much for me. Not with touch or so, no, just talking about it, eh. And to name it and what does your breast mean for you, yes a bit motherhood, whether you have breastfed or not, a bit femininity, a bit intimacy and those things, eh, just deepened and so. And at a certain moment after three hours of intensive talking, I kind of started to think, "well, this is what they call a breast, it has been with me for 62 years, and now it is ill, and it has to go." That. So uh it was also from that moment on that I felt it was not something just happening to me, but also uh a large part my own decision eh. Because I had talked to her [her niece] so intensively that I was also that strong then that I could have decided, no, perhaps I will die, but I will not do it, that breast stays on me.

In addition to Simone, there was Ann, who had explicitly parted from her old breast, although in a less distinct way than Simone. When the interviewer asked her about it, she became very emotional, as if talking about her silently performed ritual reinforced the experience of parting.

ANN: [emotional] Two days before I was operated upon, I went to the mirror more often and felt my breast more carefully, how it felt and how that was. And touched it and looked at it, and my husband also. And now that is more emotional than it was at that moment.

Some women responded to the question by saying they had not consciously performed a farewell ritual, but then went on to say that they did something that could be interpreted as a kind of farewell:

ELLEN: No, I didn't? Not consciously.

I: No?

ELLEN: Before the operation I looked once oh yes you didn't make it, so. But whether that is saying good-bye, I don't know. But further, no not really consciously, no.

And Judith, who eventually had a breast-saving surgery said:

JUDITH: Yes, beforehand, when I took a bath, then I kind of thought—while pressing it [the breast] a bit—"perhaps this will be gone soon." Yes, that is what I did until I knew for sure that I could have a breast-saving treatment. Then I tried to imagine what that would look like. But I did this only when I took a bath, then you see both breasts and, yes, then I did think about it for a moment.

Also Kathy reconstructed for herself the very idea of "saying farewell" while talking about it.

KATHY: Well I think that farewell, that was immediately when I discovered the lump. For me the switch was immediately flipped. Then eh, I also said to John immediately, eh, I know that it is cancer, because I felt it then, swollen, uh with a little hard pit in it, and then I stood up and looked in the bathroom and I also saw a little indent, exactly as it is described in the literature, so that you know, and then I knew. I said [to] John, "well my decision is whatever happens, those breasts will go." So, at that moment it happened. Yes.

In asking an unusual question, the interviewer invited the women to take another look at their experiences, to consider them in terms of saying farewell to their breasts.

Invitation to Configure an Account while Talking

Sometimes the interviewees responded to questions while saying they had not really thought about the issue at hand but then, all the same, continued to talk about it.

> INTERVIEWER: And at which moments, say, are you most conscious of your breast operation. That you are being treated for breast cancer?
> DIANE: Phew. That I do not know, yes when you are washing yourself and changing clothes, then you see your scar and then I think oh yes. But very often I take it for granted completely. And I never did this before, but I started to put body lotion or cream or whatever on because the skin in the beginning, because of radiation, has become much drier. . . . So I do that, and then I see it every day. But it is not that I have a lousy feeling about it every day but okay it is there. I can look at it in the same way I look at the scar on my arm [which I have already had for several years]. But there are also days that you get up in the morning and haven't seen anything and then suddenly feel brrr, it is not feeling well today. And then you are down, or uh, and then, you cannot give a clear reason for anything.

Another example of composing an account of something that the interviewees said they had not really thought about was provided by Ruth. To the question of whether she would plan to go swimming with or without her prosthesis, she first responded by saying that she did not know yet. When the interviewer subsequently remarked, "So you have not yet reflected on this?," Ruth said:

> RUTH: I have not thought about it, yes I did think about it, because they [nurses] explained that there are special swimsuits, which cover it [the asymmetry], but, I don't know. Maybe I won't go swimming; that is also a possibility, when it is very crowded or something with kids. . . . It is easier in the sea, then we go off the boat right into the sea. And then you don't have any trouble, even without a prosthesis and the people living there they know about it.

In both cases, the respondents were facilitated by the interviewer to reflect upon something they had not thought about before.

Invitation to an Explicit Secondary Reflection

Donna, the only respondent who conscientiously kept a diary, at a certain point used her diary to explicitly reflect on a previous interview with the interviewer.

> DONNA: I told Jenny Slatman that I don't mind touching my breast, but to be honest, I do find it rather unpleasant to touch the scar, since it is swollen. (diary extract)

Here an interview gave rise to second-order reflections. In her diary Donna mentioned her answer to a question in the interview and then reflected upon her own answer.

MAKING SENSE: PUTTING EXPERIENCE INTO WORDS

The three examples from the interviews above show in what sense the interaction between interviewer and interviewee can lead to the recounting of experiences that have not been put into words before, as well as the effects that the interview can have for the interviewee. In this process the role of the interviewer was not only the passive one of being an addressee of the story, but she was also active in initiating the reflection. In this section we further analyze the role of the interviewer and the meaning of interviewing or, more generally, the meaning of putting experiences and actions into words.

First, we consider the *Invitation to respond to a somewhat unusual question*. It is Simone in particular who expressed the importance of recounting what had happened to her. The farewell ritual and talking about her breast allowed her to make the events in which she passively participated into her own. At first the diagnosis overwhelmed her and made her feel like a victim, but after the ritual the amputation felt like her own decision.

> SIMONE: But my feeling then is, eh, I was not a victim anymore and after the conversation with the oncologist I only felt a victim. Do you understand? And that switch, that is what I also grant other people eh, that they have that opportunity to pause for a while before the breast is removed.

For Simone, talking about the events that happened to her, what Ricoeur calls mimesis^2, or configuration, implies making them her own and becoming active instead of passive. Language functions as an intermediary between experience and self. It enables the women to take a distance from their experiences, as the interview with Simone shows.

But most women who were interviewed did not engage in a farewell ritual and did not talk extensively about the breast they were about to lose. For some of them, the interview itself was the moment of putting into words what happened, which can in itself be an emotional experience. Ann said, "And now that is more emotional than it was at that moment." The distance that recounting the event of parting from her breast implies the moment of reflection and evokes emotions she did not experience while parting from her breast. The interviewer here takes the role of facilitating this moment of secondary parting.

In the case of Kathy, the realization that she has parted from her breast is evoked by the question of the interviewer. It is as if she says: if I parted, it must have been at that moment. But she also claims that she took a distance from her breast at the moment she knew it was ill. The parting, in fact, has already taken place and was initiated by the diagnosis of cancer.

The interviews with Ruth and Kathy show that the realization of having parted from the breast—that is, the awareness of their experiences—can also come about through the questions of the interviewer. Here the interview is constitutive for the interviewee's realization of what she experienced and how she acted. By putting their experiences and acts into words, the interviewees configure their experience. The interviewer here has an active role in asking the question that leads to this reflection.

Also the second aspect, the *Invitation to configure an account while talking*, alludes to mimesis[2], or configuration. The interviewer's question in this case leads to a new awareness of what the interviewee experiences or thinks. Both Diane and Ruth had not explicitly thought about the issue at hand, but while talking they started to reflect upon it. They think the issue through while talking—without coming to a firm conclusion. The interviewer's question plays an important role in evoking an awareness of their body, as, for instance, Diane's account of her washing ritual demonstrates. In the case of Ruth, the interviewer's question leads to contradictory statements, which express that she has not yet made up her mind about swimming. The interview in this case makes her formulate her doubts, the pros and cons of swimming in public.

The interviews, as narrative accounts of the women's experiences, can also allow for further reflections upon the narrated experiences. In this case the interviewee herself is the reader of her own text. Ricoeur speaks of mimesis[3] in this case, the completion of the text by the reader. It is the reader who fills in the holes, lacunae, and zones of indetermination in the text, and who in the end "carries the burden of emplotment."[14] Next to Donna, who reflects upon her own experiences in her diary, we, the researchers, also perform mimesis[3] while interpreting the interviews.

The addressee of the interviews, the second person, after having held the interviews also analyzed them and reported on them. These reflections are second-order reflections upon the first-order reflections of the interviewees. The interviews were coded, the codes were categorized, and so forth. These second-order reflections do not in themselves contribute to the experiences of the interviewees, but are directed to a scientific and medical audience.

ORIENTING ONESELF IN NEW SITUATIONS

Returning to Ricoeur's threefold mimesis, we can conclude that in the above analysis, we have not referred to mimesis[1]. The reason is that it pertains to the capacity to think about actions and experiences in terms of "what," "why," "who," and "how," and to the capacity to put actions into words.[15] This capacity is presumed rather than articulated in the interviews.

With respect to mimesis², we need to make a distinction between speaking about actions and experiences of which the interviewees were already aware and coming to awareness through speaking about them. We can see that configuration has a double function, especially in the second aspect described above, the *Invitation to configure an account while talking*, but also in the examples of Kathy and Ruth identified in the first aspect, the *Invitation to respond to a somewhat unusual question*. This double function at once implies putting into words what the interviewee had already experienced and was aware of that is now *shared* with others, and also functions as a *recognition* for the interviewee of what had happened, or what she had done or thought. In that sense the interview helps those interviewed to better understand and to orient themselves in the new situation. The questions in this respect function as "triggers" and lead not only to explicating what was not before explicit but also to a renewed awareness of their actions and experiences. Ricoeur's "ontological presupposition of language" sheds light upon this process. Here, he aims at language as a means of orienting ourselves in the world. Language is not a world in itself, nor does it constitute a world. Rather, "Because we are in the world and are affected by situations, we try to orient ourselves in them by means of understanding; we also have something to say, an experience to bring to language and to share."[16] In the interviews both aspects of language were brought to light: sharing with others and orienting oneself in situations.

Mimesis³ in our project pertains to the second-order reflection that the interviewee undertakes in further reflecting upon her experiences on the basis of the first-order reflection in the interview. But also the analysis of the interviews by the researcher can be seen as mimesis³. In this phase of analysis, the interviews are no longer first-person oral accounts but become written accounts that are coded and cut into pieces. Ricoeur distinguishes between "discourse"—as that which "intends things, applies itself to reality, expresses the world"—and "text."[17] Whereas in discourse the interlocutors share a unique spatiotemporal network (the "here" and "now" of the situation of discourse), texts do not have a situation that is common to both writer and reader. Direct references to the situation in which a conversation takes place are not present in texts. On the one hand this leads to distancing from concrete individual intentions and meaning, but on the other hand it implies the option of interpreting texts as proposed worlds that one could inhabit and in which the reader could project her own possibilities. Seen in this light, the interviews are unique texts that propose a world (the text unfolds, reveals, discovers a world[18]) that the reader—the researcher, but also the interviewee when she reads the text of the interview—can inhabit.

The role of the interviewer as a second person in this process is not only to be the receiver and facilitator for the account of the experiences of the interviewee, but with her questions she also evokes experiences and reflections upon these experiences. In this way, the interviewer supports the process of both taking a distance from events by means of the intermediating function of language, as well as relating to them.

CONCLUSION AND DISCUSSION

In this essay we have shown that in the narrative practice of interviewing within empirical-phenomenological research, the second-person perspective contributes to the configuration of a person's "lived experience." The respondents in the interviews gave voice to their experiences. For that reason, the interviews can be seen as narrative practices that not only expressed the respondents' experiences but also were (partly) constitutive of their experiences. The interviewer, as a second person in this process, played an important role. Our explicit focus on the constitutive role of the second-person perspective has repercussions for how to consider and use phenomenology within the field of health and medicine. Phenomenology has been welcomed in this field because of its presumed focus on the individual patient's voice. In the philosophical literature on the phenomenology of the body in health and medicine, it is often emphasized that the body, as it is lived (*le corps vécu*)—that is, the body from the patient's first-person perspective—should be distinguished from (and opposed to) the body as an object, a thing, as it is considered from the medical professional's perspective, which implies a third person's perspective on the body.[19]

We believe that it is not productive to stick to this dichotomy in medical practices. It seems to set and frame the scene for combat between two parties who presumably are not able to share their views. If patients' lived experiences are considered as personal and idiosyncratic to the extent that they can be shared only with fellow sufferers who have gone through similar experiences, a phenomenological approach can be easily misused to build a "power block" against the medical establishment that is based upon the body-as-object paradigm, the third person's perspective.[20] What we argue for, in contrast, is that the voice of the patient—his or her first-person perspective—and the interaction between medical professionals and patients should be considered as a narrative practice. In medical settings the medical professional not only represents a third person's perspective on patients but is also involved in narrative practices with patients. Even if a physician talks about a patient from an external point of view, from a third person's perspective—for instance, in talking about lab results—she or he is at the same time in conversation with the patient, addressing the latter as an interlocutor. It is especially in this last role that a medical professional can assist in letting the patient voice her or his lived experience.

The idea that patients should be able to tell and frame their stories has been increasingly adopted in medicine. It is especially narrative medicine that has brought attention to this issue. Narrative medicine argues for the importance and relevance of narrative training in reading and writing for healthcare professionals because of the healing effects for patients of giving voice to what they endure and of being able to frame and give meaning to their illnesses. However, also in narrative medicine we come across the distinction between the medical professional as "scientist" and the medical professional who has narrative capabilities.[21] In other words, in this context the third person's perspective of the medical professional is firmly opposed to his or her function as interlocutor. Instead, we suggest that every interaction between medical professional and patient is inherently narrative in the sense that patients as well as medical professionals aim at making sense of the situation and at mutual understanding. We do not mean to imply that further developing the narrative capacities of medical professionals—which is Charon's main aim—is not important, but we do suggest that opposing too strongly the third- and second-person perspectives in the interaction between medical professional and patient is not very productive. Instead of understanding narrative medicine as a distinct field of medical practice, we would rather understand all oral dialogues as narratives. In these dialogues, not only is the first-person perspective articulated, but the interlocutor, the second person, plays a vital role as well in evoking, co-constituting, and receiving the first-person accounts of their experiences.

ANNEMIE HALSEMA is Assistant Professor in the Department of Philosophy at Vrije Universiteit Amsterdam, Netherlands. She is the author of *Luce Irigaray and Horizontal Transcendence* (Amsterdam: SWP, 2010) and editor (with Fernanda Henriques) of *Feminist Explorations of Paul Ricoeur's Philosophy* (Lanham, MD: Lexington, 2016).

JENNY SLATMAN is Professor of Medical Humanities in the School of Humanities at Tilburg University, Netherlands. She is the author of *Our Strange Body: Philosophical Reflections on Identity and Medical Interventions* (Amsterdam University Press, 2014).

NOTES

1. This project, "Bodily Integrity in Blemished Bodies" (2011–2016), was funded by the Netherlands Organization for Scientific Research (NWO-VIDI-276-20-016).
2. Dan Zahavi, *Subjectivity and Selfhood: Investigating the First-Person Perspective* (Cambridge: MIT Press, 2005).
3. See Max van Manen, *Researching Lived Experience: Human Science for an Action-Sensitive Pedagogy* (Albany: State University of New York Press, 1990); and Linda Finlay, *Phenomenology for Therapists: Researching the Lived World* (Chichester, West Sussex: John Wiley and Sons, 2011).
4. Havi Carel, "Nursing and Medicine," in *The Routledge Companion to Phenomenology*, ed. Sebastian Luft and Soren Overgaard, 623–32 (London: Routledge, 2012).
5. Karin Dahlberg, Les Todres, and Kathleen Galvin, "Lifeworld-Led Healthcare Is More Than Patient-Led Care: An Existential View of Well-being," *Medicine, Health Care, and Philosophy* 12, no. 3 (2009): 265–71.
6. See, for the results of this study, Jenny Slatman, Annemie Halsema, and Agnes Meershoek, "Responding to Scars after Breast Surgery," *Qualitative Health Research* (2015). DOI: 10,1177/1049732315591146.
7. All interviews for this study were conducted by Jenny Slatman, the second author of this paper. We chose to write about "the interviewer," thus referring to one of us in the third person, because It is not our aim to explore specifically her personal role in the interviews, but rather her role as interviewer.
8. See especially Rita Charon, *Narrative Medicine: Honoring the Stories of Illness* (Oxford: Oxford University Press, 2006).
9. Paul Ricoeur, *Time and Narrative*, trans. Kathleen Blamey and David Pellauer, vol. 1, (Chicago: University of Chicago Press, 1984), 3.
10. Charon, *Narrative Medicine*, 138.
11. Ricoeur, *Time and Narrative*, vol. 1, 71.
12. Ricoeur, *From Text to Action. Essays in Hermeneutics II*, trans. Kathleen Blamey and John B. Thompson (London: Continuum, 1991), 82.
13. Ethical clearance for this empirical study was obtained from the ethical review board of Maastricht University Medical Center. All included respondents gave written consent to participate in this study. To protect the anonymity of our respondents, we have used fictional names. The fragments from the interviews in this section are translations of the oral interviews in Dutch, transcribed verbatim, and translated into English by the authors. To remain close to the oral accounts, we did not mend flaws and peculiarities in syntax.
14. Ricoeur, *Time and Narrative*, vol. 1, 77.
15. Ibid., 55–57.
16. Ibid., 78.
17. Ricoeur, *From Text to Action*, 81.
18. Ibid., 84.
19. Compare Drew Leder, "A Tale of Two Bodies: The Cartesian Corpse and the Lived Body," in *The Body in Medical Thought and Practice*, ed. Drew Leder (Dordrecht: Kluwer Academic Publishers, 1992); S. Kay Toombs, "Illness and the Paradigm of the Lived Body," *Theoretical Medicine* 9, no. 2 (1988): 201–226; and S. Kay Toombs, "The Temporality of Illness: Four Levels of Experience," *Theoretical Medicine and Bioethics* 11, no. 3 (1990): 227–41.

20. See also Jenny Slatman, "Multiple Dimensions of Embodiment in Medical Practices," *Medicine, Health Care, and Philosophy* 17, no. 4 (2014): 549–57.

21. See, for instance, Charon, *Narrative Medicine*, 3.

BIBLIOGRAPHY

Carel, Havi. "Nursing and Medicine." In *The Routledge Companion to Phenomenology*, edited by Sebastian Luft and Soren Overgaard, 623–32. London: Routledge, 2012.

Charon, Rita. *Narrative Medicine. Honoring the Stories of Illness*. Oxford: Oxford University Press, 2006.

Dahlberg, Karin, Les Todres, and Kathleen Galvin. "Lifeworld-Led Healthcare Is More Than Patient-Led Care: An Existential View of Well-being." *Medicine, Health Care, and Philosophy* 12, no. 3 (2009): 265–71.

Finlay, Linda. *Phenomenology for Therapists: Researching the Lived World*. Chichester, West Sussex: John Wiley and Sons, 2011.

Leder, Drew. "A Tale of Two Bodies. The Cartesian Corpse and the Lived Body." In *The Body in Medical Thought and Practice*, edited by Drew Leder, 17–35. Dordrecht: Kluwer Academic Publishers, 1992.

Manen, Max van. *Researching Lived Experience: Human Science for an Action-Sensitive Pedagogy*. Albany: State University of New York Press, 1990.

Ricoeur, Paul. *From Text to Action. Essays in Hermeneutics II*. Translated by Kathleen Blamey and John B. Thompson. London: Continuum, 1991.

———. *Time and Narrative*. Vol. 1. Translated by Kathleen Blamey and David Pellauer. Chicago: University of Chicago Press, 1984.

Slatman, Jenny. "Multiple Dimensions of Embodiment in Medical Practices." *Medicine, Health Care, and Philosophy* 17, no. 4 (2014): 549–57.

Slatman, Jenny, Annemie Halsema, and Agnes Meershoek. "Responding to Scars after Breast Surgery." *Qualitative Health Research*. Published online before print June 15, 2015. DOI: 10.1177/1049732315591146.

Smith, Jonathan A., Paul Flowers, and Michael Larkin. *Interpretative Phenomenological Analysis: Theory, Method, and Research*. Los Angeles: Sage, 2009.

Toombs, S. Kay. "Illness and the Paradigm of Lived Body." *Theoretical Medicine* 9, no. 2 (1988): 201–226.

———. "The Temporality of Illness: Four Levels of Experience." *Theoretical Medicine and Bioethics* 11, no. 3 (1990): 227–41.

Zahavi, Dan. *Subjectivity and Selfhood: Investigating the First-Person Perspective*. Cambridge: MIT Press, 2005.

14 HANNAH ARENDT AND PREGNANCY IN THE PUBLIC SPHERE

KATY FULFER

INTRODUCTION

Although reproduction was once thought to be a paradigmatic private activity, it seems common now to accept that it is part of the public realm. Pregnancy often takes place in public institutions of hospitals or other medical facilities. Public policy may regulate reproduction and infertility services in places where health care is provided by the state, or in places that seek through legislation to restrict or protect women's access to reproductive and sexual health services. Further, as Amy Mullin has emphasized, pregnant people not only make physical adjustments to their changing bodies, but they also must make accommodations within the public sphere.[1] Climbing the stairs in the public library may no longer be feasible for a pregnant person, and parental leave from work might need to be arranged. A person's context plays an important role in the public accommodation of reproduction as well: secure jobs with paid leave better support women's financial stability than those without it.

Because society seems to readily accept that pregnancy, at least partially, is situated within the public sphere, Hannah Arendt's insistence that reproduction is not a public activity may seem surprising. It cannot be a political activity, in Arendt's view, because political activities are public—that is, they are the topics of speech and action. Arendt's main concern is political agency within the public sphere. Reproduction is private because it is aimed at the maintenance of life, and as such it is unable to disclose the "who" of a person. Unsurprisingly, many feminists have been skeptical of using Arendt to discuss embodied subjectivity and reproductive justice, because she relegates reproduction to the private realm.[2] For the purposes of this essay, a firm definition of "reproductive justice" and what it involves is not required. For my purposes it is sufficient to say that reproductive justice means that women have decision-making authority over their reproductive capacities, and that reproductive justice requires the end of women's oppression that is facilitated through others' control of their reproductive activities.[3]

Contrary to some feminist skepticism, I think Arendt has important contributions to make to feminist thinking about reproduction. This essay is a first step in exploring those contributions. I contend that reproduction can indeed appear within the public realm as Arendt understands it. Further, I show why Arendt's distinctions between private and public activities do not necessarily threaten conditions for women's political agency. My motivation in turning to Arendt is to think through moral and political problems with contract pregnancy, which is the practice of hiring a woman to gestate an embryo. Whether a gestational laborer is paid or provides labor altruistically, some feminists worry about reinforcing women's relegation to the private sphere.[4] Further, contract pregnancy is prone to encouraging the idea that women be viewed not as agents but as instrumentally valuable insofar as they make healthy babies for well-off couples.[5] In the age of global reproductive travel, concerns extend to the exploitation of poor women in the global south who sell gestational labor as a means of managing acute poverty.[6] One question that arises from the transnational context in particular is that of women's agency: can women exercise agency in selling gestational labor, or is this act merely a rational choice, the least bad out of a set of inadequate options? Though I will not answer that question in this essay, I aim to show that Arendt's philosophy can make a meaningful intervention into this conversation. I will use contract pregnancy as a reference point in rethinking an Arendtian perspective on reproduction as a site of political action.

This essay is structured as follows. First, I look at how reproduction becomes public in what Arendt calls "the social," and I draw connections with Foucault's concept of biopolitics. Using the social-biopolitical as a lens reveals the oppressive aspects of contract pregnancy that obstruct women's agency. Second, I look at how contract pregnancy is made public through the exercise of agency. How an agent takes up a particular act is what determines whether that act is private or public.

CONTRACT PREGNANCY IN THE SOCIAL-BIOPOLITICAL

The Social

I challenge the presumption that reproduction is philosophically uninteresting from an Arendtian perspective because it is a private activity. Contract pregnancy provides an insightful example of the problem Arendt identifies as "the social," in which political concerns become usurped by the necessities of life. Contract pregnancy exemplifies the social because it involves the commodification of a type of labor that historically has not been understood as wage-earning work. In examining contract pregnancy as a form of social organization that Michel Foucault termed "the biopolitical," in which physical life becomes the object of governance, I argue that in the social-biopolitical the distinctions between private and activities—that is, the boundaries between *labor* and *work*—collapse. In the second part of the essay, I show how this collapse is problematic from Arendt's perspective. I also show how the collapse between *labor* and *work* explains how contract pregnancy may be understood as a public activity (although in the social-biopolitical, the public character of pregnancy is limited and is not a fully a political activity).

Speaking generally, the distinction between what is public and private is one way of understanding differences between the activities constitutive of the human condition. Action is public, as it brings people together in a shared space. Work supports and enables the public by providing durability and stability for the human world, through the use-objects that people use and share, and through art that relates meaningfulness to others. In contrast, labor is about life processes, what sustains physical life without producing anything durable. Life processes can take place without the recognition of others, away from public life. This is what makes activities of labor private.[7] I suggest that contract pregnancy may become public within the social-biopolitical. The social, which came into appearance in modernity, is the state of society in which the boundaries between the public and the private collapse. To put it another way, in the social, activities that are properly political become replaced by activities that are properly private. Freedom and conditions for agency diminish. As Arendt characterizes the social:

> Perhaps the clearest indication that society constitutes the public organization of the life process itself may be found in the fact that in a relatively short time the new social realm transformed all modern communities into societies of laborers and jobholders; in other words, they became at once centered around the one activity necessary to sustain life.[8]

Having the means to survive is important, but when the necessities of life become the entire focus of politics, then speech and action have no space to appear.

The Biopolitical

I suggest we read the problem of the social in conjunction with an analysis of the biopolitical. Much of Arendt's diagnosis of the social foreshadows Foucault's articulation of biopolitics.[9] As stated, physical life becomes the object of governance. On the surface it seems as if health is a positive political concern, especially in liberal societies that aim to promote the ability of individuals to pursue their own conceptions of the good life, which likely involves some measure of physical and mental well-being. In contrast to liberalism, which focuses on the individual, the unit of concern in biopolitics is populations, which are abstract, homogenizing generalizations.[10] With population control, it is not only the ability to live that is at stake but also that populations are made to live in a particular way. Biopolitics offers governing bodies the ability to control bodies and populations under the guise of promoting the health of individuals, which opens up the possibility that the interests of some populations might count more than those of others.

Contract pregnancy exhibits features of the biopolitical. For example, contract pregnancy may be used as a means of population control. The contract pregnancy industry in India, through recruitment practices and fertility clinic regulations, disciplines women who sell gestational labor to be the ideal workers.[11] According to these disciplinary forces, to be a good worker is to be a virtuous mother who is "cheap, docile, selfless, and nurturing."[12] The discipline of gestational laborers to be good mother-workers occurs through the rhetoric used by clinic recruiters or staff, including the language of the contract, and through the setting of the hostels where these women live.[13] First, consider the language of the contract, which is often translated only in part for gestational laborers, as contracts are in English. The contract specifies the rules the woman must adhere to while pregnant and emphasizes that she has no significant connection to the embryo. It also frames the embryo's health as being of the highest importance. The woman as an individual is not important—her health is not prioritized, and her individuality is not required at all to perform gestational labor.[14] Similarly, the rhetoric used by clinic staff and recruiters shapes the women into virtuous mother-workers while simultaneously treating each woman's labor as interchangeable or exchangeable. The fetus is "borrowing" the woman's womb, and she is to treat it as a guest. The commercial aspect is further deemphasized by one hostel matron who instructs the women in her care to view their contractual arrangements as gifts from God rather than work. Being greedy or manipulative is indicative of a poor mother and hence indicative of being a poor gestational laborer.[15]

Second, the space of the hostel, the shared living space of gestational laborers, functions to instill in them care of the fetus and docility. Clinics may require women to live in hostels in part because these women may be faced with social stigma for selling gestational labor, but the main justification is to keep a close eye on the women's pregnancies. The women's medication and naps are structured. In some cases, lunch portions are large to ensure the fetus is receiving adequate nutrition. Women may also have computer classes and English classes to help them better communicate with commissioning parties. Women's activities tend to be more structured during the first trimester. After women's pregnancies seem stable, they are given more freedom. This freedom is connected with the knowledge the gestational laborer now has about what will or will not harm the fetus.[16]

Through the contracts and other rhetoric, and through their structured living spaces, gestational laborers constitute a population that is controlled and disciplined. In executing population control, the biopolitical erases the meaningfulness of individuals or of individual acts.[17] Human bodies are regulated strictly as if they were machines, with the aim of protecting the species. In Indian contract pregnancy, the production of healthy babies can be understood to be the supreme good, and the health or well-being of gestational laborers matters only insofar as it facilitates that end. These population-control measures, rather than the well-being of individual citizens, become the primary political concern of the state. For example, the gestational contribution that these women make to the future children is not viewed as an aspect of motherhood nor as being a part of the resulting child. Rather, the image put forward by the clinic is one of temporary care and nurturing.[18] Further, the industry seeks to make all aspects of a gestational laborer's life subordinate to the well-being of the fetus.[19] For example, a woman's commitment to the health of the embryo is put above her relationships with her family. Women may receive daytime visitors in some instances, but not overnight visitors. Visits with family are treated as rewards for good behavior rather than being important to the woman's well-being.[20]

In the above example, biopolitics functions in the same way as the social does for Arendt. People are no longer viewed as unique individuals with the capacity to flourish. Rather, they must be maintained in their positions to extract the highest level of efficiency. Political agents transformed into mere workers exist to perpetuate the life of the factory/corporation/group for whom they work. New actions and individuality are not interpretable as meaningful within the social-biopolitical. Hence, Arendt would be critical of contract pregnancy for the way its biopolitical dimension exhibits population control that is typical to the problem of the social.

Becoming Public in the Social-Biopolitical

One way that we can understand contract pregnancy as a public activity is, in Arendt's terms, a version of the social-biopolitical problem. This means of becoming public occurs in a way that threatens conditions for women's agency. Contract pregnancy is a practice that merges a process of consumption with a process of fabrication. It does not fit neatly into the descriptions of labor or of work. On the one hand, it seems to be an activity of labor. As a form of reproduction, contract pregnancy contributes to the cyclical nature of maintaining the human species. Because, in Arendt's view, the activities of family life are private and aimed at supporting physical life, it seems as if pregnancy is not the kind of activity that contributes to the durability of public space.

Even though contract pregnancy does not take on all characteristics of work, it manifests some of them through its commodification within the social-biopolitical. Durable objects, the products of work, involve reification.[21] There is no reification in contract pregnancy per se, but there is instrumentality and purpose in the intention to nurture a fetus for someone else. A worker uses tools and other means to purposefully produce the fabricated object that will endure. Similarly, contract pregnancy renders a woman's body a tool. This imports a degree of objectification into how she may understand her own body.[22] Along with other tools or technologies, such as exercise, controlled diet, and prenatal care, a woman's body becomes one part of the larger mechanism of the production of children.

The social appears when consumption takes the place of durability and co-opts the public realm through the exchange economy. The biopolitical appears, at least in part, when populations of people become managed through norms targeting their physical health, their bodies, their economic class, and their survival. Contract pregnancy occurs in both of these spaces because of its synthesis of consumptive and purposive elements. In short, as part of the social-biopolitical, contract pregnancy becomes public, but it is an impoverished publicity. The social replaces the political, as the practice of contract pregnancy is indicative of how consumption becomes more important than political agency. Contract pregnancy reallocates reproductive labor's position in the private sphere and makes it an economic-political concern, because it becomes an activity that institutions (e.g., industry, government) are interested in managing.

From within the social-biopolitical, the cyclical production of babies *as products* becomes more important than the individual child who is born. Contract pregnancy makes babies appear as commodities produced for consumers, and pregnancy is valuable only insofar as it supports the consumptive systematicity of the life of the population. A pronatalist ideology cycles in the background of population politics here—babies must continually be (re)produced for people who under other circumstances might not choose or be capable of giving birth. Even in a less polemical description of contract pregnancy, conceived of as the sale of gestational services, the practice feeds into a system of consumption. Before the advent of reproductive technologies, pregnancy was an unpredictable process in which parents waited for nature to reveal what would be—a healthy child, a sick child, a boy, a girl, a miscarriage, a stillborn fetus—and in which people could not manipulate features of the child to the degree now allowed with some reproductive technologies.

The use of contract pregnancy, however, implies that people are interested in forcing certain outcomes. At the very least, one member of a commissioning party is primarily interested in having a genetically related child.[23] Attempting to control an inherently unpredictable process (fertility/infertility in this case) is a common feature of the social-biopolitical. Spontaneity is curtailed (though, as I will discuss later, it cannot be completely inhibited). This curtailment is troublesome because the spontaneous character of human agency is part of what separates agency from conformity, and it is more worrisome when it supports systems of population control. People use medical interventions all the time to attempt to "control" natural processes, such as using oral contraceptives to prevent pregnancy. But there is a difference between a woman who takes an oral contraceptive because she has decided that she prefers not to bear children at this point and a woman who does so because it is a condition of receiving social assistance. Contract pregnancy involves the problematic curtailment in the latter sense: it seeks to use a medical intervention to create a certain outcome—a child—by using the body or services of a woman who is typically of a lower economic class than the intended parents. The context surrounding contract pregnancy is one in which a gestational laborer's opportunities to exercise political agency are subordinated to the task of bearing the child.

In other words, contract pregnancy contributes to a framework in which consumption replaces agency as the highest political activity (that is, labor seeks to usurp conditions for agency). Recall that in the social-biopolitical, contract pregnancy becomes public by threatening conditions for agency rather than enhancing them. If reproduction as an activity of labor replaces political concerns, it threatens conditions for agency. Consumptive activities alone do not bestow subjectivity on human beings—human agency is much more complicated than consumption would allow. When subjectivity becomes constitutive of mere consumption, then the capitalist economy and the biopolitical threaten the ability of people to act and to flourish politically. For Arendt, consumptive activities are those that humans share with the nonhuman animal world in that such activities are connected to the continuation of the species, not the individual.[24] Creatures must consume to live, and species must consume to be able to reproduce new members of the species. Contract pregnancy challenges the rigid distinction between bodily processes as mere consumption and the function such bodily processes might play in a market economy. At the same time, many feminists worry that contract pregnancy threatens the self and the ability of women to resist oppression.

To review my argument thus far, under the social-biopolitical contract, pregnancy becomes public. However, the publicity of contract pregnancy is restricted to Arendt's conception of the social, and it does not foster agency. Instead, it maintains structures that prohibit it. Arendt is deeply concerned with how agency becomes thwarted when the social replaces the political. Because contract pregnancy is an instantiation of the social, the practice is philosophically relevant from an Arendtian perspective. But to say that contract pregnancy is an instantiation of the social, and hence is public in a warped way, does not exhaust how we might think about it from an Arendtian perspective. The social is like totalitarianism in that it can threaten agency but not completely abolish it. Just as totalitarianism contains the seeds of its own destruction, so too does the social-biopolitical; the exercise of agency has the potential to interrupt the social-biopolitical and create new, non-oppressive meanings.[25]

BRINGING CONTRACT PREGNANCY INTO THE PUBLIC SPHERE THROUGH SPEECH AND ACTION

In contrast to the social-biopolitical, I suggest that the exercise of agency brings contract pregnancy into the public realm. I do not interpret Arendt's public/private distinction as providing rigid categorical distinctions. Rather, in my view, what makes an activity public or private has to do with how that activity is taken up by agents. When reproduction becomes a commodity that can be contracted for and exchanged, it is taken up in a way that requires the recognition of others (it is not merely private). Moreover, when contract pregnancy facilitates injustices and harms, it becomes a potential subject of speech and action within the public realm.

To show that the exercise of agency can bring contract pregnancy into the public realm, I will provide two different approaches to Arendt's public/private distinction. The first I call the "location strategy." In this reading, various activities have appropriate, fixed positions in either the public or the private realm. The second approach I call the "narrative strategy," which focuses on how agents take up and make sense of activities that structure their lives. Whether an activity is considered to be public or private may shift according to how an agent takes it up. Both of these approaches have a foundation in Arendt's book *The*

Human Condition. I will tease them apart and argue that the narrative strategy is better for feminist thinking because it acknowledges how agency can be exercised within an oppressive context as a form of resistance.

The Location Strategy

The first approach to reading the public/private distinction in Arendt is through the location strategy. According to this strategy, certain activities have fixed positions in one realm. This reading appears vividly in the contrast between the Greek household and *polis* (i.e., political space) in *The Human Condition*. In the private sphere of the household, Hellenes "lived together because they were driven by their wants and needs."[26] In other words, the difficult task of surviving pushed people to pool resources and live together. The need to "master" the brutish necessities of physical life gives rise to a hierarchal structure in which men head families, and women, children, and slaves are subordinated. Unlike the relationships constitutive of this hierarchy, the polis is the space of freedom and equality. The household is structurally incapable of freedom, because it is a site of consumption. Masculine heads of household may engage politically, but only by leaving the household can they be free political agents. One might draw from Arendt to make a similar claim about work. Arendt does state that "poverty forces the free man to act like a slave."[27] We might say that to fabricate durable objects and to not be in servitude to a master, a person would need to be free (enough) from tasks of physical maintenance to engage in the work. Otherwise a person would be caught up in the tasks of physical survival and hindered in fabrication.

With the location strategy, given that the necessities of life belong to the private sphere, most of the activities women have traditionally or stereotypically engaged in belong to the private realm. These activities may include domestic labor, care work with children or elders, and reproductive labor. Arendt does argue that how activities are viewed can shift through historical periods. After all, in Plato's *Republic*, child care was arguably a shared, public responsibility.[28] However, women's work has largely been relegated to the private realm and deemed irrelevant to the public.[29] But if there is some historical contingency in how activities are viewed, perhaps the location strategy can accommodate reproduction as a public activity. We could "gender" the location strategy to ensure that reproduction holds a fixed place in the public realm. This gendering is attractive for several reasons. It appreciates the central role reproduction plays in many women's lives and that birth is a central concept for Arendt in her articulation of natality, that with each new physical life is the possibility of a new, unique agent.[30]

Despite these advantages, fixing reproduction as a public, political activity would be unsuccessful. It downplays the reproductive contribution men make, but, more significantly, it yields an essentialist view of women. To stipulate that reproduction belongs to the political, according to the location strategy, would entail a connection between reproduction and what is essentially human. As a result, women would be essentially connected with their reproductive capacities. Giving reproduction a privileged location in the public realm, as Mary Dietz puts it, "lies in accepting natality as the central category of politics (as Arendt does) and then configuring it literally as women's experience in giving birth and mothering, or figuratively as a feminist concept derived from women's 'life activity' (as Arendt does not)."[31] Not only is the location strategy, once gendered, inadequate for feminist purposes, but the concept of the self that emerges from the location strategy is also limited for feminist thinking. If the activities of the public realm have fixed locations, then the self that engages in those activities is in some sense determined by those fixed locations.[32]

The Narrative Strategy

Although there are elements of the location strategy in *The Human Condition*, Arendt is not wedded to a strict version of this reading. She makes the following claim about the location of human activities: "Historical judgments of political communities, by which each determined which of the activities of the *vita activa* [labor, work, and action] should be shown in public and which should be hidden in privacy, may have their correspondence in the nature of these activities themselves."[33] Arendt admits that the historically situated fixed positions of human activities may result from a community's judgment. Situatedness provides fluidity that the location strategy tends to underemphasize. As I aim to show, if activities are categorized as public or private on the basis of communal judgments, and if activities "may have their correspondence in the nature of these activities themselves," then we have reason to interpret "the nature of activities," or their core features, as not corresponding directly to fixed positions. This flexibility allows theorists to separate essentialist interpretations from the categories themselves and to understand particular activities, such as reproduction, as having positions that are unstable and open to change.

Seyla Benhabib resists a strict version of the location strategy, what she calls "phenomenological essentialism," for reasons similar to the ones I give, asserting that it yields an essentialist definition of women.[34] Instead, Benhabib uses what I call the narrative strategy. By "narrative," I refer to ways people engage in and talk about specific activities. How people take up activities is what determines whether they are categorized as public or private. Benhabib uses an agent-centered, narrative analysis to argue that child-rearing and family life transcend the traditional categorization of belonging in the private realm.[35] I wish to apply the same strategy to reproductive labor to show how the exercise of political agency makes contract pregnancy public.

The narrative strategy focuses on human activities themselves rather than on any allegedly fixed positions in the private and public realm.[36] The term "realm" itself implies space or place. Not only is the public realm the space of appearances, but it is also a common world, shared between people.[37] While both "a space of appearances" and "a shared, common world" are important ways of understanding the public realm, too much focus on spaces themselves privileges the location strategy over the narrative one.

According to Benhabib, in contrast to an emphasis on space, the public realm as a common world emphasizes how our shared context is socially, historically conditioned.[38] In this understanding, the public realm is contextual and made up of overlapping relations (between people, between people and objects, and so forth). As such, it allows for the boundaries between what is public and private to be more fluid. Benhabib states, "When human activities are considered as complex social relations, and contextualized properly, what appears to be one type of activity may turn out to be another; or the same activity may instantiate more than one action type."[39] How people engage in the activities partially determines "where" the activities are located, whether in the private or the public. Looking at context and at the agent acting reveals a more robust picture of the meaningfulness of an activity than what the location reading allows.

Pregnancy, and hence contract pregnancy, is an activity that can migrate between categories and between the private and public realm without having a fixed location in the world. Despite being a consumptive experience, pregnancy seems to resist being categorized as belonging entirely in the private realm. A fetus is both separate and not separate from a pregnant woman. For example, as the woman experiences them, the fetus's movements—its kicks and stretches—both belong and do not belong to herself.[40] Other relationships lead us to question the privacy of pregnancy: the woman and her partner, if she has one (whether absent or present), and the midwife or physician assisting with the birth. Though not easily thought of as political in these terms, pregnancy is shared in a way that is underplayed by Arendt's understanding of the private realm. Pregnancy can also be understood as a form of work. The pregnant woman sustains a fetus for nine months and may experience significant changes in her mental and physical self during gestation. And, as evidenced in my discussion of the social-biopolitical, contract pregnancy in particular displays instrumentality and purposiveness, which are features of Arendt's category of work.

NEW DIRECTIONS: USING ARENDT FOR FEMINIST THINKING ON CONTRACT PREGNANCY

For Arendt, the public realm consists of work (at least in the durability of objects and the exchange economy) and politics. I suggest that contract pregnancy can also enter the specifically political aspect of public space through the speech and action of political agents. Amrita Pande, an ethnographer working on transnational contract pregnancy in India, suggests that gestational laborers begin to negotiate their oppression through their shared living spaces in the hostels run by the fertility clinics.[41] There is potential here for political action. Pande describes how gestational laborers in the hostel discuss problems around their dining table. One problem is with how the women pay recruiters for bringing their willingness to sell gestational labor to the clinics. One woman suggests that the commissioning couple be responsible for paying the recruiters. The women talk about this possibility among themselves. This discussion sparks a chain of events that leads to better, less exploitative contracts. Pande states, "By the time I left the field, Divya (the hostel matron) has passed the surrogates' message to the doctor, and a special clause had been added to the contract: the intended parents would be responsible for paying any broker involved in the surrogacy process."[42] I suggest that this example shows how contract pregnancy enters into the public realm. This conversation between women in the clinic-run hostel exhibits features of political space and has implications that extend beyond the privacy of a single isolated woman. In this case, an exploitative element of the industry was changed, in part through women sharing stories about selling gestational labor.

Before I conclude, I would like to mention one additional way in which reproduction is not merely a private activity. Unlike other consumptive activities, reproduction emphasizes the experiential importance of agency.[43] Reproduction transcends its categorization as a private, consumptive activity because of the role it plays in Arendt's concept of natality, the new beginning in birth, which is the underlying basis "in which the faculty of *action* is ontologically rooted."[44] In this quotation, Arendt invokes the capacity to begin something new in its descriptive dimension as the literal capacity of reproduction to begin a new life. Birth symbolizes the power of human agency. Physical birth results in a new person, but, more specifically, it results in a new agent, whose actions have the power to shape the world.

This special status of reproduction is illustrated well in Arendt's brief discussion of love and the child. According to Arendt, two lovers in the thralls of passionate love become worldless. A lover is totally consumed with "who" her lover is and loses all attention to "what" her lover is. She is consumed with the who of her lover to the point that the world, the in-between that separates and relates human beings, is destroyed. In this picture, love binds two people together into a unity so that the lovers' respective uniqueness is suppressed. However, the birth of a child reinserts the lovers into the world: "The child, this in-between to which the lovers now are related and which they hold in common, is representative of the new world that also separates them; it is an indication that they will insert a new world into the existing world."[45] This reinsertion into the world is not political as such. It is not speech nor action. Rather, it is a reminder, a way of drawing attention back to the world and to plurality. The child represents a new beginning, a new world that will overlap and contribute to the existing one.

Analogously to the child reinserting lovers back into the world, I have been thinking through how the practice of contract pregnancy inserts women who sell gestational labor into the world as speakers and as actors. To sum up my argument, even though Arendt does not find reproduction a philosophically rich topic for discussion, I have argued that her framework does not preclude philosophical analyses of reproduction. This project is intended to be a stepping-stone that opens up Arendt's philosophy for engaging reproductive justice. I have suggested that contract pregnancy provides a rich example of the problem of the social, which I understand in conjunction with the biopolitical. Moreover, contract pregnancy need not be understood as necessarily belonging in the private realm. Through the narrative strategy, I have argued that contract pregnancy can be a public and a political activity, within Arendt's framework, through the exercise of agency. On the basis of this argument, it would be my hope that feminists working on reproductive justice and embodied subjectivity in relation to reproduction will pay heed to Arendt and the rich theoretical resources she offers us.

KATY FULFER is Assistant Professor in the Department of Philosophy and the Women's Studies Program at the University of Waterloo.

NOTES

1. Amy Mullin, *Reconceiving Pregnancy and Childcare* (Cambridge, UK: Cambridge University Press, 2005).

2. See Mary O'Brien, *The Politics of Reproduction* (Boston: Routledge, 1981); Mary G. Dietz, "Feminist Receptions of Hannah Arendt," in *Feminist Interpretations of Hannah Arendt*, ed. Bonnie Honig, 17–50 (University Park: Pennsylvania State University Press, 1995); Bonnie Honig, "Toward an Agonistic Feminism: Hannah Arendt and the Politics

of Identity," in *Feminist Interpretations of Hannah Arendt*, ed. Bonnie Honig, 135–66 (University Park: Pennsylvania State University Press, 1995); Virginia Held, "Birth and Death," *Ethics* 99, no. 2 (1989); Adrienne Rich, "Conditions for Work: The Common World of Women," *Lies, Secrets, and Silence* (New York: W. W. Norton, 1979), 38–39.

    3. Reproductive justice was a framework pioneered by women of color. It involves recognizing how broader societal and economic inequalities affect reproductive and sexual health. For an extended discussion of reproductive justice, and how it relates to contract pregnancy (which is the focal point for this paper), see Alison Bailey, "Reconceiving Surrogacy: Toward a Reproductive Justice Account of Indian Surrogacy," *Hypatia* 26, no. 4 (2011): 726–36.

    4. Debra Satz, "Markets in Women's Reproductive Labor," *Philosophy and Public Affairs* 21, no. 2 (1992): 127.

    5. Maren Klawiter, "Using Arendt and Heidegger to Consider Feminist Thinking on Women and Reproductive/Infertility Technologies," *Hypatia* 5, no. 3 (1990): 73; Jyotsna Agnihotri Gupta, "Reproductive Biocrossings: Indian Egg Donors and Surrogates in the Globalized Fertility Market," *International Journal of Feminist Approaches to Bioethics* 5, no. 1 (2012): 39–40.

    6. Gupta, "Reproductive Biocrossings," 42.

    7. The paradigm of the division between public and private is historically conditioned. It first appears, in Arendt's thought, in the Greek household, to which I return in the next section of this essay. Our understanding of public and private activities shifts according to historical contexts. For example, Arendt attributes the origin of the social realm with the Romans, a development that will shift our understanding of the public/private split. It shifts through the medieval era and in modernity. Hannah Arendt, *The Human Condition* (Chicago: University of Chicago Press, 1958), 22–24, 33–35.

    8. Arendt, *Human Condition*, 46.

    9. Michel Foucault, *The History of Sexuality*, trans. Robert Hurley, vol. 1, *An Introduction* (New York: Vintage Books, 1990), 135–45.

    10. Lorna Weir, *Pregnancy, Risk, and Biopolitics* (London: Routledge, 2006), 8.

    11. Amrita Pande, *Wombs in Labor* (New York: Columbia University Press, 2014), 64–83. Since the writing of this essay, the Indian government has taken steps to restrict access to contract pregnancy within their borders. See BBC, "India Unveils Plan to Ban Surrogacy."

    12. There are tensions with this production too. While industry ideals emphasize that good gestational laborers are nurturing and put the fetus's well-being above all other priorities, they also attempt to distance the gestational laborer from forming an emotional attachment to the particular embryo she gestates. See Pande, *Wombs in Labor*, 64.

    13. Some women may live in the fertility clinics or in hostels that are operated by the clinics. In Amrita Pande's study there were some differences in how the women living above clinics were disciplined relative to the women living in hostels. The latter tended to have more freedom of movement, for example, than the former. Nevertheless, the messaging to gestational laborers in both instances is the same. See Pande, *Wombs in Labor*, 75–76.

    14. Pande, *Wombs in Labor*, 70, 106.

    15. Ibid., 72, 92–93.

    16. Ibid., 78–79.

17. André Duarte, "Biopolitics and the Dissemination of Violence: The Arendtian Critique of the Present," *HannahArendt.Net* 1, no. 1 (2005), 7, 11–14; Miguel Vatter, "Natality and Biopolitics in Hannah Arendt," *Revista De Ciencia Politica* 26, no. 2 (2006): 149.

18. Despite attempts to deemphasize women's connection to the embryos or resulting children, some women do understand their gestational contribution to be significant for the child. See Pande, *Wombs in Labor*, 70, 147–50.

19. Serene J. Khader, "Intersectionality and the Ethics of Transnational Commercial Surrogacy," *International Journal of Feminist Approaches of Bioethics* 6, no. 1 (2013): 80.

20. Ibid., 81–82.

21. Arendt, *Human Condition*, 139.

22. Klawiter, "Using Arendt and Heidegger," 82; Elizabeth Anderson, *Value in Ethics and Economics* (Cambridge, MA: Harvard University Press, 1993), 178–80.

23. Although a gestational laborer may sometimes donate genetic material to the embryo, it is much more common that contract pregnancy is only gestational. In India, a gestational laborer is prohibited from also contributing genetic material to the embryo. Thus, gestational contract pregnancy reinforces the idea that parenthood or family connections are genetically based. This privileging of the genetic supports a broader framework that devalues care-giving work by people not genetically related to a child. See Khader, "Intersectionality," 83–84.

24. Arendt, *Human Condition*, 10.

25. Totalitarian solutions, such as Nazi Germany's concentration camps, seek to "transform human nature itself" by killing human dignity and the meaning-making capacities of persons, and by quashing spontaneity. The camps attempted to make the life and death of any individual meaningless and interchangeable with another. Arendt draws on reports from camp survivors who describe conditions that dehumanized them and treated them as "naked life." Nevertheless, totalitarian regimes will never be able to fully make this transformation, because spontaneity is a core feature of human agency. The capacity for spontaneity resides with each person and will manifest even in the struggle for physical survival. See Hannah Arendt, *The Origins of Totalitarianism*, rev. ed. (Orlando: Harcourt, 1968), 438–39, 458–59, 478–79.

26. Arendt, *Human Condition*, 30.

27. Ibid., 64.

28. Plato, *The Republic*, trans. Allan Bloom (New York: Basic Books, 1991), 457d-e, 461d-e.

29. Rich, "Conditions for Work," 213; Elizabeth V. Spelman, *Inessential Woman: Problems of Exclusion in Feminist Thought* (Boston: Beacon Press, 1988), 38–39.

30. Arendt, *Human Condition*, 9, 19.

31. Dietz, "Feminist Receptions," 28.

32. Seyla Benhabib, *The Reluctant Modernism of Hannah Arendt* (Thousand Oaks, CA: Sage, 1996), 125–27; Dana R. Villa, "Hannah Arendt: Modernity, Alienation, and Critique," in *Judgment, Imagination, and Politics*, ed. Ronald Beiner and Jennifer Nedelesky, 296–98 (Lanham, MD: Rowman and Littlefield, 2001).

33. Arendt, *Human Condition*, 1958, 78.

34. The definition of phenomenological essentialism roughly matches my description of the location strategy: "Each type of human activity has a proper 'place' in which it can be carried out." See Benhabib, *Reluctant Modernism*, 124.

35. Ibid., 172–219.
36. See Dietz, "Feminist Receptions"; Benhabib, *Reluctant Modernism*.
37. Arendt, *Human Condition*, 50–58; Benhabib, *Reluctant Modernism*, 128.
38. Benhabib, *Reluctant Modernism*, 128.
39. Ibid., 131.
40. Iris Marion Young, "Pregnant Embodiment: Subjectivity and Alienation," *Journal of Medicine and Philosophy* 9, no. 1 (1984): 48.
41. Pande, *Wombs in Labor*, 158–62, 169.
42. Ibid., 162.
43. Kimberly F. Curtis, "Hannah Arendt, Feminist Theorizing, and the Debate over New Reproductive Technologies," *Polity* 28, no. 2 (1995): 183–84.
44. Arendt, *Human Condition*, 247; emphasis added.
45. Ibid., 242.

BIBLIOGRAPHY

Anderson, Elizabeth. *Values in Ethics and Economics*. Cambridge, MA: Harvard University Press, 1993.
Arendt, Hannah. *The Human Condition*. Chicago: University of Chicago Press, 1958.
———. *The Origins of Totalitarianism*. 1951. Rev. ed. Orlando: Harcourt, 1968.
Bailey, Alison. "Reconceiving Surrogacy: Toward a Reproductive Justice Account of Indian Surrogacy." *Hypatia* 26, no. 4 (2011): 715–41.
BBC. "India Unveils Plan to Ban Surrogacy." *BBC News*. August 25, 2016. http://www.bbc.com/news/world-asia-india-37182197.
Benhabib, Seyla. *The Reluctant Modernism of Hannah Arendt*. Thousand Oaks, CA: Sage, 1996.
Curtis, Kimberly F. "Hannah Arendt, Feminist Theorizing, and the Debate over New Reproductive Technologies." *Polity* 28, no. 2 (1995): 159–87.
Dietz, Mary G. "Feminist Receptions of Hannah Arendt." In *Feminist Interpretations of Hannah Arendt*, edited by Bonnie Honig, 17–50. University Park: Pennsylvania State University Press, 1995.
Duarte, André. "Biopolitics and the Dissemination of Violence: The Arendtian Critique of the Present." *HannahArendt.Net* 1, no. 1 (2005): 1–15.
Foucault, Michel. *The History of Sexuality*. Vol. 1: *An Introduction*. Translated by Robert Hurley. 1976. New York: Vintage Books, 1990.
Gupta, Jyotsna Agnihotri. "Reproductive Biocrossings: Indian Egg Donors and Surrogates in the Globalized Fertility Market." *International Journal of Feminist Approaches to Bioethics* 5, no. 1 (2012): 25–51.
Hayden, Patrick. *Political Evil in a Global Age: Hannah Arendt and International Theory*. New York: Routledge, 2009.
Held, Virginia. "Birth and Death." *Ethics* 99, no. 2 (1989): 362–88.
Honig, Bonnie. "Arendt, Identity, and Difference." *Political Theory* 16, no. 1 (1988): 77–98.
———. "Toward an Agonistic Feminism: Hannah Arendt and the Politics of Identity." In *Feminist Interpretations of Hannah Arendt*, edited by Bonnie Honig, 135–66. University Park: Pennsylvania State University Press, 1995.
Khader, Serene J. "Intersectionality and the Ethics of Transnational Commercial Surrogacy." *International Journal of Feminist Approaches of Bioethics* 6, no. 1 (2013): 68–90.

Klawiter, Maren. "Using Heidegger and Arendt to Consider Feminist Thinking on Women and Reproductive/Infertility Technologies." *Hypatia* 5, no. 3 (1990): 65–89.

Law Commission of India. "Need for Legislation to Regulate Assisted Reproductive Technology Clinics as Well as Rights and Obligations of Parties to a Surrogacy." Government of India, Report 228, August 5, 2009.

Mullin, Amy. *Reconceiving Pregnancy and Childcare*. Cambridge, UK: Cambridge University Press, 2005.

O'Brien, Mary. *The Politics of Reproduction*. Boston: Routledge, 1981.

Pande, Amrita. *Wombs in Labor*. New York: Columbia University Press, 2014.

Plato. *The Republic*. Translated by Allan Bloom. 1968. New York: Basic Books, 1991.

Rich, Adrienne. "Conditions for Work: The Common World of Women." *On Lies, Secrets, and Silence*. New York: W. W. Norton, 1979. 203–214.

Satz, Debra. "Markets in Women's Reproductive Labor." *Philosophy and Public Affairs* 21, no. 2 (1992): 107–131.

Spelman, Elizabeth V. *Inessential Woman: Problems of Exclusion in Feminist Thought*. Boston: Beacon Press, 1988.

Spivak, Gayatri Chakravorty. "Can the Subaltern Speak?" Rev. ed. In *Can the Subaltern Speak?: Reflections on the History of an Idea*, edited by Rosalind C. Morris, 21–78. New York: Columbia University Press, 2010.

Twine, France Winddance. *Outsourcing the Womb: Race, Class, and Gestational Surrogacy in a Global Market*. New York: Routledge, 2011.

Vatter, Miguel. "Natality and Biopolitics in Hannah Arendt." *Revista De Ciencia Política* 26, no. 2 (2006): 137–59.

Villa, Dana R. "Hannah Arendt: Modernity, Alienation, and Critique." In *Judgment, Imagination, and Politics*, edited by Ronald Beiner and Jennifer Nedelesky, 287–310. Lanham, MD: Rowman and Littlefield, 2001.

Weir, Lorna. *Pregnancy, Risk, and Biopolitics*. London: Routledge, 2006.

Young, Iris Marion. "Pregnant Embodiment: Subjectivity and Alienation." *Journal of Medicine and Philosophy* 9, no. 1 (1984): 45–62.

Zaretsky, Eli. "Hannah Arendt and the Meaning of the Public/Private Distinction." In *Hannah Arendt and the Meaning of Politics*, edited by Craig Calhoun and John McGowan, 207–231. Minneapolis: University of Minnesota Press, 1997.

Zerilli, Linda M. G. "The Arendtian Body." In *Feminist Interpretations of Hannah Arendt*, edited by Bonnie Honig, 167–93. University Park: Pennsylvania State University Press, 1995.

PART 5
PRESENT AND FUTURE SELVES

15 IS DIRECT PERCEPTION ARROGANT PERCEPTION?

Toward a Critical, Playful Intercorporeity

APRIL N. FLAKNE

INTRODUCTION

Feminist phenomenology promises numerous futures. In this essay, I will consider what emerging interactionist approaches to embodied social cognition might offer to feminist phenomenologists. For the sake of convenience, I will refer to a group of related, phenomenologically inspired approaches to embodied social cognition as "direct perception" (DP).[1] I use this overarching term not to ignore significant differences between the various strands, but to focus on their central, shared claim—namely, that our perception is "smart" enough to perceive "directly" that there are other minds as well as a great deal of what supposedly goes on "in" those other minds.[2] Just how directly we perceive the emotions and intentions of others may be a matter of dispute,[3] but the point remains that primarily and for the most part we do not need to resort to inference or analogy in our everyday encounters and dealings with other mindfully embodied beings in a shared space of interaction. We do not first see movements, actions, and behaviors and then infer or deduce from them intentionality and emotional investment. Instead, we see movements and behaviors precisely as expressive of those intentionalities and emotions in the first place, and we take them up through our own bodies as such.[4] "We have," as Shaun Gallagher maintains, "a direct understanding of another person's intentions because their intentions are explicitly expressed in their embodied actions, and mirrored in our own capabilities for action."[5]

I argue that the thrust of DP as against more traditional cognitivist approaches to other minds—including DP's emphasis on understanding persons as fundamentally social, contextual, interactive, and embodied, while giving reasonable and appropriate attention to developmental psychology—ought to be attractive to feminist phenomenologists going forward. Most importantly for my present purposes, direct perception can be a key ally in defeating a dominant and damaging analogical approach to Otherness that necessarily effaces difference by always modeling the Other on oneself. However, despite this, and as with some of the phenomenological and hermeneutic theories of Otherness that DP draws upon, feminists must remain keenly attentive to ways DP risks the *replication* or even the *institution* of harmful habits of perception and interaction it claims only to *describe*. In my view, and in keeping with traditional phenomenological method, direct perception aims to unearth a founding mode of interaction with Others upon which competing theories of other minds, such as theory theory and simulation theory, may proceed in specialized circumstances.[6] In this version, direct perception builds upon classical phenomenology's thematization of lifeworlds and lived bodies as these underlie actions, explicit propositional content, objective body images, and so on. Attention to this level of inquiry is obviously vital to critical projects in feminist, or any other, phenomenological theory. But at the same time, feminist phenomenologists are wise to apply careful critical skills gleaned from feminist ethics and epistemology to ensure that this fecund ground, once exposed, does not, under the guise of neutral description and theory formation, smuggle in injurious perceptive and social practices and place their normativity beyond dispute. We must investigate, then, whether the insights direct perception offers can help orient critical practices of perception and social interaction or whether they merely serve to justify and entrench current, lopsided ones. To adopt and adapt the vocabulary of Marilyn Frye and Maria Lugones, we want to see if direct perception merely enables yet another iteration of arrogant perception or if, with some help—particularly from Lugones—it might offer tools to combat the invidious workings of such perception.[7]

In the first section of this essay, I will sketch a transcendentalist version of direct perception and show how it can be used to critique the analogical assumptions of both theory theory and simulation theory approaches to other minds. Feminist phenomenologists, I believe, have much to gain by extending this critique to analogical approaches to Others more generally, including to variants that continue to crop up within their own tradition (for example, in Edmund Husserl's own writing, despite his loud protestations to the contrary in the fifth *Cartesian Meditation*). My reconstruction here has little to do with versions of DP that some phenomenologists fear naturalize phenomenology beyond recognition. On the contrary, I maintain that DP works best when it relies on a presuppositional argument to reveal a transcendental (or at least quasi-transcendental) layer of embodied, second-person interaction beneath cognitivist and subject-centered approaches to other minds.[8] The danger of DP's conciliatory moves toward empirical psychology and the cognitive sciences, then, is less that DP might abandon the phenomenological project that inspired it, but more that it might reinscribe data meant only to bolster its plausibility back into this (quasi)transcendental layer as a structuring element of all possible social perceptions and interactions. It is against any such move that we must remain vigilant.

In the second section of the essay, in order to articulate what sort of danger this represents, I turn to Frye's indictment of arrogant perception as an example of how background assumptions can operate to suppress difference in the name of a meaningful coherence for those who profit from existing power relations. However, even while proposing her solution, I show that Frye falls back on familiar analogical approaches to the Other that defeat her own intent to liberate and to love difference. As an alternative to this, in the final section I combine Lugones's idea of world-traveling with an intercorporeity developed through direct perception's insistence on an embodied secondperson interactionist approach to Others. This combination, properly understood as playful praxis, may act as an effective strategy to counter analogical arrogance in social perception.[9]

DIRECT PERCEPTION, THEORY THEORY, AND SIMULATION THEORY

Gallagher originally offered interaction theory (IT) and direct perception (DP) to rival the currently dominant empirical approaches to "other minds." These can be conveniently grouped under the titles "theory theory" (TT) and "simulation theory" (ST). Theory theory assumes we develop and employ folk psychological theories about others' mental states—primarily beliefs and desires—in order to understand them. For example, we understand that the pirate will look for the booty where she left it, not where we happen to know it currently resides. Simulation theory," by contrast, maintains that we reenact or induce the states of others within ourselves in order to empathize with them—we put ourselves "in their shoes" to try to think and feel as they do. Objecting to both TT and ST, direct perception makes the bold claim that we can, and do, generally dispense with such mechanisms of knowledge and affect inducement insofar as we encounter "other minds" first and foremost as bodies interacting within a shared space of concern. The other is not a closed envelope whose content I must guess at from the limited perspective of my equally confined, interior space. Instead, she intervenes in my environment as an opportunity for interaction of a very special sort. I perceive in her embodied actions directed toward our shared environment multiple possibilities for embodied response while anticipating her possible responses to this response. This circuit of response-able intentions and affections is not coincidental or subsequent to the encounter with another; entering into this circuit is precisely what it means to bodily perceive an Other at all.

Still, while DP takes direct aim at TT and ST, a simple contrast between DP versus ST or TT remains misleading. On closer inspection, many iterations of direct perception mean to be much more than an empirical alternative to the other two approaches to mind reading. In fact, the strongest arguments in DP's defense are *presuppositional*: it is not so much that social cognition is best explained either by theory theory, simulation theory, or direct perception. The strong claim is that something like direct perception as an immediate perception of expressive, intentional agents and behaviors in a shared environment of concern is the precondition for anything like theory-theoretical or simulation-theoretical feats of mind reading. In Gallagher's words, direct perception is "primary and pervasive."[10] Without my ability to see that you are engaging intentionally and affectively—that is, mindfully—with your environment, the question of why, or how, or how I know you are doing so could not even arise. In classical phenomenological parlance, ST and TT are *founded* modes of intersubjectivity, while direct perception is the *founding* one.[11] This move to a founding mode of perceiving Others is at once utterly important and convincing but also cause for critical concern.

On the one hand, the phenomenological tradition informing direct perception has been quite unified in agreeing that Others are immediately given to us in a way that differs significantly from the way objects are given to us. While we might be mistaken in ascribing Otherhood to an automaton, a zombie, a fluttering curtain, or a computer program in specific (and probably quite peculiar and localized) cases, or, at the other extreme, that we might on occasion mistake a sleeping or still Other for an inert object, it is not the case that Others in general present to me first as objects whose subjectivities I must work out in addition to and after the fact of our encounter. Phenomenologically, Others are given, for example, in empathy (Husserl, Edith Stein), or alongside us (Martin Heidegger), or in shame (Jean-Paul Sartre), but they are given precisely as *Others*. With all of this, direct perception concurs. Others are given directly and perceptually as minded, intentional, embodied, affective, and engaged entities alongside us in our shared environment. On the other hand, it is disturbing how often this immediate, revealed givenness is at a second stage forgotten or covered over, not only through interested or biased and strategic concrete experience but also by the very same ingenious philosophers who exposed the Other's very givenness in affect or worldliness to begin with. So forgotten, the Other is again forced to acquit itself of an objecthood externally imposed, with the conditions of its innocence depending on its recognition of the authority of the "same"—in other words, of whatever subjectivity is established as dominant, legitimate, constitutive, or normative. The one who originally impressed us, was given to us, as an Other-subject is now reduced once more to a body, over there, to be interrogated, tested as a hypothesis: Are you really a subject? If so, you must prove you are like me; but we both know you are different, because there you are, standing over and against me, exterior, like an object: you are Other. According to a sad history of phenomenological/hermeneutic failures, the Other who is given as Other can be recognized as Other only at the price of being Othered—that is, becoming more than a mere object but less than a subject, namely, becoming *a recognition machine* for the sake of the same.[12] Can the direct perception of Others, informed as it is by a phenomenological tradition more haunted by G.W.F. Hegel than it likes to admit, guard against this ever recurrent mistake (or, perhaps more accurately, this historical sedimentation of *his- stakes*)?[13]

Direct perception tells us that Heidegger was right; we see other Dasein as other Dasein because they comport themselves toward the world alongside us as we comport ourselves toward the world. We do not (at least we do not very often), and we should not (although it not clear what might stop us), view Other Dasein as ready-to-hand and present-to-hand things. And direct perception tells us that Maurice Merleau-Ponty was also right; these comportments are embodied ones, and we, as likewise embodied, directly perceive and respond to bodily expressions as arising from and reaching toward a world that we are also always affected by and affecting. This interactive, embodied, expressive comportment toward the world forms the prethematic, implicit background against which any explicit acts of "mind reading" of the sort that concern TT and ST can take place.

Yet all of our postmodern and feminist training primes us to be wary of any move toward presuppositional, foundational, or—to use that dangerous, old-fashioned term—transcendental claims. We do and should worry whether such claims are legitimate or whether they simply bolster contingent power relations by placing them at a depth inaccessible to social criticism. Direct perception rightly draws attention away from monadic selves to embodied interactors and assures us that our perception of Others always operates according to the worldliness of these expressive bodies. But how rigid are the conditions under which such expressive bodies become legible? Is there a single code of legibility applicable to all that dictates who or what could be directly perceived, taken up, interacted with? Are we in a position to interrogate the very conditions of legibility of expressive bodies, or must we just accept them?

Feminist phenomenologists must confront these questions if we are to develop direct perception in the promising directions I believe it holds. But questioning the operations of a prethematic layer of embodied social interaction and remaining vigilant against importing contingent power relations back into this structuring layer do not amount to demanding that phenomenology be naturalized, as some critics of DP fear it does. One can retain a critical, skeptical attitude toward transcendental claims without demanding that they be subject to the same procedures of evidence-based verification as are empirical ones. In fact, in searching out productive alliances with empirical psychology and the brain sciences, proponents of DP are doing no more than following through on Merleau-Ponty's lead.[14] In pursuing this track, DP proponents have gained indicators that bolster their necessarily indirect, presuppositional proofs while multiplying "phenomena" to help disclose what it is like to interact.[15] For Merleau-Ponty, this approach meant acknowledging that the existence of a life body can never be proved by empirical, third-person means; yet attention to empirical case studies could unearth traces of this life body and prompt first-person awareness of it, cutting beneath the layers upon layers of third-person objectifications of our bodies that have become second nature. Similarly, where TT and ST raise the question of how we comprehend the intentions, emotions, and mental states of other minded beings, DP asks what it is like and how it is possible to experience other-minded beings at all, against the background of which additional questions about whether we are right about their being minded or about what they are doing with their minds might arise in the first place.

Alliances between phenomenology and empiricism may always imply risk, but they need not entail capitulation. For a phenomenology that also wants to be a critical social theory—as does "feminist phenomenology" and some of Gallagher's recent work[16]—the point is to retain the critical gap between the third-person observable data and the first- (and second-) person processes that make these possible. These founding first- and second-person processes can themselves manifest in social and historical expressions that are amenable to additional empirical study and critique in the human and social sciences. The critical phenomenological demand is to move deftly between these levels and domains without succumbing to convenient collapses between them.

The question remains how best to accomplish this. Gallagher's approach encourages a critical fallibilism to operate alongside a benevolent pluralism that disentangles his arguments for the phenomenological and presuppositional primacy of direct perception under the guise of a modified transcendental intersubjectivity (TI) from the empirical case he makes concerning its *developmental* primacy in his interaction theory, allowing each aspect to be scrutinized in its own terms as well as brought into critical dialogue with one another.

For the most part, this strategy has been fecund. One can certainly make a purely empirical case that, for example, since we can observe neonates attending to human faces and voices longer than to any other stimuli, and we can also observe that these neonates strive to imitate and respond to facial and vocal gestures almost immediately after birth, direct perceptual access to others as Others must precede highly complex cognitive acts of theory construction and at least explicit acts of simulation or empathy, since these appear to emerge much later. There also appears to be good evidence that such "primary" intersubjectivity subsists and subtends, as Gallagher maintains, even through the subsequent development of secondary (joint attention) and tertiary (linguistic ability and narrative competence) levels of complexity that depend and build upon it.[17] One can imagine the construction of experiments that might support or question these claims without advancing any position whatsoever on a transcendental interactive capacity underlying this observably early and consistent developmental layer.

Such empirical work would likely value and validate practices of caretaking in a way that might appeal to important strands of feminist ethics, phenomenological or otherwise. As such, it offers a promising intersection between direct perception and feminist concerns, but I will not pursue this further here. Instead, I want to retain the idea that such "primary and pervasive" early interaction may indeed indicate and support a (at least quasi) transcendental layer of interactivity as embodied, enactive, dialogical, and second-personal. It is precisely the primacy of this dialogical, second-person in-betweenness that, as I argue below, holds the key to a decisive break with the analogical approach to others that has damaged feminist interests. But how much can we say about this layer, based on observations we might make, before we stop up the aperture into this layer of responsive, dialogical, open-ended play between affective, mindful bodies and fill it in with biased, predecided outcomes imported from findings lodged squarely in our natural attitudes? Some of Gallagher's and Dan Zahavi's interpretations of the neonatal experiments risk doing just that.[18]

To briefly state one cause for such concern: Gallagher uses "new evidence" (neurological and developmental) supporting very early or even innate proprioception to challenge Merleau-Ponty's notion (itself supported by contemporaneous empirical studies in developmental psychology) of a body schema that develops against a backdrop of originally inchoate interpersonal boundaries.[19] Next, this supposedly proven proprioceptive capacity is translated into a transcendental "minimal self" presupposed in any encounter with others.[20] Elsewhere I argue that this move is dubious for at least three reasons: (1) the "evidence" Gallagher cites remains equivocal—all we really observe is a capacity for intercorporeal interaction, neither imitation nor improved motoric accuracy require proprioception per se; (2) such a minimal, proprioceptive self is not presuppositionally necessary, even for the account of "intersubjectivity" Gallagher presents; and (3) such a minimal self "front-loads" considerably more normative—and gender-biased—content than Gallagher and Zahavi acknowledge.[21] DP at once forefronts the in-between, intercorporeal, and interactive presuppositions of any actual encounter with a concrete other while taking a datum it believes to be confirmed empirically—the minimal, enclosed, proprioceptive self—and establishing that as a structuring element in this now allegedly primary in-betweenness (i.e., what appears to be *really* primary, by this account, is not the interaction but a minimal self). Is it not likely, though, that proponents of DP look for this primary proprioceptive self precisely because the contingent in-between they happen to inhabit values boundaries, stability, separation—and that they allow this contingent social and cultural background to construct what they maintain must be presupposed as an absolute background for observable neonatal interaction to occur?

As I will explore in the next section, such examples do put direct perception at risk of deteriorating into arrogant perception, despite the anti-analogical tools it also provides that help us dismantle the very bases of such analogical arrogance. To make good on the dismantling task, we will retain DP's presuppositional account insofar as it aims to show how any empirical research into other minds already must assume an interactive, intercorporeal—but not intersubjective—basis.[22] In such an embodied, enactive, and dialogical account, our perception of others is tied to the multiple and varied interactive opportunities they present to us. I do not ordinarily approach the other third personally and try to understand or simulate what "she" is thinking or doing, but instead interact with a "you" whose actions and intentions concern me and affect my own actions and intentions in an environment we share, act into, and continually make collective sense of.[23]

This focus on embodied, dialogical interactivity as a presuppositional argument for direct perception as it unfolds in the pragmatic and perceptual spaces between us offers the leverage that critical phenomenologists need to at last loosen the grip of the old argument from analogy that has detrimentally determined a long line of approaches to other minds.[24] To embrace it is to reinvigorate Merleau-Ponty's notion of a founding intercorporeity or the interconnection of lived bodies underneath empirical accounts of other minds. We can endorse this and, at the same time, as critical, feminist phenomenologists, take care to bracket any too thick account of such embodied interaction, such as one that depends upon a proprioceptive self, being "front-loaded" into empirical inquiries. In the next section, I will explore problems with analogical approaches to others in greater depth before I return to address how direct perception helps us escape analogizing tendencies while itself posing the threat of a reified, homogenizing lifeworld. I will then show how it could learn from the work of Lugones to plurify selves and worlds of sense-construction to make good on its best intercorporeal promises.

ARROGANT PERCEPTION AND THE ANALOGICAL APPROACH TO OTHERS

The problem with all arguments from analogy is that the model for understanding the "Other" is always myself. The terms that form the basis of the analogy may differ depending on the theory. For example, for theory theory, the terms would be mental states such as beliefs and desires, while simulation theory would speak of affects and bodily states. In either case, though, the "known" term is always myself, on the basis of which I must deduce the variable that is the other. As such, all analogical approaches reduce the Other to a series of "possible" my-selves, with potentially disastrous consequences—consequences quite well captured by Frye's term "arrogant perception."[25]

As I understand it, arrogant perception operates according to a threefold logic resulting in a stranglehold of harm. The first and second bases of this logic result from the binary relation of identity and difference inherent in any proportional analogy upon which classical approaches to other minds are based. A is to B as C is to D, but the "as" is equivocal. It means that A/B both is and is not like C/D. So the first basis of arrogant perception is that your body and behavior are to your interior mental/intentional world as my body and behavior are to mine; you are *like me*. But since the terms are nonidentical, the second move is to posit that you are *different from me* but still in ways that are *determined by me*, inevitably, since my body-mind complex is the known term. The final move in the stranglehold shifts to a dialectical resolution of the binary of identity and difference by reference to pragmatics or interest, what Frye calls "arrogating perception." Here the proportional analogy shifts imperceptibly into a *pros hen* equivocation: A is to B as C is to B (since D is taken to be strictly identical to B): you are to my body-world as I am to my body-world; your similarities and difference are structured by their perceived salience to me and mine.

By beginning with a founding worldliness and pragmatic engagement through interacting expressive bodies, direct perception takes firm aim at a model of Otherness based on simple proportional analogy. It is no longer possible to think of each side of the analogy as a discrete unit, where the invisible term—your mental life—can be inferred on the basis of some likeness between your bodily expression and my own in relation to my mental life. In DP, any object-likeness of our expressive bodies is replaced by engaged, mutual interaction in a shared space informed by but also informing our mental lives. Our bodies and behaviors are no longer conceived of as signs or symptoms of a separate and invisible mental life, but are modalities of minded embodiment in (inter)action. Nonetheless, a temptation toward pros hen equivocation remains great, since the condition of all possible legibility of the expression of otherness now becomes the one shared world between us, in and through which we interact. Such pros hen equivocation differs in important ways from the one Frye feared, however. Where Frye warned against granting a pros hen priority to a certain sort of perceivers or selves (arrogant, male ones), direct perception instead risks prioritizing a specific lifeworld as a set of shared background assumptions, rules, and conventions according to which the intentionality and expressive behaviors of others become directly perceivable to us. Following a Heideggerian theme, it is not that we see digits curling around a porcelain ring attached to a porcelain vessel, and a limb lifting this toward an abstract orifice on an indifferent fleshly plane; rather we see this whole movement *as* the act of drinking a hot beverage. We can do this because we recognize a familiar sort of embodied agent engaged with familiar things in a familiar world or context. As discussed in the first section of this essay, the danger in this update of existential hermeneutics is that direct perception might simply push the sources of arrogant perception back to a danker place, where the construction of specific norms and conventions—and therefore the sorts of selves that can appear and perceive in the worlds comprised of these norms and conventions—operates invisibly and beyond contention. In such a situation, where subjects are displaced in favor of enabling contexts, arrogant perception might pass, and get a pass, simply as "competent" perception. We will return to this problem—and possible remedies—in the final section, but first I want to look in a bit more detail at the mechanics of arrogant perception in Frye's account.

The first move in arrogant perception is analogical: I take myself as a body-mind complex to be the rubric according to which the other is able to appear as

Other at all. The other has an invisible interior life animating her moving body as my interior life expresses itself through mine. Since I can only have access to, and judge, my own interior life, I tend to assume, given similar gestures and behaviors, that the other's interior life is like my own. If it appears to deviate from mine, I may, if I am in good faith, attempt to understand any peculiarities of her situation that might explain her differences from me. But if I think I can account for these and still fail to comprehend her position or action, I judge it to be invalid or deficient. (For example, if a black youth fears an encounter with the police, a white American suburbanite might take this as an indication of guilt. Since the white suburbanite feels no reason to fear the police, she or he assumes that only wrongdoers have reason to do so.) For Frye, my needs, interests, and power position determine what happens next. I may try to discipline the other to be more like me, dismiss her altogether, or attempt to use her deficiencies to justify my use of her to further my own, always already (self-) justified, projects. In Frye's account, the attempt, if there is any, to understand the other is already structured not by what Frye still takes to be a legitimate proportional analogy, but by what has now almost imperceptibly slid into a pros hen equivocation; it is not that my health is to me as your health is to you, but rather that my health is to me as your health is to me.[26] You are healthy to the extent that you serve my health, and unhealthy/abnormal to the extent that you fail to do so. The argument from analogy sets up a single standard, but not only a single standard. It also sets up an interested perspective that reveals arrogant perception as *arrogating* perception; the substantive term in the analogy will always be one; it will always be me.

Lugones demonstrates this strangling dialectic while narrating her relationship with her mother. She loved her mother and wanted to identify with her, yet at the same time, she saw her mother as an object of abuse, including Lugones's own abuse of her. Lugones did not want to be an object of abuse, and she could not understand why the mother she loved, and so sought to identify with, seemed so willing to take on this role. But of course she needed and wanted her mother to willingly take on this role. The dynamic of the failure of projective identification leads easily, "naturally," into the second step of arrogant perception: the reification of differences into one-dimensional biases. I cannot understand why the other does not think/behave/emote as I do, or as I think I would do in her place, so I project a story that justifies the differences I notice and renders them constant. I begin to see the other only through the lens of this story. The proportional analogy breaks down, and I become the norm where she is the exception. In Frye's terms, I simplify her by reducing her to an embodiment of that exception, and then I use that exceptionality as an excuse to treat her as I need or would like her to be treated rather than as I would like to be treated (as in the golden-rule version of proportional analogy).

Emmanuel Levinas notoriously identifies the Other as what calls me into question, but it is precisely this self-questioning that analogically arrogant pros hen perception blocks. Within arrogant perception, the very structuring vision that allows the other to appear as Other at all—that is, in her simplistically analogical likeness and stereotypically stubborn difference from me—cannot itself be called into question. Instead she vacillates between a replica, a disappointment, and a curiosity, until she is finally incorporated into a story that suits my needs. But Frye, as Lugones sees, misidentifies the problem, assuming that the quick move to an arrogating, self-interested—or in my terms, pros hen equivocation—is all that ails. Frye's solution of "loving perception" strives to restore the very proportionally analogical relations that kicked off the dialectic to begin with. In other words, Frye's call for "loving perception" can be sensibly understood as a call only to eradicate the arrogating pros hen equivocation that renders the other intelligible solely according to myself and my interests: in order to love, I must reestablish her as an independent term while still retaining some relation. But of what sort could this relation between two separate terms be, if not analogical?

Frye's "loving perception" can be read in two ways that weaken both its plausibility and its desirability. First, it may merely restore the proportional analogy between self and other that direct perception teaches us is superficial, self-defeating, and avoidable, forever either shutting subjectivities off from each other completely or bridging the gap through a damaging analogy. And, second, as Frye also recognizes, it puts too much faith in individuals' ability, motivation, and responsibility to willfully alter their perception from an arrogant eye to a loving one.

A word more about each of these weaknesses: Frye's insistence that "the loving eye knows the independence of the other" while possessing "self-knowledge, knowledge of the scope and boundary of the self" appears merely to call for a restoration of a proportionally analogical approach to the other.[27] Loving perception thereby does not, in Lugones's reading, ask quite enough from us. It does not ask us to interrogate the very boundaries it assumes, to ask where these boundaries came from and at what cost our identities as independent terms in the analogy were formed. Even when it asks us to "look and listen and check and question," the questions are still being put to the object of our loving gaze from the perspective of our enclosed selves; they are not directed back at our structuring perceptions or at the presupposed boundaries encasing our bodies and minds.

Our discussion of direct perception pointed to a way out of the confines of analogical approaches to the other that begin with such dubious self-transparency and bounded selfhoods.[28] Direct perception invites us instead to focus on the spaces between us where dialogical, interactive access to others unfolds; the Other is, primarily and for the most part, an occasion for uptake and response that we cannot present to ourselves: our selves begin in and through her; we already encounter her outside of ourselves, within the world, where our boundaries have already been transgressed. Given this way out, we needn't and oughtn't be satisfied with any return to the analogical model and its harrowing dialectics between discrete terms. Moreover, we needn't, with Frye, rely so heavily on the willful decisions of (fictionally) bounded individuals to cast loving rather than arrogating eyes on others. Frye ends her essay with skepticism about whether individuals, in a man's world, would ever find the motivation to cultivate a loving eye. But even if they do find the motivation, it is not clear that such bounded individuals alone have the meaning-making resources to combat the world of premade significances created by and upheld for so long by dominant, arrogant eyes. DP's displacement from subjects to lifeworlds and relations, meanwhile, may get us out of our shells and directly interacting only to cast us, helpless, into a world that always already structures what we can see and whom we can love as we interact.

Lugones presses precisely at these points of weakness in both Frye's and DP's accounts as she critically examines the concrete operation of arrogant perception in her relationship with her mother. The awareness that she is both subject (toward her mother) and object (according to cultural expectations) of arrogant perception leads Lugones to modify Frye's notion of loving perception by offering a more phenomenologically savvy alternative of playful world-traveling. Unlike Frye, and like DP, Lugones does not understand individuals in terms of discrete self-relations and mastered intentionalities, but as participating in, constructing, and being constructed by discursively and pragmatically structured "worlds" through which we become visible and intelligible. We cannot expect to alter our perceptions, so deeply implicated in these lifeworlds, without changing the background conditions that structure those perceptions. Lugones's account can then join forces with direct perception to help us abandon the damning dialectics of arrogant, analogizing perception, but only if direct perception can resist its own temptations toward a worldly pros hen that may yet rest on a too subjective (as opposed to genuinely intercorporeal) conception of primary intersubjectivity. In the final section, I want to suggest some positive directions that a two-way alliance between Lugones and direct perception might go.

DIRECT PERCEPTION AND WORLD-TRAVELING

Lugones is clear that Frye's analogical independence is not the way she wants to love. Against discrete, independent terms, she wants to advocate loving identification and interdependence. Arrogant perception and abusive love blocked her ability to love her mother as she longed to do, and felt she could. Rather than reject identification as part of love, she wants to think through to the conditions of a kind of love that would foster and value such identification. While surely identification must not take the form of a lopsided pros hen equivocation—the arrogation of substance in one direction or the other—the flight from arrogance must not come at the price of ignorance either.[29] Lugones laments that among white Anglo women, "the more independent I am, the more independent I am left to be."[30] A respect for, or a tolerance of, difference can result in a fear to engage or even in apathy, and Frye's very loving perception can overvalue mystique or aestheticize exoticism rather than admit that we share and co-construct a common world; that the selves we can be are shaped by that world; and that responsibility to it and to each other is our combined, immense, and unending task.

Lugones's notion of world-traveling is meant to improve upon Frye's loving perception. World-traveling, in contrast to loving perception, tries to explore how we may enter into, affect, and be affected by different "worlds" in order to approach the other on her own grounds and be open to interactive possibilities when these worlds meet, transmute, and unfold. As in direct perception and in contrast to analogical perception, the substantive term is not either of the individuals' closed relation to their own interior mental or emotional life; instead, it is the world or worlds they bodily inhabit as these afford varying and variable opportunities for diverse interactions and modes of perceiving and appearing.

As Mariana Ortega has recently explored at length, Lugones's concept of world-traveling appears at once as ontologically and existentially suspect—especially from a phenomenological perspective—as it is immediately intuitive to members of marginalized groups who are forced to move between worlds in order to survive.[31] For the engaged, critical phenomenologist, any such jagged contrast between theoretical assumptions and lived experience cries out for further exploration. Marginalized experiences can easily be concealed or "forgotten" (in the sense of Heidegger and Arendt) by privileged theories and commonsense versions of "everydayness" as we move through our worlds. Retrieving them can allow us to scrutinize whether these privileged optics and practices have become rigid or even built into the conditions of possible shared life even while making life unshareable, or even impossible, for some.

World-traveling plurifies identity rather than gathering it—a move that even Ortega's sympathetic reading of Lugones finds problematic. Lugones makes the prima facie puzzling claim that we become different selves when we participate in different worlds, and Ortega is right to say that this account only gets more baffling with Lugones's idea that some function of memory nonetheless allows us to compare the multiple selves that we are and can be. Yet despite this (by no means trivial) difficulty on the level of personal identity, the idea of genuinely multiple selves can be read as following directly from phenomenology itself, where being coincides with appearing.[32] We are both constructed and self-constructing according to the possibilities of visibility, agency, and interaction afforded by the worlds (or as terminologically rigorous phenomenologists might prefer, "lifeworlds," "horizons," or "spaces of appearance") in which we participate.[33] Identity is not an invisible and stable entity or even a point of reference from which we can build an analogy to another and their identity, but is itself fundamentally world-relative. According to Lugones, since these worlds are multiple, so too must be the selves that occupy them.

Lugones balks at offering a rigid definition of "worlds," and she almost certainly did not mean to invoke the academic phenomenologists' necessarily unitary, "ultimate totality," "convergence of horizons," and so on. She prefers what she calls an "intuitive account," or what existential phenomenologists might call an ontic one. Nonetheless, I think understanding worlds as "lifeworlds"— a more or less stable backdrop of things, practices, and norms, against which variable spaces of appearance unfold—can help us tease out her claims(though much more about these worlds in their boundedness and possibilities of convergence would ultimately need to be said). In the meantime, Lugones's suggestion that such "worlds" can be experienced as bounded to the extent that selves can really be different within them should not be precipitously dismissed, especially if it can unsettle familiar phenomenological pictures and thereby make phenomenologists more alert about reifying one particular set of background assumptions as necessarily governing all possibilities of world.[34]

Direct perception could probably accept an ontic conception of worlds as just those familiar interactional contexts that ground the immediate, non-inferential perceptibility of intentional and affectively expressive bodies and behaviors where I am able to interact dialogically with you, and vice versa. Bodies become expressive in the context of worlds where their expressions can show up as significant—that is, interactionable. Taking Lugones seriously, we may well suspect that bodies participate in multiple such worlds, and that not all bodily expressions will be equally perceptible/legible in each of them. Unlike analogical inference, where each individual is first of all a closed, independent unit unto themselves, worlds for direct perception and for Lugones can be understood as zones of second-person impact and contact between persons, where identity is constructed and reconstructed through embodied acts of expression and participatory sense-making.[35] By drawing careful attention to the processes of situational, intercorporeal meaning-making, direct perception and interactionism can be deployed to help us see how specific worlds come to construct us in order both to question and to impact the various worldly constraints on ourselves and on others in their expressive bodily being.

Understood in this way, direct perception might retain a critical thrust, allowing us to focus on dynamics within specific worlds rather than exclusively on individually based inference-attitude relays. So where some worry that direct perception might close the gap that allows us to correct false or biased inferences that distort our perceptions of others, a world-traveling praxis aims to excavate features of intercorporeal interaction that might harbor these perceptual and interactional distortions to begin with. World-traveling accomplishes this by showing that no one way of perceiving or interacting exhausts all possible ways of doing so. World-traveling thereby helps us to effect the phenomenological epoché through a "making-strange" of given, familiar worlds, turning our own selves into strangers (rather than tourists, who merely flit from world to world, imposing their assumptions on "foreign" worlds), while never making the impossible demand that we become "unworldly." Nor does this approach in any way deny that attention to individual learning processes and inference correction is either possible or desirable *within* worlds; what it does is shift our gaze to generalized habits of perception that inform many individual inference-attitude relays and are facilitated by certain institutions and interaction patterns that have become "natural."[36]

Building on the lived experience of marginalized persons, Lugones's ontologically queer model of multiple worlds and plurified selves can make sure—over and over again—that direct perception's astute focus on intercorporeal interactionism and sense-making remains at the level of a very thin transcendentalism, one that recognizes our expressive, embodied dialogical interaction as the ground of all understanding of others, without letting any single empirical story about how such interactionism and sense-making plays out become *the* world of interaction. It allows us to remain skeptical about any single type of world or even a single kind of "self"—including a minimal, proprioceptive one—underlying such interactionism. There is no one way for the interactionist story to go, and the very practice of interaction will guarantee that the worlds and selves uncovered will be dynamic, bringing about collisions and convergences—even the creation of new worlds.[37] Bodies will interact with bodies, find different expressive opportunities and limitations, and be interpreted differentially in the diverse worlds to which we travel. Finally, we, the epistemic "subjects," need to be aware that our perception of others may be differentially direct in any single given world, depending on the structure of that world as well as the other worlds each expressive body also participates in. To assume that others present to us as Others through the peculiarly social and interactional opportunities they convey is one thing; to assume that we always have direct perceptual access to all others equally is another, and is to risk committing hermeneutic arrogance through a pros hen equivocation toward a single pragmatic world of structured and structuring interests and interactions. Lugones's focus on the epistemic virtue she calls playfulness, and contrasts to rule-governed play, can make this contrast clearer still.

To be playful, according to Lugones, is to be able to move between worlds precisely because one's identity—understood through embodied expressivity—is not rigidly invested in one world and its metrics of legibility. Direct perception should heed Lugones's suggestion to avoid falling into the trap of relying too heavily on an understanding of play as structured by rules and the agonistics of success defined by these very rules. In such "play," your intentional actions toward the world become intelligible to me, but only through rule-bound norms of competence and contest. I do indeed engage you directly, but generally, as Lugones points out, only as an antagonist (think of Hegelian, Heideggerian, or Sartrian models of Otherness here). To enter into another world, by this account, would be to role-play until "I" develop the requisite competencies to potentially qualify as a winner. Lugones's notion of playfulness, by contrast, is "unruly." It assumes identities are constructed in open-ended and differential relationships to others through embodied and intercorporeal processes of "participatory sense-making."[38] Worlds form more or less stable backdrops of intelligible interaction or play, but playfulness encourages us to enter other worlds in the spirit of creativity and discovery, without an eye to winners and losers.

Imagine children finding a board game at a garage sale. The instructions have been lost, maybe parts have also gone missing through the years. The board and pieces will set up certain parameters—a shared worldly basis—but the children will invent the rules of the game, adapting it as they go along. The only goal is to have fun, and inventiveness, sustained engagement, and humor will be predominant values for as long as the children continue the play. Naturally, the "worlds" the children occupy outside of the game will influence their embodied expression of these values, but so too will the expressive attitudes of the other participants, and each must be particularly attuned to the possibilities the others unfold at every minute. Such playfulness, Lugones suggests, is vital for world travel as distinct from conquest or tourism. Entering other worlds playfully means I may "identify" with you or become your partner in play and try to inhabit your world without fearing that this will undermine who I am or what I have achieved in other worlds (although it always may do just that; the outcome is uncertain). I will encounter and interact with your expressive body in ways that challenge my capacities as bits of my expressive repertoire are taken up while others fall on deaf ears and I will need to try again.

Ridding itself of reliance on rule-governed play and moving in the direction of playfulness, direct perception might turn its empirical gaze toward yet another "early" form of interaction. While folk-psychological approaches to other minds focus on the quite late stage when children can pass false belief tests, a playful direct-perception approach could encourage us to focus on the much earlier and immensely more taxing and complex cognitive processes that go on in children's nonstructured pretend play, where worlds are created and roles adopted and cast off, expanded, and taken in new directions. It is here, perhaps, that we might find keys to processes of expressive, participatory sense-making in action, as well as to understanding the sort of world-traveling that might, in any given world or pragmatic context, enable a critical eye to zero in on the institutions and relations that hamper or encourage expressive possibilities, solidarity, and love.

APRIL N. FLAKNE is Associate Professor of Philosophy at New College of Florida. She is the author of numerous essays on phenomenology, political philosophy, and ethics that have appeared in journals such as *Philosophy Today*, *Hypatia*, and *New German Critique*. She is currently completing a manuscript on the ethics of intercorporeity.

NOTES

1. I have in mind, for example, interaction theory, the "phenomenological proposal," and participatory sense-making. For a summary overview of direct perception, see Shaun Gallagher, "Direct Perception in the Intersubjective Context," *Consciousness and Cognition* 17, no. 2 (2008): 535–43. Dan Zahavi also brings out crucial continuities and divergences among several related approaches in Zahavi, "Empathy and Direct Social Perception: A Phenomenological Proposal," *Review of Philosophy and Psychology* 2, no. 3 (2011): 541–58. Gallagher has recently carefully incorporated insights from Hanne De Jaegher and Ezequiel Di Paolo's notion of "participatory sense-making" as part of his empirical research and sometimes appears to prefer the term "interaction theory" (IT) to direct perception (DP). For details about participatory sense-making as a welcome alternative to the methodological individualism of the other approaches, see De Jaegher and Di Paolo,

"Participatory Sense-Making," *Phenomenology and the Cognitive Sciences* 6, no. 4 (2007): 485–507. For Hanne De Jaegher's critique of direct social perception, see De Jaegher, "Social Understanding through Direct Perception? Yes, by Interacting," *Consciousness and Cognition* 18, no. 2 (2009): 535–42.

2. Gallagher, "Direct Perception."

3. For some of these disagreements, compare Zahavi, "Empathy and Direct Social Perception"; Joel Krueger and Søren Overgaard, "Seeing Subjectivity: Defending a Perceptual Account of Other Minds," *ProtoSociology: Consciousness and Subjectivity* 47 (2012): 239–62; and Pierre Jacob, "The Direct-Perception Model of Empathy: A Critique," *Review of Philosophy and Psychology* 2, no. 3 (2011): 519–40.

4. Pierre Jacob complains that direct perception amounts to an unattractive, "crude" behaviorism. See Jacob, "Direct-Perception Model of Empathy." But this has no warrant once we understand embodied comportments not simply as behavior but as expressive behavior. Expressive means affective-affecting—that is, able to affect, as having been impressed and directing that impression spontaneously outward to a shared world. Expressive behavior neither represents intentions and emotions (as Jacob and the traditional picture would have it), nor does it constitute them as a crude behaviorism contends. Instead, expressive behavior realizes certain flows of emotion and intention and puts them into interactive play where they can be taken up by others within an environment and recycled. Emotions and intentions are not "things" to be represented or constituted, but are energies or flows with combinatory and opportunity potentials. For related but different defenses of DP against the behaviorism charge, see Krueger and Overgaard, "Seeing Subjectivity"; and Zahavi, "Empathy and Direct Social Perception."

5. Shaun Gallagher, *How the Body Shapes the Mind* (Oxford: Oxford University Press, 2005).

6. This reconstruction is consistent with Shaun Gallagher and Dan Zahavi, *The Phenomenological Mind: An Introduction to Philosophy of Mind and Cognitive Science* (New Jersey: Routledge, 2008); Gallagher, *How the Body Shapes the Mind*; and Gallagher, "Direct Perception," although he expresses ambivalence toward a transcendentalist reading in Shaun Gallagher, "In the Shadow of the Transcendental: Social Cognition in Merleau-Ponty and Cognitive Science," in *Corporeity and Affectivity*, ed. Karel Novotny, Pierre Rodrigo, Jenny Slatman, and Silvia Stoller (Leiden: Brill Publishers, 2013). Nonetheless, I think a transcendentalist reading that fits DP into the sort of project that Heinämaa, Hartimo, and Miettine articulate is the most promising track. See Sara Heinämaa, Mira Hartimo, and Timo Miettinen, *Phenomenology and the Transcendental* (New Jersey: Routledge, 2014), 1–20.

7. For the concept of arrogant perception, see Marilyn Frye, "In and Out of Harm's Way: Arrogance and Love," in *The Politics of Reality: Essays in Feminist Theory* (Trumansburg, NY: Crossing Press, 1983); and Maria Lugones, "Playfulness, 'World'-Travelling, and Loving Perception," *Hypatia* 2, no. 2 (1987): 3–19.

8. By "quasi-transcendental" I mean, following Habermas, an inquiry that examines what accepted empirical claims must presuppose, but recognizes, fallibilistically, that these presuppositions may themselves be historically, culturally, or socially contingent.

9. In emphasizing world-traveling as praxis, I am agreeing with Mariana Ortega's interpretation of Lugones. See Mariana Ortega, "Being Lovingly, Knowingly Ignorant: White Feminism and Women of Color," *Hypatia* 21, no. 3 (2006): 56–74.

10. This locution is fairly consistent throughout Gallagher's work, even in his more empirically oriented recent work. Compare Gallagher, *How the Body Shapes the Mind*, and Gallagher, "Direct Perception."

11. Gallagher strives to separate the question of transcendental intersubjectivity from empirical questions of social cognition. See Gallagher, "In the Shadow." While this is a useful precaution, it does not deny that something quite like transcendental intersubjectivity is operative in Gallagher's work. See Gallagher, *How the Body Shapes the Mind*.

12. This dynamic is exposed most baldly in Sartre's appropriation of the master/slave dialectic in part 3 of *Being and Nothingness* and is then rigorously dissected in Beauvoir's *The Second Sex*.

13. *The Phenomenological Mind*, cowritten with Dan Zahavi, provides good insight into DP's debts to the phenomenological tradition. See Gallagher and Zahavi, *Phenomenological Mind*.

14. Gallagher and Zahavi address this concern in the second chapter of *The Phenomenological Mind*, esp. pp. 38–41. They make clear that they are not abandoning the transcendental or a priori aspects of phenomenology even as they move forward into experimental domains.

15. Gallagher and Zahavi, *Phenomenological Mind*; Shaun Gallagher, "On the Possibility of Naturalizing Phenomenology," in *Oxford Handbook of Contemporary Phenomenology*, ed. Dan Zahavi, 70–93 (Oxford: Oxford University Press, 2013).

16. Gallagher, "In the Shadow"; Shaun Gallagher and Somogy Varga, "Social Constraints on the Direct Perception of Emotions and Intentions," *Topoi* 33, no. 1 (2014): 185–89.

17. Shaun Gallagher and Daniel Hutto, "Understanding Others through Primary Interaction and Narrative Practice," in *The Shared Mind: Perspectives on Intersubjectivity*, ed. Jordan Zlatev, Timothy P. Racine, Chris Sinha, and Esa Itkonen, 17–38 (Amsterdam: John Benjamins Publishing, 2008).

18. Gallagher, *How the Body Shapes the Mind*; Gallagher, "Two Problems of Intersubjectivity," *Journal of Consciousness Studies* 16, no. 6 (2009): 292; Gallagher and Zahavi, *Phenomenological Mind*.

19. Gallagher, *How the Body Shapes the Mind*.

20. Ibid., chapters 3 and 9; Gallagher and Zahavi, *Phenomenological Mind*, chapter 9.

21. April N. Flakne, *The Affection In-Between*, forthcoming, chapters 2 and 3.

22. Beata Stawarska has insisted on the need for classical phenomenology to become "dialogical phenomenology," although she is also wary of transcendental claims. See Stawarska, *Between You and I* (Athens: Ohio University Press, 2009).

23. Gallagher draws on De Jaegher and Di Paolo's notion of "participatory sense-making" to make a distinction between "how we understand others" and "how with others we make sense of the world." See Gallagher, "Two Problems"; De Jaegher and Di Paolo, "Participatory Sense-Making." But since, as my discussion of "world-traveling" below should make clear, we precisely make sense of others via our participation with them in making sense of the world, I am not sure it is useful to maintain this distinction.

24. For a brief overview of how DP rejects the argument from analogy as it figures in theory theory and simulation theory, see Gallagher and Zahavi, *Phenomenological Mind*, 181–83. Gallagher goes into more detail in Gallagher, *How the Body Shapes the Mind*, chapter 9.

25. Frye, "In and Out of Harm's Way."
26. Ibid.
27. Ibid.
28. One only need, with Lugones, to think of mother-daughter relationships to realize these boundaries are rarely so pregiven and clear.
29. Ortega, "Being Lovingly."
30. Lugones, "Playfulness, 'World'-Travelling, and Loving Perception," 7.
31. Ortega, "Being Lovingly."
32. Hannah Arendt, *The Life of the Mind* (San Diego: Harcourt Brace Jovanovich, 1978), 19.
33. While Lugones insists that I may, through memory, first personally link my experiences in these different worlds, there is no underlying "I" with discrete boundaries that may form the basis of an analogy. When, in the midst of a current world, I remember myself behaving and appearing in varying and even contradictory ways in another world, I do so from the standpoint of who I am able to be, how I am able to act and appear, in the current world. In short, Lugones insists that the world-traveler should not be viewed as acting or role-playing when she moves between worlds; she really is different people in different worlds. Gail Weiss's example of the mother/intellectual is helpful here. See Gail Weiss, "Mothers/Intellectuals," in *Refiguring the Ordinary* (Bloomington: Indiana University Press, 2008), 181–202.
34. The obvious phenomenological objection would be that we cannot plurify worlds, since "world" is not a "thing" that can be multiplied but just is the regulative idea of a convergence of necessarily multiple horizons that we project. But, agreeing with both this understanding of world and Lugones's insistence on multiple worlds, we may readily see that there may be multiple regulating ideas of totality governing different arenas of appearance. Similarly, an Arendtian might reasonably object that while "public spaces" are multiple, world is not. I think the Merleau-Ponty inspired account of intercorporeity as bodies interactively engaged in world-making blurs the Arendtian line between worldliness and plurality in a positive way.
35. De Jaegher and Di Paolo, "Participatory Sense-Making."
36. There is much more to say about this than I can discuss here. Gallagher and Varga have begun to tackle the problems related to bias and "dehumanization" from an interactionist perspective in Gallagher and Varga, "Social Constraints."
37. For example, we should be suspicious of a notion of "innate" proprioception that gives predetermined bodily boundaries, as well as notions of "narrative competence," that might well be culturally specific. For a discussion of the latter concept, see Gallagher and Hutto, "Understanding Others."
38. De Jaegher and Di Paolo, "Participatory Sense-Making."

BIBLIOGRAPHY

Arendt, Hannah. *The Life of the Mind*. San Diego: Harcourt Brace Jovanovich, 1978.
Flakne, April N. *The Affection In-Between*. Forthcoming.
Frye, Marilyn. "In and Out of Harm's Way: Arrogance and Love." In *The Politics of Reality: Essays in Feminist Theory*, 66–72. Trumansburg, NY: Crossing Press, 1983.
Gallagher, Shaun. "Direct Perception in the Intersubjective Context." *Consciousness and Cognition* 17, no. 2 (2008): 535–43.

---. *How the Body Shapes the Mind.* Oxford: Oxford University Press, 2005.

---. "In the Shadow of the Transcendental: Social Cognition in Merleau-Ponty and Cognitive Science." In *Corporeity and Affectivity,* edited by Karel Novotny, Pierre Rodrigo, Jenny Slatman, and Silvia Stoller, 149-58. Leiden: Brill Publishers, 2013.

---. "On the Possibility of Naturalizing Phenomenology." In *Oxford Handbook of Contemporary Phenomenology,* edited by Dan Zahavi, 70-93. Oxford: Oxford University Press, 2013.

---. "The Socially Extended Mind." *Cognitive Systems Research* 25-26 (2013): 4-12.

---. "Two Problems of Intersubjectivity." *Journal of Consciousness Studies* 16, nos. 6-8 (2009): 289-308.

Gallagher, Shaun, and Daniel Hutto. "Understanding Others through Primary Interaction and Narrative Practice." In *The Shared Mind: Perspectives on Intersubjectivity,* edited by Jordan Zlatev, Timothy P. Racine, Chris Sinha, and Esa Itkonen, 17-38. Amsterdam: John Benjamins Publishing, 2008.

Gallagher, Shaun, and Somogy Varga. "Social Constraints on the Direct Perception of Emotions and Intentions." *Topoi* 33, no. 1 (2014): 185-99.

Gallagher, Shaun, and Dan Zahavi. *The Phenomenological Mind: An Introduction to Philosophy of Mind and Cognitive Science.* New Jersey: Routledge, 2008.

Heinämaa, Sara, Mira Hartimo, and Timo Miettinen. *Phenomenology and the Transcendental.* New Jersey: Routledge, 2014.

Jacob, Pierre. "The Direct-Perception Model of Empathy: A Critique." *Review of Philosophy and Psychology* 2, no. 3 (2011): 519-40.

Jaegher, Hanne de. "Social Understanding through Direct Perception? Yes, by Interacting." *Consciousness and Cognition* 18, no. 2 (2009): 535-42.

Jaegher, Hanne de, and Ezequiel Di Paolo. "Participatory Sense-Making." *Phenomenology and the Cognitive Sciences* 6, no. 4 (2007): 485-507.

Krueger, Joel, and Søren Overgaard. "Seeing Subjectivity: Defending a Perceptual Account of Other Minds." *ProtoSociology: Consciousness and Subjectivity* 47 (2012): 239-62.

Lugones, Maria. "Playfulness, 'World'-Travelling, and Loving Perception." *Hypatia* 2, no. 2 (1987): 3-19.

Ortega, Mariana. "Being Lovingly, Knowingly Ignorant: White Feminism and Women of Color." *Hypatia* 21, no. 3 (2006): 56-74.

---. *In Between: Latina Feminist Phenomenology, Multiplicity, and the Self.* New York: State University of New York Press, 2016.

Stawarska, Beata. *Between You and I.* Athens: Ohio University Press, 2009.

Weiss, Gail. "Mothers/Intellectuals." *Refiguring the Ordinary,* 181-202. Bloomington: Indiana University Press, 2008.

Zahavi, Dan. "Empathy and Direct Social Perception: A Phenomenological Proposal." *Review of Philosophy and Psychology* 2, no. 3 (2011): 541-58.

16 LEADERSHIP IN THE WORLD THROUGH AN ARENDTIAN LENS

RITA A. GARDINER

As MORE WOMEN move into leadership roles within the public sphere, there is a need for feminist phenomenologists to investigate how current leadership research fails to account sufficiently for gender and for the myriad ways we live and lead in the world. Instead, many leadership scholars focus on developing abstract models. One such model I explore here is that of authentic leadership. Specifically, in placing authentic leadership scholars in conversation with Hannah Arendt, I show how her more expansive view of leadership offers insight into the complexities regarding what it might mean to lead authentically. My main contention is that an Arendtian analysis allows us to see something that mainstream leadership theory obscures—namely, that our situated, gendered, embodied relationships influence how we lead in the world.

Thus, in what follows, I interrogate claims put forward by authentic leadership scholars so as to consider a more relational approach to leading that focuses on lived experience. By focusing on lived experience, different aspects of leadership come to the fore that serve to complicate and enrich the narrow framework put forward by some scholars. In particular, I explore the descriptive accounts of two senior women leaders to indicate a different approach to questions of authenticity in leadership that takes gendered, embodied experience into account. From their sharing of words and worlds, these accounts highlight Arendt's contention that leadership needs to be responsive to situated, embodied relationships—that is, it must account for how we lead in the world.

To begin, I lay out the main tenets of authentic leadership scholarship and then contrast scholars' claims with Arendt's conceptualization of leadership.

I show how an Arendtian approach can provide us with a richer perspective from which to understand leadership. Next, I turn to the narrative accounts. Viewing these leaders' narratives, alongside an Arendtian discussion, points to new ways of thinking about a genuine style of leadership that connects us to the world.

AUTHENTIC LEADERSHIP

In this section I consider the conceptual underpinnings of authentic leadership and contrast prevailing assumptions within the scholarship with that of Arendt as well as some recent criticism of the field. Authentic leadership is a relatively new theory in leadership studies that emerged earlier this century out of a perceived need to deal with leaders' ethical shortcomings.[1] Due to ongoing scandals in the corporate and political arenas, it was widely felt that people were losing confidence in leaders; Bill George contended that authenticity could be the solution to assuage leaders' wrongdoings.[2] Yet what began as an ethical inquiry into leadership malpractice has rapidly turned into a prescriptive theory that does little to explain fully why authenticity might be valuable to leadership praxis. Instead, the scholarship offers upbeat assertions, describing authentic leaders as "confident, optimistic, hopeful, [and] resilient."[3] These positive traits, it is argued, enable authentic leaders to have a greater likelihood in achieving personal and institutional goals. Moreover, when leaders add authenticity to their tool kit, it serves as a "leadership multiplier" that aids individual and organizational success.[4] It appears that authentic leaders not only have the wherewithal to improve employee morale through their charismatic personalities, but they also possess the ability to increase organizational effectiveness. In short, authentic leaders are perceived as not only efficient and ethical but good for the bottom line.

In much of the scholarship, however, there is a lack of attention to context and to understanding the diversity of leadership experience. This inattention, it seems to me, is fueled by the desire of some scholars to define a leader's authenticity through quantitative means. For example, it is argued that a leader's authenticity, or lack thereof, is measurable through specific techniques, such as statistical analysis. This statistical data enables scholars to prove their assertion that authentic leadership is comprised of four traits: self-awareness, relational transparency, internalized moral perspective, and balanced processing.[5] No matter the context, it is presumed that if a leader demonstrates these particular traits, she will act ethically. But this focus on leadership traits fails to describe, in any meaningful way, why authenticity is relevant to leadership.

Indeed, a critical interrogation of authentic leadership scholarship reveals that this topic is often approached from what Hannah Arendt refers to as the "Archimedean standpoint."[6] For Arendt, the Archimedean standpoint represents a perspective abstracted from the world. In the case of the positivist approach adopted by many authentic leadership scholars, what begins as a theoretical supposition becomes, over time, a "universally valid law."[7] Yet this is a law devoid of context and specificity and, as such, is not representative of lived, embodied experience. In taking up this view from nowhere, these leadership scholars privilege abstract thinking over and above the web of relationships that Arendt saw as fundamental to understanding the plural nature of human existence. Phenomenologically, we might say that authentic leadership exhibits a kind of worldlessness, since it is founded on abstract ideas that fail to convey adequately the complexity of human experience.[8]

Much of the scholarship on authentic leadership is rooted in positive psychology. Seen through the lens of positive psychology, authentic leadership offers leaders a moral script they can learn so as to perform their duties in a particular manner. However, I perceive scholars' desire for a definitive way of measuring what constitutes authentic leadership as part of a symptomatic problem in positivistic research whereby scholars confuse knowledge with meaning. As Arendt tells us, these are not the same. One of the problems is the desire to replicate empirical studies and then regard them as a form of universal truth. But what this does, as Arendt reminds us, is to mistake the quest for knowledge with that of meaning. Simply put, one cannot predict a person's ethical behavior, or lack thereof, from a set of predetermined factors, as this way of thinking ignores the role of contingency in human affairs.

Although Bruce Avolio and Ketan Mhatre maintain there is extensive empirical evidence to back up their claims about authentic leadership, critics suggest otherwise.[9] For instance, Mats Alvesson and Stefan Sveningsson contend that scholars who promote authentic leadership indulge in tautological thinking.[10] Hence, the supposition that authentic leaders are good for organizations because they act in an authentic manner is little more than circular reasoning. Such reasoning does not help us to understand what authenticity might consist of, nor to gauge whether authenticity, in and of itself, has anything to offer to leaders. In their attempt to define how authentic leaders can effect positive change, scholars fail to think through the conceptual underpinnings of authenticity.[11] What is more, in their desire to predict a leader's authenticity based on specific characteristics, scholars attempt to quantify the unquantifiable. Despite their claims, however, scholars cannot verify a leader's authenticity through empirical methods, since, as Arendt tells us, we can never know for sure whether a person is conveying the truth of their convictions or being disingenuous.[12] In their attempt to quantify a leader's authenticity, or lack thereof, these scholars inadvertently cover over what is most precious—that is, the uniqueness of each person's lived experience.

When we think alongside Arendt, we become aware that this focus on authenticity may not be helpful in explaining why leaders engage in ethical malpractice. For example, the notion that we can know whether a person's action is in keeping with their intention is erroneous. Our intentions, like our thoughts, never make an appearance in the world. Rather, it is through the revelatory power of speech and action that we come to understand one another. But whether this revealing is an indication of a person's authenticity is impossible to tell. So although a leader might appear to be authentic in the terms that authentic leadership scholars describe, we can never know for sure if that person is being genuine or not. Furthermore, Arendt maintains that while our motives may be heartfelt, our intentions become suspect when they appear before others. This is because a person's intentions may not be as they seem on the surface, since they may have ulterior motives, such as hypocrisy and deceit. Whenever there is a demand that people display their innermost intentions, according to Arendt, it effects a transformation—that is, it turns actors into hypocrites. Clearly, we cannot just assume that because a person claims to be an authentic leader this is indeed the case. Neither can we take it for granted that because our intentions are honorable they will necessarily be read that way by others. Yet it is noteworthy that what is missing from most discussions of authentic leadership is any discussion of the effects of deceit or hypocrisy.

Instead, much of the scholarship equates authentic leadership with moral goodness. But, following Machiavelli, Arendt maintains that it is not whether a leader is good that matters, but whether her actions are good for the world.[13] She also contends that natural goodness cannot make an appearance without becoming corrupted once it is made public. On the political stage, for example, this search for goodness can turn into a reckless pursuit of those whose views differ from that of the leader. Indeed, we have countless examples of regimes attempting to unearth those who are disloyal to a particular cause. But, as Arendt shows in *On Revolution*, the desire to unmask a hypocrite, such as Robespierre tried to do, is an impossible task, since we cannot see into another's soul. In any event, there is nothing to suggest that a leader's proclaimed authenticity will necessarily lead to positive societal outcomes or is, in and of itself, necessarily good.[14]

In this section I have outlined some of the conceptual underpinnings of the theory known as authentic leadership. I have suggested that scholars who put forward this theory are prone to overlook difference in favor of a more regimented approach. In their attempt to define the specific traits that make a leader authentic, paradoxically, what is being missed is the uniqueness of individual experience. This problem arises from this quest for the truth, which, many of those engaged in authentic leadership scholarship suppose, can be unearthed through statistical measurements. But this quest for the truth is erroneous, since, as previously stated, we cannot know the truth of another's intentions. Moreover, the desire for consistency through statistical measurement can lead to a flattening of individual experience. By focusing their attention on what makes a leader similar to another, scholars have not paid enough attention to particularities. In a phenomenological exploration, both aspects must be kept in view. In highlighting the drawbacks with scholars' desire to define authenticity in a categorical manner, I contend that this abstract perspective does not offer us insight into leadership. By contrast, I suggest that Arendt offers us a more nuanced perspective on leadership, as I now seek to demonstrate.

LEADERSHIP

Arendt had a very different way of conceptualizing leadership than that delineated by authentic leadership scholars.[15] For her, leadership functions best when it arises out of individuals working together rather than directed by a person in charge. When people come together over a common cause, she argues, they discover the strength that derives from collective action. This is why Arendt maintains it is possible for a small group of concerted individuals to overthrow a dictatorship. Hence, the power that comes from collective leadership can have a liberatory effect.

Arendt notes that the emphasis on the individual leader, as opposed to a more collective way of conceptualizing leadership, has a long history in Western thought.[16] She traces this narrow view of leadership back to Plato and his desire to separate thinking from action. For Plato, the contingency inherent in action was troublesome; what was required was a way to foster a sense of control. Otherwise, people were no more than puppets on a stage at the mercy of the whims of Fate. Hence, Plato wanted to build a society founded upon laws that would help to assuage the anxiety caused by the contingency of action. With this emphasis on lawmaking, we also see the emergence of the individual leader whose primary responsibility became "the capacity to rule one's self."[17] In time, this focus on self-rulership led to "the fallacy of the strong man who is powerful because he is alone."[18] Instead of the collective equality of those citizens of the *polis*, the criterion for ruling was based on a separation between the individual leader and the led. The separation between the one who envisions something and those who carry out the task ushered in a hierarchical understanding of rulership.

This view of leadership as rulership, according to Arendt, serves to debase an "authentic understanding of human freedom."[19] Fundamental to an Arendtian notion of leadership is the interrelation between human freedom and collective action. From this perspective, then, freedom and power are impossible without the ability to act in concert with others. Furthermore, the disconnection between leader and led is potentially harmful, since a leader's isolation can create an atmosphere of fear and suspicion among others. Rather than seeing the leader as no more than *primus et pares*, what we are left with is a conception of leadership that is negative vis-à-vis collective freedom, because plurality is usurped in favor of sovereignty. In extreme circumstances, as Arendt demonstrates in her assessment of why Nazi officers like Adolf Eichmann refused to take responsibility for their actions, unquestioning obedience to a leader can result in devastating consequences.[20] This is why we need to move away from a solipsistic way of thinking about leadership, which gives excessive power to any one individual.

The problem with too much focus on the individual leader, as evidenced in much of the authentic leadership literature, is that the original meaning of leadership as collective action is covered over. It is the emphasis on the power of collective action rather than individual control that makes Arendt's work so important to rethinking questions of leadership. What an Arendtian perspective brings to light, therefore, is the notion that collaboration, as opposed to control and command, must form the basis of leadership. Thus, instead of a hierarchical way of thinking about the solitary leader who decides on what others do, Arendt provides us with a relational approach to leadership.

One way to think about leadership in a relational way is through the medium of storytelling. If, as Arendt argues, storytelling is fundamental to lived experience, then it may be productive to consider how narrative accounts help us think through what a more relational model of leadership might look like. This is what I seek to explore through the descriptive accounts that follow. Before doing so, we need to understand why Arendt regarded narrative as essential to understanding how we live in the world.

NARRATIVE

For Arendt, narrative represents a central component of our lives, since it serves to illuminate each person's unique "thisness."[21] Unlike a scientific mode of writing, narrative is both unique, in the sense that a story concerns someone, and plural, insofar as stories are part of the interwoven fabric of life. What we can say is that there is a unique story for each person who lives, has lived, or will live. However, a person's unique story does not concern the individual alone, since it is part of the intricate human fabric that Arendt refers to as "the web of relationships."[22] Thus, our stories are always part of a wider societal fabric that connects us to others through time and space. Yet while we may intend to produce a truthful account of our lives, Arendt tells us that this is impossible, because we cannot see ourselves from all sides. For this reason, it is the role of the storyteller to recount another person's narrative in a meaningful way.

Through the medium of storytelling, we memorialize the actions of others. It is due to the ephemeral nature of action that we need the narrator to bear witness to the narrative accounts of others. From an Arendtian perspective, stories are plural in the sense that they are multiple but also unique in that they belong to someone. As Jacques Taminiaux observes, Arendt views narrative as revealing, not least because storytellers employ a plurality of viewpoints from which to assess a particular action.[23] Unlike philosophers, Arendt contends that storytellers are able to put themselves into the minds of others without taking a definitive stance. And it is narrative's focus on lived experience, as opposed to abstract knowledge, that may offer valuable insight into how leadership is connected to the social world.

Previously, I highlighted some drawbacks with scholars' desire to define authentic leadership in a categorical fashion. I also argued that this abstract perspective does not offer us a well-rounded view. Conversely, storytelling makes us aware of the material reality that abstract accounts overlook. As we turn our attention to the narrative accounts of two women leaders, what comes to the fore is the diversity of how ideas of leadership are affected by the actions of others. These accounts are not meant to confirm, or deny, whether these particular leaders are authentic; I have already stated that such truth-seeking is impossible to confirm, since, as Arendt tells us, we cannot see inside another's heart. Nevertheless, narrative accounts may open up ways of thinking about leadership that are more encompassing of the plurality of human experience. In so doing, narrative may provide us with a different way of thinking about leadership that is more responsive to situated, embodied relationships.

LEADERSHIP IN THE WORLD

As part of a broader investigation into authentic leadership, I interviewed ten senior women leaders in the higher education sector from three different countries. I chose to interview women because, to date, little has been written about the effect of gender on authentic leadership.[24] My primary research question was: How do senior women leaders experience authenticity, or lack thereof, in their everyday working lives?[25] Although I had anticipated that the narrative accounts these women leaders shared would be about their own actions in the workplace, the most expressive narratives were about how others, principally their mothers, had acted in a way that encouraged them not only to want to lead but also to try to make a difference. As such, these accounts point to a different way of thinking about the connections among authenticity and leadership than most mainstream scholarship that takes into account the diversity of lived experience and how this affects leaders. In what follows, I concentrate on two narrative accounts. The first account is from Jill, a college president; the second is from Laura, who runs a university research institute.

Jill grew up in a small working-class town in the northeastern part of America. In our conversation, she discussed her desire to lead in an authentic manner, which she connected with a feminist ethic of care. This connection with care and authenticity was critical to how Jill perceived her leadership responsibilities. Thinking about leadership in this manner was partially a result of earlier experiences where she had witnessed gender and class discrimination. These experiences encouraged Jill to think about leadership alongside questions of social and gender justice. In the following extract, she describes how her mother's leadership actions played a powerful role in encouraging Jill to see that it was possible to try to challenge gender and class prejudice:

> I worked with my mother in the summers in a light switch factory. I saw how institutional or organizational cultures perpetuate and reinforce classism and sexism.... There were no men on the factory floor. The men were in the loading docks, or in the catering trucks, or in the boss's office. The factory workers were women doing piecework. I saw through my mother, in her role as a shop steward, how you could confront head-on issues of classism and sexism. This engendered in me a sense of possibilities in terms of women's leadership.

In this description, we see how the factory where Jill worked alongside her mother was divided along gender lines. Her mother's willingness to take an active role as union shop steward encouraged Jill to believe that she too might have leadership potential. Her mother's union activism thus engendered "a sense of possibilities" about Jill's own future prospects.

Jill then went on to describe a difficult period in her life when, due to her mother's illness and inability to work, they were forcibly evicted from their home. The ensuing experience of homelessness led Jill to recognize the arbitrary nature of social inequity:

> I lived for a while on the streets with my mother and got to know that people often don't have control over the circumstances of their lives through no fault of their own. . . . I have seen how people have been marginalized and disenfranchised. As a consequence, I try to lead with a sense of empathy and a commitment to social justice.

Rather than viewing this experience of homelessness as a negative event, Jill told me, it offered her a deeper comprehension of the frailty of human life. This understanding led her to try to lead in an ethical way. For example, within the work environment this meant she tried to create a space where people felt able to speak about difficult issues and talk through dilemmas openly. Jill maintained that the primary purpose of a leader was to try to foster collaboration through consensus-building. In her view the leader's role is one of being a facilitator and an advocate for others. Jill's account reaffirms Arendt's notion of the leader as someone who views themselves as part of, rather than isolated from, others in her community.

We turn now to Laura, who described the powerful effects that growing up in a rural village in Jamaica had on her ideas about leadership. She told me that her village was divided along gender lines—in her words, "The designated heads of households were not those of management." This gender division of labor created leadership opportunities for women, although they were not perceived as leaders by most people in the village. Yet, in Laura's eyes the women who ran the local institutions displayed important leadership qualities such as "purpose and integrity." Moreover, it was the village women who made things happen through their concerted action. In one instance Laura described how her mother took on a leadership role by rallying support from other villagers to set about rebuilding the church after a devastating hurricane. In Laura's retelling of her mother's action, we obtain a glimpse of how one person can provide the necessary spark to arouse collective action. This type of leadership depends not on the leader's separation from others, but on their intrinsic connection to the people's lived environment.

Arendt argues that in a crisis a leader emerges organically. Therefore, in crisis situations it is not a person's positional authority that matters but whether they are willing to step up when they are needed. Although Laura told me that her mother would never have called herself a leader, for Laura, her mother was an exemplar of someone who took the necessary action to galvanize support in response to community needs.

Later in our discussion, Laura juxtaposed the freedom and joy she felt growing up with the shock of racism and feelings of marginalization she experienced as a university student in Canada. She described how these experiences shaped her views:

> Being a black woman is not alone a disadvantage, because it allowed me to be very aware of whom I was as an individual. . . . Other women who were not minorities were going to university for the ride, because the environment said you are entitled to it. But I had women role models who kept saying to me you must "defy the gods."

This experience of being marginalized encouraged Laura to think deeply about who she was and to develop her own style of leadership, modeled on those women who had taught her so much as a child. Laura told me that the voices of the village women helped her to stay strong during moments of despair. This visceral connection between Laura and the women of her village enabled her to obtain the courage needed to deal with racist taunts and feelings of isolation. Thus her account reveals how much we sediment our embodied relationships.

Laura's past experiences of racism encourage her to speak out whenever she witnesses prejudice in the workplace. As she states, "If I see a wrong, I will redress it. If you don't want me to speak about a wrong that I see, don't engage me, because I will not compromise on things that are wrong." Leadership, for Laura, means being willing to take a stand against prejudice. Additionally, she expressed her desire to be "a leader who has the capacity to change or to talk with others to change things that I alone can't change." As with Jill, we see a recognition that it is through working with others that a leader is able to effect change.

It is by sharing our stories of vulnerability that we open ourselves up to the world. I perceive links between these narrative accounts and Arendt's comparison of the parvenu and the pariah. Arendt argues that it is only the social pariah who is able to remain true to her ideals. As such, being on the margins of society can enable the pariah to "instinctively discover human dignity in general long before Reason has made it the foundation of morality."[26] In Jill's case, it was her experience of homelessness, as well as her stint as a factory worker, that made her more fully aware of social inequities. This awareness was instrumental in her desire to lead in an ethical manner. For Laura, it was the visceral, embodied connection she felt with the women of her village that enabled her to obtain the strength to overcome racial prejudice and combat loneliness. Over time, it seems that, for some leaders, being on the margins of society enables them to better understand the vulnerability and contingency of people's lives. These experiences were important to how these women leaders viewed leadership as not principally about self but rather about self in relationship.

What emerges from these women's descriptive accounts is how past events can have a lasting effect on present and future action. It is noteworthy that these women chose to share stories from their childhood as exemplars to describe their understanding of authentic leadership.[27] According to Arendt, what encourages people to treat others as equals emerges from "a childhood world in which mutual respect and unconditional trust, a universal humanity and a genuine, almost naive contempt for social and ethnic distinctions was taken for granted."[28] Our memories can guide us in remembering instances that influence our way of thinking about ethical action. Over time, we learn to emulate those whom we cherish, because they provide us with exemplars. Perhaps, in so doing, we are able to bring forth a more relational approach to leadership that has at its base a desire to care for others. For these women leaders, questions of authenticity in leadership could not be disentangled from their lived experiences. As such, these narrative accounts serve to contrast the Archimedean perspective taken up by many authentic leadership scholars and bring us back to the "little things."

CONCLUSION

By considering authentic leadership through an Arendtian lens, we discover a richer perspective that is more responsive to situated, embodied experience. We perceive that leadership shows itself in many different guises; the problem is that oftentimes we forget to look beneath the surface. Rather than focusing on a person's position in an institutional setting, these research findings suggest that current definitions of authentic leadership are too narrowly defined to explain how leadership works in everyday life. By interweaving Arendt's comments on leaders alongside these women's descriptive accounts, we perceive how leadership is intrinsically connected to a world of embodied, intersubjective relationships. These women's accounts serve to illustrate instances of positive and negative connection among people in different situations. What emerges from these narratives is recognition of the vulnerability of individual life, as well as a more relational way of thinking about leadership. This relational way of thinking meshes with Arendt's more expansive way of thinking about leadership.

Yet too often the focus on leadership is where most of us think power resides. By making institutional life the center of attention, it is possible to underestimate, or even ignore, the important leadership work that is carried out in the home or in volunteer or church groups. This situated knowledge, if considered at all, is perceived as less valuable than the "business" of leadership. This is a problem because it denies us the important leadership lessons that we learn from our mothers and other childhood mentors.

In conclusion, we need diverse kinds of stories if we are to understand the effects that leadership has on individuals and those they lead. I suggest that narrative accounts can help us rethink leadership in a way that is more open to being-in-the-world. It is time, therefore, to rethink notions of authenticity in leadership by paying closer attention to situated, embodied reality. Perhaps by doing so we will obtain more insight into ethical ways of leading that connect us to the world.

RITA A. GARDINER is Assistant Professor in the Faculty of Education at the University of Western Ontario. Recent publications include *Gender, Authenticity, and Leadership: Thinking with Arendt* (Palgrave MacMillan, 2015).

NOTES

1. In the last decade, more than 120,000 articles, books, and blog posts have been written on the topic of authentic leadership (internet search by author, November 2014).
2. Bill George, *Authentic Leadership: Rediscovering the Secrets to Creating Lasting Value* (Cambridge, MA: Harvard University Press, 2003), 1–6.
3. Bruce J. Avolio and William L. Gardner, "Authentic Leadership Development: Getting to the Root of Positive Forms of Leadership," *Leadership Quarterly* 16, no. 2 (2005): 317.
4. Adrian Chan, Sean T. Hannah, and William L. Gardner, "Veritable Authentic Leadership: Emergence, Functioning, and Impacts," in *Authentic Leadership Theory and Practice: Origins, Effects, and Developments*, ed. William L. Gardner, Bruce J. Avolio, and Fred O. Walumbwa (Amsterdam: Elsevier, 2005), 4.
5. Avolio and Gardner, "Authentic Leadership Development," 317.
6. Hannah Arendt, *The Human Condition* (Chicago: University of Chicago Press, 1958), 11.
7. Ibid., 263.
8. It is noteworthy that few publications make mention of the conceptual underpinnings of authenticity in hermeneutic, existential phenomenology. Even when phenomenology is discussed, it is often in the form of a casual gesture, such as a footnote to the work of Martin Heidegger. See, for example, P. M. Algera and M. Lips-Wiersma, "Radical Authentic Leadership: Co-Creating the Conditions under Which All Members of the Organization Can Be Authentic," *Leadership Quarterly* 23 (2011): 118–31.
9. Bruce J. Avolio and Ketan H. Mhatre, "Advances in Theory and Research on Authentic Leadership," in *Handbook of Positive Organizational Scholarship*, ed. Gretchen S. Spreitzer and Kim S. Cameron (Oxford: Oxford University Press, 2011), 772–83.
10. Mats Alvesson and Stefan Sveningsson, "Essay: Authentic Leadership Critically Revisited," in *Authentic Leadership: Clashes, Convergences, and Coalescences*, ed. Donna Ladkin and Chellie Spiller (Cheltenham, UK: Edward Elgar, 2013), 45.
11. Elsewhere, I trace the conceptual underpinnings of authenticity back through hermeneutic phenomenology to Enlightenment notions of the gendered subject. See Rita Gardiner, *Gender, Authenticity, and Leadership: Thinking with Arendt* (London: Palgrave Macmillan, 2015), 57–61.
12. Hannah Arendt, *The Life of the Mind*, ed. Mary McCarthy (San Diego: Harcourt, 2001), 40.

13. Hannah Arendt, "Collective Responsibility," in *Amor Mundi: Explorations in the Faith and Thought of Hannah Arendt*, ed. James William Bernauer (Dordrecht: Martinus Nijhoff Publishers, 1987), 151.
14. Arendt, *On Revolution* (New York: Viking Compass Books, 1963), 91–94.
15. Arendt, *Human Condition*, 189–90.
16. Ibid.
17. Ibid., 224.
18. Ibid., 40.
19. Ibid., 225.
20. Arendt, "Personal Responsibility under Dictatorship," in *Responsibility and Judgment*, ed. Jerome Kohn (New York: Schocken Books, 2003), 40–47.
21. Arendt, *Human Condition*, 181–87.
22. Ibid., 183.
23. Jacques Taminiaux, *The Thracian Maid and the Professional Thinker: Arendt and Heidegger*, ed. and trans. Michael Gendre (Albany: State University of New York Press, 1997), 16.
24. Two notable exceptions are Alice H. Eagly, "Achieving Relational Authenticity in Leadership: Does Gender Matter?" *Leadership Quarterly* 16, no. 3 (2005): 459–74; and Amanda Sinclair, "Can I Really Be Me? The Challenges for Women Leaders Constructing Authenticity," in *Authentic Leadership: Clashes, Convergences, and Coalescences*, ed. Donna Ladkin and Chellie Spiller (Cheltenham, UK: Edward Elgar, 2013), 239–52.
25. In concert with Arendt, rather than analyzing these interviews in a thematic manner, I approach these narrative accounts through her mode of visiting. For Arendt, visiting is a way we try to suspend our own ideas about a particular concept so as to take into account diverse viewpoints. These different viewpoints enable us to have a much wider frame from which to judge a particular aspect of life or a specific concept. For more on this topic, see Lisa J. Disch, *Hannah Arendt and the Limits of Philosophy* (Ithaca, NY: Cornell University Press, 1994), 157–64.
26. Hannah Arendt, *Rahel Varnhagen: The Life of a Jewish Woman*, trans. Richard Winston and Clara Winston (New York: Harcourt Brace Jovanovich, 1974), 224.
27. I think that what is going on here is similar to what Samah Sabra describes as "critical memory work." For Sabra, critical memory work serves to open up different perspectives on the world that may have been overlooked. Critical memory work differs from nostalgic remembering in that it allows us to see how the intersections of identity are experienced differently depending upon time and place. See Samah Sabra, "Reimagining Home and Belonging: Feminism, Nostalgia, and Critical Memory," *Resources for Feminist Research* 33 (2008): 1–21.
28. Hannah Arendt, *Men in Dark Times* (New York: Harcourt Brace Jovanovich, 1968), 41.

BIBLIOGRAPHY

Algera, P. M., and M. Lips-Wiersma. "Radical Authentic Leadership: Co-Creating the Conditions under Which All Members of the Organization Can Be Authentic." *Leadership Quarterly* 23 (2011): 118–31.

Alvesson, Mats, and Stefan Sveningsson. "Essay: Authentic Leadership Critically Revisited." In *Authentic Leadership: Clashes, Convergences, and Coalescences*, edited by Donna Ladkin and Chellie Spiller, 39–55. Cheltenham, UK: Edward Elgar, 2013.

Arendt, Hannah. "Collective Responsibility." In *Amor Mundi: Explorations in the Faith and Thought of Hannah Arendt*, edited by James William Bernauer, 43–50. Dordrecht: Martinus Nijhoff Publishers, 1987.

———. *The Human Condition*. Chicago: University of Chicago Press, 1958.

———. *Lectures on Kant's Political Philosophy*. Edited by Ronald Beiner. Chicago: University of Chicago Press, 1982.

———. *The Life of the Mind*. Edited by Mary McCarthy. San Diego: Harcourt, 2001.

———. *Men in Dark Times*. New York: Harcourt Brace Jovanovich, 1968.

———. *On Revolution*. New York: Viking Compass Books, 1963.

———. "Personal Responsibility under Dictatorship." In *Responsibility and Judgment*, edited by Jerome Kohn, 17–49. New York: Schocken Books, 2003.

———. *Rahel Varnhagen: The Life of a Jewish Woman*. Translated by Richard and Clara Winston. New York: Harcourt Brace Jovanovich, 1974.

Ashman, Ian, and John Lawler. "Theorizing Leadership Authenticity: A Sartrean Perspective." *Leadership* 8, no. 4 (2012): 327–44.

Avolio, Bruce J., and William L. Gardner. "Authentic Leadership Development: Getting to the Root of Positive Forms of Leadership." *Leadership Quarterly* 16, no. 2 (2005): 315–38.

Avolio, Bruce J., and Ketan H. Mhatre. "Advances in Theory and Research on Authentic Leadership." In *Handbook of Positive Organizational Scholarship*, edited by Gretchen S. Spreitzer and Kim S. Cameron, 772–83. Oxford: Oxford University Press, 2011.

Chan, Adrian, Sean T. Hannah, and William L. Gardner. "Veritable Authentic Leadership: Emergence, Functioning, and Impacts." In *Authentic Leadership Theory and Practice: Origins, Effects, and Developments*, edited by William L. Gardner, Bruce J. Avolio, and Fred O. Walumbwa, 3–43. Amsterdam: Elsevier, 2005.

Disch, Lisa J. *Hannah Arendt and the Limits of Philosophy*. Ithaca, NY: Cornell University Press, 1994.

Eagly, Alice H. "Achieving Relational Authenticity in Leadership: Does Gender Matter?" *Leadership Quarterly* 16, no. 3 (2005): 459–74.

Gardiner, Rita A. *Gender, Authenticity, and Leadership: Thinking with Arendt*. London: Palgrave Macmillan, 2015.

George, Bill. *Authentic Leadership: Rediscovering the Secrets to Creating Lasting Value* Cambridge, MA: Harvard University Press, 2003.

Sabra, Samah. "Re-imagining Home and Belonging: Feminism, Nostalgia, and Critical Memory." *Resources for Feminist Research* 33 (2008): 1–21.

Sinclair, Amanda. "Essay: Can I Really Be Me? The Challenges for Women Leaders Constructing Authenticity." In *Authentic Leadership: Clashes, Convergences, and Coalescences*, edited by Donna Ladkin and Chellie Spiller, 239–52. Cheltenham, UK: Edward Elgar, 2013.

Taminiaux, Jacques. *The Thracian Maid and the Professional Thinker: Arendt and Heidegger*. Edited and translated by Michael Gendre. Albany: State University of New York Press, 1997.

17 IDENTITY-IN-DIFFERENCE TO AVOID INDIFFERENCE

EMILY S. LEE

INTRODUCTION: THE THREAT OF ABSOLUTE DIFFERENCE

Sexual and racial differences matter. Indeed, rejecting facile understandings of sameness at the heart of universalism, philosophers of race speculate that racial differences are ontologically relevant. At the same time, absolute difference can slip into indifference. For example, Glen Loury points to disparate statistics among racial groups that occasion no alarm from the majority populations.[1] As Maria Lugones describes such indifference, "The more independent I am, the more independent I am left to be. Their world and their integrity do not require me at all."[2] My concern is that although we have yet to fully understand what difference means and what difference difference makes, absolute sameness and absolute difference are not true to phenomenological experience. Hence, I focus on the idea that although differences matter, recognizing our commonality is just as important. This essay provides a brief history of the philosophical relation between identity and difference from its metaphysical origins in monism and dualism to G.W.F. Hegel's first formulation of a dialectical relation between identity and difference. I present four relations of identity-in-difference within Maurice Merleau-Ponty's phenomenology. The phenomenological idea of identity-in-difference prevails in Merleau-Ponty's later works and functions at least nascently in his earlier works, in both its epistemic and ontologic sense. Keeping in mind this phenomenological sense of identity-in-difference with its emphasis on integration and tension, I argue for upholding the value of both difference and sameness in developing our understandings of race.

THE ONTOLOGIZING DIFFERENCE OF RACE

A widely accepted approach in race theory positions race as socially constructed. Recently, race theorists explain that such social/cultural meanings about race have sedimented so as to not only be seen as natural but to also effectively function as natural. Jeremy Weate writes, "Instead of remaining an *historical* ascription of identity (albeit a false one applied by a white mythos), the schema becomes 'naturalized' as a *condition* skin. The epidermal marks the stage where historical construction and contingency is effaced and replaced with the facticity of flesh."[3] Racial markers are so embedded in our social world that we no longer recognize these meanings as social constructions. Lewis Gordon insists that the process of naturalizing what is socially constructed makes an ontological difference: "Ontology can be regarded not only as a study of what 'is' the case, but also a study of *what is treated as being the case* and *what is realized as the contradiction of being the case*. . . . Ontologies often ascribe necessity instead of contingency to being."[4] Gordon understands ontology as including this phenomenon of treating the socially constructed understandings of race as natural because of the very real human condition in which we cannot distinguish the cultural and the natural. The cultural interweaves and embeds with the natural as they influence each other.

Advocacy of this understanding of ontology—an ontology of race—has been building within philosophy of race.[5] One particular expression that emphasizes race as difference lies in subaltern studies. Gareth Williams writes about the challenge to the efforts of colonized subjects and their descendants to remember a different history—the subalterns' history. He states, "The knowability and representability of subaltern experience—of its moments of violence, of suffering, and of many of the scars left behind by the histories of domination—is actively suppressed within the time horizon of capital itself."[6] The postcolonial period thrives on an epistemic drive that demands focusing only on the seeming advancements of capitalism. As such, history cannot help but erase—must erase—the narratives of the lives of people who do not support these grand developmentalist narratives, the lives of people who did not benefit from the so-called advancements of development and capitalism. Against forces that prioritize such a unified history, Williams and other postcolonial writers address the epistemic difficulty of conveying subaltern experiences as a distinctly separate history that cannot be wrapped within the hegemonic developmentalist narrative of history. Consistent with the post-structuralist struggle against totalizing narratives, Williams demands recognition of absolute difference—a different history and consequently different lives—and he warily regards any attempts at recognizing sameness because of its unavoidable subsumption into the dominant history.[7]

I find these positions incredibly persuasive. But with Weate's and Gordon's conclusion that racial differences constitute ontological differences and Williams's insistence on the different histories and lives of the colonized, I am concerned that these positions threaten the possibility of racially distinct subjects sharing a social horizon, living in the same world, and communicating with one another. I fear that these positions lend themselves to an understanding of racially different individuals as living radically separate lives.

THE RELEVANCE OF DIFFERENCES OF THE BODY

In contrast to the Cartesian tradition's tendency to separate the material conditions of subjectivity from thought, Merleau-Ponty scholars have argued that the particularities of human embodiment influence our cognitive development and capabilities. Perhaps most prominent among these figures is Hubert Dreyfus, who maintains that human bodies' upright postures, human bodily distinctions of front and back, as well as the limitations of human body movements impact human beings' cognitive development.[8] Dreyfus explains that the form of the input, as constrained by the material structure of the body, directly influences thought. Referring to neural networks designed to simulate cognitive processes, Dreyfus writes:

> The body-dependence of shared generalizations puts disembodied neural networks at a serious disadvantage when it comes to learning to cope in the human world. Nothing is more alien to our form of life than a network with no varying degrees of access, no up-down, front-back orientation, no preferred way of moving, such as moving forward more easily than backward, and no emotional response to its failures and successes.[9]

In other words, research with neural networks shows that embodiment intrinsically conditions cognitive development and thinking. In recent philosophy of cognitive science, much work explores cognition as extended, embodied, embedded, enactive, and amalgamated—all of this research acknowledges the integral tie of the material circumstances of consciousness.[10] The mind and the body cannot be separated; they are not different in kind. The mind does not completely or solely control the body; human embodiment conditions and structures thinking.

More than the general features of human embodiment such as two-leggedness, race theorists focus on the specific differences in embodiment, especially as reflected in the bodily differences of race. For, after all, these specific features of the body figure as "an entire orientation, a framework" for living subjectivity.¹¹ Gordon's dispute with Kwame Appiah centers precisely on the distinction between the primary/essential features of the human being and the secondary/contingent/accidental features. Gordon writes, "The problem Appiah sees with racism, that it fails to respect the abstract feature of a human being, misses the point about racism that it involves hating others in the flesh, which is a failure to respect important, supposedly contingent features of a human being."¹² Gordon challenges Appiah's prioritization of the abstract features that define all humanity over the specific features of the body that serve as the symbols of racial differences.¹³

Gordon holds that the particular or secondary features of sex and race play a significant role in social life. The question remains as to which of the two— the general or the specific features—condition cognition more. The Hegelian insight that history flows through the interchange between what human beings conceive as necessary and contingent at different periods clarifies the arbitrariness of the attribution of certain body features as primary and other body features as secondary. The attribution of certain body features as primary and others as secondary only reflects history up to the present.

IDENTITY-IN-DIFFERENCE

The two conclusions I've reached so far are these: (1) the sedimentation of socially constructed meanings about race effectively function as natural; as such, the differences of race are ontologically significant; and (2) human embodiment conditions thinking, and thus the specificities of human embodiment may also impact cognition. As persuasive as these conclusions might be, I fear that they lead to the threat that racially and sexually different subjects not only inhabit different worlds but also think differently. The flow of time could only hermeneutically reinforce and exaggerate these differences. Although it is important to dispel facile assumptions of similarity in claims about universal truths, I do not endorse the idea that differently racialized and sexualized people live in different worlds and hence in isolation from one another.

Uma Narayan warns us that too much of an emphasis on difference "ignores the degree to which cultural imperialism often proceeds by means of an 'insistence on Difference,' by a projection of Imaginary 'differences' that constitute one's Others as Other, rather than via an 'insistence on Sameness.' Failing to see that 'cultural imperialism' can involve both sorts of problems, attempts to avoid the Scylla of 'Sameness' often result in moves that leave one foundering on the Charybdis of 'Difference.'"¹⁴ In heeding Narayan's warning, let me clarify that racial and sexual differences matter, but the differences do not matter so much that they disconnect our relations with each other forever.

It is not clear exactly when philosophy birthed the idea of an identity-in-difference. Its first appearance might have been in Hegel's work *The Science of Logic*. Clearly it lies within the old debate between monism and dualism, with its slippery-slope slide into the one and the many. As Paul Weiss states, "To say nothing more than 'One' is not yet[,] as Plato long ago observed, to say anything of significance. Yet to say 'One is' is already to have said two things, and in fact to have made a distinction between Unity and Being."[15] Identity has had many incarnations: as the one, synthesis, concurrence, similarity, resemblance, consistency, or unity. Difference has also had numerous incarnations: as self-diremption, dualism, multiplicity, or the many. Perhaps the best-known instantiation of this idea sits firmly within the discussion between essence and accident in Aristotle's work.[16] By admitting the distinction between essence and accident, Aristotle reveals his interest in difference, acknowledging difference to explain change and permanence.[17] Essences are permanent; accidents change. This relationship poses an epistemic problem. Hegel insists that essences/thought must reveal themselves in the accidents/being. Hegel introduces the notion of an identity-in-difference in the dialectic movement of history between spirit and matter. With a dialectical relationship, he avoids prioritizing monism or dualism—the one or the many.

To insist not simply on a relation between identity and difference but on an identity-in-difference recognizes immediacy in their connection. Hence in place of adhering to a dialectic relation between identity and difference, where time separates identity and difference, the condition of identity-in-difference holds no such separation. As Weiss states, "The defenders of the doctrine of Identity in Difference recognize the fact that despite their diversity the One and the Many are not alien to one another in meaning or in being."[18] The immediacy of this relation frustrates some philosophers, even while motivating others.

Clearly Merleau-Ponty finds the structure of identity-in-difference enigmatic. In *The Visible and the Invisible*, he describes Hegel's dialectical movement as profound but having limitations. He writes, "Take the profound idea of *self-mediation* (médiation par soi), of a movement through which each term ceases to be itself in order to realize itself, breaks up, opens up, negates itself, in order to realize itself. It can remain pure only if the mediating term and the mediated term—which are 'the same'—are yet not the same in the sense of identity."[19] Dialectically, identity-in-difference maintains a connection/tension between the complete transcendence of the world and the total immanence of subjects in that world. Merleau-Ponty's phenomenology conceptualizes the relation of identity-in-difference otherwise. He writes in the working notes of *The Visible and the Invisible*, "That the same be the other than the other, and identity difference of difference—this 1) does not realize a surpassing, or dialectic in the Hegelian sense; 2) is realized on the spot, by encroachment, thickness, *spatiality*."[20] The second account of identity-in-difference is phenomenological. The phenomenological sense of identity-in-difference remains nascent throughout his texts—for example, in his explanations of the gestalt framework for perception and experience, and in his descriptions of embodiment and body movement that aim to avoid conceptualizing the body as either just physical/natural or the manifestations of the mind. In his last text, identity-in-difference centers on the chiasmatic relation of the visible and the invisible or the touching touched and in the element of flesh. With the structure of an identity-in-difference, Merleau-Ponty theorizes an encroachment between the particular and the general, simultaneous separation and union, and an immediate relation between being and becoming, as well as permanence and change.

To establish identity Merleau-Ponty does not rely upon the sixteenth-century constancy hypothesis, a one-to-one concordance between objects in the world and the subject's vision and representation. There is no resort to an identity of some atomistic, elemental, positive, core features. As Martin Dillon writes, within a phenomenal relation the "attribution of identity need not entail identity of attributes, and mis-identification and uncertainty become conceivable possibilities.... It also renders enduring identity intrinsically ambiguous."[21]

What kind of identity does Merleau-Ponty posit? As opposed to upholding an absolute identity, he posits an identity that is fragilely upheld by its surroundings, situation, place, context, and time—the horizon of the world. Joseph Rouse describes this relation between identity and its phenomenal field as "a transcendental field; its structures are immune to empirical revision because they are presupposed by it. Yet there is no principled way . . . to distinguish such 'structures' from what they structure."[22] In other words, the horizon plays a pivotal role in establishing identity. Identity cannot be recognized without the structuring context. As Merleau-Ponty writes, "The mediating term and the mediated term—which are 'the same'—are yet not the same in the sense of identity: for then, in the absence of all difference, there would be no mediation, movement, transformation; one would remain in full positivity."[23] Such an identity is an identity-in-difference.

In favor of the concept of identity-in-difference, let me elaborate four instantiations. First, Merleau-Ponty insists on the occurrence of a daily small miracle—that human beings can concur about seeing the same object, because perception performs a miracle. Somehow "in the course of perceptual experience, I shall be presented with an indefinite set of concordant views."[24] Given the differences in embodiment for each subject, as well as their position and perspective in the horizon, they still see and refer to the same object or scenery. Sharing the perception of an item in the world demonstrates an insistence that in our difference we reach agreement and see the same object. As Merleau-Ponty writes, "There is—and I know it very well if I become impatient with him—a kind of demand that what I see be seen by him also. . . . The thing imposes itself not as true for every intellect, but as real for every subject who is standing where I am."[25] Without this agreement, one questions whether one has actually seen the object, whether something is wrong with oneself or the other, or whether some illusion has occurred. In other words, perception performs a miracle and reaches agreement, even without completely understanding exactly how multiple perspectives coincide.

In the second instantiation, Merleau-Ponty describes the experience of embodiment as an identity-in-difference. Drew Leder elaborates three senses of embodiment. First, the distinction between the experience of the phenomenal and the objective body: "There is a 'divergence' (*écart*), a 'fission,' that stops the phenomenal and objective body from quite merging. Yet this is an identity-in-difference. The two sides of the body are not ontologically separate categories."[26] In a very important sense, the experience of one's physical body transcends one. It remains in difference. Leder captures this identity-in-difference in his description of the experience of a particular yet common material feature of our body: "My own blood belongs as much to the world as to me: enfolded into my body, it is never quite mine."[27] Second, one's perception of one's own body and the visceral experience of one's own body never quite coincide: "'Flesh and blood' expresses well the chiasmatic identity-in-difference of perceptual and visceral life."[28] Although one's own body as perceived and experienced by oneself seem to be one and the same, the two do not quite overlap. This is a familiar dissonance. Consider the well-known shock most people experience when unexpectedly encountering their own reflection in a mirror. Finally, according to Leder, one's own body as seen by others and the visceral experience of one's own body never quite coincide. Leder writes, "While phenomenologically distinct, the visceral circuit is intertwined, an identity-in-difference, with that of the body-as-visibility."[29] Although it is the same body, one's own experience and the other's perception of one's body inevitably diverge. Leder's three senses of identity-in-difference in embodiment demonstrate that embodiment is never an essential or intrinsic identity, but an identity that lies within the limits of its horizon, an identity-in-difference.

Merleau-Ponty's third instantiation of identity-in-difference addresses Paul Ricoeur's concern with an enduring identity. Ricoeur's problem centers on how to determine that an adult is the same human being as the child she once was. This question becomes especially relevant with respect to promise keeping. How does one identify a human being and hold her to a past promise when she has undergone changes in body, in personality, and in mind? Let me begin by acknowledging that Edmund Husserl shows that the ego is not "a little tag-end of the world,"[30] and that the ego upholds an identity-in-difference structure in that although the ego undergoes changes, it nevertheless maintains a connection, a recognition of itself through its changes.[31] Ricoeur begins with simple delineations between the sameness and the difference of one's identity: "*Idem* refers to a notion of identity based on Sameness. . . . *Ipse*, described as Selfhood, can incorporate change within a recognizable entity."[32] Recognizing the tendency of the ego to assume self-transparency, Ricoeur provides two reasons why the ego can reach out of these dangers. First, he insists, the "self can be the source of its own insight."[33] Second, the process of constructing a narrative can provide insight into oneself, "based on Freud's clinical work with individuals whose cure involves making narrative sense of the fragments of memory and stories that disorder their sense of identity. . . . Ricoeur notes that the subject comes to self-knowledge through the construction of a 'coherent and acceptable story' about himself."[34] Ricoeur insists that the self is not simply and forever trapped within her own narcissism or self-denial, but that she can move toward self-understanding. With a practice/methodology that provides access to self-knowledge, Ricoeur's work insists on the possibility of identifying the self through change. In place of a dualistic understanding, the sense of identity within narratives can be thought in terms of its indistinguishability in "the structure from what it structures." Merleau-Ponty's work affirms Ricoeur's position that promise keeping can be solved insofar as each person dwells within a horizon of personal history.

Finally, Merleau-Ponty's phenomenology never begins with subjects existing in complete isolation from each other—resulting in the skeptical problem of accessing other subjects. He insists that no human being lives in isolation, completely outside the purview of the experience of others. The conditions of birth highlight the impossibility of a life lived in complete isolation. Associated with this biological impossibility is the epistemic impossibility of the philosophic claim to know absolute difference. Because his subjects are embodied and situated in the world, not only does Merleau-Ponty respect each subject's unique perspective but also his phenomenology maintains a connection with other subjects. As Taylor Carman and Mark B. N. Hansen write, "If the phenomenology of perception brings about a displacement of the *cogito* from the personal, 'I' to the prepersonal 'one' (*l'on*), it likewise opens up a space of collective social existence between the first- and the third-person points of view."[35] Merleau-Ponty's position against absolute alterity denies the extremes of complete separation and union in our contact with others.

Some critics express the doubt that the structure of identity-in-difference can escape from the totalizing force of identity. Because narcissistic slippages enwrap all perception and experience, some theorists have argued that the relation between identity and difference cannot really recognize true difference; sameness subsumes all difference.[36]

I do not want to defend the dualistic and dialectical relation between identity and difference but, rather, to affirm the phenomenological structure of identity-in-difference. The idea that the structure of identity-in-difference totalizes may originate from an understanding of this structure as static. If the structure of identity-in-difference in itself develops, in that both the identity and the difference change, this becoming at the heart of the structure should properly alleviate the fear of totality.

In place of the idea that essences are somehow ready-made, that which serves as the identity or the difference does not and need not preexist the subject. Michael Baur writes, "Any distinction between the Essential and the Unessential remains a matter of perspective, and so 'the same content can therefore be regarded now as Essential and again as Unessential.'"[37] In other words, depending on the occasion, that which functions as the identity and that which functions as the difference changes. For perception, for experience of the body, for determining identity relations in time, and for experience of the other—all of these relations determine the essential and the unessential.[38] For within the phenomenological field, "every context is nonsaturable."[39] Within the structure of phenomena, of course, nothing is fully within or without our existential control. In the intersubjective context, one of the most important reasons for changes, in defining identity and difference is the role of another subject.

CONCLUSION

With the threat that the socially constructed differences of race are ontologizing and that the specificities of embodiment impact cognition, difference makes a difference, but we cannot lose sight of the shared features of humanity. Without an understanding of our common humanity, signs of indifference prevail regarding people considered to be different. Let me illustrate this. Glen Loury's definition of stigma is an alarming disparity in some social indicator within a specific population group that does not indicate something wrong in "our" society, only that something has gone wrong in "their" community. We have known for the last twenty years at least that "there are 650,000 young black men in the United States penal system today, or approximately 23% of all black men between the ages of 20 and 29 . . . [and] only 450,000 young black men are enrolled in colleges today," yet such statistics are not understood as signaling that something has gone wrong in society as a whole, only that something has gone wrong in "their" communities.[40]

Weate's and Gordon's analyses of the ontologizing consequences of the social and political situation suggest that ontology and politics are not separate. As such, much like the motivations for metaphysically and phenomenologically exploring a relation between the one and the many, or between permanence and change, perhaps we should consider our social and political conditions to be a relation between identity and difference, or identity-in-difference. By evoking the phenomenological notion of identity-in-difference, our relations with one another facilitate both an appreciation of our shared plight as well as a respect for our differences. By keeping the relation of identity-in-difference in mind, we could attend to the balance between unity and multiplicity necessary within a polity.

EMILY S. LEE is Associate Professor of Philosophy at California State University at Fullerton. She edited the anthology *Living Alterities: Phenomenology, Embodiment, and Race* (SUNY Press, 2014).

NOTES

1. Glen Loury, *The Anatomy of Racial Inequality* (Cambridge, MA: Harvard University Press, 2001), 83.
2. Maria Lugones, "Playfulness, 'World'-Traveling, and Loving Perception," *Hypatia* 2, no. 2 (1987): 7.
3. Jeremy Weate, "Fanon, Merleau-Ponty, and the Difference of Phenomenology," in *Race*, ed. Robert Bernasconi, 174–75 (Malden, MA: Blackwell, 2001).
4. Lewis Gordon, *Bad Faith and AntiBlack Racism* (Amherst, MA: Humanity Books, 1999): 133. George Yancy also voices this sedimentation of racial meanings as, "a process of *ontologization*, a process where the *being* of the Black body (and the white body) undergoes a process of radical transformation. This involves the process whereby the historically and culturally contingent markings of the Black/White body are transformed into intrinsically natural eternal dispositions." See George Yancy, "'Seeing Blackness' from within the Manichean Divide," in *White on White/Black on Black*, ed. George Yancy (Lanham, MD: Rowman and Littlefield, 2005), 248.
5. Linda Martín Alcoff writes, "There is a visual registry operating in social relations which is socially constructed, historically evolving, and culturally variegated but

nonetheless powerfully determinant over individual experiences and choices.... This visual registry cannot be fully or adequately described except in ontological terms, because the difference that racializing identities has made is an ontologizing difference, that is, a difference at the most basic level concerning knowledge and subjectivity, being and thinking." See Linda Martín Alcoff, "Philosophy and Racial Identity," *Philosophy Today* 41 (Spring 1997): 68–69. See also Charles W. Mills and his insistence that the difference of race is an ontologizing category. Mills, *Blackness Visible: Essays on Philosophy and Race* (Ithaca, NY: Cornell University Press, 1998), 9–13.

Other areas of philosophy articulate this understanding of the inextricable interrelatedness between the natural and the cultural. Feminist theorists, evolutionary theorists, and animal studies theorists speculate similar co-constituted structures. With the growing acceptance of the inseparability of the social and the natural, and their influence upon each other, philosophy of race clearly does not uniquely posit that social/cultural meanings sediment into human considerations of nature if not nature itself. See Susan Bordo, "Does Size Matter?," in *Revealing Male Bodies*, ed. Nancy Tuana et. al. (Bloomington: Indiana University Press, 2002), 33. Maxine Sheets-Johnstone writes, "The methodological significance of the hyphenated adjective, existential-evolutionary, can be capsulized in the simplest way perhaps by quoting from Merleau-Ponty's posthumous work, *The Visible and the Invisible*, and saying that there, 'reversibility . . . is the ultimate truth." See Maxine Sheets-Johnstone, "Existential Fit and Evolutionary Continuities," *Synthese* 66 (1986): 232.

6. Gareth Williams, "Subalternity and the Neoliberal *Habitus*: Thinking Insurrection on the El Salvador/South Central Interface," *Nepantla: Views from the South* 1, no. 1 (2000): 140. He cites Gyanendra Pandey, "In Defense of the Fragment: Writing about Hindu-Muslim Riots in India Today," *Representations* 37 (1992).

7. Williams exhibits suspicion of any attempts at drawing sameness, referring to notions of hybridity as "death work." He writes, "Identity and difference falter before the radical undecidability of hybrid like-being. Moreover, it appears to be through like-being that we enter the affective, corporeal, and ontological borderlands of collective identity/difference's other side: namely, opaque resemblance, open exposure, and active contagion.... After all, the origin of being-in-common in the transnational order is nothing more than the death work of immanence and of communion." See Williams, "Subalternity and the Neoliberal *Habitus*," 162. I worry that Williams's eschewing of hybridity does not provide space for any positive accounts of the lives of the many hyphenated and mixed subjects today and upholds a troubling notion of purity.

Such emphasis on unknowable difference parallels poststructuralist positions such as that of Luce Irigaray, who insists on the existence of ontological "difference." Elizabeth Grosz elaborates, writing, "When it comes to the otherness of the other (whether woman for man, man for woman, or any others) the subject is necessarily unable to see that otherness. We see nothing in the difference because difference itself cannot be grasped, made present; hence I remain blind to—but equally unable to hear or feel—a body that is sexed differently." Irigaray and Grosz hold that difference itself is unperceivable; one cannot perceive complete difference, difference in a radical sense. See Elizabeth Grosz, *Volatile Bodies* (Bloomington: Indiana University Press, 1994), 106.

8. Hubert Dreyfus writes, "In opposition to mainline cognitive science, which assumes that intelligent behavior must be based on representations in the mind or brain, Merleau-Ponty holds that the most basic sort of intelligent behavior, skillful coping, can

and must be understood without recourse to any type of representation." See Hubert Dreyfus, "Merleau-Ponty and Recent Cognitive Science," in *The Cambridge Companion to Merleau-Ponty*, ed. Taylor Carman and Mark B. N. Hansen (Cambridge, UK: Cambridge University Press, 2005), 129.

9. Ibid., 135–36.

10. See Mark Rowlands, *The New Science of the Mind: From Extended Mind to Embodied Phenomenology* (Cambridge: MIT Press, 2010); Robert Rupert, *Cognitive Systems and the Extended Mind* (Oxford: Oxford University Press, 2009); Shaun Gallagher, *How the Body Shapes the Mind* (Oxford: Oxford University Press, 2005); H. Bruun and R. Langlais, "On the Embodied Nature of Action," *Acta Sociologica* 46, no. 1 (2003): 31–40.

11. Elizabeth Grosz, "Merleau-Ponty and Irigaray in the Flesh," in *Merleau-Ponty, Interiority and Exteriority, Psychic Life and the World*, ed. Dorothea Olkowski and James M. Morley (Albany: State University of New York Press, 1999), 162. See also Mills, *Blackness Visible*, 13. Gail Weiss makes a parallel point: "We cannot refrain from the 'project of gender' even if we do not deliberately 'intend' gender as our project, insofar as we live and express our genders through our bodies. . . . Gender is a lived bodily project and hence is an integral component of human existence." See Gail Weiss, *Body Images: Embodiment as Intercorporeality* (New York: Routledge, 1999), 140–41.

12. Gordon, *Bad Faith and AntiBlack Racism*, 69.

13. At this point, recall that feminists critical of Merleau-Ponty, especially Judith Butler and Shannon Sullivan, argue that to reduce human embodiment to an anonymous subjectivity is too abstract and does not depict the very real lives of women. In other words, a significant number of voices within feminist and race theory argue that the so-called secondary/contingent features of embodiment may matter significantly in social life. Butler defends Merleau-Ponty in other respects. See Butler, "Sexual Difference as a Question of Ethics: Alterities of the Flesh in Irigaray and Merleau-Ponty," in *Feminist Interpretations of Maurice Merleau-Ponty*, ed. Dorothea Olkowski and Gail Weiss, 107–125 (University Park: Pennsylvania State University Press, 2006).

14. Uma Narayan, "Essence of Culture and a Sense of History: A Feminist Critique of Cultural Essentialism," in *Decentering the Center: Philosophy for a Multicultural, Postcolonial, and Feminist World*, ed. Uma Narayan and Sandra Harding (Bloomington: Indiana University Press, 2000), 83. Recall also in the last chapter of *Black Skins White Masks*, Frantz Fanon declares that he is a Frenchman, and that "I am a man, and what I have to recapture is the whole of the past of the world. . . . Every time a man has contributed to the victory of the dignity of the spirit, every time a man has said no to an attempt to subjugate his fellows, I have felt solidarity with his act. In no way should I derive my basic purpose from the past of the people of color." He aims to "reach out for the universal." Clearly, Fanon focuses on the sameness of blacks and whites as long as both fight for the humanity of all. See Frantz Fanon, *Black Skins White Masks*, trans. Charles Lam Markmann (New York: Grove Press, 1967), 197, 226.

15. Paul Weiss, "On Being Together," *Review of Metaphysics* 9, no. 3 (1956): 391.

16. Irving M. Copi, "Essence and Accident," *Journal of Philosophy* 51, no. 23 (1954): 706–719.

17. Ibid., 707.

18. Weiss, "On Being Together," 400.

19. Maurice Merleau-Ponty, *The Visible and the Invisible*, trans. Alphonso Lingis (Evanston, IL: Northwestern University Press, 1968), 92.

20. Ibid., 264.

21. Martin Dillon, *Merleau-Ponty's Ontology* (Evanston, IL: Northwestern University Press, 1997), 76.

22. Joseph Rouse, "Merleau-Ponty's Existential Conception of Science," in *The Cambridge Companion to Merleau-Ponty*, ed. Taylor Carman and Mark B. N. Hansen (Cambridge, UK: Cambridge University Press, 2005), 285, 287. Rouse continues to describe scientific theories as functioning similarly—that is, following phenomenological logic, not strict analytic logic. Sounding very much like Thomas Kuhn's articulation of the relation between theory and facts, Rouse writes, "Theories thus occupy an ambiguous place between us and the world. They seem to be objects with properties independent of us (we discover rather than invest their implications, for example). Yet we also use them to explore the world and, in doing so, incorporate them into our own capacities, much as a blind man incorporates his cane."

23. Merleau-Ponty, *Visible and the Invisible*, 92.

24. Maurice Merleau-Ponty, *Phenomenology of Perception*, trans. Colin Smith (New York: Routledge, 1996), 185.

25. Maurice Merleau-Ponty, "Primacy of Perception," in *The Primacy of Perception*, ed. and trans. James M. Edie (Evanston, IL: Northwestern University Press, 1964), 17.

26. Drew Leder, "A Proposed Supplement to Merleau-Ponty," *Human Studies* 13, no. 3 (1990): 210.

27. Ibid., 214.

28. Ibid.

29. Ibid., 213.

30. David R. Cerbone, *Understanding Phenomenology* (Chesham, UK: Acumen Publishing, 2006), 33.

31. John B. Brough, "Time and the One and the Many (In Husserl's Bernauer Manuscripts on Time Consciousness)," *Philosophy Today*, SPEP Supplement (2002): 142.

32. Patrick Crowley, "Paul Ricoeur: The Concept of Narrative Identity, the Trace of Autobiography," *Paragraph* 26, no. 3 (2003): 1.

33. Ibid., 3.

34. Ibid.

35. Taylor Carman and Mark B. N. Hansen, introduction to *The Cambridge Companion to Merleau-Ponty*, ed. Taylor Carman and Mark B. N. Hansen (Cambridge, UK: Cambridge University Press, 2005), 17. Drew Leder also confirms this inherent intersubjectivity in the phenomenological structure: "World and self still lack their full depth, however, until reference is made to another chiasmatic relation: that which connects me to other perceivers. My perspective and that of the other intertwine in mutual validation, while never quite coinciding." See Leder, "Proposed Supplement," 211.

36. See Peter Hallward, "Edouard Glissant between the Singular and the Specific," *Yale Journal of Criticism* 11, no. 2 (1998). See also Krzysztof Ziarek, *The Historicity of Experience: Modernity, the Avant-Garde, and the Event* (Evanston, IL: Northwestern University Press, 2001).

37. Michael Baur, "Sublating Kant and the Old Metaphysics: A Reading of the Transition from Being to Essence in Hegel's Logic," *Owl of Minerva: Quarterly Journal of the Hegel Society of America* 29, no. 2 (1998): 149.

38. Let me quote Gallagher one more time to substantiate my position here, particularly with regard to perception, but I am confident he would agree with me with regard

to body movement as well. Gallagher's explanation of perception illustrates how the act of perception in effect chooses the essence: "Where must an object be located within my perceptual field to afford an optimal perception? It depends on the sense modality with which I perceive, and on the purpose of my perception." Gallagher, *How the Body Shapes the Mind*, 140. See also T.L.S. Sprigge, "Personal and Impersonal Identity: A Reply to Oderberg," *Mind* 98, no. 392 (1989): 610.

39. Leonard Lawlor, "Dialectic and Iterability: The Confrontation between Paul Ricoeur and Jacques Derrida," *Philosophy Today* 32, no. 3 (1988): 182. Lawlor specifically refers to the work of Ricoeur and Derrida here, but clearly both philosophers work within phenomenology.

40. Patricia J. Williams, *The Alchemy of Race and Rights* (Cambridge, MA: Harvard University Press, 1991), 189–90.

BIBLIOGRAPHY

Alcoff, Linda Martín. "Philosophy and Racial Identity." *Philosophy Today* 41 (Spring 1997): 67–76.
Baur, Michael. "Sublating Kant and the Old Metaphysics: A Reading of the Transition from Being to Essence in Hegel's Logic." *Owl of Minerva: Quarterly Journal of the Hegel Society of America* 29, no. 2 (1998): 139–64.
Bordo, Susan. "Does Size Matter?" In *Revealing Male Bodies*, edited by Nancy Tuana et al., 19–36. Bloomington: Indiana University Press, 2002.
Brough, John B. "Time and the One and the Many (In Husserl's Bernauer Manuscripts on Time Consciousness)." *Philosophy Today*, SPEP Supplement (2002): 142–53.
Butler, Judith. "Sexual Difference as a Question of Ethics: Alterities of the Flesh in Irigaray and Merleau-Ponty." In *Feminist Interpretations of Maurice Merleau-Ponty*, edited by Dorothea E. Olkowski and Gail Weiss, 107–125. University Park: Pennsylvania State University Press, 2006.
Carman, Taylor, and Mark B. N. Hansen. Introduction. *The Cambridge Companion to Merleau-Ponty*, edited by Taylor Carman and Mark B. N. Hansen, 1–25. Cambridge, UK: Cambridge University Press, 2005.
Cerbone, David R. *Understanding Phenomenology*. Chesham, UK: Acumen Publishing, 2006.
Copi, Irving M. "Essence and Accident." *Journal of Philosophy* 51, no. 23 (1954): 706–719.
Crowley, Patrick. "Paul Ricoeur: The Concept of Narrative Identity, the Trace of Autobiography." *Paragraph* 26, no. 3 (2003): 1–12.
Dillon, Martin. *Merleau-Ponty's Ontology*. Evanston, IL: Northwestern University Press, 1997.
Dreyfus, Hubert. "Merleau-Ponty and Recent Cognitive Science." In *The Cambridge Companion to Merleau-Ponty*, edited by Taylor Carman and Mark B. N. Hansen, 129–50. Cambridge, UK: Cambridge University Press, 2005.
Fanon, Frantz. *Black Skins White Masks*. Translated by Charles Lam Markmann. New York: Grove Press, 1967.
Gallagher, Shaun. *How the Body Shapes the Mind*. Oxford: Oxford University Press, 2005.
Gordon, Lewis. *Bad Faith and AntiBlack Racism*. Amherst, MA: Humanity Books, 1999.

Grosz, Elizabeth. "Merleau-Ponty and Irigaray in the Flesh." In *Merleau-Ponty, Interiority and Exteriority, Psychic Life and the World*, edited by Dorothea E. Olkowski and James M. Morley, 145–66. Albany: State University of New York Press, 1999.
———. *Volatile Bodies*. Bloomington: Indiana University Press, 1994.
Hallward, Peter. "Edouard Glissant between the Singular and the Specific." *Yale Journal of Criticism* 11, no. 2 (1998): 441–64.
Lawlor, Leonard. "Dialectic and Iterability: The Confrontation between Paul Ricoeur and Jacques Derrida." *Philosophy Today* 32, no. 3 (1988): 181–94.
Leder, Drew. "A Proposed Supplement to Merleau-Ponty." *Human Studies* 13, no. 3 (1990): 209–219.
Loury, Glen. *The Anatomy of Racial Inequality*. Cambridge, MA: Harvard University Press, 2001.
Lugones, Maria. "Playfulness, 'World'-Traveling, and Loving Perception." *Hypatia* 2, no. 2 (1987): 3–19.
Merleau-Ponty, Maurice. *Phenomenology of Perception*. Translated by Colin Smith. New York: Routledge, 1996.
———. "Primacy of Perception." In *The Primacy of Perception*, edited and translated by James M. Edie, 12–42. Evanston, IL: Northwestern University Press, 1964.
———. *The Visible and the Invisible*. Translated by Alphonso Lingis. Evanston, IL: Northwestern University Press, 1968.
Mills, Charles W. *Blackness Visible: Essays on Philosophy and Race*. Ithaca, NY: Cornell University Press, 1998.
Narayan, Uma. "Essence of Culture and a Sense of History: A Feminist Critique of Cultural Essentialism." In *Decentering the Center: Philosophy for a Multicultural, Postcolonial, and Feminist World*, edited by Uma Narayan and Sandra Harding, 80–100. Bloomington: Indiana University Press, 2000.
Rouse, Joseph. "Merleau-Ponty's Existential Conception of Science." In *The Cambridge Companion to Merleau-Ponty*, edited by Taylor Carman and Mark B. N. Hansen, 265–90. Cambridge, UK: Cambridge University Press, 2005.
Sheets-Johnstone, Maxine. "Existential Fit and Evolutionary Continuities." *Synthese* 66 (1986): 216–48.
Weate, Jeremy. "Fanon, Merleau-Ponty, and the Difference of Phenomenology." In *Race*, edited by Robert Bernasconi, 169–83. Malden, MA: Blackwell, 2001.
Weiss, Gail. *Body Images: Embodiment as Intercorporeality*. New York: Routledge, 1999.
Weiss, Paul. "On Being Together." *Review of Metaphysics* 9, no. 3 (1956): 391–403.
Williams, Gareth. "Subalternity and the Neoliberal *Habitus*: Thinking Insurrection on the El Salvador/South Central Interface." *Nepantla: Views from South* 1, no. 1 (2000): 139–70.
Yancy, George. "'Seeing Blackness' from within the Manichean Divide." In *White on White/Black on Black*, edited by George Yancy, 233–63. Lanham, MD: Rowman and Littlefield, 2005.
Ziarek, Krzysztof. *The Historicity of Experience: Modernity, the Avant-Garde, and the Event*. Evanston, IL: Northwestern University Press, 2001.

18 WHAT IS FEMINIST PHENOMENOLOGY?

Looking Backward and Into the Future

SILVIA STOLLER

INTRODUCTION

The question "What is feminist phenomenology?" is not as easily answered as it might first seem. To some extent, this has to do with the term itself, since in the academic field two different terms are regularly used to designate more or less the same area: "feminist phenomenology" and "phenomenological feminism." Strictly speaking, feminist phenomenology is a feminist-oriented phenomenology, whereas phenomenological feminism can be characterized as a phenomenologically oriented feminism. In her early essay "Sexual Ideology and Phenomenological Description," Judith Butler speaks of "phenomenological feminism," whereas in her encyclopedia article Dorothea Olkowski speaks of "phenomenologically-oriented feminists" and of "feminist phenomenologists" at the same time.[1] To clarify the question, is feminist phenomenology a kind of phenomenology from a feminist perspective or a kind of feminism that is influenced by phenomenology?

The answer to the question "What is feminist phenomenology?" depends on how one views phenomenology, on the one hand, and feminism, on the other. Here, too, opinions, even among feminists and phenomenologists, vary greatly. Additionally, the perfect designation depends on one's self-understanding. For example, if a researcher is trained and educated in phenomenology and understands herself more as a phenomenologist, then she will probably prefer the term "feminist phenomenologist" for her work. If she is an expert in feminist theory and applies phenomenology for her studies, then she will perhaps call herself a "phenomenological feminist." The situation is complicated still further if someone considers herself a feminist *and* a phenomenologist at the same time or if the identification with one or the other changes. Last but not least, the nature of the relationship between phenomenology and feminism determines the character of "feminist phenomenology."

In the past, such a connection has not always been desirable. Linda Fisher has clearly reminded us of the early feminist skepticism toward phenomenology. At the beginning it was not clear whether phenomenology and feminism, with their "radically different world-views," were even compatible.[2] Ultimately, feminist phenomenology has undergone a historical transformation. Over the years, early feminist skepticism has transformed into a widely accepted new research field in its own right. The international conference "Future Directions in Feminist Phenomenology" at the University of Western Ontario in 2013 demonstrates how much feminist phenomenology has developed since its origin. The early feminist skepticism with regard to classic phenomenology has been replaced by heterogeneous research characterized by a productive application of classic phenomenology among feminist theorists.

Finally, the uncertainty concerning the historical beginning of feminist phenomenology shows how vaguely defined this point of departure really still is. Is it possible to speak of a totally new approach? Or is there a need to address this issue in terms of approximately thirty years of research? Does feminist phenomenology start with Simone de Beauvoir's *The Second Sex*? Or does the term "feminist phenomenology" apply only to research that has emerged since the awareness of such a specific approach named "feminist phenomenology"?

I would like to shed light on this issue. My starting point is the assumption that "feminist phenomenology" is an umbrella term. By definition, an "umbrella term" unites the most diverse concepts. In the case of feminist phenomenology there are very different assumptions, methods, and objects of research at stake. In order to be able to characterize feminist phenomenology, one needs to glance over the history of research in this field. That will be done in the first part of this essay. Afterward, I will look briefly at the future implications of feminist phenomenology. However, I will not provide a definition of "feminist phenomenology." Rather, I will describe how "feminist phenomenology" has been presented in the academic field in the past and what it is currently.[3]

HISTORICAL OUTLINE: TWO PHASES

Seen from the point of view of the history of philosophy, feminist phenomenology is as old as Beauvoir's *The Second Sex*, originally published in 1949. While for a long time Beauvoir was categorized as an existential feminist, she is now widely read as a phenomenologist. Feminist researchers have provided evidence that phenomenology influences her work in various ways.[4] Maurice Merleau-Ponty's influence on Beauvoir is the most obvious one and is most clearly exemplified by her use of his phenomenological term "lived experience" (*expérience vécu*) in her analysis of femininity. Moreover, she also assumes Merleau-Ponty's concept of the "phenomenal body." One can also detect a certain affinity to Martin Heidegger. Sara Heinämaa has supported the view that Beauvoir is a genuine phenomenologist, arguing that "Beauvoir's discussion of femininity and sexual difference is phenomenological in its aims and its methods."[5] For this reason, Bonnie Mann and Beata Stawarska call Beauvoir the "founder" of feminist phenomenology. They speak of her as "the most prolific and influential figure in . . . feminist phenomenology," although they consider *The Second Sex* its "founding text."[6]

While it seems obvious that Beauvoir's *The Second Sex* is strongly influenced by phenomenology, my intention is to clearly delineate two separate historical phases with respect to the history of feminist phenomenology. In the first phase, feminist phenomenology was practiced without declaring this line of thought as such. To put it another way, early researchers were "doing" feminist phenomenology but not in its name. This phase includes Beauvoir and many who came after her. What should be noted is the very fact that when Beauvoir wrote *The Second Sex*, she saw herself as neither a phenomenologist nor a feminist. It was not until much later, in the 1970s, that she committed herself to a feminist stand.

It was only in the 1980s, when a new phase of feminist phenomenology was introduced, that feminist phenomenology appeared as such. Interestingly, it was not a phenomenologist in the strict sense but a post-structuralist feminist whose early works have become eminently important in the field of feminist phenomenology. In 1981 Judith Butler wrote an article in which she criticized, from a feminist point of view, Merleau-Ponty's phenomenology of sexuality.[7] In the conclusion to her article "Sexual Ideology and Phenomenological Description," she explicitly refers to a "phenomenological feminism" and marks this as a feminist theory that makes use of Merleau-Ponty's phenomenology, expanding it around the central aspect of gender categories. Interestingly, she notes that the future of such a "phenomenological feminism" does not lie so much in phenomenological philosophy "but in the works of philosophical feminism to come."[8] In general, making use of phenomenology in the fields of feminist theory and gender studies is a main characteristic of feminist phenomenology. Classic phenomenology is used as a helpful resource for gender issues. Carol Bigwood's self-declaring article "Renaturalizing the Body (With a Little Help from Merleau-Ponty)" is symptomatic of this tendency that has characterized feminist phenomenology up to now.[9]

But a further step in establishing feminist phenomenology had to follow: its academic institutionalization. Visible signs of this are conferences, academic anthologies, and lectures on the topic of feminist phenomenology as well as the foundation of organizations. This move began in the 1990s and started in the United States. The following cornerstones must be mentioned. In 1994 Linda Fisher and Lester Embree organized a research symposium on the topic of "Feminist Phenomenology," a conference that can be hailed as the founding event of institutionalized feminist phenomenology. In 2000 feminist phenomenology arrived in Europe as well, when the first international workshop on "Feminist Phenomenology" took place in Vienna.[10] This workshop was followed by a series of international conferences, which were all held in the name of the "Feminist Phenomenology Group," a network of international experts in feminist phenomenology.[11] Three edited volumes have come out of these events. They currently count as standard literature in feminist phenomenology. The first one is dedicated to the concept of alterity, the second volume focuses on time and temporality, and the third takes up Beauvoir's important work on old age.[12]

Other classics are edited volumes that explicitly address the new tradition of feminist phenomenology. In the late 1990s the first academic anthology, *Phänomenologie und Geschlechterdifferenz* (*Phenomenology and Sexual Difference*), was published in German, followed by *Feminist Phenomenology*, a collection of conference papers.[13] Finally, in 2005 another German volume, expanded to include hermeneutics, *Feministische Phänomenologie und Hermeneutik*, appeared.[14] Today these works are seen as classics and have substantially contributed to promoting feminist phenomenology at universities. Special issues in American philosophy journals followed, for example, in *Continental Philosophy Review* and *Janus Head*.[15] Finally, in the 1990s the first monographs in philosophy were published.[16]

During this period, feminist phenomenology further emerged in academic discourse. In philosophical seminars as well as in women's studies programs, individual texts ascribed to feminist phenomenology became part of the curriculum—for example, Iris Marion Young's essay "Throwing Like a Girl: A Phenomenology of Feminine Body Comportment, Motility, and Spatiality" (1989).[17] Her account, developed in this article, "combines the insights of the theory of the lived body as expressed by Merleau-Ponty and the theory of the situation of women as developed by Beauvoir."[18] What makes it specifically feminist is Young's gender perspective on the issue of motility and her conclusion that women reveal a different bodily comportment—for example, when throwing a ball. What her analysis shows is that this different bodily comportment is not biological but instead has to do with the situation of unequal gender relations where women experience their bodies both as objects and subjects. Young's rich description of the modalities of "feminine bodily existence" was extremely influential in feminist phenomenology research.[19]

Finally, the establishment of academic organizations has also contributed to the establishment of feminist phenomenology. In addition to the international network Feminist Phenomenology Group, there is also the Society for Interdisciplinary Feminist Phenomenology, founded by Bonnie Mann and Beata Stawarska at the University of Oregon in 2006.

Looking back at the historical benchmarks allows us to trace both the beginning of feminist phenomenology and its historical development. When considering its inception, distinguishing between a narrow and a broader understanding of feminist phenomenology seems to be helpful. In the initial phase of the mid-twentieth century, philosophers applied feminist phenomenology without being conscious of it as such. This is the case with Beauvoir. Characterizing her as the founder of feminist phenomenology is an attempt to subsequently categorize her philosophy within the tradition of feminist phenomenology, whereas she herself did not understand her work in these terms. From the 1980s on, feminist phenomenology became increasingly more established and institutionalized. This came about first and foremost through an increasing awareness and ultimately found expression in its academization. In a broad sense, one can speak of roughly sixty years of feminist phenomenology if Beauvoir is designated as its starting point. In a narrower sense, one can claim thirty years of such history if the starting point is identified with the academic establishment of the term.

THE RESEARCH OF EARLY FEMALE PHENOMENOLOGISTS

In the following, I delve into the contextual characterization of feminist phenomenology and the question of who is to be considered a feminist phenomenologist in the early phase of this movement. For the first time in the history of phenomenology, female phenomenologists and their specific contributions to phenomenology have come into focus. From a historical perspective, this was the first task of feminist phenomenologists.

The German philosophers Edith Stein (1891–1942), Gerda Walther (1897–1977), and Hannah Arendt (1906–1975) are the most important figures in this early stage of the history. Stein was a student of the founder of phenomenology, Edmund Husserl, in Germany and later became his assistant in Freiburg.

Her dissertation on empathy and her study on the "nature" of women from a Husserlian perspective and against the background of Roman Catholicism have met with particular interest.[20] Gerda Walther, also Husserl's student, and the first woman to receive a postdoctoral qualification at a German university in philosophy, has become known for her focus on the phenomenology of mysticism. Linda Lopez McAlister has labeled Walther an "original thinker" who represented views that are of particular interest for feminist theory because she "reached many of the same conclusions that feminist philosophers have reached—decades before we did."[21] Arendt, Heidegger's student, did not consider herself to be a feminist philosopher; nonetheless, her work became enormously influential among feminist philosophers and phenomenologists. In particular, her political thinking has been taken up by many feminist theorists, among them Seyla Benhabib, although Arendt's phenomenological background itself has been an object of research for many years in mainstream phenomenology as well as in feminist phenomenology. According to Bonnie Mann and Beata Stawarska, "Although few women became internationally renowned scholars in the discipline of phenomenology, Edith Stein and Arendt also count as important historical figures within the phenomenological movement and they bring a woman's intellectual perspective to the discipline."[22] While it seems that Stein and Walther are at the margins of contemporary feminist phenomenology, Arendt is among the most popular philosophers in feminist phenomenology today. However, as important as this historical research was and still is, it nonetheless does not overlap with what one today calls feminist phenomenology. To put it differently, historical research is part of feminist phenomenology, but the field is not restricted to the historical research of female phenomenologists. Therefore, another hallmark of feminist phenomenological must be introduced.

PHENOMENOLOGY AS A RESOURCE

One of the most important, if not the most important, characteristics of feminist phenomenology is the application of phenomenological theory to feminist issues. At first, feminist theorists were skeptical of classical phenomenology. Linda Fisher, in her enlightening contribution "Phenomenology and Feminism," called attention to a series of difficulties posed by the convergence of phenomenology with feminist theory.[23] This skepticism corresponds to a basic skepticism of feminist theoreticians with regard to mainstream philosophy, with its masculinity, androcentrism, and misogyny, as was symptomatic in the early phase of feminist philosophy. In addition, the very fact that Husserl's phenomenology was considered an idealistic philosophy based on a theory of consciousness that ignored embodied existence was another hindrance for feminists to deal with in terms of phenomenology.

Interestingly, feminist phenomenology has gone far in doing away with this skepticism. This does not mean it has become less critical of the philosophical male tradition. It simply means it has replaced its tendency toward a negative attitude with a tendency toward a positive one. In contemporary works, the phenomenological tradition is used as a tool to address central issues that arise in a feminist context. An apt example is Carol Bigwood's article "Renaturalizing the Body (With a Little Help from Merleau-Ponty)."[24] A classic representative of phenomenology, Merleau-Ponty can now "help" address key issues in classic feminism—in this case, the problem of naturalizing the body. In her "feminist reappropriation," Bigwood argued that Merleau-Ponty's phenomenology of the body represents a model of the body that leads neither to biological determination nor to cultural relativism and, as such, allows for the development of a "feminist philosophy of the body."[25] In other words, classics in phenomenology are no more the mere object of feminist concern but rather of feminist interest, if not to say of feminist need.[26] Certainly, this does not mean that Merleau-Ponty research remains untouched by the feminist skepticism mentioned above. As was the case with the work of other male phenomenologists, feminists from the beginning have also criticized the gender-neutrality and androcentrism of Merleau-Ponty's philosophy and did not stop when, for the first time, other feminists started to make positive use of his work.[27] However, the difference lies in the changed feminist attitude toward the classics. While initially phenomenologists were the object of feminist critique, now their works have become a helpful resource for feminist theorizing. For many feminists Merleau-Ponty has been one of the most promising phenomenological theorists. This has to do with his transformation of Husserlian phenomenology from a "transcendental phenomenology" to a phenomenology of embodied existence, whereby embodiment is no longer merely a part of phenomenology, and embodied existence is no longer simply one characteristic of human existence but its very condition. In the course of the transformation of Husserlian transcendental phenomenology into an existential phenomenology, which is particularly characteristic of the French tradition, phenomenology has come to posit experience as situated. If experience is understood as being situated in the body of concrete subjects of experience, then it is possible to describe the experiences of subjects of different genders, including the collective experiences of women in comparison to the experiences of men, as well as the very different gender experiences that vary from woman to woman on the basis of unique gender identities.[28]

While Merleau-Ponty is without doubt among the favorites, in the 1990s there was an increasing tendency to turn to other classical phenomenologists for feminist thought, despite their, in part problematic, views from a feminist perspective. Today almost every phenomenologist is fair game for feminist phenomenology, even though certain tendencies and affinities are apparent. Among them is the French phenomenologist Paul Ricoeur, whose work has also been discovered to support feminist theory.[29] He not only left behind an immense philosophical oeuvre, but he also provided an interesting essay on sexuality.[30] Tina Chanter, in her work *Ethics of Eros*, set the path for a feminist adaptation of the phenomenology of Emmanuel Levinas in the 1990s. Even Heidegger has become interesting to scholars of feminist theory. His ontological hermeneutics, as Veronica Vasterling has shown, can contribute to an important feminist issue: the relationship between nature and culture. Even the work of Edmund Husserl, the founder of phenomenology, is no longer avoided. An example is the work of Christina Schües, who opened up Husserl's phenomenology to a feminist approach of generativity.[31] Also Sara Heinämaa's work has a strong emphasis on Husserl. Her specific contribution to feminist phenomenology consists in showing that Beauvoir's *The Second Sex* is not only influenced by phenomenology in general but also can be understood only from within the framework of Husserl's phenomenology.[32] She even claims that Beauvoir's account of woman's embodiment "is deeply indebted to Husserl's phenomenology."[33] Debra Bergoffen's feminist reading of Beauvoir takes a similar direction; she argues that Beauvoir, as a phenomenologist, "reworks Husserl's theory of intentionality" and that she "follows Husserl to retrieve the lived body for philosophy."[34] Work with the classical thinkers is now so extensive that a satisfactory overview is no longer possible. However, what characterizes this branch of feminist phenomenology is a positive attitude toward the phenomenological tradition and a productive application of various phenomenological terms and approaches for feminist purposes.

Another development in the context of feminist philosophy can be held responsible for the recent flourishing of feminist phenomenology. That is, the opening of feminist philosophy with regard to classical phenomenology can in great part be traced back to the post-structuralist feminist criticisms of phenomenology that thrived in the 1990s and relied on one-sided arguments. The critical response from phenomenologists focused on the overemphasis on language or discourse and the criticism of experience in postmodern or post-structuralist feminism. In 1998 Sonia Kruks wrote, "But in the last few years interest has grown again, as theorists have sought insights from the tradition that might move theory beyond the impasses that postmodernism now seems to present."³⁵ In other words, it was necessary to revise the poststructural criticism of phenomenology and reevaluate phenomenology and its basic concepts. It was not only post-structuralist philosophy in general but post-structural feminism in particular that had a share in this denunciation. An article by the post-structuralist historian Joan W. Scott, in which the notion of experience is heavily critiqued, became extremely influential in this respect.³⁶ It had a major influence on feminist debates and led to the "discrediting" of reliance on any account of experience.³⁷ Elizabeth Grosz went so far as to conclude that experience had become a "dirty word."³⁸ Rather than positing experience as an origin of knowledge, Scott argues for the necessity of "historicizing" experience.³⁹ Another post-structuralist critique of phenomenology as a philosophy of experience concerns the purported immediacy of perceptual experience; post-structuralists assume that experience has always already been interpreted. More politically, Scott argued that the recourse to experience is in danger of reproducing ideological systems. As well, any recourse to so-called women's experience as an authentic gendered experience was critiqued from the post-structuralist perspective. Scott, for example, argued that such an assumption means to falsely "universalize the identity of women." Finally, feminist post-structuralists believe that conceptualizations of knowledge based on experience do not explore the discursive character of experience, whereas, they argue, every experience is a discursive experience or, as Scott puts it, a "linguistic event."⁴⁰ However, the question raised by feminist phenomenologists is whether the post-structural critique of experience, in particular Scott's, can in fact be applied to phenomenology. I have argued in detail elsewhere that it cannot be done successfully, at least not to the works of Husserl and Merleau-Ponty.⁴¹ Linda Martín Alcoff also critically noted that the feminist reception of phenomenology could be ascribed to a series of misunderstandings, arguing that characterizing phenomenology as a transcendental phenomenology does not do justice to the rich potential of phenomenological philosophy.⁴²

At this point we see a debate emerging among feminists. The primary goal is no longer a critical stance toward the male tradition but a debate within the field itself: feminist phenomenology versus post-structural feminism. Since this debate is now long-standing, it is possible to draw some conclusions. Although initially phenomenology and post-structuralism seemed to be irreconcilable antagonists, contemporary gender research shows that the two in fact meaningfully complement each other.⁴³ Johanna Oksala seems to move in the same direction by following her sharp criticism of feminist phenomenology with what she refers to as a "post-phenomenological reading" from a post-structuralist perspective in order to constitute a "radically revised" phenomenology of gender. Such a feminist phenomenology would "give up a complete phenomenological reduction to transcendental subjectivity," demand a "critical distance" from one's own experience, and, in its reflective step, concentrate on "experiences that are foreign to us."[44]

PHENOMENOLOGICAL METHOD

Another essential characteristic of phenomenology is its method: the so-called phenomenological description. Merleau-Ponty goes to the heart of the matter when he says, "Phenomenology is accessible only through a phenomenological method."[45] One can proceed from the assumption that feminist phenomenology, at its core, is characterized by the application of the phenomenological method. However, while, in principal, this cannot be denied, certain problems begin to emerge in considering the specifics of the methodology and how it is applied by feminist phenomenologists.

For Husserl, the phenomenological method consisted of a description of the objects in the way they were viewed by the observer—that is, the essential "phenomenon" in phenomenology. According to Husserl's "principles of all principles," it is about the application of intuition, the "rightful source" of all phenomenological understanding. He is convinced that *every originary presentive intuition is a legitimizing source of cognition*, that *everything originarily* (so to speak, in its 'personal' actuality) *offered* to us *in, intuition' is to be accepted simply as what it is presented as being*, but also *only within the limits in which it is presented there.*"[46]

Phenomenological description, according to Husserl, is actually a very specific method that entails various precise steps. It starts with distinguishing two different approaches of relating to the world. Husserl differentiates between a "natural attitude" and a "phenomenological attitude." The "natural attitude" is the attitude by which we intuitively relate to the world. It would be wrong to assume that phenomenology deals simply with a pure description of the natural world. The real phenomenological method starts with expounding on the problems of the natural approach, whereby phenomenologists must bring about a change in the approach: they do not just live in this natural world anymore, but instead have to make it their object. They are no longer intuitively relating to the world, but are instead consciously directed toward the world. With the next step phenomenologists implement the so-called phenomenal *epoché*, whereby they suspend all judgment about the being of the object. Husserl calls this the *"method of parenthesizing."*[47] The phenomenologist consciously "parenthesizes" all judgment about "being-in-the-world." In the next methodological step, the "phenomenological reduction," the being parenthesized through the phenomenological *epoché*, is led back to the *appearing for* the phenomenologist—that is, the actual "phenomenon" of phenomenology and the actual object of phenomenological description. In this way the "phenomenon" has appeared, to a certain extent, as an "artificial" object: it is from this point on an object that has been robbed of its "naturalness."

It seems, however, that one of the peculiarities of phenomenological research is that almost no one who calls herself a phenomenologist ever really applies this phenomenological method in the strict sense. This goes for classical phenomenology as well as for feminist phenomenology. One can even go so far as to say that no one applies the Husserlian method, at least not in this very *specific* way. Feminist phenomenologists do not, or only rarely, make use of the phenomenological method in its strict sense. Rather, they tend, for the most part, to limit themselves to the description of experience without applying these various, separated steps of the phenomenological method. This tendency has to do with Husserl's specific methodological approach, on the one hand, and the transformation of his phenomenology into a variety of diverse phenomenological approaches, on the other.

For this reason we need to differentiate in feminist phenomenology between instances where the phenomenological method is applied in a narrow Husserlian sense or in a broad phenomenological one that relies on descriptions of experience. With the latter, we must ask how such an approach can even be termed a phenomenological method, for what is in fact specifically phenomenological about this description.

In contemporary research, feminist phenomenologists use phenomenology to describe, in a more or less strict sense, *lived experiences*. In this respect they follow a model that Merleau-Ponty called the "pre-reflective experience"—that is, the lived experience underlying its reflection. Iris Marion Young's famous essay "Throwing Like a Girl" is a good example of this approach inasmuch as in her analysis she concentrates on the "primordial structures of existence," as did Merleau-Ponty.[48] However, she does not follow the steps of phenomenological description in the sense described above. Rather, she herself calls her reference to the phenomenological method "loosely" applied.[49] In fact, in her own words, her phenomenological method consists of the description of female experiences "from the point of view of the subject."[50] Motherhood, pregnancy, menopause, menstruation, and birthing continue to be central issues in feminist phenomenology even among the younger generation of scholars. The reproductive female body is a permanent resource for teaching and research in feminist phenomenology.[51] I would argue that the smallest common denominator of this research is the source of experience—that is, of the first-person perspective and the consideration of the lived dimension in the lifeworld.

Others, however, do not strive so much for a phenomenological description of gendered experiences in a narrow sense but try to grasp a specific phenomenological concept and make it pertinent to a feminist approach. This approach is still relatively focused on "practical applications," since these phenomenological concepts are directly integrated into feminist theory. Merleau-Ponty's terms of "chiasm" and of "flesh" or "anonymity"; Ricoeur's term of "narration"; Heidegger's "thrownness" (*Geworfenheit*); Levinas's "alterity" and his notion of the "feminine"; and Arendt's "natality" are only a few such examples.[52]

Feminist phenomenologists in a third, and perhaps the largest, group critically take up the various theories, arguing why, for example, the so-called phenomenal body is very important for a gender theory, or addressing the relationship of phenomenology to post-structuralism;[53] they use phenomenology to criticize problematic approaches within gender studies.[54] Or they try to make Beauvoir into a phenomenologist, to name only a few examples.[55]

Given these diverse orientations in the research of feminist phenomenology, the following preliminary conclusion can be drawn: Feminist phenomenology is a theoretical approach that, at its core, deals with descriptions of lived experience; it fundamentally applies the phenomenological method to feminist research in a more or less strict sense; and it also applies phenomenological concepts making use of them within a feminist framework. Finally, it critically discusses the intersection of phenomenology and feminist theory.

INTERDISCIPLINARITY

A characteristic of contemporary feminist phenomenology is its interdisciplinarity. Feminist phenomenology has left traces across diverse academic disciplines. It is no longer just a subdiscipline of philosophy but is rather often an applied approach. Indeed, the rich potential of the phenomenological tradition is also responsible for the interdisciplinary character of feminist phenomenology, allowing Eva-Maria Simms and Beata Stawarska to claim that "the strength of phenomenology lies in its interdisciplinary appeal."[56] This appeal corresponds well with feminist theory and gender studies that have been interdisciplinary from the very beginning.[57] This application of feminist phenomenology outside philosophy has in turn led to opening up philosophy to other disciplines.

In fact, feminist phenomenologists consistently respond to current research developments in a variety of fields. Today, for example, feminist phenomenologists critically engage with the cognitive sciences.[58] Another important area is the health sciences, which has gained momentum in the last few years, as evidenced by the recent, groundbreaking volume *Feminist Phenomenology and Medicine*, which provides insights into medical practices from the perspective of phenomenology and feminism. Another new and important field of interdisciplinary research is disability studies, with which the feminist perspective has become more and more integrated.[59] Simms, who is educated as a philosopher, has also significantly contributed to making feminist phenomenology fertile ground in the field of psychology. Among other studies, her book on the phenomenology of the child is worth being mentioned.[60] Along with Sara Ahmed's study on *Queer Phenomenology*, feminist phenomenology has entered queer studies. In addition, phenomenology has slowly been discovered by masculinity studies. Timothy Laurie, for example, has raised the question of how masculinity is addressed in the works of Heidegger and Beauvoir.[61] Recently, feminist phenomenology has also entered the field of aging in focusing on Beauvoir's widely neglected work on the subject.[62] In sports studies Jacquelyn Allen-Collinson for one uses feminist phenomenology to analyze female sporting embodiment, in particular female distance running.[63] And in film studies, Kate Ince, for example, draws on Merleau-Ponty in order to read Agnès Varda's cinema as fruitful for a "feminist existential-phenomenological approach," and puts it into the context of feminist phenomenology.[64] Among others, Alcoff has opened the phenomenological field to critical race studies. In her book *Visible Identities*, she offers "a phenomenological account of racial identity as it is lived in the body of various racialized subjects at a given cultural moment."[65] More recently, Emily Lee has edited a collection on embodiment and race and has an essay on difference in this volume, and Mariana Ortega has published a monograph on Latina feminist phenomenology in which she draws important connections between the writings of women of color who draw on experience and feminist phenomenology.[66] This admittedly small selection still shows an extensively broad development that feminist phenomenologists have set in motion with regard to other areas of study.

Due to this interdisciplinary character, the question posed at the beginning of this essay about whether one is dealing with phenomenological feminism or feminist phenomenology can be addressed anew. Feminist phenomenology is no longer limited to the field of philosophy. Although philosophy is well represented in feminist phenomenological research, there are numerous examples of feminist phenomenology being taken up in other disciplines.

THEORETICAL AMPLIFICATIONS: HERMENEUTICS AND POST-STRUCTURALISM

Since the beginning of its institutionalization, feminist phenomenology has experienced two clear theoretical developments. On the one hand, it has been extended through the approach of hermeneutics; on the other hand, feminist phenomenology has opened up in the direction of post-structuralism, which means it is no longer limited to classical phenomenology. As far as hermeneutics goes, it is clear that classical hermeneutics has developed from phenomenology. Hans-Georg Gadamer's main work, *Truth and Method*, is indebted to Husserlian phenomenology. Lorraine Code, in the collected anthology *Feminist Interpretations of Hans-Georg Gadamer*, argues that "Gadamerian hermeneutics—in which knowing is engaged, situated, dialogic, and historically conscious—has much to offer to feminists."[67] Moreover, it is well known that Heidegger refers to a *phenomenological* kind of hermeneutics. Another classical phenomenologist, Paul Ricoeur, also speaks of hermeneutics, though of a narrative kind. In other words, developing research in the area of feminist phenomenology with regard to philosophical hermeneutics makes perfect sense.[68]

Somewhat more difficult to achieve is incorporating feminist phenomenology into post-structuralism. Unlike hermeneutics, phenomenology and post-structuralism have been at odds with each other for many decades. The differences seemed irresolvable, in part due to the ongoing critical post-structuralist reading of phenomenology, which drew clear lines in order to stress the disparity between the two approaches. While phenomenology considered itself a philosophy of experience, it was precisely this term that incensed post-structuralists, especially the phenomenological description of experience, as I have already discussed. As a consequence, for some time, feminist phenomenology had a hard time dealing with the flourishing post-structural feminism of the 1990s. Oksala argues that phenomenological descriptions of the female body are in danger of becoming an "essentializing move" even if their descriptions are based on Merleau-Ponty's phenomenology of the body: "If any first-person description by a woman is understood as a phenomenological account and then generalized by turning it into a description of eidetic female embodiment, we end up with a female body that is essentialized."[69]

At the same time, however, the post-structural criticism made a new positioning of the relationship between phenomenology and post-structuralism possible with regard to feminist phenomenology. Feminist philosophers like Alcoff tried to rehabilitate the phenomenological term for "experience." I also showed in my own work that, for the most part, Scott's critique of the term "experience" did not apply to phenomenology.[70] On the contrary, I argued that in many aspects phenomenology and post-structuralism overlap. They both—each in their separate ways—have a "construction" of experience as their starting point. In addition, I have recently shown that the phenomenological term of the horizon in its indeterminacy comes very close to Butler's theory of the impossibility of fully determining gender identity.[71]

A certain approaching of post-structuralist phenomenology from the side of feminist phenomenologists begins to slowly emerge. There are references not only, or exclusively, to classical phenomenology but also to post-structuralist philosophy, and often at the same time. Veronica Vasterling, for example, made Jean-François Lyotard and Jacques Derrida, among others, accessible to feminist phenomenology.[72] Dorothea Olkowski strongly refers to the approach of Gilles Deleuze in her phenomenological-feminist work.[73] In my work I have read texts by Husserl and Merleau-Ponty together with the works of Judith Butler.[74] Finally, even though Johanna Oksala was greatly influenced by Michel Foucault and is especially critical of phenomenology—in certain circumstances—she still views a "phenomenology of gender" as a realistic possibility.[75]

These examples clearly demonstrate that the line between phenomenology and post-structuralism can no longer be drawn as clearly in the framework of feminist phenomenology. Phenomenology and post-structuralism in many respects do have a lot in common. Not only do they come out of the same historical tradition of continental philosophy, but also post-structuralist concepts have become more and more related to phenomenological research.[76] Consequently, a sharp demarcation between these two philosophical traditions has been deemed unproductive by many, which allows us to draw another conclusion: feminist phenomenology is no longer limited to the classics of phenomenology; it also relies on post-phenomenological approaches like philosophical hermeneutics and post-structuralism. When Johanna Oksala, in her critical reading of classical phenomenology, argues that feminist phenomenology should not consolidate but rather "destabilize" phenomenological thinking; that traditional phenomenology—in particular, transcendental and eidetic phenomenology—should be replaced by generative phenomenology, including a phenomenology of the event; and when, finally, she calls for a feminist phenomenology as an "open question," then one can say that this openness has already begun.[77]

CONCLUSION: THE FUTURE OF FEMINIST PHENOMENOLOGY

Feminist phenomenology is a research approach in which phenomenology and feminist theory enter into a constructive relationship. Historically, this occurred for the first time with Simone de Beauvoir's theoretical major work *The Second Sex* in 1949, but this approach was not institutionalized until the late 1980s, when there was growing research in the name of feminist phenomenology. Among these research activities we can count the exploration of female phenomenologists as well as dealing with gender issues through phenomenological means. These are very diverse accomplishments and dependent on the particular phenomenological tradition to which they refer. In the meantime, feminist phenomenology has grown into an interdisciplinary research approach in its own right that has also been known to, if necessary, incorporate other philosophical approaches such as phenomenological hermeneutics and post-phenomenological post-structuralism. Among its smallest common denominator one can count the study of gender-relevant issues from a perspective of lived experience—that is, from a first-person perspective. Due to the heterogeneous phenomenological tradition, feminist phenomenology itself is also essentially marked by heterogeneity. Ultimately, this is also why it refers to itself as a still open movement. In my view, the future of feminist phenomenology can be sustained only by continuing to preserve its heterogeneity and cultivating its diverse orientations. It was never—as is the case with phenomenology itself—a fully developed theory. As Ricoeur mentions, the history of phenomenology can also be described as a history of Husserlian heresies.[78] Feminist phenomenology will remain successful if it continues to present itself as an open, flexible movement and knows how to make use of its plurality. Here lies the future of feminist phenomenology. One can also refer to Merleau-Ponty's definition of phenomenology in his work *Phenomenology of Perception* and in a modified form apply it to feminist phenomenology: feminist phenomenology "*allows itself to be practiced and recognized as a manner or as a style, or that it exists as a movement, prior to having reached a full philosophical consciousness.*"[79]

SILVIA STOLLER is University Docent in the Department of Philosophy at the University of Vienna (Austria) and also teaches at the University of Graz (Austria). She is editor of *Simone de Beauvoir's Philosophy of Age: Gender, Ethics, and Time* (Berlin: De Gruyter, 2014) and (with Karel Novotný, Pierre Rodrigo, and Jenny Slatman) *Corporeity and Affectivity: Dedicated to Maurice Merleau-Ponty* (Leiden: Brill, 2014).

NOTES

1. Judith Butler, "Sexual Ideology and Phenomenological Description: A Feminist Critique of Merleau-Ponty's *Phenomenology of Perception*," in *The Thinking Muse: Feminism and Modern French Philosophy*, ed. Jeffner Allen and Iris Marion Young, 85–100

(Bloomington: Indiana University Press, 1989); Dorothea E. Olkowski, "Feminism and Phenomenology," in *The Edinburgh Encyclopedia of Continental Philosophy*, ed. Simon Glendinning (Edinburgh: Edinburgh University Press, 1999), 332.

2. Linda Fisher, "Feminist Phenomenology," in *Feminist Phenomenology*, ed. Linda Fisher and Lester Embree (Dordrecht: Kluwer Academic Publishers, 2000), 3.

3. For an overview, also see the following articles on feminist phenomenology or on the relation of feminism and phenomenology: Helen Fielding, "Feminism," in *Routledge Companion to Phenomenology*, ed. Sebastian Luft and Søren Overgaard, 518–27 (New York: Routledge, 2012); Fisher, "Feminist Phenomenology"; and Linda Fisher, "Phenomenology and Feminism: Perspectives on their Relation," in Fisher and Embree, *Feminist Phenomenology*, 17–38; Johanna Oksala, "What Is Feminist Phenomenology? Thinking Birth Philosophically," *Radical Philosophy* 126 (2004): 16–22; and "Phenomenology of Gender," *Continental Philosophy Review* 39 (2006): 229–44; Olkowski, "Feminism and Phenomenology"; and Eva-Maria Simms and Beata Stawarska, "Introduction: Concepts and Methods in Interdisciplinary Feminist Phenomenology," special issue, *Janus Head* 13, no. 1 (2013): 6–16. A bibliography on feminist phenomenology and hermeneutics can be found in Silvia Stoller, Veronica Vasterling, and Linda Fisher, *Feministische Phänomenologie und Hermeneutik* (Würzburg: Königshausen and Neumann, 2005).

4. See, for example, Debra B. Bergoffen, *The Philosophy of Simone de Beauvoir: Gendered Phenomenologies, Erotic Generosities* (Albany: State University of New York Press, 1997); Sara Heinämaa, *Toward a Phenomenology of Sexual Difference: Husserl, Merleau-Ponty, Beauvoir* (Lanham, MD: Rowman and Littlefield, 2003). I have critically addressed the question of the extent of the phenomenological influence on Beauvoir. See Silvia Stoller, *Existenz—Differenz—Konstruktion. Phänomenologien der Geschlechtlichkeit bei Beauvoir, Irigaray, and Butler* (Munich: Wilhelm Fink, 2010).

5. Heinämaa, *Toward a Phenomenology of Sexual Difference*.

6. See the website of the SIFP (Society for Interdisciplinary Feminist Phenomenology), http://sifp.uoregon.edu/history; and Simms and Stawarska, "Introduction: Interdisciplinary Feminist Phenomenology," 7.

7. The article "Sexual Ideology and Phenomenological Description: A Feminist Critique of Merleau-Ponty's *Phenomenology of Perception*" first appeared in Allen and Young, *Thinking Muse*. In a footnote Butler explains that her essay was originally written in 1981.

8. Butler, "Sexual Ideology and Phenomenological Description," 99.

9. Carol Bigwood, "Renaturalizing the Body (with a little help from Merleau-Pony)," *Hypatia* 6, no. 3 (1991): 54–73.

10. I organized this workshop. Participants came from the Netherlands (Annemie Halsema, Veronica Vasterling), Germany (Sabine Gürtler, Bettina Schmitz), Switzerland (Gabrielle Hiltmann), and Canada (Linda Fisher).

11. The series started in 2002 when Veronica Vasterling from Radboud University, Nijmegen, The Netherlands, organized the next conference on "Feminist Phenomenology and Hermeneutics." A year later, in 2003, the Swiss philosopher Gabrielle Hiltmann from the University of Basel arranged a conference on the topic of "Alterity and Sex/Gender: Phenomenological Reflections in Ethics." In 2006 the conference "Time in Feminist Phenomenology" took place at the University of Vechta in Germany, organized by Christina Schües together with Gabrielle Hiltmann. On the occasion of the

one-hundredth anniversary of Beauvoir, I ran another conference in Vienna in 2008 on Beauvoir's monograph *The Coming of Age*. The most recent event in this series is the international conference "Future Directions in Feminist Phenomenology," held at the University of Western Ontario in London, Canada, in 2013, organized by Helen Fielding.

12. Helen A. Fielding et al., eds., *The Other: Feminist Reflections in Ethics* (New York: Palgrave Macmillan, 2007); Christina Schües et al., eds. *Time in Feminist Phenomenology* (Bloomington: Indiana University Press, 2011); and Silvia Stoller, ed. *Simone de Beauvoir's Philosophy of Age: Gender, Ethics, and Time* (Berlin: Walter de Gruyter, 2014).

13. Silvia Stoller, and Helmuth Vetter, eds. *Phänomenologie und Geschlechterdifferenz* (Vienna: WUV-Universitätsverlag, 1996); Fisher and Embree, *Feminist Phenomenology*.

14. Stoller et al., *Feministische Phänomenologie und Hermeneutik*.

15. Lanei Rodemeyer and Sara Heinämaa, eds., "Feminist Phenomenologies," special issue, *Continental Philosophy Review* 43, no. 1 (2010); Eva-Maria Simms and Beata Stawarska, eds., "Feminist Phenomenology," special issue, *Janus Head* 13, no. 1 (2013). Several volumes in the series "Re-reading the Canon," edited by Nancy Tuana and published by Pennsylvania State University Press, also play an important role in the history of feminist phenomenology insofar as some of the included essays focus on the phenomenological background of a classic philosopher, as, for example, the volume on Merleau-Ponty (see Dorothea E. Olkowski and Gail Weiss, eds., *Feminist Interpretations of Maurice Merleau-Ponty* [University Park: Pennsylvania State University Press, 2006]), on Jean-Paul Sartre (Julien S. Murphy, ed., *Feminist Interpretations of Jean-Paul Sartre* [University Park: Pennsylvania State University Press, 1999]), on Levinas (Tina Chanter, ed., *Feminist Interpretations of Emmanuel Levinas* [University Park: Pennsylvania State University Press, 2001]), on Heidegger (Nancy J. Holland and Patricia Huntington, eds., *Feminist Interpretations of Martin Heidegger* [University Park: Pennsylvania State University Press, 2001]), and of course on Beauvoir (Margaret A. Simons, ed., *Feminist Interpretations of Simone de Beauvoir* [University Park: Pennsylvania State University Press, 1995]).

16. It must not go unnoticed that during this time Helen Fielding's dissertation was among the first ones. See Helen A. Fielding, "Beyond the Surface: Towards a Feminist Phenomenology of the Body-as-Depth," PhD diss., York University, 1996.

17. Iris Marion Young's text is one of the earliest texts of modern feminist phenomenology. It was first delivered as a lecture in 1977 at the conference of the Midwest Division of the Society for Women in Philosophy and then appeared again later in Allen and Young, *Thinking Muse*.

18. Iris Marion Young, "Throwing Like a Girl: A Phenomenology of Feminine Body Comportment, Motility, and Spatiality," in Allen and Young, *Thinking Muse*, 54.

19. For a critical adaptation of Young's article, see Dianne Chisholm, "Climbing Like a Girl: An Exemplary Adventure in Feminist Phenomenology," *Hypatia* 23, no. 1 (2008). In contrast to Young, Chisholm stresses the category of the lived body over the category of gender in order to do justice to female experiences that, strictly speaking, fall out of Young's narrow 1977 descriptions of feminine motility and spatiality. For Chisholm, the famous American rock climber Lynn Hill is a good example of how women's motility does not have to be considered negatively. Today's sports culture demonstrates that feminine bodily comportment can no longer be described in terms of typical incapability.

20. Edith Stein, *On the Problem of Empathy*, trans. Waltraut Stein (Dordrecht: Springer, 1964); Edith Stein, *Essays on Woman*, 2nd ed., trans. Freda Mary Oben and ed. Luce Gelber and Romaeus Leuven (Washington: ICS Publications, 1996). For more on Stein and her difficult relationship to Husserl, see Theresa Wobbe, *Das Weibliche. Edith Stein Jahrbuch*, vol. 2, "Sollte die akademische Laufbahn für Damen geöffnet werden..." *Edmund Husserl und Edith Stein.* (Würzburg: Echter, 1996). On the feminist roots of Stein, see Antonio Calcagno, *The Philosophy of Edith Stein* (Pittsburgh: Duquesne University, 2007).

21. Linda Lopez McAlister, "Dr. Gerda Walther: German Feminist Philosopher," in *Against Patriarchal Thinking: A Future without Discrimination?*, ed. Maja Pellikaan-Engel (Amsterdam: VU University Press, 1992), 69.

22. See the SIFP website, http://sifp.uoregon.edu/history.

23. See Fisher, "Phenomenology and Feminism."

24. This article appeared in a special issue of *Hypatia*, dedicated to *Feminism and the Body* and edited by Elizabeth Grosz (1991).

25. See Bigwood, "Renaturalizing the Body," 57, 61.

26. Alcoff argues that while she takes it as a given that phenomenology "needs" feminism, she also suggests that feminist theory could "benefit" from phenomenology, which can provide a "helpful corrective" against the shortcomings of post-structuralist feminism. See Linda Martín Alcoff, "Phenomenology, Post-structuralism, and Feminist Theory on the Concept of Experience," in Fisher and Embree, *Feminist Phenomenology*, 39–40.

27. Exemplary for the feminist criticism of Merleau-Ponty is Butler's early critique of his gender-neutral description in his *Phenomenology of Perception*. See Butler, "Sexual Ideology and Phenomenological Description." Another example is the debate between Shannon Sullivan and me. While Sullivan argues that Merleau-Ponty's reflections on anonymous corporeality ignore the very fact of gender difference, I argue that his concept of anonymity provides feminists with the helpful idea of difference as a process of differentiation. See Shannon Sullivan, "Domination and Dialogue in Merleau-Ponty's *Phenomenology of Perception*," *Hypatia* 12, no. 1 (1997): 1–19; Silvia Stoller, "Reflections on Feminist Merleau-Ponty Skepticism *Hypatia* 15, no. 1 (2000): 175–82; and Shannon Sullivan, "Feminism and Phenomenology: A Reply to Silvia Stoller," *Hypatia* 15, no. 1 (2000): 183–88.

28. Alcoff, "Phenomenology, Post-structuralism, and Feminist Theory," 39.

29. See, for example, Pamela Anderson, "Rereading Myth in Philosophy: Hegel, Ricoeur, and Irigaray Reading Antigone," in *Paul Ricoeur and Narrative: Context and Contestation*, ed. Morny Joy (Calgary: University of Calgary Press, 1997); and Annemie Halsema, "Reflexionen über Identität in einer multikulturellen Gesellschaft—Ein Dialog zwischen Ricoeur, Irigaray und Butler," in Stoller et al., *Feministische Phänomenologie und Hermeneutik*.

30. See Paul Ricoeur, "La sexualité: La merveille, l'errance, l'énigme," *Espirit* 289 (1960): 1665–75. Unfortunately, this study is still unknown in feminist research.

31. See Christina Schües, "The Birth of Difference," *Human Studies* 20, no. 2 (1997): 243–52; "Generative Phänomenologie in feministischer Perspektive," in Stoller et al., *Feministische Phänomenologie und Hermeneutik*.

32. In the past, feminist research has explored not only the phenomenological background of Beauvoir but of other classics in feminist theory, too, such as that of Luce Irigaray (Annemie Halsema, "Phenomenology in the Feminine: Irigaray's Relationship

to Merleau-Ponty," in *Intertwinings: Interdisciplinary Encounters with Maurice Merleau-Ponty*, ed. Gail Weiss, 63–83 [Albany: State University of New York Press, 2008]) and even Butler (Stoller, *Existenz—Differenz—Konstruktion*; and Silvia Stoller, "Expressivity and Performativity: Merleau-Ponty and Butler," *Continental Philosophy Review* 43 [2010]: 97–110). In a remarkable reading of Beauvoir's *The Ethics of Ambiguity* and Irigaray's *Sharing the World*, Anne Van Leeuwen has shown that there is an "important affinity between Beauvoir and Irigaray." See Anne Van Leeuwen, "Beauvoir, Irigaray, and the Possibility of Feminist Phenomenology," *Journal of Speculative Philosophy* 26, no. 2 (2012): 474.

33. Heinämaa, *Phenomenology of Sexual Difference*, 17.

34. Debra B. Bergoffen, "From Husserl to Beauvoir: Gendering the Perceiving Subject," in Fisher and Embree, *Feminist Phenomenology*, 57–58. See also Bergoffen, *Philosophy of Simone de Beauvoir*.

35. Sonia Kruks, "Existentialism and Phenomenology," in *A Companion to Feminist Philosophy*, ed. Alison M. Jaggar and Iris Marion Young (Malden, MA: Blackwell Publishers, 1998), 66.

36. Joan W. Scott, "Experience," in *Feminists Theorize the Political*, ed. Judith Butler and Joan W. Scott, 22–40 (New York: Routledge, 1992).

37. See Alcoff, "Phenomenology, Post-structuralism, and Feminist Theory," 44.

38. Elizabeth Grosz, "Merleau-Ponty and Irigaray in the Flesh," *Thesis Eleven* 36 (1993), 40.

39. Scott, "Experience," 33.

40. Ibid., 37, 25, 31, 34.

41. See Silvia Stoller, "Phenomenology and the Poststructural Critique of Experience," *International Journal of Philosophical Studies* 17, no. 5 (2009): 707–737.

42. Alcoff, "Phenomenology, Post-structuralism, and Feminist Theory."

43. Stoller, *Existenz—Differenz—Konstruktion*. Contrary to Oksala, however, I do not believe that feminist phenomenology requires dispensing with classic phenomenology in the strict sense. As I have shown elsewhere, if one is willing to read phenomenology with different eyes, one can find post-structuralist assumptions in classical texts of phenomenology—for example, that by way of the phenomenological concept of intentionality experience is always already an interpretation. See Stoller, "Phenomenology and the Poststructural Critique of Experience."

44. Johanna Oksala, "Phenomenology of Gender," *Continental Philosophy Review* 39 (2006): 240, 241.

45. Maurice Merleau-Ponty, *Phenomenology of Perception*, trans. Donald A. Landes (London: Routledge, 2012), viii.

46. Edmund Husserl, *Collected Works*, vol. 2, *Ideas Pertaining to a Pure Phenomenology and to a Phenomenological Philosophy* (The Hague: Martinus Nijhoff, 1983), 44.

47. Ibid., 60.

48. Young, "Throwing Like a Girl," 58.

49. Young, *Throwing Like a Girl*, 12.

50. Ibid., 13.

51. See Caroline Lundquist, "Being Torn: Toward a Phenomenology of Unwanted Pregnancy," *Hypatia* 23, no. 3 (2008): 136–55; Sarah LaChance Adams, *Mad Mothers, Bad Mothers, and What a "Good" Mother Would Do: The Ethics of Ambivalence* (New York: Columbia University Press, 2014).

52. For chiasm or flesh, see Grosz, "Merleau-Ponty and Irigaray in the Flesh"; Tina Chanter, "Wild Meaning: Luce Irigaray's Reading of Merleau-Ponty," in *Chiasms: Merleau-Ponty's Notion of Flesh*, ed. Fred Evans and Leonard Lawlor (Albany: State University of New York Press, 2000); and Dorothea E. Olkowski, "Chiasm, the Interval of Sexual Difference between Irigaray and Merleau-Ponty," in *Rereading Merleau-Ponty: Essays beyond the Continental-Analytic Divide*, ed. Lawrence Hass and Dorothea E. Olkowski (Amherst, MA: Humanity Books, 2000). For anonymity, see Megan M. Burke, "Anonymous Temporality and Gender: Rereading Merleau-Ponty," *philoSOPHIA* 3, no. 2 (2013): 138–57; Sara Heinämaa, "Personality, Anonymity, and Sexual Difference: The Temporal Formation of the Transcendental Ego," in Schües et al., *Time in Feminist Phenomenology*, 41–59; Silvia Stoller, "Gender and Anonymous Temporality," in Schües et al., *Time in Feminist Phenomenology*, 79–90; and Gail Weiss, "The Anonymous Intentions of Transactional Bodies," *Hypatia* 17, no. 4 (2002): 187–200. For narration, see Annemie Halsema, "The Time of the Self: A Feminist Reflection on Ricoeur's Notion of Narrative Identity," in Schües et al., *Time in Feminist Phenomenology*, 111–31. For thrownness, see Mechthild Nagel, "Thrownness, Playing-in-the-World, and the Question of Authenticity," in *Feminist Interpretations of Martin Heidegger*, ed. Nancy J. Holland and Patricia Huntington, 289–306 (University Park: Pennsylvania State University Press, 2001). For alterity, see Chanter, "Wild Meaning." For natality, see Schües, "The Birth of Difference"; Christina Schües, *Die Philosophie des Geborenseins*, 2nd ed. (Freiburg: Alber, 2016); and Adriana Cavarero, *Relating Narratives: Storytelling and Selfhood*, trans. Paul Kottmann (New York: Routledge, 2000).

53. For the first, see Simone de Beauvoir, *The Second Sex*, trans. and ed. H. M. Parshley (New York: Vintage Books, 1989), and for the second, see Alcoff, "Phenomenology, Post-Structuralism, and Feminist Theory"; Stoller, *Existenz—Differenz—Konstruktion*.

54. See Alcoff, "Phenomenology, Post-Structuralism, and Feminist Theory"; Fielding, "Feminist Phenomenology."

55. Heinämaa, *Toward a Phenomenology of Sexual Difference*.

56. Simms and Stawarska, "Interdisciplinary Feminist Phenomenology," 9.

57. One indication of this interdisciplinary direction is the Society for Interdisciplinary Feminist Phenomenology, which emphasizes the interdisciplinary orientation of feminist phenomenology even in its name. Another clear indication of the interdisciplinary character is the international conference "Future Directions in Feminist Phenomenology" at the University of Western Ontario, London (Canada), where the spectrum of interdisciplinary approaches was extremely broad; many of the essays from this conference appear in this volume.

58. See, for example, April Flakne's essay in this volume.

59. See Gayle Salamon, "The Phenomenology of Rheumatology: Disability, Merleau-Ponty, and the Fallacy of Maximal Grip," *Hypatia* 27, no. 2 (2012): 24–60; Linda Fisher, "The Illness Experience: A Feminist Phenomenological Perspective," in *Feminist Phenomenology and Medicine*, ed. Kristin Zeiler and Lisa Folkmarson Käll, 27–46 (Albany: State University of New York Press, 2014).

60. Eva M. Simms, *The Child in the World: Embodiment, Time, and Language in Early Childhood* (Detroit: Wayne State University Press, 2008).

61. Timothy Laurie, "The Ethics of Nobody I Know: Gender and the Politics of Description," *Qualitative Research Journal* 14, no. 1 (2014): 64–78. In the future it will be interesting to see how feminist phenomenology interacts with masculinity studies.

This is particularly interesting since masculinity studies is a field still for the most part ignored by mainstream feminism.

62. Simone de Beauvoir, *The Coming of Age*, trans. Patrick O'Brian (New York: W. W. Norton, 1996).

63. Jacquelyn Allen-Collinson, "Feminist Phenomenology and the Woman in the Running Body," *Sport, Ethics, and Philosophy* 5, no. 3 (2011): 297–313.

64. Kate Ince, "Feminist Phenomenology and the Film World of Agnès Varda," *Hypatia* 28, no. 3 (2013): 602–617.

65. Linda Martín Alcoff, *Visible Identities: Race, Gender, and the Self* (Oxford: Oxford University Press, 2006). See also Alia Al-Saji in an interview with Emma Ryman on feminist phenomenology, race, and perception. Emma Ryman, "Feminist Phenomenology, Race, and Perception: An Interview with Alia Al-Saji," *Rotman Institute of Philosophy* (blog), 2013.

66. Emily S. Lee, ed., *Living Alterities: Phenomenology, Embodiment, and Race* (Albany: State University of New York Press, 2014); Mariana Ortega, *In-Between: Latina Feminist Phenomenology, Multiplicity, and the Self* (Albany: State University of New York Press, 2016).

67. Lorraine Code, ed. *Feminist Interpretations of Hans-Georg Gadamer* (University Park: Pennsylvania State University Press, 2003), 4.

68. See Stoller et al., *Feministische Phänomenologie und Hermeneutik*.

69. Oksala, "Phenomenology of Gender," 232. However, it must be noted that feminist phenomenologists have themselves always been critical of essentializing gender, arguing that the embodiedness and situativeness of the gendered subject resist any gender essentialism. See, for example, Fisher, "Feminist Phenomenology"; and Helen A. Fielding, "'The Sum of What She Is Saying': Bringing Essences Back to the Body," in *Creation, Resistance, Flight: Feminist Enactments of French Philosophy*, ed. Dorothea E. Olkowski (Ithaca, NY: Cornell University Press, 2000).

70. Stoller, "Phenomenology and the Poststructural Critique of Experience."

71. According to phenomenology, a perceived object is surrounded by temporal and spatial horizons. Since the focus of perception is directed against the object, its horizons remain indeterminate, which means not fully or clearly determined, however co-perceived they are in their indeterminacy. Husserl adds that the indeterminacy of the horizon can never fully be determined. Stoller, "The Indeterminable Gender: Ethics in Feminist Phenomenology and Poststructuralist Feminism," *Janus Head* 13, no. 1 (2013): 17–34.

72. Veronica Vasterling, "Dekonstruktion der Identität: Zur Theorie der Geschlechterdifferenz bei Derrida," in *Phänomenologie und Geschlechterdifferenz*, ed. Silvia Stoller and Helmuth Vetter, 132–47 (Vienna: WUV-Universitätsverlag, 1997).

73. See Dorothea E. Olkowski, "Body, Knowledge, and Becoming-Woman: Morpho-Logic in Deleuze and Irigaray," in *Deleuze and Feminist Theory*, ed. Ian Buchanan and Claire Colebrook, 86–109 (Edinburgh: Edinburgh University Press, 2000).

74. See Silvia Stoller, "Konstruktionen von Geschlecht: Wiederholung und Wiederaufnahme bei Butler und Merleau-Ponty," *Tijdschrift voor Filosofie* 70, no. 3 (2008): 563–88; and Stoller, "Expressivity and Performativity."

75. Oksala, "Phenomenology of Gender." In fact, Butler defends Merleau-Ponty against Irigaray's critiques. See Judith Butler, "Sexual Difference as a Question of Ethics: Alterities of the Flesh in Irigaray and Merleau-Ponty," in *Feminist Interpretations of*

Maurice Merleau-Ponty, ed. Dorothea E. Olkowski and Gail Weiss, 107–125 (University Park: Pennsylvania State University Press, 2006).

76. This argument, for example, was made by Tina Chanter in her reference to Irigaray's philosophy when she wrote that the "post-phenomenological thinking" still belongs to the phenomenological tradition in its criticism of that tradition. See Tina Chanter, *Ethics of Eros: Irigaray's Rewriting of the Philosophers* (New York: Routledge, 1995), 3, 9.

77. Oksala, "What Is Feminist Phenomenology?," 21.

78. Paul Ricoeur, *A l'école de la Phénoménologie* (Paris: Vrin, 1987), 9.

79. Merleau-Ponty, *Phenomenology of Perception*, lxxi.

BIBLIOGRAPHY

Adams, Sarah LaChance. *Mad Mothers, Bad Mothers, and What a "Good" Mother Would Do: The Ethics of Ambivalence*. New York: Columbia University Press, 2014.

Ahmed, Sara. *Queer Phenomenology: Orientations, Objects, Others*. Durham, NC: Duke University Press, 2006.

Alcoff, Linda Martín. "Phenomenology, Post-structuralism, and Feminist Theory on the Concept of Experience." In Fisher and Embree, *Feminist Phenomenology*, 39–56.

———. *Visible Identities: Race, Gender, and the Self*. Oxford: Oxford University Press, 2006.

Allen, Jeffner, and Iris Marion Young, eds. *The Thinking Muse: Feminism and Modern French Philosophy*. Bloomington: Indiana University Press, 1989.

Allen-Collinson, Jacquelyn. "Feminist Phenomenology and the Woman in the Running Body." *Sport, Ethics, and Philosophy* 5, no. 3 (2011): 297–313.

Al-Saji, Alia. "Bodies and Sensings: On the Uses of Husserlian Phenomenology for Feminist Theory." *Continental Philosophy Review* 43, no. 1 (2010): 13–37.

Anderson, Pamela. "Re-reading Myth in Philosophy: Hegel, Ricoeur, and Irigaray Reading Antigone." In *Paul Ricoeur and Narrative: Context and Contestation*, edited by Morny Joy, 51–68. Calgary: University of Calgary Press, 1997.

Beauvoir, Simone de. *The Coming of Age*. Translated by Patrick O'Brian. New York: W. W. Norton, 1996.

———. *The Second Sex*. Translated and edited by H. M. Parshley. New York: Vintage Books, 1989.

Bergoffen, Debra B. "From Husserl to Beauvoir: Gendering the Perceiving Subject." In Fisher and Embree, *Feminist Phenomenology*, 57–70.

———. *The Philosophy of Simone de Beauvoir: Gendered Phenomenologies, Erotic Generosities*. Albany: State University of New York Press, 1997.

Bigwood, Carol. "Renaturalizing the Body (with a little help from Merleau-Ponty)." *Hypatia* 6, no. 3 (1991): 54–73.

Borren, Marieke. "Feminism as Revolutionary Practice: From Justice and the Politics of Recognition to Freedom." *Hypatia* 28, no. 1 (2013): 199–213.

Burke, Megan M. "Anonymous Temporality and Gender: Rereading Merleau-Ponty." *philoSOPHIA* 3, no. 2 (2013): 138–57.

Butler, Judith. "Sexual Difference as a Question of Ethics: Alterities of the Flesh in Irigaray and Merleau-Ponty." In *Feminist Interpretations of Maurice Merleau-Ponty*, edited by Dorothea E. Olkowski and Gail Weiss, 107–125. University Park: Pennsylvania State University Press, 2006.

———. "Sexual Ideology and Phenomenological Description: A Feminist Critique of Merleau-Ponty's *Phenomenology of Perception*." In Allen and Young, *Thinking Muse*, 85–100.
Calcagno, Antonio. *The Philosophy of Edith Stein*. Pittsburgh: Duquesne University, 2007.
Cavarero, Adriana. *Relating Narratives: Storytelling and Selfhood*. Translated by Paul Kottmann. New York: Routledge, 2000.
Chanter, Tina. *Ethics of Eros: Irigaray's Rewriting of the Philosophers*. New York: Routledge, 1995.
———, ed. *Feminist Interpretations of Emmanuel Levinas*. University Park: Pennsylvania State University Press, 2001.
———. "Wild Meaning: Luce Irigaray's Reading of Merleau-Ponty." In *Chiasms: Merleau-Ponty's Notion of Flesh*, edited by Fred Evans and Leonard Lawlor, 219–36. Albany: State University of New York Press, 2000.
Chisholm, Dianne. "Climbing Like a Girl: An Exemplary Adventure in Feminist Phenomenology." *Hypatia* 23, no. 1 (2008): 9–40.
Code, Lorraine. ed. *Feminist Interpretations of Hans-Georg Gadamer*. University Park: Pennsylvania State University Press, 2003.
———. *What Can She Know?* 3rd ed. Ithaca, NY: Cornell University Press, 1993.
Fielding, Helen A. "Beyond the Surface: Towards a Feminist Phenomenology of the Body-as-Depth." PhD diss., York University, 1996.
———. "Feminism." In *Routledge Companion to Phenomenology*, edited by Sebastian Luft and Søren Overgaard, 518–27. New York: Routledge, 2012.
———. "'The Sum of What She Is Saying': Bringing Essences Back to the Body." In *Creation, Resistance, Flight: Feminist Enactments of French philosophy*, edited by Dorothea E. Olkowski, 124–37. Ithaca, NY: Cornell University Press, 2000.
Fielding, Helen A., Gabrielle Hiltmann, Dorothea E. Olkowski, and Anne Reichhold, eds. *The Other: Feminist Reflections in Ethics*. New York: Palgrave Macmillan, 2007.
Fisher, Linda. "Feminist Phenomenology." In Fisher and Embree, *Feminist Phenomenology*, 1–15.
———. "The Illness Experience: A Feminist Phenomenological Perspective." In *Feminist Phenomenology and Medicine*, edited by Kristin Zeiler and Lisa Folkmarson Käll, 27–46. Albany: State University of New York Press, 2014.
———. "Phenomenology and Feminism: Perspectives on their Relation." In Fisher and Embree, *Feminist Phenomenology*, 17–38.
Fisher, Linda, and Lester Embree, eds. *Feminist Phenomenology*. Dordrecht: Kluwer Academic Publishers, 2000.
Gadamer, Hans-Georg. *Truth and Method*. 2nd ed. Berkeley: University of California Press, 2008.
Grosz, Elizabeth. Introduction. *Feminism and the Body*. Special issue, *Hypatia* 6, no. 3 (1991): 1–3.
———. "Merleau-Ponty and Irigaray in the Flesh." *Thesis Eleven* 36 (1993): 37–59.
Halsema, Annemie. "Phenomenology in the Feminine: Irigaray's Relationship to Merleau-Ponty." In *Intertwinings: Interdisciplinary Encounters with Maurice Merleau-Ponty*, edited by Gail Weiss, 63–83. Albany: State University of New York Press, 2008.
———. "Reflexionen über Identität in einer multikulturellen Gesellschaft—Ein Dialog zwischen Ricoeur, Irigaray und Butler." In Stoller et al., *Feministische Phänomenologie und Hermeneutik*, 208–234.

———. "The Time of the Self: A Feminist Reflection on Ricoeur's Notion of Narrative Identity." In Schües et al., *Time in Feminist Phenomenology*, 111–31.

Heinämaa, Sara. "Personality, Anonymity, and Sexual Difference: The Temporal Formation of the Transcendental Ego." In Schües et al., *Time in Feminist Phenomenology*, 41–59.

———. *Toward a Phenomenology of Sexual Difference: Husserl, Merleau-Ponty, Beauvoir.* Lanham, MD: Rowman and Littlefield, 2003.

Holland, Nancy J., and Patricia Huntington, eds. *Feminist Interpretations of Martin Heidegger.* University Park: Pennsylvania State University Press, 2001.

Husserl, Edmund. *Collected Works.* Vol. 2. *Ideas Pertaining to a Pure Phenomenology and to a Phenomenological Philosophy.* The Hague: Martinus Nijhoff Publishers, 1983.

Ince, Kate. "Feminist Phenomenology and the Film World of Agnès Varda." *Hypatia* 28, no. 3 (2013): 602–617.

Kruks, Sonia. "Existentialism and Phenomenology." In *A Companion to Feminist Philosophy*, edited by Alison M. Jaggar and Iris Marion Young, 66–74. Malden, MA: Blackwell Publishers, 1998.

Laurie, Timothy. "The Ethics of Nobody I Know: Gender and the Politics of Description." *Qualitative Research Journal* 14, no. 1 (2014): 64–78.

Lee, Emily S.. *Living Alterities: Phenomenology, Embodiment, and Race.* Albany: State University of New York Press, 2014.

Lundquist, Caroline. "Being Torn: Toward a Phenomenology of Unwanted Pregnancy." *Hypatia* 23, no. 3 (2008): 136–55.

McAlister, Linda Lopez. "Dr. Gerda Walther: German Feminist Philosopher." In *Against Patriarchal Thinking: A Future without Discrimination?*, edited by Maja Pellikaan-Engel, 65–69. Amsterdam: VU University Press, 1992.

Merleau-Ponty, Maurice. *Phenomenology of Perception.* Translated by Donald A. Landes. London: Routledge, 2012.

Murphy, Julien S., ed. *Feminist Interpretations of Jean-Paul Sartre.* University Park: Pennsylvania State University Press, 1999.

Nagel, Mechthild. "Thrownness, Playing-in-the-World, and the Question of Authenticity." In *Feminist Interpretations of Martin Heidegger*, edited by Nancy J. Holland and Patricia Huntington, 289–306. University Park: Pennsylvania State University Press, 2001.

Oksala, Johanna. "Phenomenology of Gender." *Continental Philosophy Review* 39 (2006): 229–44.

———. "What Is Feminist Phenomenology? Thinking Birth Philosophically." *Radical Philosophy* 126 (2004): 16–22.

Olkowski, Dorothea E. "Body, Knowledge, and Becoming-Woman: Morpho-Logic in Deleuze and Irigaray." In *Deleuze and Feminist Theory*, edited by Ian Buchanan and Claire Colebrook, 86–109. Edinburgh: Edinburgh University Press, 2000.

———. "Chiasm, the Interval of Sexual Difference between Irigaray and Merleau-Ponty." In *Rereading Merleau-Ponty: Essays Beyond the Continental-Analytic Divide*, edited by Lawrence Hass and Dorothea E. Olkowski, 339–54. Amherst, MA: Humanity Books, 2000b.

———. "Feminism and Phenomenology." In *The Edinburgh Encyclopedia of Continental Philosophy*, edited by Simon Glendinning, 323–32. Edinburgh: Edinburgh University Press, 1999.

Olkowski, Dorothea E., and Gail Weiss, eds. *Feminist Interpretations of Maurice Merleau-Ponty*. University Park: Pennsylvania State University Press, 2006.

Ortega, Mariana. *In-Between: Latina Feminist Phenomenology, Multiplicity, and the Self*. Albany: State University of New York Press, 2016.

Ricoeur, Paul. *A l'école de la phénoménologie*. Paris: Vrin, 1987.

———. "La sexualité: La merveille, l'errance, l'énigme." *Esprit* 289 (November 1960): 1665–75. Also available at http://www.jeune-catholique-moulins.cef.fr/wp-content/uploads/2013/05/Texte-de-Paul-Ricoeur.pdf.

Rodemeyer, Lanei, and Sara Heinämaa, eds. *Feminist Phenomenologies*. Special issue, *Continental Philosophy Review* 43, no. 1 (2010).

Ryman, Emma. "Feminist Phenomenology, Race, and Perception: An Interview with Alia Al-Saji." *Rotman Institute of Philosophy* (blog). http://www.rotman.uwo.ca/blog.

Salamon, Gayle. "The Phenomenology of Rheumatology: Disability, Merleau-Ponty, and the Fallacy of Maximal Grip." *Hypatia* 27, no. 2 (2012): 24–60.

Schües, Christina. "The Birth of Difference." *Human Studies* 20, no. 2 (1997): 243–52.

———. "Generative Phänomenologie in feministischer Perspektive." In Stoller et al., *Feministische Phänomenologie und Hermeneutik*, 46–66.

———. *Die Philosophie des Geborenseins*. 2nd ed. Freiburg: Alber, 2016.

Schües, Christina, Dorothea E. Olkowski, and Helen A. Fielding, eds. *Time in Feminist Phenomenology*. Bloomington: Indiana University Press, 2011.

Scott, Joan W. "Experience." In *Feminists Theorize the Political*, edited by Judith Butler and Joan W. Scott, 22–40. New York: Routledge, 1992.

Simms, Eva M. *The Child in the World: Embodiment, Time, and Language in Early Childhood*. Detroit: Wayne State University Press, 2008.

Simms, Eva-Maria, and Beata Stawarska, eds. "Introduction: Concepts and Methods in Interdisciplinary Feminist Phenomenology." Special issue, *Janus Head* 13, no. 1 (2013): 6–16.

———, eds. Special issue, *Janus Head* 13, no. 1 (2013).

Simons, Margaret A., ed. *Feminist Interpretations of Simone de Beauvoir*. University Park: Pennsylvania State University Press, 1995.

Stein, Edith. *Essays on Woman*. 2nd ed. Translated by Freda Mary Oben, edited by Luce Gelber and Romaeus Leuven. Washington: ICS Publications, 1996.

———. *On the Problem of Empathy*. Translated by Waltraut Stein. Dordrecht: Springer, 1964.

Stoller, Silvia. *Existenz—Differenz—Konstruktion. Phänomenologien der Geschlechtlichkeit bei Beauvoir, Irigaray, and Butler*. Munich: Wilhelm Fink, 2010.

———. "Expressivity and Performativity: Merleau-Ponty and Butler." *Continental Philosophy Review* 43 (2010): 97–110.

———. "Gender and Anonymous Temporality." In Schües et al., *Time in Feminist Phenomenology*, 79–90.

———. "The Indeterminable Gender: Ethics in Feminist Phenomenology and Poststructuralist Feminism." *Janus Head* 13, no. 1 (2013): 17–34.

———. "Konstruktionen von Geschlecht: Wiederholung und Wiederaufnahme bei Butler und Merleau-Ponty." *Tijdschrift voor Filosofie* 70, no. 3 (2008): 563–88.

———. "Phenomenology and the Poststructural Critique of Experience." *International Journal of Philosophical Studies* 17, no. 5 (2009): 707–737.

———. "Reflections on Feminist Merleau-Ponty Skepticism." *Hypatia* 15, no. 1 (2000): 175–82.

———, ed. *Simone de Beauvoir's Philosophy of Age: Gender, Ethics, and Time*. Berlin: Walter de Gruyter, 2014.

Stoller, Silvia, and Helmuth Vetter, eds. *Phänomenologie und Geschlechterdifferenz*. Vienna: WUV-Universitätsverlag, 1996.

Stoller, Silvia, Veronica Vasterling, and Linda Fisher, eds. *Feministische Phänomenologie und Hermeneutik*. Würzburg: Königshausen and Neumann, 2005.

Sullivan, Shannon. "Domination and Dialogue in Merleau-Ponty's *Phenomenology of Perception*." *Hypatia* 12, no. 1 (1997): 1–19.

———. "Feminism and Phenomenology: A Reply to Silvia Stoller." *Hypatia* 15, no. 1 (2000): 183–88.

Van Leeuwen, Anne. "Beauvoir, Irigaray, and the Possibility of Feminist Phenomenology." *Journal of Speculative Philosophy* 26, no. 2 (2012): 474–84.

Vasterling, Veronica. "Dekonstruktion der Identität: Zur Theorie der Geschlechterdifferenz bei Derrida." In *Phänomenologie und Geschlechterdifferenz*, edited by Silvia Stoller and Helmuth Vetter, 132–47. Vienna: WUV-Universitätsverlag, 1997.

———. "Zur Bedeutung von Heideggers ontologischer Hermeneutik für die feministische Philosophie." In Stoller et al., *Feministische Phänomenologie und Hermeneutik*, 67–95.

Weiss, Gail. "The Anonymous Intentions of Transactional Bodies." *Hypatia* 17, no. 4 (2002): 187–200.

Wobbe, Theresa. *Das Weibliche. Edith Stein Jahrbuch*. Vol. 2. "Sollte die akademische Laufbahn für Damen geöffnet werden. . ." *Edmund Husserl und Edith Stein*. Würzburg: Echter, 1996.

Young, Iris Marion. *Throwing Like a Girl and Other Essays in Feminist Philosophy and Social Theory*. Bloomington: Indiana University Press, 1990.

———. "Throwing Like a Girl: A Phenomenology of Feminine Body Comportment, Motility, and Spatiality." In Allen and Young, *Thinking Muse*, 51–70.

INDEX

Page numbers in italics refer to figures and tables.

absolute subject (the), 111, 113, 114, 119, 120, 122
action(s), ix, xi, xiii, xvi, xvii, xxn66, xxv, xxvi, xxxi, 7, 9, 10, 11, 12, 13, 15, 28, 32, 33, 49, 51, 52, 69, 70, 73, 77, 79, 80, 82, 83, 93, 94, 95, 103, 105, 128, 132, 133, 189, 190, 245, 246, 250, 251, 252, 257, 258, 259, 261, 264, 266, 267, 268, 269, 277, 278, 280, 284, 287, 293, 294, 302–309 passim; collective, 303, 304, 307
affect, xxvi, 94, 97, 100, 179n67, 281, 285, 295n4; affects, xiv, 24, 68, 102, 285; affections, 8, 15, 280; affective, xvi, 8, 25, 28, 94, 98, 103, 155, 156, 165, 179, 280, 283, 291, 295n4, 323n7
affectivity, 9, 15
agency, vii, viii, ix, xi, xii, xiii–xiv, xxix, xxxi, 38, 72, 80, 81, 158, 162, 168, 187–188, 257, 258, 259, 262–265, 267, 268, 269, 291
aging, v, xi, xxx, 203, 205–209, 211, 215, 340
Ahmed, Sara, 340
Alaimo, Stacy, xiii, 187, 188, 190
Alcoff, Linda Martín, 322n5, 336, 340, 341, 346n26
Allen, Jeffner, 141, 142, 150
Allen-Collinson, Jacquelyn, 340
Al-Saji, Alia, 349n65
ambiguity, 12, 15, 71, 111, 112, 113, 184, 185, 186, 187
Andersen, Paul, 71, 72, 78
androcentrism, 141, 150, 333, 334
Anishinaabe (*pl.* Anishinaabeg; *also spelled* Anishinabek), xiv, xxvii, 157–159, 163, 168, 173, 174, 175n3, 176n6
Archimedean Point, 93, 301, 309

architecture, xxv, 66, 71, 74, 75, 77, 78, 83, 141, 146
Arendt, Hannah, xiii, xvi, xixn50, xxn60, xxxi, xxxii, 4, 93, 96, 98, 99, 101, 102, 103, 108n56, 218, 257–269, 270n7, 271n25, 290, 297n34, 299, 300, 301, 302, 303–305, 307, 308, 309, 311n25, 332, 333, 339
Aristotle, xxvii, 21, 317
arrogant perception, xxxiii, 279, 284, 285–286, 288, 289, 290
Austin, J. L., 128–130, 131–134, 136n21
authenticity, 299, 300–303, 306, 309, 310, 310n8
authentic leaders, 300, 301
authentic leadership, xxxii, 299–306, 309, 310n1

Bachelard, Gaston, 225
Bahduri, Bhubaneswari, 37
Barad, Karen, xiii, xiv, xv, 17n37, 187, 188
Bateson, Gregory, 70, 72, 82
Baton Rouge, 81
Beauvoir, Simone de, viii, xxv, xxvi, xxxii, 4, 12, 15, 16, 25, 27, 29, 30, 31, 47–49, 51, 60, 62, 82, 110–119, 120, 121, 122n8, 126–128, 134, 184–186, 187, 196n9, 205–214 passim, 216n17, 329–330, 331, 332, 335, 339, 340, 343, 347n42
being, vii, x, xii, xiii, xv, xvi, xxiii, xxvii, xxviii, 28, 29, 35, 63n12, 71, 74, 84n10, 92, 97, 100, 103, 108n56, 110, 111, 141, 142, 143, 145–149, 157, 158, 159, 162, 169, 172, 176n6, 183–195 passim, 195n5, 189nn40–41, 218, 292, 314, 317, 318, 322n4, 323n5, 323n7, 337; ways or styles of being, 33, 38

355

Benhabib, Seyla, 198n41, 266–267, 333
Bennett, Jane, xiv
Bergoffen, Debra, xxvi, 31, 122, 335
Bergson, Henri, xxvii, 13, 14–15, 225
Bierria, Alisa, 80
Bigwood, Carol, 330, 334
bioethics, 218, 223–224, 225
bio-phenomenology, 219, 224–226, 227, 228, 233, 234
biopolitics, 223, 258–264, 267, 269
biotechnology, 219, 221, 222, 224–225, 228, 233
birth, 49, 226, 228, 231, 233, 263, 265, 266, 267, 268, 269, 283, 320, 338
bleeding, 23, 25, 29, 30, 57
body, x, xi, xv, xxix, xxx, 4–15 passim, 16n4, 21–39 passim, 55, 68, 69, 70, 73, 92, 93, 94, 95, 98, 100, 113, 115, 117, 122, 141, 142, 146, 147, 149, 150, 157, 160, 161, 162, 164, 167, 169, 170, 171, 172, 173, 177n6, 179n49, 179n67, 185, 186, 187, 192, 198n40, 203, 205, 208, 209, 210, 212, 213, 214, 215, 215n3, 218–234 passim, 235n11, 237n25, 238n46, 244, 247, 251, 253, 262, 263, 281, 282, 284, 285, 286, 287, 293, 294, 315, 316, 318, 319, 320, 321, 322n4, 323n7, 330, 331, 334, 335, 339, 340, 341, 345n19; as an object, 253; image, xxix, xxx, 201, 205, 210, 214, 215, 216n10, 278
Bordo, Susan, 323n5
Bourdieu, Pierre, 203
Braidotti, Rosi, 186–188
breast amputation, 243, 244, 250
breast cancer, xxx, 242, 244, 245, 247, 248, 249, 250
breast saving, 243, 244, 248
Brouwer, L. E. J., 13–14
Butler, Judith, xii, xviiin33, 63n12, 64n38, 324n13, 328, 330, 342, 346n27, 349n75

Calcagno, Antonio, xviin9, 346n20
Carel, Havi, 236n22
catastrophe, 67, 74, 102
Cavarero, Adriana, 198n41
Cézanne, Paul, 92
Chanter, Tina, 335, 350n76
Charon, Rita, 245, 254

chiasm, 141, 147, 159, 160, 161, 162, 165, 166, 168, 172, 211, 339, 348n52; chiasmatic, 318, 319, 325n35; chiasmic, xxviii, 158, 159, 168; chiasmically, xxx
Chisholm, Dianne, 345n19
class, 38, 73, 100, 112, 113, 117, 131, 205, 262, 263, 306
classic phenomenology, 296n22, 329, 330
clinamen, 12
closed system, xxvi, 93, 96, 97
Code, Lorraine, 341
cogito, 35, 208, 31; double-cogito, 30, 42n41; tacit cogito, 145; un-cogito, 11
cognitive sciences, xxxii, 315, 323n8, 340
commodification, 262
conditio humana, 227
consciousness, xi, xxvii, xxix, xxx, 5–6, 7, 8, 9, 12, 13, 15, 27, 35, 59, 112, 141, 144–146, 155, 157, 158, 159, 162, 163, 165, 166, 170, 171, 183, 184–186, 188, 189, 190, 197n33, 189n40, 208, 221, 226, 232, 315, 334; collective consciousness, 26; human consciousness, 155, 156, 160, 162, 163, 167, 169, 171, 172, 180n67, 180nn77–78; mnidoo consciousness, 169; philosophical consciousness, 343; self-consciousness, 33
consciousnessing, 162, 169; world-, 180. *See also* Mnidoo: worlding
couple (the), 112, 114–115, 121, 122, 129
cyberbullying, xxvi, 92, 95, 97, 105, 106n20, 107n51. *See also* online bullying
cyberspace, xxvi, 95, 96, 97
cyborg, 73
cyclical, 21, 35, 91, 98, 262

Davis, Angela, 80
death, xii, xxvi, 26, 30, 31, 32, 36, 38, 39, 55, 56, 82, 92, 95, 102, 105, 106n19, 107n27, 170, 204, 221, 229, 233, 234, 235n12, 271n25; death drive, 49; death work, 323n7
Deleuze, Gilles, xiii, xiv, xv, xixn47, xxv, 6, 7, 8, 49–51, 55, 56–57, 58, 59, 62, 63n12, 66, 67, 68, 69, 70, 83n7, 102, 108n59, 179n67, 342
Derrida, Jacques, xii, 184, 342

deterritorialization, 58, 67
diacritic, xxvii, 148, 149, 150
dialectic, 3, 12, 50, 51, 55, 110, 142–143, 145, 148, 285, 287, 288, 289, 313, 317–318, 321
Dietz, Mary, 266
difference, xiv, xixn47, xxvi, xxviii, xxxii, xxxiii, 9, 47, 67, 68, 71, 72, 73, 77, 80, 85n32, 98, 110–119 passim, 121, 122, 127, 142, 148, 149, 150, 151, 158, 165, 175n4, 180n67, 186, 203, 213, 221, 278, 279, 285, 286, 287, 288, 290, 303, 313–322, 323n5, 323n7, 330, 340, 346n27
direct perception, xxxii, xxxiii, 277–285, 286, 288, 289, 290, 291–294, 294n1, 295n4, 295n6
disability, xi, xxx, 203–207, 211, 212, 21n26, 223; studies, 106n14, 207, 211, 340
Dotson, Kristie, 131
doubling negatives, 51
Douglas, Mary, 31, 204
Dreyfus, Hubert, 315, 323n8
duration, 13, 29

écart, 68, 73, 84n19, 148, 164–166, 168, 319
embodied, viii, ix, xi, xii, xv, xvii, xxix, xxx, xxxii, xxxiii, 3, 4, 5, 11, 14, 34, 35, 69, 84n15, 91, 93, 103, 104, 106n14, 114, 142, 145, 155, 157, 160, 161, 168, 171, 173, 176n6, 179n64, 183, 185, 189, 190, 208, 227, 257, 269, 277, 279, 280, 281, 282, 283, 284, 285, 286, 292, 293, 295n4, 299, 301, 305, 308, 309, 310, 315, 320, 334, 349n69
embodied dialectic, 12
embodied social cognition, 277
embodiment, viii, xxiv, xxvii, 4–7, 8, 9, 11, 12, 15, 16, 26, 35, 37, 115, 141, 168, 218, 227, 232, 233, 244, 286, 287, 315, 316, 318, 319, 321, 324n13, 334, 335, 340, 341
empirical research, 236n18, 238n44, 284, 294n1
empiricism, x, xii, xiv, 93, 144, 226, 234, 282
encroachment, 318
erotic, 49, 60, 113, 114
ethical, viii, xvii, xxx, 11, 66, 96, 113, 163, 175n6, 176, 183, 184, 194, 195, 223, 228, 231, 232, 234, 238n39, 255n13, 300, 301, 302, 307, 308, 309, 310. *See also* bioethics

Evans, Ieshia, 81, *81*
excluded middle, 14
existence, viii, x, xxvi, xxvii, 13, 14, 25, 29, 60, 67, 72, 83, 91–105 passim, 105, 113, 117, 120, 130, 142, 144, 155, 160, 165, 169, 171, 173, 176n6, 188, 191, 204, 211, 212, 213, 215, 219, 227, 231, 232, 282, 301, 321, 323n7, 324n11, 332, 334, 338; anonymous existence, 70, 92; coexistence, 82, 96, 161, 176n6; plane of existence, xxvi, 11, 12; pre-personal existence, xv, 92
existential phenomenology, 310n8, 334
experience, ix, x, xiii, xv, xxiv, xxvii, xxix, xxx, xxxii, 5, 7, 13, 15, 18n52, 24, 25, 29, 30, 51, 52, 58, 69, 70, 73, 74, 78, 79, 80, 84n19, 91, 92, 93, 94, 95, 96, 97, 102, 104, 105, 111, 118, 125, 126, 141, 145, 158, 160, 161, 162, 167, 168, 169, 170, 171, 172, 173, 176n6, 177n9, 183, 186, 187, 188, 190, 191, 192, 193, 194, 205, 206, 207, 209, 210, 212, 214, 218–234, 237n25, 237n28, 242, 243, 244, 245, 247, 248, 250–254, 267, 281, 297, 300, 303, 306, 307, 308, 313, 318, 319, 320, 321, 334, 335, 336, 337, 338–339, 340, 341, 342, 347n43; lived, xxxii, 134, 161, 174, 189, 207, 208, 211, 212, 242, 246, 253, 290, 292, 299, 301, 302, 304, 305, 306, 309, 330, 338, 339, 343; embodied, ix, xxxii, 208, 309, 332, 334; extreme or traumatic, xxvii, 97, 191, 193, 194; gendered, xxvii, 150, 266, 299, 336, 339, 345n19; living, vii, ix, xii, 97, 103; perceptual, 68, 69, 160, 161, 164, 165, 172, 179n64, 210, 319, 336; subaltern, 314

Fanon, Frantz, 324n14
felicity (of speech acts), 126, 129, 130, 131, 132, 133, 134, 135
feminine, 4, 27, 31, 47, 49, 50, 60, 63n13, 117, 120, 122, 125, 127, 128, 204, 244, 332, 339, 345n19
feminist phenomenology, vii–ix, xvi, xviiin8, xxiv, xxix, xxxi, xxxii, xxxiii, 3, 4, 16, 92, 105, 125, 128, 134, 141, 184, 195, 227, 277, 282, 328–343, 344n2, 344n11, 345n15, 345n17, 346n26, 347n43, 348n57, 349n69

feminist speech act theory, 125, 126, 128, 131
Feuerbach, Ludwig, xxiii
field, x, xi, xiv, 6, 7, 8, 9, 67, 68, 69, 70, 78, 108n59, 141, 142, 144, 145, 146, 148, 149, 150, 158, 159, 160, 161, 162, 166, 187, 190, 232, 245, 318, 321; perceptual, 11, 68, 145, 170, 210, 326n38; transcendental, x, 145, 147, 148, 150, 318
Fielding, Helen A., xxvi, 215, 344n3, 345n11, 345n16
figure/ground, 142, 144
film studies, 340
Finlay, Linda, 236n22
first person perspective, xxx, 236n22, 237n25, 242, 243, 245, 253, 297n33, 339, 343
Fisher, Linda, 329, 331, 333, 344n3
flesh, vii, ix, xv, xvi, 26, 27, 28, 30, 60, 66, 67, 68–69, 70, 71, 73, 82, 83, 83n7, 113, 114, 129, 141, 147, 148–149, 150, 154, 159, 162, 188, 213, 230, 233, 286, 314, 316, 318, 319, 339, 348n52
fold, ix, 68, 161, 185, 186, 189, 190, 197n33, 319
form, xxvii, xxviii, xxxii, 7, 8, 9, 11, 12, 14, 15, 22, 37, 38, 49, 54, 56, 59, 66, 70, 73, 75, 77, 78, 79, 98, 101, 106n22, 114, 115, 116, 118, 121, 126, 128, 133, 136n21, 144, 146, 147, 159, 161, 184, 187, 189, 209, 214, 216n16, 220, 222, 225, 245, 246, 259, 262, 265, 267, 294, 301, 315, 343
Foucault, Michel, xii, 50, 184, 188, 189, 221, 235n12, 258, 259, 342
fraternity, 114
freedom, 4, 12, 16, 73, 113, 116, 119, 120, 121, 151, 185, 259, 261, 265, 270n13, 304, 307; docile, 120; domesticated, 119
Freud, Sigmund, xxv, 49, 50, 51, 59, 63n13, 63n22, 210, 320
Frye, Marilyn, 278, 279, 285–290

Gadamer, Hans-Georg, 341
Gallagher, Shaun, xxxivn21, 277, 29, 280, 282–284, 294n1, 296n10, 11, 13, 14, 23, 24, 297n36, 37, 325n38
gap, 10, 160, 165, 170, 172, 210, 282, 288, 292. *See also* lacuna

Garland-Thomson, Rosemarie, 203
gashka'oode (entangled), 158
gender, viii, xii, xviiin33, xxviii, 4, 22, 24, 26, 27, 33, 34, 37, 38, 39, 40, 73, 79, 118, 125, 126, 127, 128, 129, 130, 131, 132, 134, 141, 149–150, 151, 205, 216, 224, 227, 265, 266, 284, 299, 306, 307, 310n11, 324n11, 330, 331, 332, 334, 336, 337, 339, 342, 343, 345n19, 346n27, 349n69
gendered speech, 126, 128
generative dimension, 218; structures, 225, 233
gestalt, xxviii, 11, 13, 142, 143, 144–145, 146, 147, 148, 149, 318; psychology, 142, 144, 148
gestell (enframing), 100, 103
Gines, Kathryn T., 118
Goffman, Erving, 205
good dialectic, 141, 143, 149, 150. *See also* hyperdialectic
Google, xxiii, 97, 107n27, 192
Gordon, Lewis, 314, 315, 316, 322
Grosz, Elizabeth, 27, 31, 186, 187, 188, 213, 323n7, 336
Guattari, Félix, 56, 57, 58, 59, 62, 179nn66–67

habit, xi, xxix, 5, 39, 40, 58, 106n14, 128, 131, 210, 213–214, 217n30, 221, 243, 244, 278, 292
habitus, 136n22, 203
Hadid, Zaha, 75
Hallowell, A. Irving, 174n2
Halsema, Annemie, xxx, 242, 255n6, 344n10, 346n32, 348n52
Haraway, Donna, 72, 73, 78, 85n42
Hartman, Saidiya V., 81
Hartsock, Nancy, 73, 85n33
Hass, Lawrence, 84n10, 15, 348n52
Havis, Devonya N., 79, 80, 81
health, xxx, 28, 232, 242, 243, 253, 257, 260, 261, 262, 270n3, 287; health-care, xxx, 243, 254, 340; healthy, 222, 230, 258, 261, 263, 287
hearing, v., 30, 33, 52, 125, 126, 135, 221, 232, 235n9
Hegel, G. W. F., xxiii, 3, 16n1, 110, 111, 119, 142–143, 148, 185, 281, 293, 313, 316, 317, 318

Heidegger, Martin, xii, 96, 100, 101, 103, 142, 146, 147, 158, 160, 183, 280, 281, 290, 310n8, 330, 333, 335, 339, 340, 341, 345n15; Heideggerean, 286, 293
Heinämaa, Sara, viii, 16n4, 295n6, 330, 335
Hekman, Susan, xiii, xiv
Henry, Michel, 225, 237n25
hermeneutic, 222, 237n23, 278, 281, 286, 293, 310n8, 310n11, 316, 331, 335, 341, 342, 343, 344n3, 344n11
high-altitude thinking, 142, 147; thought, 143
Hogan, Linda, xxviii, 154, 155, 162, 169, 172
hooks, bell, 73, 78, 79, 80, 82, 118
Hornsby, Jennifer, 129, 131, 133
Husserl, Edmund, viii, xxvii, 5, 142, 158, 225, 226, 236n22, 237n26, 237n28, 278, 280, 320, 332, 333, 335, 336, 337, 338, 342, 346n20, 349n71; Husserlian, 29, 333, 334, 338, 341, 343
Hypatia, xxv, 32–36, 37, 39, 40
hyperdialectic, xxviii, 141–142, 145–146, 147, 149, 151. *See also* good dialectic

idea, viii, ix, xxiv, xxxiii, 3, 5, 6, 7, 8, 9, 10, 11, 12, 29, 67, 69, 71, 74, 79, 81, 83, 110, 112, 114, 115, 116, 117, 118, 119, 122, 144, 146, 150, 184, 186, 189, 222, 223, 224, 226, 229, 234, 235n8, 244, 247, 248, 254, 258, 271n23, 279, 291, 297n34, 301, 305, 307, 311n25, 313, 316, 317, 321, 346n27
idealism, x, xi, xii
identity-in-difference, xxxiii, 313, 317–322
illocutionary disablement (or silencing), 126, 127, 129, 131, 134, 136n22
illocutionary force, 126, 129, 130, 134, 135
indifference, xxvi, xxxii, 8, 71, 84n26, 91, 95, 96, 97, 98, 99, 100, 101, 104, 159, 169, 286, 313, 321
inequity, 126, 130, 132, 205, 306. *See also* power
interdisciplinarity, xxxii, xxxiii, 28, 211, 332, 339, 340, 343, 348n57
internet, 95, 96, 97, 98, 99, 105, 107n51, 310n1
interrelational(ity), viii, ix, xi, xvi, xvii, xxviii, 105, 132, 157, 158, 165, 168, 169, 176n6, 180n67, 193, 228, 304

intersubjective, xxvi, 4, 36, 111, 112, 113, 120, 122, 160, 162, 168, 178n11, 187, 189, 190, 284, 309, 321
interviews, 223, 236n11, 242–253 passim, 255n7, 255n13, 311n25; interviewee, 243–253 passim; interviewer, 242–253 passim, 255n7
intimacy, 83, 112, 114, 115, 121, 122, 247
intra-action, xiii, 188
intuition, xxiv, xxvii, xxviii, 3, 7, 8, 13–14, 15, 91, 102, 103, 149, 157, 337
Irigaray, Luce, xii, 4, 22, 25, 31, 323n7, 346n32, 348n52, 349n75, 350n76
Iwamoto, Lisa, 66

Johnson, Basil, 158, 174n1, 175n6
Johnson, Galen, 70, 71, 74, 84n19, 26
Jones, Lisa, 81, 86n60

Kafka, Franz, 56, 57
Kant, Immanuel, xxvii, 39, 220, 237n28
Kepes, György, 69, 70
Kozel, Susan, 96
Kristeva, Julia, 35, 204, 216n5
Kruks, Sonia, 335
Kuhn, Thomas, 235n4, 325n22

Lacan, Jacques, 120
lacuna, 160, 170; lacunae, 251; lacunary, 146, 149. *See also* gap
Langton, Rae, 129, 130, 133
Latour, Bruno, 188, 189, 196nn27–29
Lawlor, Leonard, 326n39, 348n52
leaders, 131, 299–302, 305–310
leadership, xxxii, 299–310, 310n1
l'ecriture feminine, 27
Leder, Drew, 319, 325n35
Le Dœuff, Michèle, 3, 14, 16n1, 30
Lee, Emily S., xviiin30, xxxii, 313, 322, 340
legibility, 23, 25, 35, 37, 80, 282, 286, 293; illegibility, 25, 34, 35, 37
Leloup, Jean, 191, 197n34
Lévi-Strauss, Claude, 110, 111, 178n12
life, xv, xxiii, xxv, xxx, xxxi, 10, 13, 14, 15, 21, 26, 27, 29, 30, 31, 38, 39, 51, 52, 54, 55, 57, 66, 67, 70, 73, 79, 92, 93, 95, 96, 97, 102, 106n20, 107n27, 111, 118,

119, 121, 141, 142, 164, 169, 176n6, 184, 191, 203, 206, 209, 211, 215n3, 219–234, 235nn11–12, 237nn23–25, 237n30, 242, 257, 259, 260, 261, 262, 265, 266, 267, 268, 271n25, 282, 286, 287, 289, 290, 305, 306, 307, 309, 311n25, 315, 316, 319, 320, 324n13
lines of flight, 60, 62
lived (living) experience, vii, ix, xii, xxxii, 97, 103; 134, 161, 174, 189, 207, 208, 211, 212, 242, 246, 253, 290, 292, 299, 301, 302, 304, 305, 306, 309, 330, 338, 339, 343. *See also* experience
Lorde, Audre, 80, 123n18
Loury, Glen, 313, 321
Lugones, Maria, xxxiii, 278, 279, 285, 287–294, 295n9, 297n28, 297nn33–34, 313
Lynn, Greg, 66, 75, 77

maieutic role, 243
making-sense, 79, 250, 254, 296n23
Malabou, Catherine, 94, 106n13
Mallin, Samuel B., 171
manifesto, vii, 72
manifold, xxviii, 24, 67, 68, 69, 70, 74, 83n7, 183, 185
Manning, Dolleen Tisawii'ashii, xiv, xxviii, *154, 155, 164, 167, 171,* 174, 180n67
Manning, Rose Mshkode-bzhikiikwe baa (mother), 157, 175n3
Markopoulou, Fotini, xixn62, 69
Marx, Karl, xxiii, 142
masculine, 24, 47, 51, 119, 122, 204
masculinity studies, 340, 348n61
masochism, 48–56, 63n13
materiality, 115, 121, 157, 170, 188, 218, 221, 228, 232
Mauss, Marcel, 229, 230, 238n34
McAlister, Linda Lopez, 333
meaning of life, xxx, 219, 222, 224, 225, 226, 227, 228, 231, 233, 234
medicine, xxiv, 6, 206, 218, 219, 221, 222, 223, 224, 225, 227, 229, 233, 234, 235n11, 236n22, 243, 253, 254
menopause, 36, 208, 209, 338; menopausal, 24, 31, 35; post-menopausal, 22, 118

menstruation, 21–40, 338
Merleau-Ponty, Maurice, viii, ix, x, xi, xii, xiv, xv, xvi, xxn62, xxiii, xxiv, xxvii, xxviii, xxix, xxxii, xxxivn15, 5, 8, 9, 12, 15, 28, 66, 68, 69, 70, 71, 73, 74, 82, 83, 83n7, 84n10, 84n19, 85n26, 92, 93, 94, 96, 105, 106n14, 118, 141–151, 154 (fig. 9.1), 155, 157, 158–168, 170, 171, 176n6, 177n9, 178n11–12, 178n18, 179n49, 179n64, 180n71, 180n77, 185, 196n9, 198n40, 206, 207, 209, 210–215, 216n21, 217n30, 224, 226, 229, 230, 232, 261, 282, 283, 285, 297n34, 313, 315, 317, 318, 319, 320, 321, 323n5, 323n8, 324n13, 330, 331, 334, 335, 336, 337, 338, 339, 340, 341, 342, 343, 346n27
method, 3, 5, 6, 13, 18n52, 49, 50, 56, 58, 59, 74, 103, 142, 145, 149, 224, 225, 236n18, 301; feminist phenomenological, 329; phenomenological, 5, 103, 207, 226, 236n22, 242, 278, 330, 337–339
methodology or methodologies, 50, 91, 320; feminist, vii; feminist phenomenological, vii, viii, xxxii, xxxiii; phenomenological, ix, 5, 337
milieu, x, 6, 8, 9, 10, 12, 99, 100, 104, 142
mimesis[1]–prefiguration, 245
mimesis[2]–configuration, 245, 246, 250, 251, 252, 253
mimesis[3]–refiguration, 246
mind, xiii, xiv, xv, xxix, xxxi, 4, 5, 13, 14, 23, 34, 103, 108n56, 142, 147, 157, 160, 168, 173, 180n78, 185, 186, 277, 278, 279, 280, 281, 282, 283, 284, 285, 286, 288, 294, 305, 315, 318, 320, 322, 323n8
mitsein, 111, 112–115, 116, 121, 122, 122n5
Mnidoo (*also spelled* Manidoo, Manidou, Manitou, etc; *pl.* Mnidoog); xx, viii, 155–159, 161, 163–174, 174n1, n2, 175n3, n4, 176n6, 177n8, 179n66; ancestors (grandparents), 166, 173–174; entanglement, 168; knowing, 177; ontology, 158, 163–164, 166; world- (visible and invisible tangibles), xxvii, 156–157, 159, 168–169, 173, 180n78; -world-self, 169, 172–173, 180n78; self, 169–170, 172–173, 180n78; -self-world, 180n67; wave, 164,

166, 173; worlding, v, 155–156, 158–159, 161, 167, 171-172.
modernism, 35, 220
Moi, Toril, 126
Montaigne, Michel de, xxviii, 184, 195n2
morphology, 147
Mullin, Amy, 257
murmuration (starling organization), 158, 165, 168, 169, 173
Murphy, Robert, 204, 205
myth of femininity, 119, 120, 121

Narayan, Uma, 316
narrative, xxx, 22, 30, 39, 58, 59, 80, 97, 98, 193, 194, 223, 228, 230, 236n22, 243–246, 254, 264, 265, 266, 267, 269, 283, 297n37, 304, 305, 306, 309, 311n25, 314, 320, 345; accounts, 251, 300, 304, 305, 306, 308, 309, 310; counter-, 37; medicine, 243, 254; practice, 243, 246, 253
negative, 14, 47, 48, 51, 52, 55, 56, 71, 72, 78, 116, 127, 145, 161, 204, 209, 210, 211, 213, 304, 307, 309, 334
neonate imitation, 283
neuroscience, xxiv, 5, 6, 10, 222
new material feminism(s), xiv
Newton, Isaac, 100
Newtonian physics, 101, 102
Nietzsche, Friedrich, xxv, 47, 60, 61, 62, 63n12, 183, 186, 190
Nii Kina Ganaa (All my relations/All my relatives), 157, 165, 170, 172, 174, 177n10. *See also* Mnidoo: ancestors (grandparents)
Nonequilibrium, 67, 84n14
non-normative bodies, 207
normal abnormalities, xviiin24, xxx, 203
normalization, 212, 221

Ojibwe (*also* Chippewa/Ojibwa/Ojibway), xxviii, 156, 157, 158, 159, 163, 173, 174n2, 175n3, 175n6, 178n10, 180n80
Oksala, Johanna, 336, 341, 342, 344n3, 347n43
old age, 95, 203, 204, 205, 206, 207, 208, 209, 212, 214, 217n26, 331

Olkowski, Dorothea E., xiii, xiv, xviin3, xixn62, xxiii, xxiv, 3, 16, 28, 31, 42n41, 67, 69, 70, 71, 72, 101, 102, 106n24, 108n59, 185, 215, 234, 238n50, 328, 342, 344n3
online bullying, 95
ontological, vii, x, xiv, xviiin33, xxvii, xxviii, 9, 27, 28, 39, 139, 141, 142, 150, 158, 173, 187, 189, 191, 192, 193, 195, 223, 252, 268, 290, 292, 313, 314, 315, 316, 319, 323n5, 323n7, 335
ontology, ix, xii, xiii, xiv, xvi, xxvii, xxviii, 24, 29, 39, 141, 142, 149, 150, 155, 158, 159, 162, 163, 164, 184, 188, 189, 190, 314, 322
open system, xxv, 67, 79, 82
oppression, xii, xviin5, xxviii, xxxii, xxxvii, 80, 110, 114, 116, 117, 119, 121, 141, 184, 185, 258, 264, 268
Ortega, Mariana, vii, xviin2, 290, 291, 295n9, 340
other (the), xxvi, 7, 8, 25, 32, 36, 48, 60, 70, 71, 72, 83, 84n19, 103, 110–114, 116, 117, 118, 121, 122, 135, 148, 150, 166, 172, 208–209, 223, 229, 278, 279, 280–281, 285–289, 290, 293, 294, 318, 319, 321, 323n7, 325n35
other-than-human, xiv, 155, 158, 162, 168, 173, 174n2, 177n6. *See also* thing-memory

Pande, Amrita, 268, 270n12, 13, 271n18
parametrics, 66, 74, 75, 77, 83, 101, 104
pariah, 117, 308
Parsons, Rehtaeh, 95, 96, 97, 102, 105, 106n20, 107n27
perceptual norms, 204, 205, 206, 207, 210, 212, 213, 214, 215n3, 216n10, 217n30
perlocution, 129, 131, 132, 133, 136n21
phenomenological description, xii, 328, 330, 337, 338, 339, 341. *See also* method: phenomenlogical
philosopher, xii, xxiii, xxiv, xxv, xxvii, 4, 6, 21, 22, 27, 32, 33, 35, 37, 68, 102, 126, 144, 146, 147, 174, 184, 207, 281, 305, 313, 317, 326n39, 332, 333, 340, 341, 344n11, 345n15
philosophy, xi, xii, xxiii, xxiv, xxv, xxxii, 3, 4, 6, 7, 8, 16, 24, 25, 30, 33, 34, 41, 70, 101, 102, 105, 110, 122, 125, 135, 141, 143, 144, 147, 149, 158, 159, 163, 175n3, 177n9, 183,

184, 195, 215, 221, 234, 237n24, 254, 258, 269, 294, 314, 315, 317, 322, 323n5, 329, 330, 331, 332, 333, 334, 335, 336, 339, 341, 342, 343, 345n17, 350n76
physical (the), 8, 9, 12, 79, 101, 132, 232
plane of thought, xxiv, 3, 5, 6
Plato, 33, 34, 265, 303, 317
Platonic, 25, 33, 34, 39, 40, 75
playfulness, 293, 294
PMS, 40
point of view, viii, x, xiii, xiv, xv, 5, 8, 11, 70, 92, 93, 94, 96, 102, 254, 329, 330, 338
posthumanism, 188, 221
postmodern, xii, xiii, xiv, xvi, 16, 62, 66, 67, 75, 78, 85n43, 91, 92, 101, 102, 103, 281, 335
post-structuralism, 336, 339, 341, 342, 343
post-structuralist, xii, xiii, 143, 183, 314, 330, 335, 336, 341, 342, 346n26, 347n43
power, x, xiii, xiv, xvi, xxxiii, 7, 26, 33, 35, 48, 49, 53, 54, 56, 70, 73, 78, 80, 81, 82, 83, 118, 126, 127, 128, 130, 131, 132, 134, 154 (fig. 9.1), 189, 195, 204, 210, 214, 216n17, 222, 223, 224, 227, 233, 235n12, 238n34, 253, 268, 279, 281, 282, 287, 302, 303, 304, 309. *See also* inequity
prejudice, 207, 208, 306, 308
pre-perceptions, 206, 207, 215
pre-reflective, 158, 159, 166, 168, 194, 338; non-reflective, 158; pre-linguistic, 180n71, 194; pre-personal, xv, 69, 92, 97, 159, 160, 168, 170, 180n67; pre-reflection, 160; pre-reflectively, 172
Prigogine, Ilya, 67, 82
private realm or sphere, xxxi, 96, 97, 98, 99, 106n22, 257, 258, 259, 262, 264, 265, 267, 269, 270n7
prostitute, 117, 119
public/private distinction, 264, 265
public realm or sphere, xxxi, 79, 96, 97, 98, 99, 105, 106n22, 107n34, 257, 258, 259, 262, 264, 265, 266, 267, 268, 270n7, 299

queer studies, 340

racialization, xxxii
racism, 118, 307, 308, 316

reciprocity, 47, 73, 82, 110, 115, 121, 131, 133, 176n6, 196n29
Rehmann-Sutter, Christoph, 237n23
relatedness, 150, 227
relation, viii, ix, xiii, xiv, xv, xvi, xvii, xixn50, xxxiii, 7, 9, 47, 58, 67, 71, 77, 82, 84n26, 93, 94, 98, 101, 103, 105, 111, 121, 127, 145, 148, 149, 157, 158, 165, 172, 177n10, 179n67, 183, 184, 186, 187, 189, 192, 193, 195, 196n29, 203, 218–234, 238n34, 244, 267, 279, 281, 282, 285, 286, 288, 289, 290, 294, 313, 317, 318, 321, 322, 322n5, 325n22, 325n35, 332
relational, vii, ix, 32, 67, 68, 78, 79, 80, 83n7, 92, 94, 99, 101, 103, 104, 105, 111, 113, 122, 150, 158, 160, 170, 195, 198n41, 218, 219, 224, 226, 299, 300, 304, 309; fields, 67; perspective, 223, 227
relativity, 93, 102, 111
reverse, 161, 164, 165, 166; reversal, 168; reversed, 161, 171; reversibility, 27, 28, 38, 68, 160, 161, 172, 323n5; reversible, 103, 160, 161, 163
Ricoeur, Paul, xxx, 244–246, 247, 250, 251, 252, 320, 335, 339, 341, 343
Rodemeyer, Lanei, viii
Rouse, Joseph, 318, 325n22

Sacher-Masoch, Leopold Von, v, xxv, 47, 50–58, 60, 62n5, 63n11–n12, 63n28
Sade, Marquis De, 50–56, 58, 60
sadism, 48–56
Salamon, Gayle, 348n59
Salomon, David, 71, 72, 78
Samah, Sabra, 311n27
sameness, xxxii, 98, 104, 161, 313, 315, 320, 321, 324n14
Sands, Rita Naakwegiizhigokwe (elder/aunt), 175n3, 176n6, 178n10
Sartre, Jean-Paul, 5, 7, 8, 12, 13, 142, 143, 183, 195n5, 196n9, 209, 280, 296n12
Saussure, Ferdinand de, 135, 142, 147
savior siblings, 220, 228, 230, 231, 232, 233, 238nn44–45
Schneider, 94, 95, 210, 211, 212, 214
Schües, Christina, xxx, 16n4, 105, 218, 234, 335, 344n11

Scott, Joan W., 336, 341
second-person perspective, 243, 253, 254
second sex (the), viii, xxv, xxxii, 12, 21, 25, 30, 47, 48, 51, 110, 111, 112, 114, 116, 117, 126, 184, 185, 206, 207, 296n12, 329, 330, 335
self, xiii, 7, 8, 37, 48, 50, 60, 67, 71, 142, 151, 159, 163, 167, 169, 170–173, 180n78, 184, 187, 188, 194, 198n41, 208, 216n21, 218, 222, 226, 227, 232, 250, 264, 266, 267, 284, 285, 288, 292, 303, 308, 320, 325n35
sensation, x, xiv, xv, xxvii, 7, 13, 15, 100, 103, 167, 228
sense-making, 73, 243, 245, 292, 293, 294n1
seven directions teachings, 163
sexual difference, 110, 112, 114, 115, 121, 127, 317, 330
silencing (or illocutionary disablement), 126, 127, 128, 129, 131, 134, 136n22
Simms, Eva-Maria, xvi, xviiin28, xxvii, xxviii, 141, 151, 339, 340
Simons, Margaret A., 118
simulacrum, 6
simultaneity, 93, 94, 102, 104, 163, 165, 170, 172
simultaneous, ix, 13, 30, 68, 70, 96, 99, 104, 105, 148, 150, 156, 161, 164, 167, 170, 171, 174, 318
situated woman, 3–4
Slatman, Jenny, xxx, 242, 239, 254, 255nn6–7, 343
slave, 48, 58, 110, 112, 113, 114, 115, 116–121, 122n8, 265, 296n12
social context, xxvi, 126
social imaginaries, 193–194
social realm, 98, 186, 259, 270n7
space, x, xi, xiii, xxvii, 9, 13, 18n52, 71, 75, 77, 79, 83, 85n26, 93, 94, 95, 96, 97, 98, 99, 100, 101, 102, 103, 104, 105, 134, 147, 154, 159, 161, 162, 163, 165, 170, 172, 190, 195, 208, 210, 213, 214, 219, 259, 260, 261, 262, 265, 267, 268, 277, 279, 284, 286, 289, 291, 297n34, 305, 307, 321
Spelman, Elizabeth, 16, 122n8
Spivak, Gayatri Chakravorty, xii, 37, 38, 39
Spuybroek, Lars, 66, 74, 75
Stawarska, Beata, xi, xviiin30, xxvi, 125, 135, 136n22, 296n22, 330, 332, 333, 339

stigma, 260, 321
stigmatization, xxx, 205, 207, 211, 223
Stoller, Silvia, vii, xviin8, xxxi, xxxii, 328, 343, 344n3, 347n43, 349n71
Stonefish, Mona Kahawane, Elder, Aunt, 169, 175n3, 176n6, 178n10
stroboscopic, 167, 168
structuralism, 142, 143, 188
structure, viii, x, xi, xiii, xv, xvi, xviiin28, xixn50, xxiv, xxix, xxx, xxxi, xxxii, 3, 9, 10, 11, 12, 13, 14, 18n37, 28, 29, 37, 49, 50, 57, 59, 62, 66, 67, 75, 78, 79, 80, 81, 83, 91, 92, 97, 98, 99, 100, 102, 104, 105, 141–150 passim, 157, 159, 160, 162, 163, 168, 171, 174, 175n4, 189, 219, 220–228 passim, 230, 233, 237n28, 264, 265, 289, 293, 315, 317, 318, 320, 321, 323n5, 325n35, 338
Structure of Behavior, 142, 143, 144
subjectivity, xii, xixn47, xxiii, xxiv, xxviii, 25, 29, 38, 110, 111, 112, 122, 127, 159, 162, 183, 184, 185, 187, 190, 195, 208, 225, 237n25, 257, 263, 269, 281, 315, 316, 323n5, 324n13, 337
Sullivan, Shannon, 324n13, 346n27
symbolic (the), xiii, 8, 9, 62, 171, 224
systems, xiii, xxv, 9, 18n52, 24, 67, 68, 70, 71, 72, 75, 77, 78, 79, 82, 91, 92, 102, 103, 105, 111, 142, 143, 144, 145, 147, 167, 175n3, 180n68, 190, 263, 336

Taminiaux, Jacques, 142, 305
thermodynamics, 67, 102
thing-memory, 156, 177n8. *See also* other-than-human
third-person perspective, 211–212, 243
time, x, xv, xxvii–xxviii, xxxi, xxxiii, 5, 12–14, 35–37, 69, 77, 93–98, 100–105, 147, 163, 165, 172, 174, 195, 210, 213–214, 219, 245, 305, 314, 316–318, 321, 331; impersonal, 91–93, 97, 99, 101, 105; objective, 26, 91–93, 96, 100–101, 103–105; personal, xxvi, 91, 92, 93, 94, 95, 97, 98
Todd, Amanda, 97–99, 102, 104–105
transcendence, xiv, 4, 31–32, 113, 142, 145–146, 160–161, 165, 237n25, 317
transcendental, xi, 144, 158, 160, 226, 237n28, 278, 279, 283–284, 296n14;

claims, 281–282, 296n22; field, 145, 147, 148n2, 318; intersubjectivity, 283, 296n11; phenomenology, 226, 334, 336, 342; quasi-, 279, 295n8; reality, 237n25, 295n6; subject viii, ix; subjectivity, 225, 263, 337; transcendentalism, 292; transcendentalist, 278; transcendentally, 160
transformation, xxiv, xxxii, 7, 49–50, 59–60, 62, 63n12, 68, 70–72, 145, 163, 193, 302, 318, 329
transhuman, 222
transhuman paradigm, vi, 218, 221, 223–225, 233–234
transhuman practices, 221, 223, 225, 227, 228
transplantation medicine, 218, 225
Trinh T. Minh-ha, 103
Tuana, Nancy, 187, 345n15

unified body, 162, 167, 169, 173
uptake, 128, 131–134, 289

Van Leeuwen, Anne, 347n32
vassal, 116, 119–120, 122
Vasterling, Veronica, 107n34, 335, 342, 344n11
Venus in Furs, 57
violence, 8, 38–39, 51, 80, 99, 111–112, 118–122, 198n39, 314
visibility, 25–27, 35, 159, 291, 319
vital (the), 8, 11–12, 15
vulnerability, 26, 74, 111–114, 120, 208, 227, 308–309
vulnerable, 74, 80, 95, 111, 128, 131, 206, 227

Waldenfels, Bernhard, 220
Walther, Gerda, 332–333
weak ontology, 184

Weate, Jeremy, 314
Webb, Sarah L., 79
Weiss, Gail, xi, xxx, xxxivn21, 85n32, 216n10, 216n16, 297n33, 324n11
White, Stephen K., 184
whole, xi, xxviii, 8, 11, 48, 70, 112, 120, 141–142, 144–147, 149–151, 158, 161, 163, 190, 246
Wilde, Oscar, 216n16
Williams, Gareth, 314
Wittig, Monique, 122n5
women leaders, 299, 305–306, 308–309
world, viii–xvii, xxiv, xxvi–xxvii, xxix–xxxiii, 4–5, 7–10, 14, 28, 30, 68, 70, 81, 84n15, 84n19, 91–100, 102–105, 116, 121, 142–149, 156–161, 163–174, 177nn6–7, 179n49, 180n67, 180n77, 183–190, 193, 211–215, 217n30, 226–227, 232, 237n23, 237n25, 252, 267–268, 269, 281, 289, 291–294, 295n4, 297nn33–34, 299–300, 308, 310, 316–318, 320, 337–338; interrelational world, ix–xi, xvi; lifeworld, xxx, 225, 242, 278, 285–286, 289–290, 291, 339; lived world, 68–69; living world, ix, xxvi; social and/or cultural world, x, xii, 126, 134, 219, 305, 314; worlded, 159, 161, 163, 165; worlding, 158. *See also* Mnidoo: worlding
world-traveling, xxxiii, 279, 290–292, 294, 295n9, 296n23, 297n33
Worms, Frédéric, 233, 238n49

Yancy, George, 332n4
YouTube, 97–99
Young, Iris Marion, 24–25, 331–332, 338, 345n17

Zahavi, Dan, 283–284, 294n1, 296nn13–14, 294n24

www.ingramcontent.com/pod-product-compliance
Lightning Source LLC
Chambersburg PA
CBHW071437300426
44114CB00013B/1475